REAL
SOLUTIONS

REAL
SOLUTIONS

Taxes

Poverty

Pollution

Health Care

Immigration

College Costs

Common Sense Ideas For
Solving Our Most Pressing Problems

Michael L. Walden

Wisdom House Books

REAL SOLUTIONS

Published by Wisdom House Books, Inc.
Chapel Hill, North Carolina 27516 USA
1.919.883.4669 | www.wisdomhousebooks.com

Wisdom House Books is committed to excellence in the publishing industry.

Book design copyright © 2020 by Wisdom House Books, Inc. All rights reserved.

Cover and Interior Design by Ted Ruybal

Published in the United States of America

Paperback ISBN: 978-0-578-67556-5
LCCN: 2020913348

POL028000 | POLITICAL SCIENCE / Public Policy / General
POL024000 | POLITICAL SCIENCE / Public Policy / Economic Policy
BUS022000 | BUSINESS AND ECONOMICS / Economic Conditions

First Edition

25 24 23 22 21 20 / 10 9 8 7 6 5 4 3 2 1

TABLE OF CONTENTS

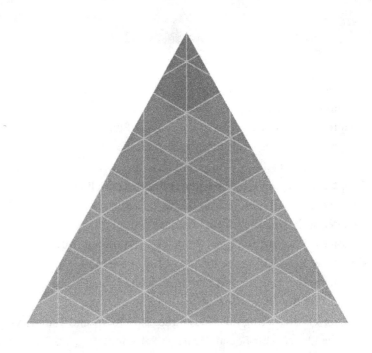

ACKNOWLEDGMENTS

This book has been over forty years in the making. I began teaching and talking about the economic issues of the day in the late 1970s, first to my classes and then to public audiences. As time went on and I matured as an economist, teacher, and public speaker, I began to formulate ideas about solutions to the issues. Of course, the major issues have changed throughout the decades. For example, in the 1970s, high inflation and high interest rates were top priority concerns. Today, some policymakers consider inflation and interest rates to actually be too low! In contrast, health-care costs and income inequality were barely discussed in the 1970s, and yet in the 21st century few politicians and policy-makers can get away with ignoring them.

My first thanks go to the students I have taught and audiences I have spoken to during my career. They have kept me on my toes about economic issues and ways of addressing them. Also, my colleagues current and past have always been generous sounding boards and sources of advice. I'll always remember my first department head, the late Bill Toussaint, who set a low bar for me by saying, "Mike, just don't say anything stupid." I hope I have exceeded that bar, especially in this book.

The professionals at Wisdom House Books—including Ted Ruybal, Clara Jackson, Diane Woodfin, and Megan Gower—have made this book substantially better in both content and appearance.

Then, of course, there is my wife Mary. Always an inquisitive person, she has never let me get away with explanations only an economist would understand. Her demands for clarity have resulted in a book that hopefully is both substantive and accessible to a wide audience. Also, a tip of my hat is due to my demanding confidant, Buddy Ray Raish.

INTRODUCTION

People want solutions to the problems they observe and experience, but the solutions offered are often too complex or too impractical. Half-hearted solutions make the provider of the solution feel accomplished even though nothing changes. Simplistic platitudes sound good but do not offer policy content.

This situation is unfortunate because the list of issues and problems that we face today is daunting. Look at education; recent achievement in K-12 schools has been flat.[1] Even though college enrollments have reached record levels in the 21st century, one-third of college students require remedial training prior to taking college courses.[2] College tuitions have been soaring, which should motivate students to graduate on time.[3] Instead, only slightly more than half finish in six years, and many of the rest don't finish at all.[4]

Two necessities of life—health-care and housing—are becoming out-of-reach for more and more people. Rather than stemming rising health-care costs and making care more affordable, the

Affordable Care Act (a.k.a. "Obamacare") seems to have worsened the situation. Medical bills may as well be written in Greek, and no one seems to know how costs are determined. At the same time, cities are expanding with trendy apartments and luxury condos, but average working people can't afford these units, so they have to endure long commutes from outlying areas where their paycheck can be stretched further.

And speaking of paychecks and jobs, it seems like there are only two types: high-paying and low-paying, with little in-between. The great middle-class, which once dominated our country, is now a shadow of its former self. One reason that kids go to college today, even if they have no interest, is they think there are only two options in life—getting a college degree or being poor! Even if you have a college degree, doesn't it seem like you need to know someone to get ahead? Isn't the job market rigged in favor of those with connections and against those (often women and minorities) without?

Creating more frustration is our tax system. Most people know they have to pay taxes, and they want to support schools, roads, police and firefighters, and the military. But did the same people who created medical bills also write the tax laws? For most of us, if something can't be understood, it can't be trusted. Has the tax code been complicated to hide the favoritism it gives to those supporting political campaigns or paying for top accountants?

If we have it bad, what about our kids and grandkids? Unless politicians get their act together quickly, won't the national debt bankrupt future families? Will tomorrow's generations still be able to benefit from programs such as Social Security and Medicare? What will the environment look like? Will future generations be living with oppressive summers, rising sea levels, droughts, and floods caused by global warming? Maybe this is why the average household saves very little. Shouldn't we all just party today because it's all downhill from here?

These paragraphs haven't been very heartening, but they describe how many, maybe most, people feel. Perhaps it's why teenagers today are more depressed than ever.[5]

Is there anything we can do? Are there real solutions to these real-life problems? Fortunately, the answer to both questions is a definite *yes*. Yes, there are things we can do, and yes, there are solutions! In fact, there are actually commonsensical solutions. It's why I wrote this book.

In the chapters ahead, I'll take on your fears, frustrations, and worries about the economic situation now and in the future. With each problem, I'll try to explain what's happening, why it's happening, and whether it will continue. In some cases, I argue that the situation is not as grave as many think, but in other cases I argue that the situation may be worse. I'll also discuss some of the simple but incorrect solutions offered for each issue, which I term "fake solutions." Then I'll give practical, "real solutions" that will address— and in many cases, solve—the problem. Other, similar books often address these problems but fail to identify specific solutions. They end with generalities, which leave the reader feeling helpless and wanting more. In this book, I'll give you more. My explanations and recommendations will always be clear and straightforward, without any of the unclear, ivory-tower mumbo-jumbo that plagues similar books.

Now, a little about me. I am a professional economist who has taught at North Carolina State University for over 40 years. I have "enlightened" thousands of students in the classroom, and I have written hundreds of academic articles and reports as well as a dozen books.

Unlike many academics, I have not spent all my time in classrooms, in my office, or talking to my colleagues. A large part of my professional time has been working with businesses and their employees, non-profits and their members, state and local governments, elected officials, and a variety of clubs and organizations. I have recorded a daily radio program for more than four decades and have written a biweekly newspaper column for two decades. Each year, I average 80 talks and presentations to a variety of groups throughout North Carolina, and I have also been frequently (about 3,000 times at last count) interviewed by both print and air media. I am honored to have received several national and state awards for these efforts, among them the *Order of the Long Leaf Pine* from the Governor of North Carolina.

I get out and talk to real people in real jobs, and I have heard the questions about their worries, hopes, and dreams. I can talk corporate finance to businesses, but I can also talk kitchen table economies to families.

It is important for you to know this is not intended to be a political book. I have not written it to promote a particular political point of view or philosophy. My intention is not to support or oppose any elected official or candidate. But I do have some biases—or beliefs—based on my training and experience as an economist, and here they are:

First, I believe in the power of incentives. The quickest way to get someone or some organization to do something is to give them an incentive to do it. Often this is a financial incentive, but it doesn't have to be.

Second, people will pay more attention to their decisions if they have "skin in the game." This means a person has a stake (usually financial) in an outcome over which they have some influence. If they can either benefit or lose from an outcome, they will care more about what actually occurs.

Third, prices are influenced by supply and demand. Oops, I just slipped into (what some would consider) economic mumbo-jumbo. Supply is simply how much of a product or service businesses will provide when they are paid a certain price. Demand is how much of a product or service users will buy when they pay a specific price. More supply reduces prices, while less supply raises prices. It's the opposite with demand; more demand raises prices, while less demand reduces prices.

Fourth, competition is good for buyers. The more companies trying to get your business, the more the companies will cater to buyers' needs, and the more likely prices will be lower.

Fifth, I believe in evidence-based recommendations. One myth about academics is that their recommendations are only based on what happens in theory with little care for practical outcomes.

While I am sure there are some academics like this, most that I know, especially economists, are not. In this book, my analysis and recommendations are backed up with facts and evidence.

Sixth, I believe recommendations should be made using common sense. Too often "experts" hide behind complexity and claims that problems and their solutions are too complicated for the average non-expert to understand. This is B.S.! Physicists may be able to make this argument, but not social scientists like economists, sociologists, and psychologists. Economics can be complicated, so it can be easy for someone like me to say: "Just trust me, the explanation is too complicated." I have always believed economic relationships should be explained in everyday language. I've always followed this approach in the classes I've taught. (And as a bonus, this is my same recommendation I have for investment advisers. If advisers can't explain an investment in terms you can understand, then get a new adviser!)

Seventh—and lastly—I believe in individual choice as much as possible. I think that the freedom to make one's own decisions is one of the most attractive features of our country. I've been told this many times by foreign-born students. This doesn't mean I believe in anarchy, particularly when one person's actions can adversely affect others. Still, when motivating someone to do something by their own free will is an option, I'll choose that route over ordering a person to make a specific choice. I see the most important role of education as equipping people with the skills and information necessary to make choices benefiting them the most.

There you have it. You know who I am, what I'm trying to do in this book, and how I'll try to do it. And one last thing: I'm an optimist by nature, so I believe we can find solutions to almost any problem! In the chapters ahead, I hope I can convince you to agree with me.

Introduction Endnotes

1. National Assessment of Educational Progress, *The Nation's Report Card*, 2019. Findings for two complementary measures for college-bound students, the SAT and ACT, show the same results (College Board, *2016 College-Bound Seniors Total Group Profile Report, and ACT, Inc., The ACT Profile Report—National*).

2. Chen and Simone, U.S. Department of Education, 2016.

3. College Board, "Tuition and Fees over Time."

4. National Student Clearinghouse Research Center, *Completing College: Eight-Year Completion Outcomes, Fall 2010 Cohort.*

5. Twenge, "Why So Many Teens Today Have Become Depressed."

CHAPTER ONE

THE MISSING INGREDIENT IN K-12 EDUCATION

IF WE JUST TRY THIS TEACHING METHOD

I t was a cold winter day at the White House in 2002. Several leading politicians, including Democrat Ted Kennedy (the "lion of the Senate" and keeper of the Kennedy name), were crowded around Republican President George W. Bush as he signed the "No Child Left Behind" (NCLB) legislation. The bill had been a bipartisan effort, particularly between Kennedy and Bush. NCLB promised to raise educational standards and performance for all children in public schools, regardless of race, ethnicity, and background. There were smiles all around as the politicians claimed that finally the nation had the K-12 school system on track to correct the educational mistakes of the past. They claimed NCLB would offer each and every child an educational experience that would develop their individual talents and potential to the fullest.[1]

In 2015—only thirteen years since it was adopted—Congress scraped NCLB. In the eyes of many it had been a failure. Indeed, the data show average school performance hadn't budged in the 21st century.[2] Even more importantly, the gaps among racial groups still persisted.

Critics say NCLB imposed too many federal regulations on local schools, most notably the frequent testing requirements, so students' learning could be evaluated. Many parents and teachers argued that the constant exams created chronic apprehension among students and motivated teachers to "teach to the test," rather than making learning fun and responsive to individual student needs.[3]

The sorry experience of NCLB isn't the first time the education system has adopted with much fanfare a new teaching method, only to toss it away a few years later when it didn't appear to work. In the last four decades, the educational bureaucracy has jumped from one initiative to another, claiming with each jump that the new plan was "the one," and rarely explaining why previous plans didn't work. A partial list of the teaching strategies include: group learning, computer learning, team teaching, standardized teaching, home schooling, charter schools, smart boards, common core, teaching fellows, teaching assistants, teaching mentors, school uniforms, school spirit, master's degrees for teachers, project-based learning, challenge-based learning, high-speed internet access, race-to-the-top, and competency-based grading systems. The head spins! I wonder how much time and money have been spent in recent decades introducing new teaching initiatives, training teachers and staff to implement the initiatives, and then finding some other teaching method when the current one fails to bring expected results.

Despite all of the experimentation with alternative teaching programs, recent research shows little success in the last half-century in closing the achievement gap between high-performing and low-performing students.[4] If a major goal of K-12 education is to level the playing field between students of different socio-economic backgrounds so they start life with the same opportunities, then what schools have been doing doesn't seem to be working.

I've put this chapter addressing K-12 education first because it is a springboard for improving many of the other issues discussed in this book, such as achieving success for college students, reducing income inequality, closing gender and racial pay gaps, and responding to the challenge of technology in the workplace.[5] I tell my audiences, "It all starts with K-12," meaning if we make gains in early education, those gains will multiply through many parts of life.

So how do we improve K-12 education? Read on.

△ IT'S NOT THE TEACHER

Full disclosure: I have been married to a teacher for over forty years. Mary is retired today, but she taught for a total of 32 years in several school systems. I can say from experience that she worked very hard. It's often said that teachers have it easy because they get summers off; I'm going to be polite here and respond with one word—wrong! Mary had four weeks of worry-free vacation in the summer, which is not out-of-line with the length of vacations of other college educated workers.[6] But then the workshops would start (especially if a new teaching method was being introduced), scheduling meetings would be held, and lesson plans would be reworked, particularly if the constantly-evolving teaching methods were being implemented.

Of course, there are bad teachers just like there are bad engineers, bad plumbers, bad car dealers, and even bad college professors. Some school systems make it difficult to get rid of bad teachers, and certainly this should be changed. But overwhelmingly, most teachers want their students and schools to succeed. They realize successful student outcomes reflect positively on them, on their students, and on the community. So, what's stopping them?

△ THE MISSING INGREDIENT

I like to eat, but I'm not very good at cooking. My best dish is scrambled eggs. The upside is that scrambled eggs are versatile; they can be dressed up for all meals—breakfast, lunch, or dinner! I suspect if I lived alone, scrambled eggs would be my go-to course.

Fortunately, Mary is a great cook, and sometimes I hang around the kitchen and watch her use a number of ingredients and magically turn them into a five-star restaurant worthy dinner. When she cooks, my wife is actually demonstrating an economic principle. Most products result from combining several inputs (ingredients) in just the right proportions. If the amount of seasoning, the level of cooking temperature, or the length of cooking time is too much or not enough, the meal is ruined.

Successfully teaching students also requires combining several ingredients in the correct proportions. Among them are the teacher's training and skills, the teaching materials and techniques, the quality of the school building and classrooms, and the support and dedication of the school's leadership and staff. I'll lump together these ingredients affecting a student's learning and call them *school factors*. When looking for ways to improve K-12 education, most of the discussion focuses on these school factors.

To complicate matters, student learning is shaped by more than teachers, books and tests, and school buildings; it is also impacted by inputs outside the classroom and school. A student's family is a big factor. A young person's performance at school will be influenced by the level of family support, particularly by parents. Both of my parents were high school dropouts, yet they valued education, seeing it as the path to a future they could not reach. Even after a long day working outside in the heat or cold as a carpenter, my father would drill me on my spelling, correct my math, and critique my handwriting. When I took high school subjects too advanced for my father to help, he still made sure I studied every night, constantly repeating, "You want to get an education so you don't have to work as hard as I do." My mother also supported me by making sure I always had a lunch to take to school, tracking my sleep time, and volunteering with the school PTA (Parent-Teacher Association).

A neighborhood conducive to learning is also important. I don't mean neighbors reading to other parents' children or helping them with homework (although these actions would be commendable). Instead, I mean that students should reside in a safe and low-crime neighborhood, one in which they won't be distracted—or worse, harmed—by gunshots, drug-runners, late night parties and violence, and screaming police sirens. And, of course, the worst-case scenario is when the student's parents or siblings are involved in these activities.

I have a term for the family and neighborhood inputs impacting child learning. It is *home factors*. Now, here's the big revelation: in recent decades, some home factors have become a bigger negative influence on learning for a greater number of students.[7] And while educational leaders have known this, there has been very little they have been able to do about it.

△ FAMILY, NEIGHBORHOOD, SOCIAL MEDIA, AND LEARNING

From a broad perspective, it looks as if there have been numerous disturbing trends in the home factors impacting student learning. In the family, single parenthood is higher, divorce is considered normal, and a larger percentage of school-age children are classified as living in poor households. In neighborhoods, residential segregation is more widespread, violent gangs are often prevalent, and drugs are still an issue. Then there's the home factor that doesn't fit neatly into the family or neighborhood category, it really spans both. This factor is *social media*. In recent years, social media usage among students has exponentially increased, and we are now beginning to learn of the technology's adverse consequences on both student behavior and student learning.

Let's come down to ground level and examine each of these individual factors in more detail. First is single parenthood. Over one-third (35%) of K-12 students were in single-parent households in 2015, almost three-times the rate as in 1970.[8] For Black students, the levels are even higher: 61% of African-American students lived in single-parent households in 2015, up from 35% in 1970.[9]

I'm NOT suggesting single parents are bad or incompetent. Most aren't. Most want the best for their children and work hard to provide it. But raising children takes both time and money. With two parents, the time input (like the things my parents did to motivate me to achieve as a student) can be divided between them. But with one parent, especially one who may be working multiple jobs to financially support the household, it's often difficult if not impossible to find the needed time to assist children in their studies. There are single parents who can do it, and they are superheroes, but we shouldn't expect all single parents to be this capable.

Unfortunately, the evidence is strong that children from single-parent households, on average, don't do as well in school or in many other aspects of life as children from two-parent households.[10] One recent study tracked over 6,000 K-12 students and found that, even after accounting for other characteristics like household income and the parent's education, children from single-parent households completed less schooling (meaning they dropped-out at a higher rate) than children from two-parent households.[11] Even more concerning, the disadvantage for the single-parent kids grows larger over time; if students don't do as well in school, their lifetime incomes will be lower, as found in a Harvard University analysis of over 20 million individual work histories.[12] Interestingly, similar results to the Harvard study have been found from other countries, suggesting the challenges of single parenthood are worldwide.[13]

Yet, what about the argument, "It's better to have a single parent than two parents when one is abusive to the spouse or children." In this case, I agree—it is better to have just one parent, but one who is caring and supportive.[14] What is even better are two parents who are caring and supportive.

After rising in the mid-20th century, divorce has remained relatively stable in recent decades.[15] Still, some children have issues accepting the divorce, and wonder if they were the cause of their parent's breakup. If joint custody occurs, children may have trouble accepting a schedule of moving back and forth between the biological parents. When living in a blended family with a stepparent and stepchildren, there may be problems with "fitting in" and determining proper relationships roles. There is also the possibility of the parent or stepparent adopting a "too strict" or "too lenient" policy with the child.

All of these potential issues stemming from divorce can adversely affect a student's school performance. Academic studies have shown children living in remarried or blended families are more likely to repeat grades, are absent more often, earn lower grades, and have parents who are less involved with schools than children living with their original parents.[16]

Poverty is another factor in student learning. One in every five school children today come from families with incomes below the poverty level, a third larger than in 1970, and the proportions are higher for non-white children.[17] Once again, poverty doesn't guarantee a child will do poorly in school, especially today where there are numerous social safety net programs like Food Stamps, Medicaid, housing vouchers, and nutrition assistance to supplement a family's income. But for some households, poverty may create issues like lack of self-respect, questions about social standing, and arguments over how to use limited financial resources. These conflicts can easily influence a child's interest in school and even their relationships with other students. Moreover, teacher turnover rates tend to be higher in high-poverty schools, with an adverse impact on consistent instruction and teacher-student bonding.[18] It should be no surprise that research has found correlations between poverty and student outcomes in test scores, graduation rates, and disciplinary issues.[19]

For many students, simply walking home from school can be risky. In 2012, almost a third (30%) of parents said their neighborhoods were "usually safe," and 13% said their neighborhoods were "never or sometimes safe." Combining these two responses means 43% of parents thought their neighborhood was less than "always safe," which shows no improvement from a similar survey conducted five years earlier.[20] Such neighborhoods make it difficult for students to do homework or even think about school. A 2011 study tracking 4,100 children found that growing up in unsafe neighborhoods significantly reduced their chances of graduating from high school. [21]Unsafe neighborhoods also make alternate forms of structure more attractive to children and adolescents. If there is little parental guidance, for example, gangs can offer the supervision, protection, and leadership that youths crave and need.

A new challenge to learning is the internet. I can remember when the internet was invented (yes, I'm that old), and there were big expectations about how it would advance both our economy and society. While many of these expectations have been fulfilled, there have also been some unintended consequences, and we are now realizing many of these revolve around social media.

Social media can be addictive. Lives have been ruined and careers lost because individuals can't control the amount of time spent on social media, as well as internet gaming and texting. In fact, there are now professional centers where individuals are checked-in for weeks at a time to cleanse themselves of their social media addiction. These centers are very similar to those for alcoholics.[22]

Social media addictions can start at an early age and easily derail learning. In my recent years of teaching university undergraduates, I've noticed a significant climb in the number of failing grades in my classes. Initially, I was puzzled because the difficulty of my tests hadn't changed, and, if anything, I had become a better teacher due to my multiple decades of experience. Then it dawned on me that the smartphones, laptops, and tablets that students were supposedly bringing to class for note-taking and accessing slides and other visuals weren't, in many cases, being used for those purposes. Instead, students were spending their class time surfing the web, using social media, and watching movies! Many professors are now banning electronics from their classes and forcing students to take notes the old-fashioned way—writing by hand.

But the problem can begin earlier. The local public-school system in the county where I live (Wake County, North Carolina) initially encouraged students to use personal computer technology in classes to access information, takes notes, and communicate with other students. Later, the school system reassessed this policy as teachers discovered students didn't always use the devices for educational purposes. It was found personal information technology was giving students access to many of the more troubling sides of society. Wake

County Schools now has a 17-point set of rules and regulations managing and monitoring internet usage in classrooms.[23]

There is now almost universal use of technology like smartphones by children, with most being introduced to the devices by their first birthday.[24] Research has shown that as personal computer technology has become more capable and more accessible, both time spent on homework and time reading have declined.[25] Is this a coincidence or is there a cause and effect?

Then there's the serious problems of bullying and depression. Bullying in schools has always occurred. I can remember an incident in my fifth-grade class in the early 1960s. The teacher, who was elderly and close to retirement, would take "rest breaks," meaning she would take a short nap at her desk while the students were supposed to work on assignments. During one of these breaks, a student who happened to be the largest kid in the class picked up another student and stuffed him in the trash can. The rest of the kids snickered when the teacher—now awake from her "rest break"—struggled to pull the kid out of the can. The perpetrator was discovered and sent to the principal for discipline.

I smile about this incident now, but bullying is a serious problem and it appears to have been made worse by social media. While physical bullying continues, social media has enabled another type of bullying: *cyber bullying*. Social media can easily be used by groups of students to criticize, embarrass, and intimate others. Multiple studies report cyber bullying occurring to about 40% of the teenagers in the U.S.[26] Sometimes cyber bullying even leads to the death of victims. For others, it can lead to a philosophical or even physical withdrawal from school, actions which certainly are not conducive to educational success.

Another adverse educational impact of social media is student depression. Several recent studies have unfortunately found an increase in symptoms of depression or a reduced feeling of life satisfaction, especially among children, teens, and females.[27] Many social media sites allow others to register approval or disapproval of postings at a user's site. A 2016 analysis found that users receiving disapprovals on social media sites were more likely to develop symptoms of depression and anxiety.[28] Depressed students are more prone to miss school, fail to do assignments, and fail in courses.[29]

△ FAKE SOLUTIONS

Expenditures per pupil in K-12 schools were 38% higher in 2017 than in 1990, and they are expected to rise about 1% annually for the next decade.[30] Importantly, the increases are on top of the increase in the general cost-of-living (a.k.a. "inflation"). Hence, we have been putting enough extra money in K-12 education to keep up with general inflation, and then some. But this has just been enough to essentially maintain the status quo, allowing a modest decline in class size and a little bit of a bump in teacher pay (after-inflation) over time.

Instead, the K-12 establishment is relying on what it has always banked on to achieve student gains: new teaching strategies and techniques. Today's plan appears to be the use of technology for individualized learning combined with group solutions to problems (does anyone but me see the incompatibility between these two approaches?). This new supposed pathway to success has already gotten pushback from parents who complain of eyestrain and headaches suffered by their children from so much screen-time, as well as reduced learning when problems are solved by a group of students.[31]

Another failed approach used by today's schools is the idea of achieving success through the setting of goals. In 2014, Wake County Public Schools set a graduation rate goal of 95% by 2020. In 2017, with three years to go, the system wasn't close with a graduating rate of 87%. Beyond this, a graduation rate doesn't guarantee student learning if standards are reduced in order to increase the number of students receiving a diploma. A high graduation rate sounds good, but what does it mean? In fact, evidence shows literacy rates haven't changed in a decade, and almost one out of 5 high school graduates are still functionally illiterate.[32]

Those who head our K-12 schools need to stop grasping for the next "magic solution" and setting these feel-good goals. Instead, those who hold the purse strings for public schools must step up to the challenge with a surge of new resources to improve the learning environment for students both inside and—perhaps arguably more important—outside the classroom.

△ REAL SOLUTIONS

Efforts to improve the performance of students in K-12 schools have focused on school factors, for the obvious reason that these are the most direct components school boards, county commissioners, and legislators can change. While there are certainly further changes that should be made to school factors, which I outline below, my major point is that we need an equal push to address the challenges posed by home factors if we want to achieve gains for more students. Here are my recommendations:

For School Factors

1. Pay teachers more both to attract and keep the best educators. Teachers make a difference in children's education, and increasing teacher salaries motivates better qualified individuals to be teachers and to stay in teaching. This is found from both national and international studies.[33] Many people, including some teachers, discount the importance of salaries by saying the "joy of teaching" is the biggest reward from the profession. I applaud individuals who think that way, but at some point, the "first law of economics" kicks in; if you want more of something, pay more. In this case, we want more of the best and the brightest choosing teaching as a career and remaining in the field.

   Even when accounting for their slightly longer vacation and job security, teachers are still paid about 30% less than comparably trained professionals.[34] This is probably one reason why top college students usually don't pursue careers in teaching. In fact, college students pursuing a major in education typically rank in the bottom third of national standardized scores.[35]

If we want better results from K-12 schools, we need to attract better teachers. Indeed, two-thirds of individuals who have left teaching say sufficiently higher pay would bring them back.[36] However, with higher pay, tenure should be ended. Tenure grants teachers a job-for-life after they've worked a certain number of years. If teachers want to be paid like the professionals they are, they should accept the risks. Teacher contracts should be of a limited time period, and teacher performance should be reviewed on a regular basis. If teachers fail to meet set standards, they should be subject to dismissal.

2. Reduce class sizes. Do you think a teacher can give the same amount of individual attention and help to each student if there are 30 students in the class versus 20 students in the class? This isn't a trick question—the answer is no. More individual attention can be provided, and the classroom can be better controlled and managed, with fewer students. If not, why do parents sometimes pay for individual tutors?

A study in Tennessee showed how powerful lowering class sizes can be on student performance.[37] Reducing class size by one-third had the impact of improving a student's score from average—meaning their score was in the middle of the distribution of all scores—to being in the upper 40% of student scores. The improvement occurred because teachers had more time to spend with each child and there were fewer distractions. Smaller class sizes lead to greater student gains than the gains from maintaining class sizes but adding teacher assistances. Importantly, the results were long-lasting and even greater for minority students.

3. Selectively use technology, if at all. Technology is one of those educational bandwagon initiatives educators often embrace as the key to improving student outcomes, but as with most innovations, there are both promises and pitfalls associated with technology. The job of schools is determining how to minimize the pitfalls while maximizing promises. Student-owned technology should be banned from the classroom. If technology is used in the classroom, it should be owned and operated by the schools and used for specific tasks, such as allowing students to perform lessons individually at their own pace with instantaneous assistance and monitoring by the teacher. Use of the technology by students for personal communications should be blocked by the school, as should access to all but school-approved websites.

But schools and elected school boards should also ask themselves how necessary technology is for learning. Is it just the latest fad—something tangible the schools can point to in order to convince parents they are on the cutting-edge and are up-to-date in teaching methods? A 2016 international study on the use of technology in K-12 schools found no benefits for learning; in fact, in some cases, learning declined.[38] There is some evidence that excessive use of technology actually reduces students' concentration and comprehension.[39]

4. Add Pre-K classes. Children's early experiences have tremendous impacts on shaping their lives.[40] It's now widely accepted that adding a quality Pre-K program for three and four-year-olds can enhance both cognitive (thinking, reasoning, understanding, development of a knowledge base) and non-cognitive (persistence, self-discipline, focus, confidence, teamwork) abilities and lead to improved economic outcomes, although some research suggests the non-cognitive gains are more permanent than the cognitive improvements.[41] The path-breaking work on this issue has been done by one of my personal heroes, economist James Heckman, who, among his many accolades, has received the Nobel Prize in Economics.[42] When Professor Heckman speaks on this topic, I listen! One of his most notable findings is that the benefit/cost ratio to investing in pre-K education is as high as 9-to-1 with benefits to the student's lifetime earnings, as well as the reduced public costs for welfare, crime, and health-care are included.[43]

For Home Factors

1. Expand the use of school social workers. Many students living with challenging family and neighborhood circumstances need guidance and intervention to achieve a successful education. Social workers are experts at spotting students experiencing such problems and working with them and their families to develop remedies. Social workers can be the link between a student's home life and school life.

2. Expand after-school programs that combine fun, learning, and exploration. The time after school when many youths are unsupervised is often a time of trouble; without guidance, kids can take wrong turns that lead them away from education or worse. Why not use the available space and time after formal school hours for learning without the concern for tests and grades? Let some students explore academic subjects in more depth, but also provide opportunities for others to enjoy acting, crafts, art, and, of course, sports. If possible, secure local experts and role models to volunteer their time to introduce students to topics and pursuits away from the classroom. Keep the cafeteria open so students' stomachs can be nourished along with their brains, and re-arrange school busing systems so transportation home can be provided for students needing it.

3. Provide the option of "boarding schools." Boarding schools allow students to learn and live at the same location. Schools become homes for students. I don't mean students sleep in the classrooms; specially designed dorms, or boarding rooms, are attached to the schools, where students live, eat, play, and sleep after school hours. This arrangement is best used for students who come from extremely disruptive home and neighborhood environments. The boarding school minimizes the student's exposure to these disruptions and offers a safe and supportive environment. Boarding schools cost twice as much per student as conventional schools, but the research to date suggests they can be successful.[44] Of course, students would only attend boarding schools with the consent of their parents or guardians.

4. Address the negative influences of social media on learning. Most distractions and disruptions from social media occur outside of school, so we need a national conversation, and the enlistment of parents and technology companies, about reducing the downsides of social media and overuse of technology by our children and young adults.[45]

The recommendations I have made are in the context of public schools. This is because a large majority—87% according to the latest data—of elementary and secondary school students attend public schools.[46] But my focus on public schools should not be taken as ignoring the important educational work done by private schools, home schools, and charter schools. However, these educational alternatives often don't face the same kinds of challenges as public schools. Obviously, for home schooling, the home factors are controlled because the teaching is almost exclusively done by parents, and private and charter schools also usually have strong parental support since parents are directly engaged in their selection.[47]

△ WHAT WILL IT COST AND WHAT WILL IT RETURN?

I've outlined some ambitious and extensive changes for K-12 schools, and the changes won't come cheaply. Raising teacher salaries, reducing class sizes, adding social workers, expanding after-school activities, adding Pre-K for three and four-year-olds, and providing the option of boarding schools will cost billions of dollars nationally on top of what's already being spent.

Yet there will be significant payback. With more young people successfully engaged in education, youth crime—which is often a gateway to adult crime and long-term imprisonment—should fall. There's also evidence that successful educational outcomes are associated with better health, which means that improving the results for K-12 education will also lower national health-care costs.[48] And, if more young people are improving their educational results in K-12, more of them will be ready for college work and won't require the cost and time of remedial courses when they attend either two-year or four-year colleges.

However, the big payoff from students doing better in school is in improved productivity and pay of the workforce. Three academics estimated that improving the educational outcomes from the K-12 school system could be worth $500 billion of additional economic production for each of the next eighty years.[49] This is because a young person who successfully and competently completes school makes a better worker, and better workers make better and more products and services. By failing to have K-12 schooling benefit all kids, we're making the economic pie shared by all of us smaller.

And there's more! Successful graduates, employed in fulfilling and well-paying jobs, will have more resources to make supportive and loving homes for their children as well as functioning and safe neighborhoods for their communities. The number of at-risk children in schools should eventually fall, and with the drop, some of the additional educational expenditures (like social workers, after-school programs, and boarding schools) could eventually be curtailed.

Here are my estimates on both the costs and benefits of improving

K-12 schools. I've skipped the boring details about the calculations, which you can find in the appendix. The big picture is that I'm increasing teacher salaries by 30% to be comparable to the salaries of similarly trained professionals of college graduates with a bachelor's degree. I'm reducing average class sizes by one-third and adding enough teachers to staff the extra classes. I'm adding social workers to have one per fifteen students, and I'm expanding public education to include Pre-K classes for all three and four-year-olds. I'm increasing after-school activities to serve half the student body, and I'm building/staffing enough boarding schools to accommodate half the number of students living in challenging family and neighborhood circumstances. I've estimated the annual costs for each of these proposals, and I've also estimated the annual benefits in terms of additional income to students, and reduced crime, health-care costs, and public assistance to society.

Without the option of boarding schools, the annual cost is $378 billion, a 70% increase in current K-12 funding, but less than 2% of national income.[50] Including the option of boarding schools increases the annual cost to $415 billion, a 97% jump over current K-12 spending and just slightly over 2% of national income. But I estimate annual benefits to be $784 billion—very close to previous calculations. This means every additional dollar spent when boarding schools are not an option returns $2.07, and every additional dollar spent when boarding schools are an option returns $1.89. I'd say this is a good deal, and it's also the right thing to do!

The additional resources devoted to K-12 education, as well as the expected benefits from the improved K-12 system, won't happen overnight. It will take time to hire more teachers and social workers, establish boarding schools, develop more after-school programs, and install Pre-K classes. The payoff of a more productive economy with less crime and better health won't occur until years down the road, but clearly history is on our side. Improved school systems and better educational outcomes have always led to a better economy and higher standards of living.[51]

Still, the money will have to be spent first before the benefits start flowing. And the benefits won't necessarily flow to the schools once they do occur. Most of the payback will go to graduates through higher earnings and to society through broader economic success and reduced costs for social problems. Taxpayers will either have to be convinced the additional spending is a good investment, or they will have to be shown what other parts of public spending will be cut to pay for the added school funds. You'll need to read more to find which path I recommend.

▲ SUMMING UP

The educational system is the backbone of our economy and society. Better educated and trained students result in more productive workers, a higher standard of living for more people, and more lives that meet their potential. We need a "surge" in Pre-K-12 school spending to make education work for all kids. Without it, we'll continue to spin our wheels and see disastrous results in lives unfulfilled and neighborhoods undeveloped. It's an investment we have to make, and one that will more than pay for itself.

Chapter 1 Endnotes

1. The White House, "President Signs Landmark No Child Left Behind Education Bill."

2. National Assessment of Educational Progress, *op. cit.*

3. Jackson, Abby, "3 Big Ways No Child Left Behind Failed."

4. Hanuskek and Peterson, "The Achievement Gap Fails to Close."

5. For research on the importance of education to income inequality and social mobility, see Chetty, Friedman, Hendren, Jones, and Porter, "The Opportunity Atlas: Mapping the Childhood Roots of Social Mobility," and Card, Domnisoru, and Taylor, "The Intergenerational Transmission of Human Capital: Evidence from the Golden Age of Upward Mobility." For research on the link between success in K-12 and success in college, see Bound, Lovenheim, and Turner, "Why Have College Completion Rates Declined? An Analysis of Changing Student Preparation and Collegiate Resources."

6. Riggs, "The Myth of a Teacher's Summer Vacation," and U.S. Bureau of Labor Statistics, "Average Paid Holidays and Days of Vacation and Sick Leave for Full Time Employees."

7. Banerjee, "A Systematic Review of Factors Linked to Poor Academic Performance of Disadvantaged Students in Science and Math in Schools."

8. National Center for Education Statistics, *Digest of Education Statistics,* 2017, Table 102.10.

9. Pew Research Center, *More than Half of Black Children Now Live with a Single Parent.*

10. McLanahan and Sawhill, "Marriage and Child Wellbeing: Introducing the Issue."

11. Ziol-Guest, Duncan, and Kalil, "One-Parent Students Leave School Earlier."

12. Chetty, Hendren, Jones, and Porter, "Race and Economic Opportunity in the United States: An Intergenerational Perspective." Chetty et al.

13. Yaw, "The Effect of Single Parenting on Student Academic Performance in Secondary Schools in Brunei."

14. Shoener, "Two Parent Households Can Be Lethal."

15. "Effects of Divorce on Children's Education," *Marripedia.*

16. Child Trends, *Children in Poverty.*

17. *Impact of Poverty on Student Outcomes,* Hanover Research, January 2015.

18. *Ibid.*

19. Child Trends, *Neighborhood Safety.*

20. Jargowsky and Komi, "Before or After the Bell? School Context and Neighborhood Effects on Student Achievement," in Harriet Newburger, Eugenie Birch, and Susan Wachter (eds.), *Neighborhood and Life Changes: How Place Matters in Modern America.*

21. Wodtke, Harding, and Elwert, "Neighborhood Effects in Temporal Perspective: The Impact of Long-Term Exposure to Concentrated Disadvantage on High School Graduation."

22. Kessler, "What I Learned in 12 Weeks of Therapy for Social Media Addiction."

23. "Board Policy 3225 – Technology Responsible Use," *Wake County Public Schools.*

24. Kabali, Irigoyen, Nunez-Davis, Budacki, Mohanty, Leister, and Bonner, "Exposure and Use of Mobile Devices by Young Children."

25. "Monitoring the Future: A Continuing Survey of American Youth," University of Michigan.

26. Bhat, "Cyber Bullying: Overview and Strategies for School Counselors, Guidance Officers, and All School Personnel."

27. Twenge, *IGen: Why Today's Super-Connected Kids are Growing up Less Rebellious, More Tolerant, Less Happy—and Completely Unprepared for Adulthood*; Orben, Dienlin, and Przybylski, "Social Media's Enduring Effect on Adolescent Life Satisfaction."

28. Seabrok, Kern, and Rickard, "Social Networking Sites, Depression, and Anxiety: A Systematic Review."

29. Saringo-Rodriguez, "Studies Show Depression Affects Academic Progress, Causes Stress and Chemical Imbalance."

30. National Center for Education Statistics, *op. cit.*, Table 236.15.

31. Jackson, Rebecca, "The Case Against Group Projects: What Parents and Teachers Can Learn from Them"; Eckard, "Guidelines Needed for Screen Safety at School."

32. Lattier, "Did Public Schools Really Improve American Literacy?"

33. RAND Education, *Effect of Teacher Pay on Student Performance*; Dolton and Gutierrez, *Teachers' Pay and Pupil Performance*.

34. Alegretto, Corcoran, and Mishel, *How Does Teacher Pay Compare? Methodological Challenges and Answers*; Baker, Sciarra, and Farrie, *Is School Funding Fair: A National Report Card?*

35. Bertrand, "Here's the Average SAT Scores for Every College Major."

36. Podolsky, Kini, Bishop, and Dariling-Hammond, *Solving the Teacher Shortage: How to Attract and Retain Excellent Educators*.

37. Mosteller, "The Tennessee Study of Class Size in the Early School Grades."

38. Organization for Economic Cooperation and Development, *Innovating Education and Educating for Innovation*.

39. Jones, John, "How Does Electronic Reading Affect Comprehension?"

40. Almond, Currie, and Duque, "Childhood Circumstances and Adult Outcomes: Act II."

41. Cornelissen and Dustmann, "Early School Exposure, Test Scores, and Noncognitive Outcomes"; Bailey, Sun, and Timpe, "Prep School for Poor Kids: The Long-Run Impacts of Head Start on Human Capital and Economic Self-Sufficiency"; Hendren and Sprung-Keyser, "A Unified Welfare Analysis of Government Policies."

42. Heckman, *Giving Kids a Fair Chance*; Heckman and Krueger, *Inequality in America: What Role for Human Capital Policies?* For a review of other research, see President's Council of Economic Advisers, *The Economics of Early Childhood Investments*. Of course, many children can thrive and develop strong learning habits outside of formalized pre-schools (see McDonald, *Unschooled*).

43. Heckman, Moon, Pinto, Savelyev, and Yavitz, "The Rate of Return to the HighScope Perry Preschool Program." Heckman et al.

44. Curto and Fryer, "The Potential of Urban Boarding Room Schools for the Poor."

45. Riley, *Be the Parent, Please*.

46. National Center for Education Statistics, *op. cit.*, Tables 203.10, 205.10, and 206.10.

47. Bifulco and Ladd, "Institutional Change and Coproduction of Public Services: The Effect of Charter Schools on Parental Involvement"; Noel, Stark, Redford, and Zukerberg, "Parental and Family Involvement in Education, from the National Household Education Surveys Program 2012."

48. Heckman et. al., op. cit.; Mitra, *Pennsylvania's Best Investment: The Social and Economic Benefits of Public Education.*

49. Hanushek, Peterson, and Woessmann, *Endangering Prosperity.* This estimate is based on achieving the economic productivity levels of Germany.

50. U.S. Bureau of Economic Analysis, U.S. *Economic Accounts.* National income is gross domestic product, or the value of everything produced in the economy during a year. The latest year available is 2016.

51. K. Jackson, "Does School Spending Matter: The New Literature on an Old Question."

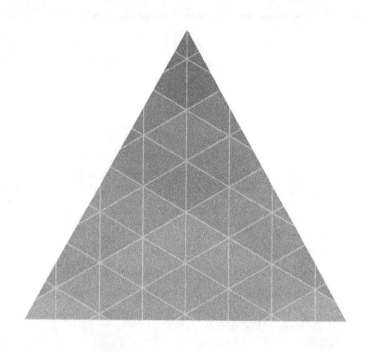

CHAPTER TWO

BRINGING COLLEGE COSTS DOWN TO EARTH

STARTING LIFE BEHIND

I n 1969, the year I entered college, one year of college tuition and fees for full-time students cost, on average, $2,302 at four-year, publicly supported colleges and universities. Almost fifty years later in 2016, average annual tuition and fees at the same institutions cost $8,804. This represents a 282% increase.[1] Now, before you say, "Yes, but everything costs more today, so big deal," I will point out that these costs are *after* removing the general rise in the cost-of-living (also called inflation). In fact, both costs are using the purchasing power of dollars in 2016, and therefore, as economists would say, the 282% increase is in "inflation-adjusted dollars."

Here's another way of looking at the rise in college costs: in 1969, annual college tuition and fees took 4.2% of average household income. In 2016, these same costs took 12% of average household income.[2] (Costs for room and board aren't included because individuals would have similar costs even if they weren't in college.) You get the point (probably a point I didn't need to make), that college costs have been rising significantly faster than other costs and faster than our income.

Now, sure, colleges and other organizations offer scholarships and grants to some students, which don't have to be repaid. But even this help hasn't kept up with rising tuition rates. In fact, subtracting scholarships and grants from tuition and fees to obtain a measure called "net tuition and fees" reveals that this expense has risen even faster than regular tuition and fees during the last four decades.[3]

The gigantic increase in college costs has created a new term in our financial vocabulary: *student loan debt*. No one ever heard of this when I started college in 1969, and I don't think the concept had been developed. Most kids, like me, financed their college education with a little help from their parents and by working part-time jobs.

Student loan debt is now the fastest-growing type of debt, standing at $1.3 trillion in 2016, and rising a whopping 500% since 2001—even after removing general inflation![4] In fact, the average student at a public college or university ends up with $27,000 in student loan debt.[5] And this includes those who graduate as well as those who don't.

Economists think the emergence of student loan debt has had a profound impact on the important decisions of today's young households.[6] Graduates saddled with student loan debt have to delay buying homes, furniture, and appliances. It is estimated today's newly minted college graduates take seven years longer to purchase their first home than my generation.[7] Student loan debt also appears to be delaying current college grads from having children.[8] All these changes could be one of the reasons why the economic recovery from the Great Recession of 2007-2009 was the slowest since World War II.[9]

When my father returned from the Second World War and became a carpenter, he rented an apartment with my mother and immediately began saving money to buy a home. Even when I graduated from college, I had very little debt so I followed in my father's tracks by renting a modest apartment and socking away money so my wife and I could eventually purchase our first home. Most of today's young people who graduate from college are unable to follow that sort of path. They start in the hole with five-figures of college debt, which puts a big dent in their goals of home-owning and even starting a family. The big question is why? Why has college become so expensive?

△ LOOKING BEHIND THE VEIL OF COLLEGE COSTS

There's an old saying in both business and journalism, "Follow the money." This means if you're trying to understand a story, a transaction, or even a mystery, tracing the flow of money between people and companies can often lead you to the answer. If we want to understand the rise in college costs, we should follow the flow of money through colleges. There are two types of college money flows to trace: revenues received by colleges, and expenditures made by colleges.

Table 2-1 shows changes in expenditures and revenues for four-year public colleges and universities during this century (2000-2017). The dollar amounts are all adjusted for general inflation and use the purchasing power of dollars in 2017. The dollar amounts are also expressed "per full-time equivalent (FTE) student." Because both college expenses and college revenues differ for part-time and full-time students, the concept of FTE was developed to allow the combination of the two.

What or who are the culprits behind rising college costs? Increases in the salaries of professors did beat general inflation by 15% points, but this works out to be less than 1% per year. In fact, the average salary of college faculty has risen only one-fourth as fast as the average salaries of all workers over the last 45 years,[10] and, contrary to what often is claimed, the teaching loads of college faculty haven't dropped.[11]

CATEGORY	2000	2017	Total Percentage Change
EXPENDITURES			
Teaching salaries[a]	$6,176	$7,129	15.4%
Teaching equipment[a]	$2,284	$5,410	**136.9%**
Student support services	$1,414	$2,107	**49.0%**
Research	$4,669	$5,269	12.9%
Public service	$1,982	$2,037	2.8%
General support	$7,723	$7,376	-4.5%
Scholarships	$1,680	$1,520	-9.5%
Other	$1,952	-$42[b]	-
Total	$27,880	$30,798	10.5%
REVENUES			
Tuition and fees	$6,809	$9,868	**44.9%**
Federal government	$4,500	$5,734	27.4%
State government	$12,718	$9,075	**-28.6%**
Private & local government	$2,337	$3,200	**36.9%**
Other	$1,516	$2,921	92.7%
Total	$27,880	$30,798	10.5%

Source: National Center for Education Statistics; [a] earliest data are for 2004; [b] reflects transfers from other years

Table 2-1. Expenditures and Revenues for Four-Year Public Colleges and Universities from 2000 to 2017, per Full-Time Equivalent Student in 2017 Purchasing Power Dollars.

College administration offices, groundskeepers, and utilities services—all captured by the category "general support"—don't seem to be a culprit. In fact, spending on these academic activities actually fell between 2000 and 2017 after adjusting for inflation. Analysis over a longer time period finds the same result.[12]

Instead, the two largest categories behind the jump in college costs during the century are a nearly 137% rise in spending on teaching equipment and an almost 50% hike in student service expenses. The extra spending on teaching equipment makes sense; classrooms like the ones I began teaching in during the 1970s used a blackboard and chalk as equipment, whereas today's classrooms have the latest in computers, touch-screens, video capabilities, and, of course, Wi-Fi access. While I have found computer-generated slides a big improvement over my chalk drawn graphs, I also know many students are distracted from learning when their personal technology devices are available for checking messages and surfing the web. This has raised questions about the benefit of new technology in the college classroom.[13]

According to the U.S. Department of Education, student support services "includes salary, benefits, supplies, and contractual fees for staff providing attendance and social work, guidance, health, psychological services, speech pathology, audiology, and other support to students."[14] I don't deny the need to give academic guidance and counseling to students, but that has been part of my job as a professor. Each year I am assigned advisees who, if they stay in college, I mentor until they graduate. Yet the large jump in student support services spending suggests more college students today are having broader personal and social issues. Maybe some of these stem from the fact that 40% of students entering four-year colleges and universities have to take some remedial courses.[15] This is another reason to take the steps to improve student performance at the K-12 level that I outlined in Chapter 1.

You might be wondering what "public service" is in Table 2-1. It means college faculty and staff taking academic information and research out of the classroom and into the community. I know, because I've participated in this kind of activity during my years as a university professor. In my case, I have worked with state agencies on economic development, and I've done around 3,000 workshops and presentations on economic issues and policy alternatives throughout the state. Public service work is typically funded out of government and private grants, not student tuition and fees.

There's been a longstanding debate about the role of sports on college campuses, specifically whether those sports use funds that could be spent on academics. Although not shown separately in Table 2-1, there are subsidies to college athletics. While the teams of big-name schools may be financially self-sufficient, a 2014 study published in the *Chronicle of Higher Education* estimated that student fees pay almost $1 billion annually (average for 2010-2014) to support Division I college sports teams. If subsidies provided by the colleges and state governments are added, the annual bill increases to $2 billion.[16]

On the revenue side, the table shows the big increase in student tuition and fees, by $3,000 or 45%, after subtracting general inflation between 2000 and 2016. This increase was needed to help replace the more than $3,000 reduction in funding from state governments. And why did state governments reduce their funding of higher education? There's a one-word answer: *Medicaid.* Medicaid is the federal-state jointly funded program to assist lower-income households with their medical expenses. As a result of expanding the number of people eligible for Medicaid, plus the rising cost of medical care, states have had to increase from 20% to 40% the share of their total spending allocated to Medicaid between 2000 and 2016. All of this is to say that every extra dollar spent on Medicaid has resulted in 43 cents less spent on public four-year colleges.[17]

What if we wanted to roll back tuition and fees to where they were in the year 2000? This would be over a 30% reduction in costs from 2016. We could accomplish this by reducing spending on teaching equipment and on student support services. For example, cutting $693 from the 2016 student support services budget would still leave it at the same level *per student* as in 2000. Likewise, trimming $2,366 from the teaching equipment budget in 2016 would put it one-third higher *per student* than in 2000. The total savings of $3,059 ($693 + $2,366) would get tuition and fees to what they were in 2000.

Why don't we see at least some colleges and universities doing something like this? It's because they can't. Higher education institutions don't have total control over their campuses!

△ THE COLLEGE CARTEL

You may have heard of a drug cartel or an oil cartel, and although you may not exactly know what a cartel is, your gut tells you it's not good. In this case your gut is right, economically speaking. A cartel is a group of companies that coordinate some of their activities in order to stifle competition and earn larger profits. Competition can be stifled in different ways. In the case of drug cartels, competition is literally eliminated through violence! Oil cartels, the most famous being OPEC (Organization of Petroleum Exporting Countries), enforce their rules in a more civilized way by using diplomacy and negotiation to have member countries limit their oil production in order to support a set price.[18]

Economists believe competition is good and limiting competition is bad. Competition forces businesses to go head-to-head against each other to win the hearts, minds, and wallets of consumers. Businesses do this by offering a better product, a lower price, or both. Yes, competition can be messy with winners and losers, and so we need referees (mainly rules and laws established by government), and consumers need to do their homework so they are not tricked by a business competing unfairly. But for the most part, competition has been shown to improve well-being and standards of living better than any other economic system.[19]

Colleges operate as a form of a cartel through accreditation. To be accredited—a sort of "seal of approval"—colleges must follow rules established by accrediting organizations. These rules are extensive, covering faculty credentials, course content and program, library facilities, administration, planning and evaluation, student support services, measurement of student achievement, and physical support like buildings and equipment. Periodic reports must be submitted and visits accepted from the accrediting organizations for a college to keep up its standing.[20] And while the organizations don't directly control tuitions and fees charged to students, the requirements for meeting the standards certainly put a floor on those charges.

Here is the most important fact about college accreditation: for a student to be eligible to receive federal aid and subsidies—which have become increasingly important as college costs have soared—the college the student attends must be accredited.[21]

So, let's say some college wanted to reduce tuition costs by cutting student support services. Could they do it? Not necessarily. They might run afoul of the accrediting organization's standards and risk losing their accreditation. And what if there's a college whose administrators and faculty think "outside the box" and develop a new way to deliver college course, but in an unconventional way? Well, good luck getting accredited! And if the innovative thinker's program isn't accredited, good luck getting the students in need of aid any financial help!

In a big way, then, college accreditation keeps all colleges and universities doing the same thing, perpetuating the same kinds of spending and inhibiting experimenting with new ways of delivering college education more effectively. This is unfortunate, because in our history it has frequently been the "odd-balls" (those following their own path) who develop breakthrough innovations that advance society.[22]

Do students or their parents care if a college is accredited? They may not think they do, but word gets around when a school is not.

A lack of accreditation hurts a college's reputation and ability to attract students. In fact, since the quality of a college is difficult for most to evaluate, studies have shown that a college's reputation is a big-deal in a young person's decision for selecting a school, as well as in the ultimate pay-off from a degree.[23] Fortunately, there are now some colleges with different structures and programs that have been accredited. They are mainly of the "online" variety, like Perdue University Global and Western Governors University. However, it can still take years for institutions who want to experiment with new formats to please the accrediting taskmasters and get their stamp of approval.[24]

For the most part, the college cartel, enforced by accreditation, protects colleges and universities that don't rock the boat, cements spending patterns as normal and expected, and justifies tuition increases to meet the standards of the accrediting know-it-alls. But there's another enforcer in this process, and its color is green.

△ THE ENABLER OF EASY MONEY

In most markets, when the price of a product or service rises, people buy less. Economists believe so strongly in this idea that we call it the "iron law of demand" (demand is the odd way economists refer to buying). So, when house prices rise, fewer homes are sold. Or when gas prices go up, drivers eventually reduce or alter their driving so they buy less gas.

However, the iron law of demand doesn't appear to apply to colleges. While college tuition and fees have been rising during the last fifty years, more, rather than fewer, high school graduates have been going to college. In 1969, I was part of only 55% of high school grads who moved on to higher education. Today the rate is up to almost 70%.[25]

How could this happen? The answer is there were enablers, mainly in the form of relatively easy money for students to borrow. Indeed, two recent studies have linked the rise of college tuition and fees to the growing abundance of money for college borrowing, with much of this money coming from the federal government. The research found that every $1 increase in federal student aid is associated with a 60-cent increase in college tuition and fees.[26] Thirty years before these studies, William Bennett, a former U.S. Secretary of Education, made the same point; he argued that the availability of government assistance reduced students' resistance to higher tuitions and allowed colleges to increase their costs.[27] There are also ways for student borrowers to repay a relatively small fraction of their loan for several years and then have the rest forgiven.[28]

In short, colleges have a sweet deal. They have cover from accrediting organizations that keep at bay innovating administrators and faculty who find ways to cut costs and tuitions. They have an enabler, mainly in the form of the federal government, who pumps credit to students so they can pay the higher rates. They have students who are convinced they have to attend college to get a good job. And finally, since repaying student loans is years in the future, students set worries aside about rising costs and mounting debt.

Still, what's the problem? As long as the system works to make college students and society better-off, who cares? But does our college system really work, especially for students?

△ IS COLLEGE WORTH IT—TO STUDENTS AND TO SOCIETY?

The good news is that going to college appears to be worthwhile, as long as the student graduates. The latest data show the average college graduate earns about $30,000 more per year than the average high school graduate, which translates to an 84% bump in annual pay and $1 million more in earnings over a typical work career.[29] College grads also have lower unemployment rates than high school grads, and fewer individuals with a college degree live in poverty.[30]

But there are two pieces of bad news. After rising for almost four decades, the increase in pay for a college graduate compared to a high school graduate—known as the *college premium*—appears to have stopped, at best, and perhaps begun to decline, at worst. We're not talking about a massive drop; instead, the college premium is down a couple of percentage points since 2015.[31] To quote the author of a recent study of salaries of college grads, one of the reasons for the fall in the college premium is "a general weakening in the demand for advanced cognitive skills."[32] Uh-oh! Translated, this means employers are finding they don't need as many college grads.

In fact, this same concern has been raised by the federal government. One report from the U.S. Bureau of Labor Statistics, the agency that tracks unemployment numbers and makes job forecasts, estimates less than 30% of jobs really need a college degree. Yet we're on a pace to produce a much larger supply.[33] So, the college wage premium may have topped out because college grads are now so common, or, more ominously, it may be because college grads aren't as valued as they used to be. I'll explore this worrisome reason in a little bit.

The second piece of bad news is that students are not graduating on time. Two independent tracking services show between 35% and 40% of undergraduate students don't have a degree by the end of six years in school, and the majority of those have dropped out of school.[34] What's worse, almost one-third of the dropouts have college debt.[35] And statistics show having some years in college but not getting a degree increases earnings only marginally above what a high school grad receives.[36] For students who drop out of college and don't get a degree, college isn't a good financial deal.[37]

Now, let me get back to my "uh-oh" state above. I'm sure you've heard a large percentage of college grads ends up getting jobs *not* in their major. One study found only 27% of college graduates had a job matching their major[38], and 30% were in jobs that didn't even require a college degree.[39] What's going on? Isn't the whole point of going to college to get a degree in a particular field and then find a job in that field? Why else would someone hire a college grad, and, more specifically, why would a business hire a college grad to do a job they weren't trained in college to do?

Bryan Caplan may have the answer. Who's he? Bryan Caplan is a very smart economics professor at George Mason University. In his relatively short career, he has taken on weighty questions—like whether people always vote in their self-interest—and achieved a level of national fame. His recently wrote a book about higher education, and in it he answers the question of why a business would hire a college graduate if the job didn't require a college degree.[40]

Caplan's simple answer is that many businesses don't hire college grads because of their degree; the businesses expect to teach most of what the grad needs to know on-the-job. Instead, businesses hire college grads because of what having a college degree "signals" about the individual. The degree signals three major characteristics: intelligence, work ethic, and conformity. The college grad needs to have some level of intelligence to be admitted to a college and then to finish. The college grad has to apply some level of work effort to successfully finish courses. Lastly, the college grad has to display some conformity, like taking courses he/she doesn't like or attending classes when he/she could be sleeping, in order to graduate.

These are low standards, but since grade inflation has hit colleges [41]and study time by college students is much lower today than in the past,[42] employers have a difficult time discerning what a college grad really knows. The point is, businesses assume that the desirable traits of intelligence, work ethic, and conformity are higher in college graduates than in individuals who don't attend college or drop out. Since these traits are difficult to perceive before someone is hired, businesses simply use a college degree as a ready screening device.

Signaling desirable personal traits to employers is not limited to individuals with college degrees. One reason job seekers are often told to dress well, be well groomed, and exhibit manners on job interviews is that these are observable features an employer may correlate with being a good worker. Caplan is also not the first to talk about the signaling effect of a college degree.[43] However, he is the first to make an estimate of the value of signaling from a college degree versus the value of the learned skills from the degree. He says, on average, 80% of the value of a college degree comes from what it signals to employers about the graduate's work-related capabilities, and only 20% of the degree's value is based on the specific skills or knowledge the graduate learned in college.

Of course, not everyone agrees with Caplan.[44] Other researchers have pegged the signaling value of a degree at 30%.[45] Yet even if you think his 80% number for the signaling value of a college degree is too high, a lower value like 30%, 40%, or 50% is still jaw-dropping and troubling. Any of these lower numbers would suggest a tremendous waste of time and money to society in teaching college students many subjects they won't use to earn a living. And if the reply is, "Yes, but they will appreciate those courses later in life"—I don't see any widespread evidence of that. In fact, analysis shows the average college student retains very little of what she or he was taught.[46] Furthermore, later in life when individuals are stable in their job and family, there are plenty of opportunities to study philosophy, art history, a foreign language, or the classics if they so wish.

So, one of the reforms we need in higher education is a system that allows employers to better know what specific skills a college graduate has mastered. But before I address this in the solutions section, let me turn to one other big issue in college education: the high cost of books.

△ HOW DID TEXTBOOKS GET SO EXPENSIVE?

Here's a pop quiz. Which of the following items had the largest price increase between 2001 and 2018: medical care, gasoline, college textbooks, or college tuition and fees? If you answered college textbooks, you know where I am going!

I have been a college professor since the late 1970s, but it wasn't until the late 1990s that I started to get questions from students about the price of their textbooks. I'd always assigned textbooks based on which ones I thought were the best (for full disclosure, some of them were written by me), and students would always ask where the books were available and if they could buy cheaper earlier editions (I usually answered "yes" to the second question). But in the late 1990s, many students said they were spending several hundred dollars each semester on books.

What happened to the college textbook market exactly parallels what has happened to the prescription drug market, which I'll discuss in depth in Chapter 4. Consolidation occurred, meaning the number of textbook publishers dramatically shrunk to about five today.[47] In economics, when competition falls, prices usually rise. Additionally, the remaining book publishers seemed to borrow a page from the automakers' handbook; in the 1950s, car companies found they could increase sales and profits by introducing new models each year. Sometimes the models had real improvements, like power steering and radios (yes, radios!), but often the changes were just cosmetic.

Textbook companies have increasingly done the same thing. They frequently commission new editions of textbooks (which authors willingly write because they earn more royalties) and argue that past editions are not usable because they're out-of-date. If the professors who choose these books buy into this logic, then students are deterred from purchasing older, cheaper editions, and the textbook companies are guaranteed a whole new round of sales.

Therefore, professors deserve some of the blame. Like doctors writing prescriptions, they assign what they consider to be the best available textbooks, and usually these are the latest editions, and since professors have no "skin in the game" (that is, they pay none of the costs), the textbook's price often isn't a factor in their choice of assigned books. Although students may complain, the enabler of easy-to-get college loan money means they can finance their book purchases just like their tuition and fees.

△ FAKE SOLUTIONS

In a nutshell, here's the explanation for high and rising college costs. High school graduates see a financial incentive in going to college, and salaries in the labor market back up that perception. As college costs rise, more students rely on borrowing money in order to pay for attending. The federal government is a big source of these funds, currently holding 83% of total student loan debt.[48] For students to qualify for loans, the college they're attending must be accredited. Accrediting agencies impose similar academic and non-academic standards on colleges, which work to impede innovation and competition.

So, ready buyers (the students) with available credit, combined with conformity and little competition, is a perfect recipe for rising prices. Plus, the ultimate users of the college grads (employers) seem to care little about what the graduate learned; they just want college graduates!

The major fake solution to this problem makes college free to students and has the federal government pay for all student loans.[49]

The solution is "fake" because it doesn't solve any of the underlying problems driving college costs.

There are several problems to making college free. First, nothing is ever free. While parents don't directly pay for the free K-12 education their children receive, they and other households indirectly pay for it though their property taxes (and yes, renters pay property taxes as a component of their rent) as well as through a variety of state and federal taxes. It would be the same situation for college education; some form of public funding through increased taxes or reductions in spending would need to be found. One "college free" plan is estimated to cost $1.3 trillion over ten years.[50]

Second, once something becomes funded by the government, this is almost a sure way to ensure costs will continue to rise. As we'll later see with the government's big health care programs, once government provides the funding, there will be intense political pressure to see that the funding continues and expands. Students, professors, and their supporters who have a lot to lose without government support will keep up a constant drumbeat for more, more, more government support.

Third, having "skin in the game" grabs one's attention and usually makes the payee work harder. While children in K-12 are likely not yet cognitively developed enough to make the connection between society's payment for their education and their commitment to learning, college students are.

Let's face it, college life is not that bad—I know, as I was once a college student and have observed students for over four decades.

If someone else is paying the bill, there's just not that motivation to put our nose to the grindstone to finish on time. For many college kids, the six or seven-year plan is fine, but if the student is paying at least some of the bill, either now or later, there will be more motivation to study and graduate quickly. In fact, a sociological study of college students found just this. As the author states, outside financial help—in this case from parents—motivated students to "dial down their academic efforts."[51]

Yet, maybe the biggest problem with the "make college free" solution is it cements the spending patterns, policies, and programs that colleges now have, many of which are mandated by the accrediting agencies. There's no motivation for colleges to become more efficient, streamlined, or innovative. And remember, every dollar unproductively spent on college could be spent in many other, potentially productive, ways. As you'll see, pushing colleges and college students to be more productive and efficient with their and our money and time is the goal of my "real solutions."

There's a corollary fake solution to "make college free" that says, "make colleges pay if students don't succeed." In this case, success occurs if students are able to repay their loans within a certain time period. If they don't, then the college would repay a portion of the loan, especially if it's a government loan. The assumption behind this idea is colleges will work harder to make sure students are successful since they know they will be on the hook for some of the loan if students flounder.[52]

I read this fake solution as just another "Let's make lawyers even richer" scheme. How, or who, determines if a college grad can't repay his loan on account of the failure of the college? What if the grad was lazy, incompetent, or picky about their jobs? I foresee a mountain of lawsuits filed by both graduates and colleges. Furthermore, if colleges and government then become more careful and restrictive in making student loans, I predict an additional surge of lawsuits.

No, the solution to costly colleges isn't to make them free or to shift the blame and responsibility if students are unsuccessful. Instead, the key to recapturing the purpose of college as a place of true leaning at a reasonable cost is based on a couple of simple, real solutions.

△ REAL SOLUTIONS

I recommend two major changes to shake-up college education, spur innovation and competition, reduce costs, and, perhaps most importantly, allow employers to easily understand what graduates have learned.

The first recommendation is *mandatory national exams for each college major.*[53] Such tests are already administered for accountants, and lawyers take state versions of a standardized exam. Several financial planning organizations use mandatory exams to earn their certification, as does the Internal Revenue Service for private sector enrolled agents who work with individuals owing large amounts of unpaid taxes. These exams for each major would be developed by leading teachers and professionals in their fields.

One obvious advantage of such mandatory exams is they would easily communicate to employers and others what the graduate knows. Now they're guessing. Potential employers may look at a graduate's GPA (grade point average) or transcript of courses, but with widespread grade inflation the numbers can be hard to trust. Some employers may use the reputation of the college as a "signal" for the quality of the graduate's education, but that can cause good graduates from lesser-known schools to be overlooked. However, with a national exam, there is no guessing about what the grad knows. And for those graduates who fear they'll have a bad test day, the rules could allow multiple attempts for passing. In fact, most of the organizations already using standardized national exams allow several retakes.

The second advantage of mandatory exams is—when combined with my second recommendation—it will incentivize a variety in learning methods. Individuals learn in different ways. Some are motivated self-leaners, others master information best through repetition, while still others comprehend knowledge most success-fully working with groups.

Individuals also have different time frames for learning. Some want to follow high school with college before they make other commit-ments, like marriage or a family, while others may want to change careers in middle age and then seek more schooling. Some college students enjoy the full experience of courses in a wide range of fields, compared to others who only want to learn a specific set of skills. Finally, the financial wherewithal of students to afford college differs.

However, for most of today's students, there's only one path for college: go to a brick-and-mortar college for four (but likely more) years, study courses in a major but also in numerous other areas (many of which the student has little interest in or will never use), deal with the various distractions of college life, and finally graduate with a diploma. And yes, this plan will cost a bundle and leave the student in debt.

If the goal of college is learning a major and becoming competent in it, then who cares how you accomplish that? People who are self-learners may require little guidance and external motivation. Some individuals may learn best by watching videos over and over. For many years, my lectures were taped, and students could access them whenever they wanted. I had many students honestly tell me they learned best by watching the videos and then emailing me questions. I had other students who obviously thrived on the live, in-person interactions provided in a classroom setting. The point is, with performance on a national exam used as the ultimate measure of a student's knowledge, there will develop many options for learning.

However, for learning options to expand, my second recommendation will need to be adopted: end college accreditation requirements.[54] The accrediting organizations keep colleges in a straitjacket and inhibit new thinking about improving learning and lowering costs. Eliminating accreditation will allow colleges to rethink and re-access the kind of education they offer and how they offer it. Many colleges will continue as they are, offering a full menu of courses, in-person learning, and amenities (student support services, access to cutting-edge research, sports teams) that most colleges now support. I'll call these full-service colleges. But alternatives and hybrids will also be developed, like online or cyber colleges, colleges offering training in specific skills, colleges offering specialized academic assistance to students, rapid-paced colleges taking only a year or two, and colleges aligned with specific businesses.[55]

One concern is that, without accreditation, there will be a proliferation of "fly-by-night," low-quality colleges that dupe students into paying for worthless degrees. But remember, any student with a degree will still have to take the national exam to be fully certified in a particular major or skill. Therefore, I recommend the remedy of annually publishing the passage rate for each major's national exam for all colleges. That way, prospective students can judge the success of colleges in educating their students. Also, if a college has a low success rate, prospective students will have to judge if it is the fault of the college or of the students. Either way, individual colleges will be motivated to take actions to improve poor success rates or risk the likely possibility of having no students!

Would my proposals mean the end of our country's great universities, which are known worldwide for both their teaching and research? Of course not! There would still be plenty of smart students who want to work with possible Nobel Prize winners on path-breaking research. And there would still be governments and private businesses who want to fund that research. But not all students care to be in that kind of environment. They want to get in and get out of college fast, learn a specific skill or field, and then start making money. Therefore, I would expect there would end up being a range of colleges, from those focusing only on undergraduate education to those with both undergraduate and graduate education, funded research, and public service.

How would these two recommendations help reduce book prices? With more competition for students and no limitations imposed by accrediting agencies, professors and colleges could experiment with using different forms of texts, like the copies of notes I used or non-current editions of books. By studying how student performance on the national standardized tests varied with the type of textbook used, professors could determine if the latest and glossiest textbooks really contributed to learning.

Here's the question you've all been waiting to ask: would my two recommendations for college education reduce college costs and make college more affordable? My answer is, yes they would, and let me tell you how.

Let's say you want to start a college. Your college will be focused only on teaching, so you need two inputs—professors to teach and space for classes. Let's consider the professors' costs first. Each student takes a full load of 5 three-credit-hour courses per semester. Since the average college teaching load for professors is four classes per semester,[56] you'll increase the average professor's nine-month salary by 25% to $109,000 annually.[57] With an average of 30 students per class and a teaching load of five classes, a professor teaches 150 students per semester. This makes each professors' costs, per student and per semester, equal to $54,500 (the professors' per-semester salary) divided by 150, or $363. For a student taking five classes during a semester, the cost of the professors' time and expertise is $363 x 5, or $1,815. For two semesters, the annual cost per student for professors is $3,630.

Now, look at space costs. With an average of 30 students per class and a rule of 18.3 square feet per student, you need a 550-square foot classroom.[58] With the annual per square foot rent at $43,[59] yearly costs for the space are $43 x 550, or $23,650. But the room can be used for more than five hours daily. Using proper scheduling, you'll be able to use each room for ten hours of daily classes. This means the per semester room costs ($23,650/2, or $11,825) are shared by 30 x 10, or 300 students, making the cost per student equal to $11,825/300, or $39.42. With each student enrolled for both semesters per year, the annual cost per student for the room is $79 (rounded).

The total cost annual per student to fund instruction and space is therefore $3,630 + $79, or $3,709. This is only 41% of the current average annual tuition and fees per student at public four-year colleges.[60]

Notice you've budgeted for the typical college year, which is two semesters. Hence, you are not assuming use of the room during the summer, even though you've paid for it. The professors' salary is also for nine months. So, if the space was used for summer school, you could charge for another semester and easily pay the professor.

You have doubtless noticed that a cafeteria, parking, sports teams, study halls, a library, professors' offices, a student support center, research labs, administration, and college outreach (another name for public service) were not included. This is because the college I've outlined is bare bones, including only faculty, classrooms, and students. Students and professors are assumed to do their work at home, eat at home or at a nearby restaurant or pack a lunch, communicate by email, pay for their own parking, do research online, and cheer for professional sports teams.

This exercise shows how much college costs could be reduced. Yet maybe the reductions are overdone. Perhaps some rooms for professors or a restaurant or cafeteria are needed. If so, instead of cutting college costs by almost 60%, maybe we can only reduce them by half. Among four-year public colleges, a 50% cut in spending would still save almost $160 billion annually.[61] This is double the annual amount of state and local public appropriations to colleges and universities.[62] If this money could be redirected to K-12 education, it would pay for around 40% of the recommended surge in K-12 spending outlined in Chapter 1.

Before wrapping-up this chapter, there's one more reason why colleges need to be transformed. The traditional customer base of colleges is dropping. Low birth rates and a slow growing U.S. population have led experts to predict the number of young people going to college will drop by 6% between 2018 and 2030.[63] At the same time, other experts forecast advances in technology that could eliminate up to half of today's occupations, while, hopefully, creating new ones.[64] If true, this means there will be millions of unemployed workers who will need to be retrained for different occupations in the coming decades, and many, maybe most, of these new students will be older than today's typical college student, possibly even with a family to support, meaning they will need to be retooled with specific occupational skills in a short period of time. Colleges will have to adapt, innovate, and become more efficient and less costly to deal with these changing circumstances.

State public policy can help by converting a portion of traditional unemployment compensation programs to educational vouchers.

Unemployment compensation programs are designed to help workers who are temporarily unemployed due to recessions. The underlying assumption is they will return to work when the recession ends. But workers who lose jobs because their occupation has been eliminated will need to acquire new skills. Converting what they would receive from unemployment compensation to a lump sum voucher to be used for education can put them on track to new careers in the new economy.

The bottom line is, the current college model has to be "shaken up."

▲ SUMMING UP

While there's much to celebrate about our colleges, there are also big issues including high prices, exploding student debt, expansion of non-teaching functions, mediocre graduation rates, lack of innovation, and a dismissal by many employees of what graduates have supposedly learned. To confront and correct these deficiencies, colleges need to be pushed out of their collective comfort zones and compete for students and win the approval of employers. Eliminating accreditation and instituting national exams for each major are two ways to bring efficiencies and enhanced excellence in our institutions of higher learning. To assist workers losing their jobs due to "technological unemployment," unemployment compensation programs should be converted to educational vouchers.

Chapter 2 Endnotes

1. National Center for Education Statistics, *op. cit.*, Table 330.10. If both public and private colleges and universities are included, the increase from 1960 to 2016 was 220%.

2. Federal Reserve Bank of St. Louis, "Real Median Family Income in the United States."

3. National Center for Education Statistics, *op. cit.*, Table 330.10.

4. Federal Reserve Bank of New York, *Quarterly Report on Household Debt and Credit.*

5. College Board, *Trends in Student Aid*, 2017.

6. Weirsch, *The Cost of College: Student Loan Debt on the Rise.*

7. CPA Practice Advisor, "Student Loan Debt Delays Homeownership by Millennials by 7 Years," Sept. 18, 2017.

8. Kolko, "Millennials Delay Marriage and Kids, but Are Still Eager to Become Homeowners."

9. Morath, "Seven Years Later, Recovery Remains Weakest of the Post World War II Era."

10. National Center for Education Statistics, op. cit.; U.S. Bureau of Labor Statistics, "Current Employment Statistics." The comparison is for 1971 to 2016 in constant purchasing power dollars. The comparisons are made for all faculty as well as faculty categorized by rank (full, associate, and assistant professor).

11. Greenbery and Moore, *Faculty Workload Policies at Public Universities.*

12. Helland and Tabarrok, "Why Are the Prices So Damn High?"

13. Berdik, "To Ban or Not to Ban: Teachers Grapple with Forcing Students to Disconnect from Technology."

14. National Center for Education Statistics, op. cit., Appendix B, Definitions.

15. Chen and Simone, *op. cit.*

16. Wolverton, Hallman, Shifflett, and Kambhampti, "The $10 Billion Sports Tab."

17. National Association of State Budget Officers, *State Expenditure Report*. In 2017 purchasing power dollars, states spent $58 billion more in Medicaid in 2016 compared to 2000.

18. Nasrawi, "Iraq: Oil Overproduction is Tantamount to Military Aggression." There was one recent exception to the diplomatic style of OPEC. Iraq's invasion of fellow OPEC member Kuwait in 1990 was supposedly due in part to Kuwait ignoring agreed-upon oil production limits.

19. Cowen and Tabarrok, *Modern Principles of Economics*. For a contrary view of competition, see Alfie Kohn, *No Contest: The Case against Competition.*

20. "Accreditation of Colleges and Universities: Who's Accrediting the Accreditors?" *The Best Schools.*

21. Burke and Butler, *Accreditation: Removing the Barrier to Higher Education Reform.*

22. Hartford, *Fifty Inventions that Shaped the Modern Economy.*

23. MacLoad, Riehl, Saavedra, and Urquiola, *The Bog Sort: College Reputation and Labor Market Outcomes.*

24. Burke and Butler, *op. cit.*

25. McFarland, Hussar, de Brey, and Snyder, *The Condition of Education 2017.*

26. Lucca, Nadauld, and Shen, *Credit Supply and the Rise in College Tuition: Evidence from the Expansion in Federal Student Aid Programs*; Gordon and Hedlund, *Accounting for the Rise in College Tuition*.

27. Bennett, "Our Greedy Colleges."

28. Pant, "REPAYE: Everything You Need to Know about the Revised Pay as You Earn Program"; "Secret Ways to Get Student Loan Forgiveness," *The College Investor*.

29. U.S. Bureau of the Census, "Mean Earnings of Workers 18 Years and Over by Educational Attainment, Race, Hispanic Origin, and Sex, 1975-2015."

30. Pew Research Center, *The Rising Cost of Not Going to College*.

31. Valletta, *Recent Flattening in the Higher Education Wage Premium: Polarization, Skill Degrading, or Both?*

32. *Ibid.*

33. Pathe, "Too Many College Grads? Or Too Few?"

34. Digest of Education Statistics, op. cit., Table 326; National Student Clearinghouse Research Center, *Snapshot Report: Yearly Success and Progress Rates*.

35. Mui and Khimm, "College Dropouts have Debt but No Degree."

36. Weissmann, "Is Going to College Still Worth It if You Drop Out?"; U.S. Bureau of the Census, *op. cit.* The Census data show an increase of about $3,000 in annual income for an individual with some college but no degree compared to an individual with a high school degree. This is far below the $30,000 salary bump if the individual obtained a 4-year college degree.

37. Benson, Esteva, and Levy, "Dropouts, Taxes, and Risk: The Economic Return to College Under Realistic Assumptions."

38. Plumer, "Only 27% of College Grads have a Job Related to their Major."

39. Cooper, "New York Fed Highlights Underemployment among College Graduates."

40. Caplan, *The Case Against Education*.

41. Jascik, "Grade Inflation, Higher and Higher."

42. Burke, Amselem, and Hall, "Big Debt, Little Study: What Taxpayers Should Know about College Students' Time Use."

43. Cappelli, *Will College Pay Off?*

44. Carr, "Is Education a Waste of Time?"

45. Aryal, Bhuller, and Lange, "Signaling and Employer Learning with Instruments."

46. Arum and Roksa, *Academically Adrift*.

47. Weissmann, "Why Are College Textbooks So Absurdly Expensive?"

48. Mislinski, Jill, "The Fed's Financial Assets: What is Uncle Sam's Largest Asset?"

49. Quintana, "Free College Plans Such as Elizabeth Warren's Are Pretty Pricey. Some Say her Plan Would Benefit the Rich Most."

50. *Ibid.*

51. Hamilton, "More is More or More Is Less: Parental Financial Investments during College."

52. Pollock, Alex, "Colleges Need to Have Skin in the Game to Tackle Student Loan Debt."

53. Charles Murray, *Real Education*. Murray has offered this recommendation.

54. Vedder, *Restoring the Promise*. A long-time analyst and critic of higher education, Vedder also recommends college accreditation be eliminated or radically reformed.

55. Craig, *A New U*; and Kirp, *The College Dropout Scandal*.

56. "What is the Typical Teaching Load for University Faculty?" *Higher Ed Professor*.

57. Digest of Education Statistics, op. cit., Table 316.10.

58. "Classroom Design Overview," *Space Planning Working Group*.

59. Carr, "Average Office Rents Might Keep Rising Until 2018."

60. Digest of Education Statistics, *op. cit.*, Table 330.10.

61. Digest of Education Statistics, *op. cit.*, Table 334.10.

62. *Ibid*, Table 333.30.

63. Grawe, *Demographics and the Demand for Higher Education*.

64. Frey and Osborne, "The Future of Employment: How Susceptible are Jobs to Computerisation?"

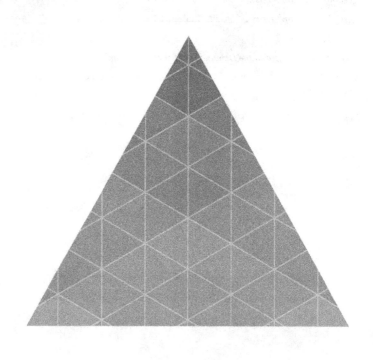

CHAPTER THREE

PAYING FOR MOVING FROM HERE TO THERE

SUNDOWN ON THE AUTO AGE?

It has only been about 120 years since the automobile made its appearance in our economy, but what an impact it has had! How and where we live and work, why some regions have expanded while others have decayed, how our environment has changed, and even how we parent and interact with our children have all been impacted by the auto. It's no overstatement to say that the last 120 years has been the Age of the Automobile.

The automobile has given us the freedom to be mobile. Unlike our ancestors over a century ago, we can live miles from our work, access a wide range of stores and amenities, and reside in remote locations where the real estate is cheaper. We can drive to other states and regions for vacations, and we can send our children to colleges hundreds of miles away and still expect frequent visits from them (often for doing laundry!). As soon as they become of driving age, many of our children want a vehicle so they can enjoy the same mobility.

Trucks have also been part of the age of the Age of the Automobile, and they too have transformed our daily lives by delivering products from all over the world to our doorsteps. Exotic and rare products that were inaccessible only decades ago are now common and available every day. Trucks are linked to another recent transportation innovation, the ocean cargo carrier. The ocean carrier has made buying products from halfway around the world as easy and common as buying from the next town was in the 19th century.[1]

There are worries that, despite the positive impacts that the invention of the auto has brought, there are also undeniably negative consequences. Air pollution from gasoline powered engines, sprawl from auto-enabled, low density suburbs, and a lack of community created by our always-on-the-go culture have been blamed on our reliance on the auto.

Yet there are signs that the Age of the Automobile may be ending, or at least changing dramatically. After declining for six decades, the percentage of households not owning a vehicle stopped dropping in the first decade of the 21st century. Many young households, including the Millennials (born between 1980 and 2000) and the newest generation, the I-Gens (born after 2000), have turned their backs on cars and are embracing new transit options like ride-sharing.[2] Even the good old-fashioned peddle-power of bicycles has experienced a resurgence in use, especially in big cities, along with their cousin, (electric) e-scooters.[3] Many cities are now establishing designated bike lanes to accommodate the cycling and scootering commuters. Then there are new transit options such as rides on demand—or ridesharing—offered by companies like Uber and

Lyft, who are also leaders in the so-called "gig" economy.[4] Around the corner may be driverless (or autonomous) vehicles.

The younger generations are also living differently, with many preferring to live in high-density cities where walking to work, shopping, restaurants, parks, and entertainment venues are easily available. In many cases, empty-nest retirees have joined them. Overall, this change has revived many inner cities in the country. While it is too early to say that these different living patterns will persist, it is clear that many people have changed how they want to live, where they want to live, and what kind of mobility method they will use.[5]

If these trends continue, some futurists expect our transportation will be dramatically different in the decades ahead. Indeed, traditional auto ownership may fall to as little as 10% to 20% of all households.[6] These experts see most of us moving around using a combination of mass transit, on-demand rides, and driverless vehicles. And vehicles won't be privately owned, but instead rented per-ride or per-trip from regional parking lots. If these forecasts are even close to correct, there will be positive changes in household budgets that free up thousands of dollars annually from unneeded car payments, auto insurance, and maintenance costs.

But there will also be challenges with funding the surfaces on which we move, mainly roads and rails. In fact, there are already problems.

△ CRACKS IN THE PAVEMENT

My paternal grandfather operated a small farm in southwestern Ohio in the early 20th century. Cars and trucks were just beginning to be used, but roads were little more than ruts carved out by the vehicles' wheels. When it rained, the ruts turned in to mini creeks, and forget about trying to navigate the "roads" during the winter weather!

My grandfather was elated when a private company used bricks and crushed rock to pave the rutted road in front of his farm running to the nearest town. Now he could reach the town quickly and safely. The "catch" was that it was a toll road, meaning the private company recovered its costs by charging drivers each time they used the road. But my grandfather didn't care; he easily covered the toll costs by reducing the losses to his farm products, such as eggs, by driving on the smoother and more reliable road.

Early roads were private ventures, and users understood they had to pay to use them. Eventually, two factors changed this system of road financing and operation. First was the massive expansion in auto use and the booming creation of new roads. While the impact of the roads was positive, the proliferation of private roads created headaches for drivers. For example, two connected but separately owned toll roads meant drivers had to stop twice to pay the tolls (remember, this was decades before smart phones and mobile payments!). The downtime of interrupting a trip to pay tolls multiplied when drivers used several private roads.

The second factor impacting toll roads and ultimately creating today's system of road finance was the Great Depression of the 1930s. This economic calamity bankrupted many companies, including those in the toll road business. Bankrupt road companies could not maintain existing roads, let alone build new ones.[7]

The solution to both problems was a government takeover of roads. With roads now essential to the economy, most people considered them to be a necessary service—meaning a service that couldn't be interrupted by the whims of the economy—and which should be financed by a reliable source of revenue. What was this reliable source of revenue? Gasoline! Initially discarded as waste when oil was first discovered in the mid-1800s, gasoline became perfect fuel for the automobile's internal combustion engine. Gas stations popped up all across the country as the automobile and road industries rapidly grew. Since vehicles needed gas to run, and since there was an approximate proportionality between gas used and miles driven, a gas tax was the perfect way to charge drivers for their use of the roads.

While gas tax revenues are the major source of revenue for roads, the reliance on gas taxes varies by state.[8] Some states use taxes on vehicle sales, license fees, and even property taxes when local governments are part of road building and maintenance. The federal government is also involved with its own tax on gasoline.

The gas tax model of financing and maintaining roads worked well for decades, but in the 21st century, major cracks appeared in the system. One crack is a reluctance to adjust the tax rate for inflation. Inflation reduces what every dollar can purchase, so when inflation occurs, more dollars must be spent to achieve the same result. Gas tax rates are measured in cents per gallon, so inflation means the cents per gallon must be periodically increased to generate the same purchasing power of gas tax revenues. Since 1994, the inflation-adjusted federal gas tax rate (tax per gallon) has dropped by one-third. [9]Most states have also not adjusted their gas tax to fully incorporate inflation.[10]

Another crack is rising fuel efficiency. Higher fuel efficiency means we're able to drive more miles per gallon. Average fuel efficiency has consistently trended upward since the late 1990s, and these gains are expected to accelerate with continued improvements in engine design and reductions in vehicle weight.[11] While this is certainly good for drivers (as well as for the environment), is also means the gas tax rate has to be increased to maintain the tax revenue collected per mile driven. But it hasn't. When both improved fuel efficiency and inflation are factored in, gas tax revenues per mile driven are lower today than they were in the 1990s.[12]

A third crack just now emerging is the use of alternative energy to run cars, like electric and hybrid (a combination of battery and gas), and possibly natural gas fuels. These alternatives are not subject to the gas tax. Although some states have levied special fees on fuels, the alternatives—specifically electric—are already costing states millions of dollars in lost gas tax revenues annually. With forecasts of rapid growth in alternative fuels, motor fuel revenues may fall by 40% by 2040.[13]

These cracks are leading to two large breakdowns in our road financing system. First as already noted, gas tax revenues have already been falling when adjusted for inflation and fuel efficiency. This crack will quickly become a chasm, as some forecasts suggest gas tax revenues will practically dry up unless tax rate increases of close to $2 per gallon are imposed (yes, you read this correctly; the gas tax would have to *rise* by almost $2 per gallon.[14] Second is a worry of a breakdown in road quality. Starved of adequate expansion and maintenance because of falling revenues, our nationwide system of roads and bridges is now receiving near-failing grades for adequacy and safety. In their latest annual report (2017), the American Society of Civil Engineers gives the nation's highways a grade of D, with a steady decline in the grade over the past decade. Bridges rank a little better at C+.[15] Drivers are wasting 6.9 billion hours annually in congested traffic, which is equivalent to 42 hours per driver. This "downtime" has a monetary value of $160 billion, and the amount has doubled in just the past decade, even after taking out general inflation. Highway fatalities have also begun to rise in recent years. Some experts think the recent rise in highway fatalities is partially linked to the decline in highway quality.[16]

△ FEWER ROADS IN OUR FUTURE?

Today's transportation system is moving us backward, not forward, with increased congestion, unsafe roads and bridges, and more dangerous driving conditions. Clearly, a factor behind these problems is lack of adequate money, mainly due to our unwillingness, or inability (or both), to make necessary adjustments to the workhorse of road finance: the gas tax.

If this was the only issue, it could be easily fixed. Gas tax rates per gallon could be raised, although I recognize this would require some heavy political lifting. But such a simple solution won't be enough. This is because we are likely living through the greatest changes to surface mobility during the century of the automobile age. Not only are new fuels being developed and used, but changes in vehicle technology and other technologies may reshape how we commute and how much we commute, and both will impact our need for roads.

For example, perfecting driverless vehicles should lower needed road capacity because these vehicles can be programmed to reduce congestion through traffic coordination and route selection. Also, telecommuting (a.k.a. working from home), after decades of never booming as many expected, may finally be ready to take off as high-speed internet, live conferencing, and—in the future—virtual reality, make home work spaces more viable.[17] It's expected that tens of millions of workers could take advantage of at-home working in order to have more time with their family and avoid lengthy and frustrating commutes, as was experienced during the COVID-19 pandemic.

The bottom line is we may not need as many vehicles and roads in the future as we think, even with population growth. Today in the US, there are 4 million lane-miles of roadway and 269 million vehicles[18] in a country with a population of 330 million.[19] If, for example, vehicle ownership fell by 33% and the average mileage in per-person commuting dropped by 25%, then in 2050, even with a forecasted population of 439 million people, we'd actually need 30% fewer lane-miles of roads.[20]

Still, we will need to continue upgrading, maintaining, and, in growing regions, building new roads as well as other public transportation infrastructure like mass transit, long-distance rail transit, and transportation depots and hubs. We need a modern method of financing this spending that will keep up with the rapid transformation expected in how we move.

△ FAKE SOLUTIONS

There are three types of fake solutions for financing our mobility. One looks at financial resources—in particular, different kinds of taxes to fund roads. The other recommends dramatically changing our method of mobility to significantly reduce reliance on roads and gas taxes. The third is a version of the second: a renewed interest in light-rail as a mobility mode.

Some observers simply say, if gas taxes aren't doing the job, and if it is difficult to increase gas tax rates, then just look for other taxes to fill the void. Two possibilities that have been offered are property taxes and sales taxes.

Let's first consider using property taxes to make up for the shortfall in gas tax revenues. An argument can be made that roads increase the values of nearby properties. Therefore, it should be nearby property owners who foot the bill for the roads. Since property taxes are used in all states, it should be simple to add some pennies per dollar of property value to fund and maintain roads. Since all states, to a varying degree, already allocate a portion of property taxes for road projects, the logic of using property taxes to finance roads is already in place.[21]

Another suggestion is to tap sales taxes to finance roads. Again, the idea is since virtually everyone pays sales taxes, and since everyone also benefits either from driving on roads or using products that are transported on the roads, there again is at least a general relationship between benefits and costs. Virginia recently decided to take this route (pun intended) when it diverted some of its sales tax revenues to transportation projects.[22]

There are problems with these ideas. For property taxes, research shows residents like to be close, but not too close, to roads. Owners of structures directly on roads can actually experience declines in the values of their properties due to noise and debris.[23] Thus, the relationship between access to roads and property values is complicated and not easily measured in a straightforward way.

The issue with sales taxes is the likelihood benefits and costs will vary widely among individuals. Sure, everyone benefits from roads, but not to the same extent. Take two people who spend the same amount of money and pay the same sales taxes. One doesn't drive and buys mostly locally-made products. The other drives frequently and purchases many products shipped long distances. Certainly, the two individuals are not benefiting from roads to the same degree. Yet they would pay the same amount in sales taxes used to finance roads.

Then there are the folks who want to rearrange where and how we live and commute in order to reduce our need for both individual vehicles and roads. They want us to live in high-rises and use mass transit like buses, light rail, or even subways where feasible.[24] In this hypothetical world, there would be little need for gas taxes or any tax to pay for roads, because using roads for mobility would be a thing of the past.

I know many people who would like to live in a Manhattan-style community, where people can easily walk to stores, restaurants, and even to work. I have no problem with developers proposing and offering this type of lifestyle, but I see two flaws in the thinking. First, not everyone will want to live this way, and second, we still need a way to finance the mass transit options.

And since I mentioned light rail, this form of transportation is enjoying an increase in interest as a way to move people and reduce congestion. In the Southeast, where I live, Atlanta has had a small light rail system for years, Charlotte is building one, and the Raleigh-Durham metro area has talked about it. Although I enjoy using light rail, I'm not a fan for a couple of reasons. It is costly, especially compared to buses. Construction costs are much higher due to acquiring land, laying tracks, and building depots. Operating costs have also been found to be more expensive than for buses.[25]

Light rail is also inflexible. Once the tracks are laid, they're hard to move without enormous expense. Light rail assumes the volume of people moving between locations remains the same, even though historically we know this isn't true. Although central cities have enjoyed a revival in recent years, their regional power is still much less than it was a century ago.[26] The residential layout of metropolitan areas has changed dramatically in past decades and will continue to do so in the future. Building light rail "locks in" travel patterns that may only be temporary.

For this reason, light rail should be relegated to highly dense cities where commuting patterns will likely persist, such as in New York City. Light rail is also feasible for highly traveled routes to destinations unlikely to move, such as airports, hospitals, or downtowns. For other mass transit options, buses using dedicated lanes offer the most flexible and cost-beneficial alternative to individual vehicles.

I'll close this section by mentioning that several states have recognized the challenges created by inflation and rising fuel efficiency on the adequacy of the gas tax in funding roads. As of 2017, 21 states have included some method of adjusting the gas tax rate for inflation. One state—Georgia—not only adjusts the gas tax rate for inflation but also for changes in fuel efficiency.[27] While helpful, these methods don't deal with the issue of alternative fuel sources, so to be generous, I'll label them a "half fake" solution.

△ REAL SOLUTIONS

Instead, the real solution to road and public mobility financing is to implement a "public mobility fee," or *Pumfee*. Pumfee would replace all current taxes and fees used to finance public transportation services, including public roads, bridges, buses, and commuter trains, with the one exception being airports. The current system of airport financing, which charges taxes and fees to passengers and cargo users, has worked reasonably well and would continue.[28]

The idea of Pumfee is simple; if you move on a public surface, such as a road, or in a public vehicle like a bus or train, you pay a fee. How you move—whether in a car, bus, or train—and how far you move (miles), determines the fee. The fuel used to move you has nothing to do with the fee. Payments could easily be split between different governmental units (federal, state, local) depending on the amount of financing of the transit mode provided by each level of government.

The Pumfee is really a mileage fee implemented by modern technology. For privately owned vehicles, technology will be installed (eventually at the factory) that will record mileage driven. The mileage information will be transmitted to a data collection location, and monthly bills will be sent to the vehicle owners (and if someone other than the owner drives the vehicle for some of the miles, it's up to the owner to negotiate compensation). Ultimately, payments would be made automatically as each trip occurs using mobile payment services, as is now done with ridesharing services like Uber and Lyft.

There are three adjustments that can easily be made to the Pumfee to address particular circumstances of traveling. Pumfee rates per mile can be adjusted for the weight of vehicles. Heavier vehicles that create more wear and tear on roads would pay a higher mileage than lighter vehicles.[29] Pumfee rates can also be adjusted by time of day to encourage drivers to take alternative routes or alternative modes of transportation when popular routes are congested. Finally, Pumfee rates can, and should, be automatically adjusted over time for general inflation or, perhaps better, for the change in transportation construction costs.

For public busses and trains, transit issued cards would be scanned as a rider entered and exited the conveyance, with mileage then recorded and the rider later paying the bill or immediately paying with a credit card on file. But like vehicle payments, eventually payments would be done using mobile payment devices.

The idea of a mileage fee to finance publicly financed transportation modes is not new. It's actually been around for over 25 years, and some localities and states have experimented with the method. But there's always been public resistance, with fears of invasions of privacy by the government through the collection of information for individual transit trips. I vividly experienced this resistance when, a couple decades ago, I wrote an opinion piece for the local newspaper praising the concept of a mileage tax. I later received a letter (email was in its infancy then, and social media didn't exist) stating that if I or anyone else tried to record the letter writer's mileage, we would confront a shotgun! Talk about a negative reaction.

But times and generations have changed. Today's youth—who will be middle-aged in a few decades—have grown up with technology, mobile payment services, posting personal information on social media, and experiencing new forms of fuel and transit. Polls show young adults are more in favor of a mileage fee as a way of financing transportation than older adults.[30] While this solution has been discarded in the past with little support, mileage fees like Pumfee should have an easier time being accepted in the future.

There is an argument that transportation modes that reduce harm to the environment, such as hybrid and electric vehicles, should be charged a lower, or perhaps no, Pumfee.[31] I agree there are types of vehicles that can lower environmental degradation, but I disagree the modes should get a partial or complete pass on the Pumfee. The modes should pay the Pumfee for use of roads. Varying impacts on pollution of transportation modes and other economic activities should be addressed separately, and I do so in Chapter 11. So please, put your pollution concerns on hold until then.

Now, let's get down to specifics. The most comprehensive research on road mileage taxes has been done by economists at the University of Arizona and the Brookings Institution.[32] Their calculations show a mileage tax of 2.2 cents per mile for vehicles would replace the revenue generated by the combined federal and state gas tax. I've done some number-crunching using published data on miles driven and current federal and state revenue devoted to road transportation, and have come up which an average mileage tax of 2.6 cents per mile.[33] So let's compromise and say the mileage fee would be between 2 and 3 cents per mile. And don't forget it would be increased each year to keep up with either general inflation or changes in road construction costs.

The 2 to 3 cents per mile is an average across all vehicles. But all vehicles aren't created equal for their "wear and tear" on roads, with some SUVs creating almost 4 times more damage to roads than sedans.[34] So, the Pumfee would need to be calibrated to the road deterioration created by the vehicle; that is, being lower for smaller, light-weight vehicles and higher for larger, heavier ones.

There are two needed adjustments for buses. The average bus creates 400 times more road wear and tear per mile than the average sedan, and the Pumfee for buses would need to recognize this fact. [35]However, countering their extra wear and tear on roads is the fact buses carry more people, especially during peak commuting periods. Therefore, buses take a large number of other vehicles off the roads, which reduces traffic congestion and saves both time and money for commuters. The Pumfee should recognize these benefits of buses by reducing the bus Pumfee by the per passenger benefit of reduced congestion, while at the same time adding a cost to the Pumfee for extra wear and tear on roads. This would require a lot of number-crunching and a lot of explaining to commuters, but it could be done. I envision localities using roadside digital message boards to alert both vehicle drivers and bus riders of the Pumfee rates at various travel times.

Pumfee is flexible, fair, and financially capable of adjusting to the massive changes expected to come in transportation. If we move using public resources, Pumfee compensates those resources. What's more natural and obvious than that?

Now that I have mobility covered, let's move on to something that may be even more essential—our health.

▲ SUMMING UP

The current method of using the gas tax to finance public transportation investments like roads is inadequate, and it is causing rising congestion, longer commutes, and unsafe roads. A new financing mechanism based on mileage driven as well as weight and type of vehicle is a needed replacement. A public mobility fee, or Pumfee, is proposed as the replacement for the gas tax and other road and transportation financing methods. The Pumfee is completely versatile and flexible and is not dependent on a particular fuel or travel model. Anytime a person uses a transportation option that has been publicly financed, a Pumfee is charged. Eventually the Pumfee will be easily and seamlessly implemented using GSP and mobile payment services.

Chapter 3 Endnotes

1. Levinson, *The Box: How the Shipping Container Made the World Smaller and the Economy Bigger*.

2. Gershgorn, "After Decades of Decline, No-Car Households are Becoming More Common in the U.S."

3. Copeland, "Biking to Work Increases 60% in Past Decade."

4. Hathaway and Muro, "Ridesharing Hits Hyper-Growth."

5. Florida, "The Comeback and Competition of the Inner City."

6. "From Horseless to Driverless," *The Economist*.

7. Lee and Miller, "The Rise, Fall and Rise of Toll Roads in the United States and Virginia."

8. Scarboro and Bishop-Henchman, *How Are Your State's Roads Funded?*

9. Puentes, "The Problem with the Gas Tax in Three Charts."

10. Auxier, "Reforming State Gas Taxes."

11. U.S. Energy Information Agency, *Annual Energy Outlook 2018*.

12. Federal Reserve Bank of St. Louis, "Moving 12-Month Vehicle Miles Traveled," and Tax Policy Institute, "Motor Fuel Tax Revenue."

13. Regan, "The Motor Fuel Tax."

14. Parry, Walls, and Harrington, "Automobile Externalities and Policies."

15. American Society of Civil Engineers, 2017 *Infrastructure Report Card-Roads*.

16. Britschgi, "America's Roads Are Getting Bumpier and More Dangerous."

17. Sintia. "How Soon Will You Be Working from Home?"

18. Federal Highway Administration, *Highway Statistics 2016*.

19. U.S. Bureau of the Census. "U.S. and World Population Clock."

20. Ortman and Guarneri, "U.S. Population Projections: 2000 to 2050."

21. Craig, G., "What Do Property Taxes Pay For?"

22. Murphy, "Virginia Ahead of Curve in Transportation Funding, but Revenue Lags Projections."

23. Levkovich, Rouwendal, and van Marwijk, "The Effects of Highway Development on Housing Prices."

24. Michigan Land Institute, 10 Principles of New Urbanism.

25. MacKenzie, "The True Operating Costs between Bus and Light Rail."

26. Fogelson, *Downtown: It's Rise and Fall, 1880-1950*.

27. Pula, Variable Rate Gas Taxes.

28. De Leon, "Airport Financing and Development."

29. Lindeke, "Chart of the Day: Vehicle Weight vs. Road Damage Levels." The "wear and tear" of vehicles are not proportional to the vehicle's weight, but increase faster than the weight increases.

30. Agrawal, *Gas Taxes and Mileage Fees: What Does the Public Think?* Schleith, *Implications of Electric Vehicles on Gasoline Tax Revenues.*

31. Davis and Sallee, "Should Electric Vehicle Drivers Pay a Mileage Tax?"

32. Langer, Maheshri, and Winston, "From Gallons to Miles: A Disaggregate Analysis of Automobile Travel and Externality Taxes."

33. Federal Highway Administration, *Highway Statistics 2016*; U.S. Bureau of the Census, *State and Local Government Finance.*

34. Lindeke, *op. cit.*

35. *Ibid.*

CHAPTER FOUR

KEEPING HEALTHY WITHOUT BREAKING THE BANK

A GOOD OLE MYSTERY

My maternal grandfather died in 1956. The irony was that he had a doctor's appointment in the morning, was declared healthy, and then later that afternoon dropped dead. My grandfather's doctor was well regarded; he cared for many of my older family members, some of whom lived almost into their nineties. It's just that he was using the tools and techniques of his day, many of which are considered primitive today. Medicine has made enormous progress in just the past six decades.

Think about heart issues: two of my grandparents, as well as my mother, died from heart complications. My mother had a bad heart from birth, and she really needed a new one. But thirty years ago, heart transplants were rare and risky. Not anymore! In 2017, over 3,200 heart transplants were done in the U.S., up from only 57 in 1980.[1] While certainly not as common as pulling a tooth, heart transplants are becoming more regular and more successful each year. On the horizon are artificial hearts that could ultimately make heart disease as outdated as polio.[2]

My point is we are doing more with health care than ever before, and the advances will likely keep coming. Of course, these treatments, operations, procedures, and highly skilled doctors and support staff cost money, and this is money that wasn't spent before medical care became so advanced.

We certainly are paying more for today's health care. In 1970, an average of $1,800 (in 2017 purchasing power dollars) was spent per person on health care. In 2017, that number was over $11,000—a 500% increase.[3] In just the three years between 2016 and 2019, the monthly premium for a standard health insurance policy paid by a 27-year-old non-smoker rose 63% in dollars with the same purchasing power.[4] The bite health-care spending has taken from our total economic pie rose from a mere 6% in 1960 to 18% in 2017. [5]The 18% economic share of health-care is more than the manufacturing and the tech sectors combined.[6]

I know what you're thinking: if we're getting better medical care, then we have to pay more. Where's the problem?

One potential problem could be that we're actually getting poorer health-care results than other countries. Critics cite higher infant mortality rates and lower life expectancies in the U.S. compared to Europe as examples.[7] However, defenders of our healthcare system fire back by arguing that the health outcome measurements aren't comparable between the U.S. and Europe, and personal factors that affect health, such as obesity, are more prevalent in the U.S. Further, data show that the U.S. has better treatment results for major diseases like cancer, heart problems, and diabetes,[8] and for elderly patients.[9]

For an alternative way to examine what we're getting for our health-care dollar, look at these numbers from the federal government, which track health-care prices *after* accounting for improvements in quality of care. Between the fifteen years from 1935 and 1950, the average consumer product price and health-care price increased at exactly the same rate: 119%. However, between 1960 and 2018, the average consumer price jumped over 700%, whereas health-care prices shot up more than 2,000%![10] In contrast, during that same time period, the average worker's wage rate increased 820%[11] and average household income improved by 790%.[12] The point is, health-care costs have far outstripped the ability of the average person to afford them.

If better care and more capabilities aren't driving health prices higher, then the mystery is, what is? Maybe one clue is the decade of the 1960s. Prior to then, health-care prices were rising in step with other prices, and after the 1960s, these prices began their exponential rise. What was happening to the health-care industry in this decade?

In this chapter, I'll try to solve two mysteries. The first is the tremendous rise in health-care prices starting in the 1960s. The second and likely harder mystery is how can we bring health-care prices back to earth and still make health care adequate, accessible, and affordable for all. However, before I put on my detective hat, let's address a fundamental question about health care. Is it different than other products and services we use?

△ IS HEALTH CARE DIFFERENT?

Often, when I talk to friends and relatives about health care and health-care prices, they quickly stop me and say, "Certainly you're not going to use that economics dribble and apply it to health care, are you? Health care is too important to be concerned with prices, costs, and profits!" If it's a relative who makes the statement, and if I want to stay on good terms with that person, I usually change the subject or walk away because their attitude is entrenched and virtually immovable. Why risk a family spat? To others, I might respond that while for most, being healthy and well is the first goal of life, other parts of life are also important. Still, however, we want a society where the "three A's" of health care are met: adequacy, accessibility, and affordability.

Economics is essential to realizing this goal. In fact, a strong argument can be made that economics is essential to making the three A's of health care a reality. At the core of economics is the reality we—as individuals and as a society—seek many things that make us happy. Surely good health is one, but so too are food, shelter, transportation, and entertainment, to name a few. Yet while we understand that there is a long list of factors affecting our happiness, we also know we have limited resources at any point in time. Households, businesses, and even governments have only a certain amount of revenues for spending. Sure, borrowing from tomorrow is an option to increase spending today—but at the cost of less in the future.

Economics was created as a discipline to help people think through how to use our limited resources among our unlimited needs and wants in order to achieve the highest level of happiness. It accomplishes this by motivating us to compare the alternative benefits from spending more on one good or service to another good or service. The objective is search for the good or service that gives the highest benefit relative to each dollar spent.

If I get a $1,000 raise, for example, I might have three alternative uses for it: purchasing a new suit so I look good and am taken seriously in my public appearances, buying more nutritious food so I improve my health, or paying for new flooring in our home's foyer which will make my wife, and me, very happy.

Again, one of my argumentative relatives might respond by saying, "This economics mumbo-jumbo might make sense for your measly $1,000 raise, but medical care should be given all the resources it needs. Doctors and hospitals should never have to make choices when life, death, and wellness are on the line."

I'm feeling assertive now, so for this particular relative I have in mind, here's how I'd answer: "Really, you twit! Then let's take all the money you spend on those cruises you take twice a year and donate it to the local hospital charity. And while we're at it, let's do the same for the cases of wine you drink, and for the golf games you play."

The problem is, every person, company, or government agency says they can use more resources. If given unlimited funds, those monies will be spent, even if that's not necessarily what's best for society. A hospital could pay $1 million for a new MRI machine, which would provide more patient diagnoses and possibly save more lives. However, it could also provide nutritious food for thousands of families for a year, thereby improving their health and extending their lifespans. Or, the money could pay for hundreds of bicycles that would give thousands of hours of fun to poor children. These tradeoffs are tough, and the choices aren't clear.[13] Economics forces us to recognize and evaluate alternative ways to use our limited resources.

I'll not try to decide how resources should be split between health-care, food, children's bikes, and the thousands of other spending possibilities. That would be presumptuous and dictatorial because I would be imposing my values on other people's choices. Instead, my goal is more modest but also more satisfying: find ways to meet the three A's of health-care at a lower cost. That's a win for consumers of health care (everyone) and a win for companies that produce other goods and services.

The first step in accomplishing this mission is to search for clues behind the exploding costs of health-care, particularly after the 1960s.

△ CLUE ONE: DEMAND

The first clue is "demand." I know, I promised to be jargon-free in this book, but I really can't get away from the economics term, "demand" (later I will refer to its sister term, "supply"). In economics, demand refers to the amount of a product or service buyers are willing to purchase at a set price. I think a better term would be "purchase," but I can't change the 140-year history of modern economics. Thus, for the first clue of demand, I'm looking at factors that would change the amount of medical care services consumers in the country would want to purchase at any given price. Further, when demand does increase and nothing comparable happens to increase the availability of medical services ("supply"), the ultimate price of the product or service rises. But I'm getting ahead of myself!

Demographics is one factor of demand, specifically the percentage of the nation's population over age 65. At age 65, the need for medical care rises significantly—I can personally attest to that. In fact, one-third of all medical care spending in the country is for individuals over this age, even though they only account for 15% of the population.[14] By 2050, however, over one-in-five (22%) of individuals in the country will be 65 or over.[15] In economics language, the increase in the relative size of the elderly population has increased the demand for health-care services, and it will continue to do so.

Government payment for health-care is another factor of demand. In 1965, the federal government passed the Medicare and Medicaid programs. This was the first time the government became directly involved in paying for health services for segments of the general population, with the exception being government supported medical payments for veterans. Medicare helps pay for health services of people 65 and over. Medicaid assists low-income individuals with paying for health services. Medicare and Medicaid are now two of the top three federal government spending programs (the third being Social Security). The Affordable Care Act (popularly known as "Obamacare") allowed states to expand Medicaid to a broader population.

The creation of Medicare and Medicaid increased the demand for health, but it also has had a second impact. By taking the funding of a significant part of the health-care industry out of private consumers' hands and putting it into political hands, Medicare and Medicaid changed the dynamics of prices in health care. In a market where most consumers pay for a product out of pocket, rising prices can eventually cause us to hit a wall and effectively say, "I can't pay for anymore." When we stop buying, a brake is effectively put on the price increases.

Government is different because it's run by politicians who aren't using their own money to pay for government programs like Medicare and Medicaid. When health-care prices rise, there is political pressure by consumers (and particularly those over age 65) to have even more government money allocated to paying their medical bills. Often, this is easy for politicians to pass because who can be against health care? And if they borrow the money to pay for the increased spending, they don't face the wrath of current taxpayers. This puts government funding of health care—through Medicare and Medicaid—on an escalator of continually increased spending.

To see if this creates a problem, particularly for health-care prices, we then have to look at "supply."

△ CLUE TWO: SUPPLY

In economics, the opposite of "demand" is "supply." Supply is the amount of a product or service providers attempt to sell at a given price. More important to the discussion here, if supply increases *faster* than demand increases, then the price of the product or service drops, but if supply increases *slower* than demand increases, the price rises.

We already know the demand for health services has been increasing during the last five decades. What about supply? From 1970 to 2015, the number of doctors in the country has really jumped, rising 225%.[16] This is far more than the total population growth of 52%[17] and, more importantly, the growth rate of the population age 65 and over of 140%.[18] These numbers would suggest no supply problem, and, since supply growth was greater than demand growth, would imply a downward pressure on medical prices.

However, some groups claim this analysis is too simplistic. Based on the growing elderly population and expansion of health-care needs for that population, medical schools argue there is actually a shortage of doctors, and the shortage will only grow unless training programs are expanded.[19] Of course, keep in mind that medical schools have a vested interest in getting more "business" in training physicians.

Things become a little clearer when looking at the supply of nurses. Between 1970 and 2015, the number of registered nurses in the country expanded 61%,[20] slightly higher than total population growth (52%) but far shorter than the 140% increase in the elderly population. Since the elderly population is such an important driver of health-care usage, I read these results as demand growth outstripping supply growth, and hence putting upward pressure on health-care prices.

Another important measure of health-care supply is the number of available hospital beds. Here the trend is very interesting; between 1975 (earliest year of available data) and 2015, the number of hospital beds dropped by almost 40%.[21] But before you respond, "Ah-ha, mystery solved!" note that more medical treatments are being done on an out-patient basis, meaning no overnight stays. Also, the average length of stay for patients in hospitals has dropped by almost half in the last four decades.[22] Rather than the reduction in hospital beds suggesting a decline in supply, it can represent an improvement in efficiency.

Thus, the findings on changes in the supply of health care are inconclusive. But even if there is more supply, if the added supply is controlled by fewer hospital firms, the result could be less competition and higher prices. To see how, let's go to the next clue.

△ CLUE THREE: OLIGOPOLY

Oh, oh, here's another economics term: *oligopoly!* Once again, I apologize, but I think I can convince you it will be worth learning another piece of economists' secret language. Here's a painless explanation: when many businesses compete for your purchases, economists call this situation, "competition." When only one company exists to sell a particular product or service, that company is called a "monopoly."

Every firm would like to be a monopoly, because then they don't need to worry about customers going elsewhere if they don't like the price or quality of their product/service. The only choice consumers have is to go without that product or service sold by the monopoly. The monopoly is therefore in the driver's seat and can charge higher prices compared to what they would charge if faced with competitors.

Hence, competition is good for consumers and monopoly is bad. Then what is an oligopoly? It stands in-between competition and monopoly—it's where more than one firm exists, but not many. But as long as there's some competition, does it matter? Actually, it does; with only a few firms selling to consumers, the firms are motivated to engage in "strategic behavior" rather than outright competition.

Each firm knows a price cut will almost immediately be met by a similar price cut from the other companies. Since this will leave all of them worse off, each company is reluctant to cut prices. The firms are content to avoid competition and rake in the revenues from their piece of the total customer pie. As long as the firms avoid entering into specific price-fixing or other anti-competitive agreements, federal laws prohibiting anti-competitive behavior are not violated.[23]

What does this have to do with health-care, you ask? Plenty, because the health-care market has become less competitive and more oligopolistic (say that word ten times!) in recent decades.[24] Between 1998 and 2015, there were over 1,500 hospital mergers, resulting in many local markets being controlled by one large hospital system. The same has happened to health-care insurers, with the two largest insurers controlling a majority of the business in over half of local markets. There's even been consolidation among medical suppliers and distributors, with only a handful of each now existing.[25] To add to the list, individual doctors' offices, like the one my parents used in my youth, are disappearing. Just short of half of primary physicians are now affiliated with a hospital system that guarantees them patients as well as supporting staff and specialists.[26]

My wife and I experienced this situation a couple of years ago when our family doctor, "Dr. Bob," retired. We had been his patients for almost forty years. He had a small office and two employees: a nurse and a secretary. We considered Dr. Bob not just our doctor, but also our friend. With a limited practice and intimate knowledge of his patients, he could always work us in to his schedule the same day we called about some ache or pain.

Try as we did, we couldn't find anyone comparable to Dr. Bob as a replacement. A big part of the reason being that the Raleigh-Durham area where we live is dominated by three large health-care systems: Duke, UNC, and Wake Med. Together, the three systems control an astonishing 92% of the market.[27] We chose Duke, mainly due to the location of its office to our home. The physicians and staff are certainly cordial, professional, and competent, but there's an atmosphere of an "all business" attitude. They're just not Dr. Bob!

A variety of reasons have been offered to suggest why the provision of health-care has become less competitive and more oligopolistic (there's that word again). Some say bigger is more efficient and less wasteful. It's also argued that complying with government medical programs (Medicare and Medicaid) and private insurance companies has become so complicated that only large companies with an expert staff can do it.[28]

In my opinion, the overriding motivation for consolidation among health-care firms is profit; companies in an oligopoly structure make higher profits than companies in a competitive structure. Any elementary economics textbook will show that competition drives profits down to a level just high enough to compensate owners to endure the risks, uncertainty, long hours of running a business, and doing constant battle with competitors who want to take away all your customers.[29] Running a business requires lengthy workdays and making seemingly endless tough decisions. If little companies can merge in to a few big companies, they can declare a truce on competition, divide up the market, and each make bigger profits.

And that's exactly what has happened in health-care. In 2016, three of the top ten industries with the highest profit rates were in health-care. The profit rates of the health-care sectors were 33% to 66% higher than the average profit rate for all companies.[30] A study in Indiana confirmed high profit rates for individual hospitals.[31] Although non-profit hospitals technically don't earn profits, they do earn something termed *operating surplus*, which is usually paid to executives and used to fund hospital buildings. Equating operating surplus to profit shows that non-profits are just as profitable as their for-profit cousins.[32]

How do these oligopolistic health-care giants make their big profits? By none other than pushing up prices from what they would be in a competitive market. Lots of studies show this.[33] They also use strategies competitive firms can't, like pressuring their doctors to make all referrals to other doctors within the hospital system where they can capture more profits,[34] or requiring their doctors to use more expensive pharmaceuticals.[35]

Another tactic is "market segmentation." Rather than selling the same product or service to all consumers at the same price, oligopoly firms like big hospital systems divide buyers into groups based on each group's sensitivity to prices. A good example is prescription drugs. Customers using insurance pay a higher price, while consumers paying with cash pay a lower price for the exact same drug.[36] Why? Because customers using insurance will have much of the higher price paid by their coverage—they don't care as much about the price. Indeed, until recently, it was illegal for pharmacists to tell customers that paying cash could significantly reduce the price of prescription drugs.[37]

To rub more salt into the wound, analysis shows no relationship between high drug prices and pharmaceutical innovation.[38] That is, drug companies would continue to research and develop new pharmaceutical products even if they were paid lower drug prices!

The replacement of physicians like Dr. Bob with health system giants represents more than trading in the old way of delivering health-care with a new way; it also represents a change in the structure of health-care that shifts economic power and leverage from the patient to the provider.

But shouldn't the government be protecting little consumers from giant companies by using regulations and other tools since it has regulatory powers over health-care? Does the government use those powers to help patients or to help the big health-care oligopolies maintain their power? The answer is in the next clue.

△ CLUE FOUR: REGULATION

Government regulation is supposed to protect individuals from things that can harm them and for which they have no defense. The lack of a defense can be because people have no ability to detect the harm or no ability to evaluate and judge the harm.

Financial regulations are a good example. Many people don't have a good understanding of financial concepts. I can remember my parents—both of whom were innately smart but never finished high school—sitting at the kitchen table with a loan broker. The broker was describing the terms of a loan, the interest rate my parents would pay, and how the loan was such a good deal. I didn't know it then, but I now know my parents had absolutely no clue what the broker was saying. Back then, interest rates could be manipulated to make them seem less costly than they really were. Fortunately, there are now federal regulations standardizing how loan interest rates are calculated, thereby allowing borrowers to more easily understand and compare loan terms.

The federal government presumably has our backs with medical care in several ways. The Federal Drug Administration (FDA) is in charge of overseeing the development of new prescription drugs. It requires pharmaceutical companies to jump through many, many hoops before a new drug can be prescribed and sold. Of course, I—and I suspect you—are grateful for this oversight. We certainly don't want to be taking prescription drugs that haven't been thoroughly tested and might harm us.

The question isn't the concept of oversight, but the degree of that government oversight. The typical prescription drug requires between seven and fifteen years of development and evaluation before it hits the market.[39] The total cost can be several hundreds of millions of dollars to over $2 billion per drug.[40] Critics argue part of the reason for this time and cost is the cautiousness of the FDA in the approval process, which includes several clinical trials. [41]The FDA is focused on making sure flawed drugs don't reach the market and cause harm. However, the downside of this approach is that drugs that are good and can help people take longer to reach the market, which means people who can be helped by the drug have to wait and suffer longer.[42] In 2018, this cost was eliminated for terminally ill patients when legislation was passed allowing them access to experimental drugs and treatments.[43]

To its credit, the FDA has been working to quicken its drug approval system. The agency now has a "fast track" approval process that can shave years off the time when the drug hits the market.[44] Still, more can be done, like accepting drug approvals from other countries which have high quality systems (European Union, Canada, Japan, and Australia), greater consultation with doctors and patients about the use of a drug prior to its final approval, and collaboration with non-profit drug certification organizations.[45]

Prescription drugs are also regulated by the U.S. Patent Office. Our country encourages inventors by giving them a protected time period to recover their significant costs, which is called a patent. During this period, which is usually ten years after the drug has reached the market, no one else can copy and sell the newly invented product or service.[46]

Pharmaceutical companies are heavy users of patents for prescription drugs. It's during the patent period that companies expect to recover most of their drug development costs. Once the patent expires, other companies are free to manufacture and sell the drugs. These alternatives are called "generic drugs." Since the generic drug manufacturers did not incur the costs of developing the original prescription drug, they are usually much cheaper. The federal government has estimated that, on average, generic drugs are 75% cheaper than non-generic brand name-drugs.[47]

The system tries to play fair with the prescription drug developers. Recognizing the costs developers incur, they are given a temporary monopoly market for sales—meaning there are no competitors during the monopoly period of the patent. The cost of the prescription drug will be high during this period. After that, competition is opened up and drug prices fall. Seems like a reasonable system, right?

Except that prescription drug developers have found a way around it. As the patent period nears its end, drug developers will often release a "new and improved" version of the drug. This tactic is called *ever-greening*. Often, the new version is only marginally different than the original and so doesn't require as much testing, evaluation, nor (importantly) new expenses. Yet pharmaceutical companies will still file for a new patent and, if granted, the patent will delay for another period of years the marketing of cheaper generics! Lower priced generic copies of the earlier version can still be sold, but pharmaceutical companies will use advertising to push the new patented-protected version.[48] Also, doctors may be motivated to use the higher priced version if they are reimbursed by Medicare the cost of the drug plus a percentage of that cost.[49] Medicare must pay the prevailing price for a drug, which, of course, is what the manufacturer charges.[50] With 3 billion claims processed annually, Medicare's resources are stretched too thin to exercise much scrutiny over health-care providers.[51] What a system!

Ever-greening is quite common. For example, between 1989 and 2002, two-thirds of the 1,035 drugs approved by the FDA were modified versions of existing drugs.[52] Generic drug producers can go to court to stop ever-greening, but they can be deterred by high court costs. Also, generic companies can drop a lawsuit after being offered a financial settlement by the company using the ever-greening technique.[53]

Although technically not a regulatory agency, Medicare is a key government player in health-care because the program pays the majority of medical costs for the elderly. Congress has directed that Medicare set the prices it pays to health-care providers for treatments and procedures. Alright, you're probably thinking, "At least this means Medicare is keeping a lid on health-care prices." Except for one big problem: the group charged with periodically establishing prices has a large representation from the health-care industry itself. Many of the members in the price-setting group are from the American Medical Association, which represents health-care providers. Not only are the foxes not guarding the henhouse, they are actually living inside the henhouse! Academic studies of price setting decisions by Medicare have concluded the process has largely been controlled by the health-care industry.[54]

Regulations on immigration are also part of the health-care cost debate. Foreign-trained doctors are already a substantial part of the supply of medical professionals, with their numbers accounting for 25% of all doctors practicing in the U.S.[55] Yet it can be difficult and time-consuming to add to this supply. Doctors trained in other countries must complete their residency requirements in the U.S., which can take up to seven years. Once the residency is completed, the doctor must return to his or her home country for at least two years, unless a waiver is granted. Finally, to practice in the U.S., the foreign-trained doctor must have a family member or employer sponsor them.[56]

In addition, there are regulations imposed by states potentially impacting the cost of health-care. One is a holdover from national legislation passed in the 1940s which allows states to regulate health insurance policies sold within their boundaries.[57] Unfortunately, states can effectively limit competition by setting standards and requirements that may deter other companies from participating in the market. For insurance companies to pay claims and maintain affordable prices, they must sell in large markets with a variety of health risks. National markets meet this requirement better than state markets, and, as a result, state regulated insurance markets can mean higher priced health insurance policies—a conclusion found in some, but not all, empirical analyses.[58]

Many states have endured battles between different medical professionals over what each state can and cannot legally do. The most common has been between physicians and physician assistants. Physicians are fully trained medical doctors, while physician assistants have substantial medical training but lack the "M.D." credential. Many states have severely curtailed the tasks physician assistants can perform, and these restrictions are often supported by physicians.[59] The question becomes: are physicians protecting their patients, or are physicians protecting their turf and income? It is common sense that if lower-cost physician assistants are capable of doing some tasks in place of higher-cost doctors, then health-care costs will be somewhat lower. The studies looking at this question agree with the commonsensical conclusion.[60]

Another issue is state licensing regulations impacting the relocation of medical professionals to states with growing medical demand. States require licenses for many occupations, with health-care occupations among the most numerous,[61] yet licensing requirements in all states aren't necessarily the same. This means when a registered nurse moves from New York to North Carolina, he/she may have to jump through some hoops such as taking tests or courses in order to continue practicing in the new state. While certainly doable, again research shows these requirements create barriers for workers moving across state lines. In doing so, the regulations can perpetuate higher health-care costs in states where the use is greater than the supply of health-care facilities and personnel.[62]

There are regulations in many states controlling the amount of equipment medical practitioners can purchase. These regulations are termed "certificates of need," (CON) and they are used in 35 states.[63] Say Dr. Smith wants to purchase an MRI machine for her office. She foresees enough use from it that payments from consumers, insurance, and government will more than cover the costs. But Dr. Smith can't buy the MRI unless the state is satisfied there is a "need" for it. Furthermore, the state says a "need" only occurs if Dr. Smith's use of an MRI won't take customers away from other doctors who also have an MRI, thereby causing those doctors to lose revenue and possibly not be able to pay for their machines.

This is one way government bureaucrats control the economy, and it's illogical on many fronts. Firstly, how can the state predict the uses of MRI machines in different doctors' offices? Secondly, even if a doctor loses money from using an MRI machine, those losses may be covered by better diagnoses generated by the MRI that then reduce costs elsewhere. And thirdly, allowing doctors to make their own decisions about equipment purchases enhances competition in health-care and ultimately puts a dampening effect on medical care prices.

But most importantly for our discussion about health-care costs, rather than reducing costs, CON can actually increase them. How, you ask? Simply by reducing effective competition. Suppose my old doctor—

Dr. Bob—wanted to go up against the gigantic health-care systems by purchasing an MRI machine, figuring he could keep many patients who valued this kind of technology. If state regulators denied Dr. Bob's request on the grounds that the local health-care systems had enough MRI's to serve the community, then this would just be another nail in his practice. He, and others like him, denied the ability to put up a good fight, would simply leave the field to the oligopolistic health-care system giants, who could use their tools to further boost prices and profits. Again, there is research to back up this conclusion.[64]

The federal government has numerous laws prohibiting certain types of business behavior that can lead to non-competitive markets. Ironically, under the direction of Congress, the government does not enforce some of these laws for components of the health-care industry. For example, when medical supply manufacturers make payments to their distributors as a way of acquiring contracts with hospitals, the hospitals will often get a "cut" of these fees. Obviously, this gives preference to some manufacturers of medical supplies over others, which is why the agreements are usually prohibited. However, an exemption has been given to the health-care sector.[65]

While government regulations are supposedly in place to help and protect us, in the health-care area many of them ironically seem to limit competition, protect the giant providers, and boost the prices you and I pay. Politics seems to be at work here; between 1997 and 2015, the pharmaceutical industry was the largest contributor to U.S. congressional campaigns, out-spending the second largest contributor by 43%, and not far behind were political contributions from hospitals and health-care professionals.[66]

△ CLUE FIVE: CONFUSION, CAREFREE, AND CODES

Although I'm almost 70, I still have vivid memories of my parents taking me to the doctor in the 1950s. I was always scared to see Dr. McClellan, probably because he was the person who gave me shots, looked down my throat with what appeared to be a popsicle stick, and tapped my legs and arms with a rubber hammer. I was particularly unhappy with him when he told my parents I needed to lose some weight. There went desserts for several months. Yet, as an economist, I still remember how my parents paid for the appointment. There were no insurance cards to show or forms to complete. Credit cards didn't exist then, and my parents rarely used checks. Instead, my father would pull out his wallet and simply pay with good-old cash. And, my father wasn't a wealthy man.

My point is that paying for health-care then was as simple as paying for groceries today—at least for those of us who pay for groceries with paper money. Dr. McClellan gave my parents an itemized bill, my father looked it over, and, if he agreed with everything, paid Dr. McClellan in cash. Paying for health-care was a simple transaction.

Contrast that process to today: try reading a medical bill, assuming you can obtain one! You might as well attempt to read Greek. Expenses are itemized by codes and short-cut names that often make no sense. On top of this, many of the expenses frequently appear outrageously high. Those who know say this is because there is massive cross-subsidization in medical care.[67] The unpaid costs of those who can't pay for everything are shifted to other patients who can. The patients paying more either don't complain because they don't know, or if they do, they don't care because the government or insurance will pick up most of the bill.

My wife is a big-time price comparer. Prior to purchasing anything that costs more than $20, she meticulously scans advertisements and websites to see where she can get the best deal. Consumer advocates would applaud my wife's diligence because they argue comparison price-shopping is a vital part of maintaining competition. Yet try doing this with health-care! Although there have been a few experiments in some states with doctors' offices and hospitals posting prices for specific treatments and procedures, the experiments haven't been widespread and consumers have largely ignored them.[68]

Doesn't it seem odd that consumers of health-care wouldn't want to take the time to price-shop for the best deals on doctor's visits and operations? In fact, if we all did this, wouldn't consumers hold the medical providers' collective feet to the fire and force them to lower prices and only charge us for the medical care we actually use?

Why don't consumers appear to care about health-care prices? Ironically, the answer is based on something that looks like a positive, but is actually a negative. It's the fact that most of the money used to pay for health-care doesn't come directly out of our pockets *at the time the payment is made*. Government (federal, state, and local) pays 45%, businesses and other private entities pay 27%, and individuals pay 28%.[69] Most of the government bill is paid through the two big federal programs, Medicare and Medicaid. The bulk of the business and private contribution is paid by insurance, and the individual bill is mainly through insurance deductibles and co-pays. After we pay those deductibles and co-pays, we don't really care about the bill.

"But wait, wait," you say. "Don't individuals ultimately pay the taxes funding Medicare and Medicaid? And wouldn't insurance premiums paid by businesses for their employees' health- care simply be a substitute for larger paychecks?"

Indeed, these comments are all absolutely true, but irrelevant to my point that individuals pay little of a medical bill at the time the payment is made. At the time the medical bill is issued, individuals (you and I) immediately pay only 28 cents of every dollar of cost. As a result, we have relatively little "skin in the health-care game."

This is the curse of using other people's money! By doing so, we inevitably drive up total spending. To understand the curse, try this experiment the next time you go to dinner with friends: convince them to split the total bill, and each person will pay the same amount regardless of how much he or she eats. If it's a group of friends you frequently dine with, you will find that this "equal payment system" results in most people eating and spending more than if they only paid for their own food. Actual experiments of comparing spending when each diner pays his own bill versus having the bill split equally confirms this happens.[70] Why do the diners overeat and over-spend? Because they're using "other people's money," just as in the case of medical care! With other people's money on the line, we feel we can be more carefree about costs.

With our guard down and other people's pockets open, health-care providers enforce their power through coding. In billing for medical costs, the key in getting the highest reimbursement rate from the government or insurance is determined by the code. Every medical treatment, procedure, product, or service has a code, and each code has a different reimbursement rate. Where there's a choice, providers like hospitals and doctors have an incentive to use the code with the highest reimbursement rate.[71] There's actually a term for this in the industry. It's called *up-coding*.[72]

Of course, the possibility of financial audits puts limits on this practice. But the federal funders (Medicare and Medicaid) ultimately face no limits on their spending, since what they spend is determined by the claims they receive. And while private insurance companies may balk at some expenditures, the reality is that their profits are derived from a percentage of their volume of business. They fear that if they complain too much to hospitals, the big hospital systems will stop doing business with them.[73] Also, insurance companies can simply pass higher expenses to policyholders (businesses and individuals) and argue that those were the costs received from health-care providers.

△ PUTTING THE CLUES TOGETHER

These five clues suggest the deck is stacked with incentives leading toward ever higher costs and prices in health-care. An aging population and the entry and expansion of government payments for medical care through Medicare and Medicaid are constantly creating and enabling greater and greater use (demand) of the health-care system. By itself, this would be enough to drive up prices. Add to this federal and state restrictions on expanding the supply of medical care, the consolidation of medical care providers into non-competing and manipulative economic giants, government regulations that support these trends, and a passive customer base allowing all this to happen (because other people's money is used to pay the bills), and we have the perfect recipe for a medical care system that vacuums in money and is morphing into an ever-growing financial web which is virtually controlling our lives.

It's said that a picture is worth a thousand words. In the case of health-care, make that 3.5 trillion words, with each word representing $1.00 of the total U.S. health-care spending in 2017.[74] My picture of the U.S. health-care system and why costs have continued to rise is in Figure 4-1.

Start with an increase in health-care costs charged by providers (1). This leads to higher costs for the insurance companies, who then respond by raising premiums (2A). Deductibles and co-pays made by patients also rise (2B). Insurance companies then pass on their higher costs to employer-provided insurance plans (3). Research shows employers reduce wages paid to workers to compensate for the higher costs (4).[75] Lobbyists for workers, such as unions, as well as lobbyists for the health-care providers, pressure Medicare and Medicaid to pay for more of the costs (5 and 6). All the while, the FDA as well as other government rules and regulations contribute to the size and power of the health-care complex.

Some argue the U.S. health-care system is dysfunctional, implying there are flaws in its organization and operation,[76] and that if we just add a program here or expand coverage there everything will be fine.

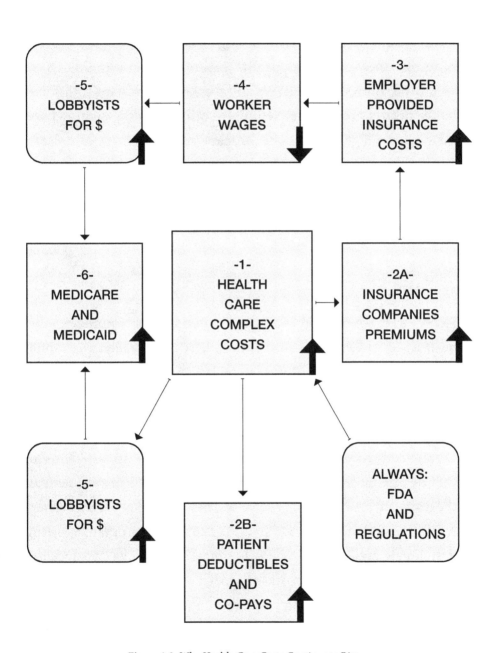

Figure 4-1. Why Health-Care Costs Continue to Rise

I disagree. The U.S. health-care system is not dysfunctional. In fact, it is perfectly functional for the incentives it faces. The large oligopolistic health-care systems are acting exactly as we would expect to maximize their power and profits. Insurers conform to this power by passing on costs to patients and workers. Importantly, this system is perpetuated by the seemingly endless funding coming from the big federal government health-care programs.

To change our health-care system, we have to totally alter the incentives that we have today. As I'll examine next, there are both fake ways and real ways to do this.

△ FAKE SOLUTIONS

Here I'll examine four proposed solutions for improving our health-care system: "Medicare-for-All," a national health system, price controls, and the Affordable Care Act. Each has flaws that don't directly address the problem of incentives in our current system, and this is why I label all four proposals as "fake."

One widely recommended solution to the various problems of U.S. health-care is to simply expand government involvement in the payment of costs. This idea is generally called *Medicare-for-All*.[77] It's based on the notion that Medicare—the program assisting individuals aged 65 and over—has worked fairly well. Advocates tout low administration costs for Medicare, the success of Medicare Part D in controlling drug costs, and the clout Medicare can have over health-care providers due to its enormous size. They argue Medicare-for-All could improve health-care *and* lower costs.[78]

Some versions of Medicare-for-All would allow it to compete with private insurers; other versions would eliminate private insurers and have Medicare be a "single payer." In both versions, however, the overriding rationale is the same: if Medicare can work for the elderly, why not let it also work for the non-elderly? Germany, France, and Japan are examples of countries using this system.

Hold on, though. If we're going to expand Medicare because it works so well for the elderly, then let's first see if it really does work well. Let's consider administrative costs. Medicare supporters say the program pays only 3% of its budget for administration, compared to between 12% and 14% for a typical health insurance program.[79] Therefore, supporters continue, replacing private insurance with Medicare would save a bundle of money, maybe $500 million annually in spending that doesn't even pay for health-care.[80]

Unfortunately for supporters, this is an "apples to oranges" comparison. Since the current Medicare program is exclusively for the elderly, Medicare is able to "piggy-back" on the Social Security Administration for much of its paperwork. When comparisons are made accounting for this fact, Medicare's alleged administrative cost advantage disappears. Yet even without this fact, since Medicare patients are elderly, and they typically have much higher medical expenses than the non-elderly, administrative expenses as a percentage of total medical expenses should be lower for Medicare. Adjustments accounting for the elderly composition of Medicare users show higher, not lower, administrative costs compared to private insurance.[81] Therefore, it is inaccurate to assume that Medicare's expansion to the entire population would be a big saver of administrative costs.

In 2006, under its new Part D program, Medicare expanded to include coverage of prescription drugs. Initially, there appeared to be an association of the new program with a slowdown in prescription drug price increases. However, a decade after the program began, both drug prices and payments per program recipient were accelerating.[82]

Since Medicare alone pays for around one-quarter of all health-care services, and it picks up a whopping two-thirds of the elderly's medical expenditures, Medicare-for-All advocates argue that the program can use its buying power to enforce lower medical costs.[83] Indeed, over the decades Medicare has been in existence, the program has attempted to do just this, yet the agency has always faced a big roadblock in these efforts: politics. Medicare can be overruled by Congress, which holds its purse string. Typically, if there is an effort by Medicare to roll back, or even to just contain costs, there is pushback and pressure from Congress to stop. And, of course, behind the pressure from Congress are political contributions from the health-care industry.[84] Political clout usually tops the best of bureaucratic efforts.[85]

Then there's the matter of the price tag of Medicare-for-All and paying for that price tag. Economists specializing in the health-care sector estimate a Medicare-for-All type plan could increase federal spending on health-care by 70% over a decade.[86] Obviously, taxes of some kind would need to be raised or added to fund the plan, unless, of course, Congress just borrows the money!

Thus, the problem with Medicare-for-All is that it doesn't address any of the incentives in today's health-care system that leads to ever-increasing costs. In fact, Medicare-for-All just expands these incentives by having Medicare involved in paying for much more of our health- care, not just for the health-care of the elderly. At least today, there's a modicum of competition between the health-care providers, insurers, Medicare, businesses, and patients. Especially with the single-payer version of Medicare-for-All, these components are collapsed into one payee: Medicare, which would be the focus for all the lobbying and political pressure working against transparency, competition, and common sense.

A *national health system* (NHS), as practiced in the United Kingdom, Spain, and Scandinavian countries, is the ultimate in government control of health-care. In the pure version of this model, there is one payee for health-care—the government—and there is also only one provider—again, the government. Medical practitioners, including doctors, nurses, and technicians, work for the government; they are government employees. All hospitals, doctors' offices, and other medical facilities are owned and operated by the government. In contrast, in the Medicare-for-All system, the government pays the bills, but health-care providers and facilities are still private.

Supporters applaud the concept of an NHS, especially those who believe health-care is fundamentally different and should not be subject to typical economic constraints. Backers of an NHS see it as the most decent and best way of providing health-care to all. No prices, no insurance premiums, no worries about drug costs, no exorbitant salaries paid to doctors, and no sky-high profits earned by pharmaceutical companies and hospital systems. The government pays for everything. Sick people just have to show up at a doctor's office or hospital and care will be provided with no questions and no concerns about payment.

That last word, payment, signals the first issue with an NHS. With the federal government paying all health-care expenses, the health-care component of the federal budget would explode. Using the 2018 federal budget, the federal government spent over $1 trillion on health-care, including Medicare, Medicaid, children's health-care, and veteran's health-care spending. If the federal government took on paying *all* health-care expenses in the country, that annual amount would soar to $3.5 trillion.[87]

Then the next question would be how to pay for that extra government spending? One answer is to borrow the funds, but doing so would send annual federal borrowing to levels never before seen, without hope of ever being reduced. Hence, any serious proposal for an NHS has to include new tax recommendations. A variety of ideas have been set forth, including simply increasing income tax rates—primarily on the rich—or instituting a new federal sales tax.[88]

A second issue with an NHS is the amount of micro-management required from the government. Employment in an NHS would be eight times more than the number of military personnel and with a budget five times bigger than the Pentagon's.[89] The comparisons to the U.S. Postal Service are even more dramatic, with an NHS being 48,000 times larger in spending and 27 times bigger in personnel. [90]Every decision about salaries, equipment, the numbers and types of operations and treatments, the number of hospitals—the list goes on and on—would have to be made by government managers and bureaucrats. And let's face it, government bureaucracies aren't known for their efficient use of money and speedy actions. Do we really want the same kind of managers who have given us $600 military toilet seats, $7,600 coffee makers, and post offices closed at peak customer times running our health-care?[91]

If you think countries having an NHS hear no complaints about health-care, think again! One of the ways governments can keep NHS spending in check is to lengthen the time until care is administered. For example, someone like me who has had chronic shoulder pain would be very happy to hear that an NHS would cover rotator cuff surgery. That is, I would be happy until I learned it would be almost a five-month wait for the next available operation.[92] Waits in emergency rooms of British NHS-run hospitals can be as long as 12 hours,[93] and seniors wait an average of over two times longer to see a specialist than in the U.S.[94] Sometimes particular kinds of care are simply prohibited, especially if the patient is older.[95]

Last, if you're worried about political influence in our current health-care system, then see what happens when the government controls the entire system. I predict political contributions to Washington politicians would increase exponentially as all the players in health-care would try to rig the multitude of components and decisions in the NHS to best serve their purposes.

Some say the answer to our health-care systems is not Medicare-for-All or an NHS, but it is to keep our current health-care systems and regulate prices.[96] We could set up something that might be called a *Health-Care Prices Board* composed of representatives from government, health-care providers, and patients. The Board would establish "fair and reasonable" prices for treatments, surgeries, office visits, hospital stays, insurance, etc. The Board takes away all the tricks, schemes, and power used by the health-care industry to keep prices high and then make them even higher. So, problem solved!

What could be wrong with something so simple and logical and which gets to the heart of our health-care system problems? Let me count the ways! Number one, the amount of information an outside group would need to set prices is enormous, meaning the price-setting system will be extremely complicated. Those providing the information (the health-care institutions) will be motivated to manipulate, or "game," the data to give themselves the highest possible price.

Number two, health-care institutions will claim there are many unique factors affecting their situation which warrant "special" (read "higher") prices for themselves. Indeed, there are always unique factors for any business or provider, but the challenge for the Health-Care Prices Board would be to separate "real factors" from "fake factors."

Number three, there have been several examples of states implementing price controls for healthcare, and the conclusion is that they failed to have any restraining effect on total health-care prices. A big reason—reflecting the first two points—is the complexity of the price-control process. Most states have abandoned the price controls.[97]

Number four is a more nuanced problem with price controls that economists recognize, but many non-economists dismiss. Economists argue prices, and in particular, changes in prices, provide information very valuable to any competitive market. Let's say in the Raleigh area the hourly wage rate of plumbers is surging. This reveals there's more plumbing work available than there are plumbers to do the work. The rise in the wage rate is an enticement for more plumbers to move to Raleigh, for more workers already in Raleigh to become plumbers, and for the local community college to expand its training programs for plumbers. When these things happen, plumbers' wage rates will moderate.

Without the ability to change plumbers' wages, we wouldn't necessarily know why plumbers weren't returning customers' calls. Sure, some economist (yours truly?) could do a survey and detect the plumbers' shortage, but it would take time to gather and analyze the data. In contrast, prices (wage rates are the price of workers) change rapidly. For any competitive market to function properly and allow resources to freely and quickly move to where they are most valued, we need to have prices change. The problem in health-care is we don't have a competitive market where prices truly reflect the cost and value of work. The solution is we need to create a competitive health-care market. How we do this will be detailed below.

The last fake solution is the *Affordable Care Act* (ACA), better known as "Obamacare." The ACA was supposedly a solution to solving the health-care system's high prices and inadequate coverage. The key features of the ACA were: (1) expanding Medicaid (the federal government's program for helping lower-income people pay for health-care) by raising the income limit for qualifying for the program, (2) requiring businesses above a certain size to provide health insurance to their employees or pay a penalty, (3) requiring individuals not covered by (1) or (2) to purchase health insurance or pay a penalty, but providing subsidies to households under certain income limits in their purchase of health insurance, (4) mandating certain features in health insurance policies, and (5) basing premiums paid by an individual for health insurance on characteristics of their community and not of themselves.[98]

For many reasons, the ACA is not fully working. While the plan resulted in more people being covered by health insurance, this was primarily due to the Medicaid expansion. Despite assurance from ACA supporters that no one would lose their existing health insurance plan, 1 million people did because their insurer did not comply with the new coverage requirements. An additional 3 to 5 million people lost health insurance coverage from employers who decided that paying the penalty was cheaper than complying with the ACA rules.[99]

The ACA relied on private insurers competing for uninsured individuals' business, but the opposite appears to have transpired. Numerous insurers dropped out of the ACA, leaving many communities with few to no participants.[100] A major reason was the community rating system. Here insurers were required to charge everyone in the same geographic area the same insurance premium. This requirement totally ignored the insurance industry's long-used practice of charging more to higher-risk and less healthy individuals, for the simple reason such individuals are expected to have more insurance claims. This requirement caused many insurance companies to simply not participate in the ACA. Since healthier individuals paid more than their health risks suggested, many of them also chose not to participate in the ACA.[101] Another problem was that the financial penalties for those not buying health insurance were very low, and as a result, many people simply waited until they became sick to buy health insurance—a practice that created losses for insurers and further dissuaded insurance companies from working with the ACA.[102]

What about the cost of health insurance? ACA backers promised the plan would significantly lower the cost of health insurance. [103]While this has been the result for lower-income households who qualified for the expanded Medicaid or large government subsidies, higher-income households have paid significantly more for health insurance since the ACA was enacted.[104] There was, however, one clear winner from the ACA: hospitals. Both hospital revenues and profitability have soared since the program was enacted in 2010.[105]

The ACA is also hindered by its "one size fits all" feature, requiring certain provisions be in each health insurance policy. The superior alternative would have been to allow individuals to customize policies with the provisions they wanted, and premiums would have fallen as a result.[106]

To top it all off, the biggest flaw with the ACA is its philosophy, which is to expand the footprint of government (Medicaid expansion) and to put requirements on insurers and businesses. Left out was the individual health-care consumer. A more effective philosophy puts consumers in the driver's seat by giving them the financial resources to force competition among health-care providers. This will be the basis for my "real" solutions.

△ REAL SOLUTIONS

A "real" solution for health-care addresses each of the "clues" I examined earlier, as well as changes the incentives illustrated in Figure 4-1 that constantly push toward higher costs and prices. I categorize these real solutions into two parts. One part addresses the supply of health-care providers, and the other addresses how consumers pay for health-care. The purpose of these proposals is to change incentives to make the health-care system meet the "three A's" of affordability, adequacy, and accessibility.

Let's address the issue of supply of health-care providers. We need to increase the number of health-care professionals by expanding medical school enrollments, reducing residency training times without sacrificing quality, boosting the number of nurses (especially male nurses who have lost jobs in manufacturing), expanding the tasks performed by physician assistants and nurses, and allowing more foreigners trained in medical sciences to apply for jobs and permanent worker status in the U.S. States also need to modernize and modify their occupational licensing to facilitate easier movement of medical professionals between states. This could be most swiftly accomplished by ending state occupational licensing and moving to national licensing. State certificate-of-need laws should be eliminated, and the federal government should enact legislation allowing health insurance companies to sell policies across state lines.

Policies promoting large corporate health-care oligopolies need to be reversed. Rather than facilitating further creation and growth of these systems, regulators at both the federal and state levels need to move in the opposite direction and encourage and promote more individual, competing health-care companies. This means being cautious and possibly skeptical in approving further mergers and consolidations of health-care firms. It is also time for government regulators to reexamine existing health-care firms and decide if they are using anti-competitive practices. If the conclusion is "yes," then the firms may deserve serious fines or "breaking-up."

At the same time that the power and influence of big medical companies are being curtailed, smaller medical providers should be encouraged to develop modest health-care clinics that are staffed by physician assistants and located in pharmacies and "big box" stores. It's estimated that such clinics can handle as much as one-quarter of typical medical problems[107] and are 30% to 40% less expensive than traditional doctors' offices.[108] For issues beyond their scope, physician assistants would refer patients to doctors or specialists. Because these clinics would keep the same hours as the home store, and because the home stores are conveniently located and used by large numbers of individuals, it's expected their presence would encourage more people to seek medical care when needed.[109]

There's recently emerged another "small" health-care model. These are single or two-doctor offices taking patients on a monthly subscription basis and not using health-care insurance. Typical monthly rates might range between $100 and $150 depending on family size, with the subscription entitling patients to unlimited visits and a specified range of tests. The offices frequently have been able to negotiate reduced prices for other tests as well as pharmaceutical drugs.[110]

I call these "1950s doctors' offices," because they remind me of Dr. McClellan's office I visited as a child. However, while today's 1950s doctors' offices do not use insurance, patients would still want to carry health insurance for larger expenses related to medical procedures, operations, and hospital stays.

Turning now to the regulation of the health-care industry, several changes should be made to the major industry regulator, the FDA. With evidence suggesting pharmaceutical drug development costs are significantly lower than reported by the companies,[111] the patent protection period should be reduced from seven to five years. Health benefits from any proposed new drug should be compared to the benefits from existing drugs, not to a placebo.[112] After the patent protection period expires, consumers should be allowed to purchase generic versions of drugs from both domestic and safe foreign sources, such as Canada.

The FDA should continue efforts to speed the approval process for new pharmaceuticals. Also, the agency should forcefully and rapidly discontinue the ability of drug companies to engage in "ever-greening," where patent periods are expanded due to minor and insignificant changes to the drug. Hopefully common sense will prevail, but if not, a public board or panel independent of the pharmaceutical industry should be charged with determining if changes to existing drugs warrant a new patent period.

And while I'm focusing on the federal government, Congress should remove from the law any exemptions for the health-care industry from anti-competitive laws.

Last is the issue of medical malpractice laws, and whether changes need to be made in those laws. Certainly, we want to maintain the ability of patients to sue doctors and hospitals for errors they've committed in treatments and procedures. However, in our increasingly litigious society, medical malpractice costs, including settlements as well as insurance, now account for almost 2.5% of all health-care spending.[113] The concern is that this has led to the practice of "defensive medicine," where medical professionals use extra treatments and tests they consider of limited value, but they do so in order to guard against potential claims of malpractice.

Interestingly, current research shows that the quality of patient care is not worse where malpractice law suits are prohibited.[114] This is consistent with the idea that practicing defensive medicine provides little help to the patient, even though it adds to costs. Although I'd like to see more research conducted, the initial conclusion suggests medical malpractice laws should be closely examined and possibly revised to make the standards for lawsuits higher, thereby curtailing their occurrence. Limits should be considered for non-economic damages, and lawsuits should only be allowed after arbitration has been attempted.

While the "supply" changes I've offered here are important in reforming our health-care system, they won't be enough unless there are corresponding changes to the "demand" side. The primary problem on the payment side of health-care can be summed up in four words: no limit on spending. Unlike most government programs and certainly all household and business budgets, the two, big federal government health-care programs, Medicare and Medicaid, are open-ended. While Congress may set expectations for their annual spending, ultimately there is no limit on the yearly total spending of Medicare and Medicaid. As I've discussed, health insurance companies also are not adverse to higher spending because they simply pass those costs on to employers, who then pass them on to workers via lower wages.

We need two major changes on the demand-side of health-care. First, we need a constraint on spending, where a limit is set each year for what is spent on medical care. This means there would be no automatic pass-through of costs created by the health-care system. Second, we need both providers and patients to have "skin in the game," so they know "other people's money" isn't always there to pay the bills. For patients, this means they need to be directly involved in the payment of medical costs.

I see two ways of doing this. My preferred method is for the government to require everyone to have health insurance. Those who can afford the insurance would pay out of their own pocket. Those who couldn't would be financially assisted by the government with a health-care voucher, however, with the requirement not to reduce the size of the voucher dollar for dollar with increases in the person's ability to pay. Also, the size of the voucher would be greater for those individuals with special health-care needs, such as pre-existing conditions.

My optimal solution may not be possible due to a legal ruling striking down the ACA mandate that individuals purchase health insurance.[115] However, one possible way around this may be to have each state mandate the health insurance requirement, and then have the federal government provide the necessary subsidy funds for vouchers to each state.

If neither of these plans pass legal mustard, then my fallback plan directly provides households and individuals with government vouchers to assist in the purchase of health insurance policies. As in the first plan, the size of the vouchers would be scaled by the income and age of the individual, as well as by medical situations like pre-existing conditions. The size of the voucher would be slowly phased out as the income of the individual or household rose. The voucher could only be used to purchase health insurance. Although most households would need to add some of their own money to purchase policies, the expectation is that with the government helping with the purchase, and with the knowledge health insurance is a necessity, a very high percentage of households would "take the deal." Individuals and households would be free to purchase additional health insurance beyond that available with the government vouchers using their own funds.

I also see an important role for the government—likely the U.S. Department of Health and Human Services—in setting standards for health insurance policies. In particular, there should be minimum standards for the coverage of doctor and hospital expenses, and provisions regarding coverage that is clearly stated in plain, everyday language. However, there should be enough flexibility in the standards to allow individuals to customize policies to their own preferences. As discussed earlier, inflexibility in insurance policy provisions has been an issue with the health insurance policies established by the ACA.

There are several benefits to my plan. As revealed earlier, half of individuals with health insurance currently receive it as a benefit through their employer. However, if the person leaves the company, they lose their health insurance until they get a new job. My plan eliminates this problem by making health insurance portable: your insurance goes with you; it is not tied to your employer.

My plan ensures full coverage of health insurance for all, particularly those with limited financial resources. Poor households and households near the poverty line would receive the greatest financial assistance in their purchase of health insurance. Higher-income households would pay for most of their health insurance out of their own pockets. But from a financial standpoint measured in lost income from being ill or injured, households with ample income have the most to lose from being without adequate insurance. Hence, the motivation of higher-income households to buy their own insurance is strong. In fact, multiple studies have shown the amount of health-care sought by individuals is unrelated to any tax benefits or similar governmental subsidies they might receive.[116]

The current oligopolistic system combined with health-care consumers using mostly other people's money has prevented competition from working its magic to moderate prices and promote quality. My recommendations for the supply-side will create enhanced competition in the provision of health-care. And with consumers again shopping around, making their own health insurance decisions, and having financial "skin in the game," the price and quality comparisons would return to the demand-side of the industry.

Putting financial resources into households' hands to purchase the kind of health insurance they desire, combined with greater competition among health insurance providers, should prompt innovative ideas in financing health-care. One is the development of a market for "pre-birth health insurance"—the idea of purchasing health insurance for an individual prior to birth. Since pre-existing conditions of the individual would not be known, the price associated with the probability of such conditions would be evenly spread throughout all newborns and reflected in the average price of the policy. It follows the idea that insurance markets work best when it is not known in advance who will be inflicted by a disease or deformity. With this information unknown, everyone pays the same cost that includes coverage for the risk.

Further, such policies could potentially be bought for the lifetime of the individual. Also, similar to life insurance, there could be two versions of payments. One, which corresponds to term life insurance, would increase premiums as the probability of the individual needing medical treatment increased. Typically, this would mean the annual premiums would increase with age. Alternatively, like whole life insurance, premiums could be constant over time, meaning more is collected than is needed to cover risks in the early years of life and less is collected to cover risks in the later years of life. Yet the over-collection in the early years of an individual covers the under-collection in the person's later years.

Now on to finances. Notice that my plan eliminates the current federal health-care payment programs of Medicare, Medicaid, the Children's Health Insurance Program (CHIP), veterans' medical care, and the ACA subsidies. Also, the loss of business tax revenues due to the deductibility of employer-provided health insurance would be recovered.[117] In 2018, the total of these six categories of savings was $1.3 trillion.

Assuming most of the health vouchers would be used for households with incomes below the median income (which is three times larger than the poverty level),[118] $1.3 trillion would be enough to provide each household with almost $20,000 annually for the purchase of a health insurance policy. This is actually slightly more than the current annual cost for a non-subsidized standard family health insurance policy.[119]

Yet again—so I'm clear—all households under the median income wouldn't receive $20,000. Some households would get more if they have special health needs, or are aged, and are below the poverty level. Others with higher income (but still below the median) would get less, but with the reductions in the voucher always made in a way to still encourage households to earn more income. But here's the big conclusion: it appears government funds are already available to implement a health insurance voucher program.

Actually, the voucher program could become more affordable over time for two reasons. First, several studies have determined the non-competitive practices of the current health-care system have resulted in prices much higher than necessary. One study estimated 30% of health-care costs are due to unnecessary procedures, treatments, and prescriptions.[120] Another study showed hospital charges ten times the cost of the care.[121] So over time we could easily see health-care costs fall as greater competition emerges.

Second, advances in technology should have cost-reducing impacts on health-care. Innovations such as remote treatment via the internet, improved diagnoses using artificial intelligence, virtual medical assistants, and body-sensors that alert health professionals to an individual's emerging health problems before they occur (and before expensive treatment is needed) could make health-care more effective as well as cost-efficient.[122]

Here's another piece of good financial news from my plan: private employers who provide health insurance coverage to their workers will be relieved of this obligation. Today, this benefit annually costs employers an average of about $5,700 for a single worker and $14,000 for a worker and their family.[123] Current research shows companies pay for half of this expense by reducing the worker's salary. So, for the 156 million workers who receive health insurance coverage at work, they could be in for a big pay raise if my voucher plan was implemented.[124]

The solution to reducing health-care costs without sacrificing coverage and quality is to increase supply, competition, and efficiency in the provision of health-care, while at the same time giving consumers both the resources and incentives to make providers cater to their needs and their finances. These are the characteristics of a productive and performing market, something—unfortunately—we do not have in health-care now.

▲ SUMMING UP

Although some claim concerns about costs and spending should be kept out of health-care, it's the lack of these concerns and the absence of a competitive market that have brought us the unsustainable high costs. We need a two-front attack to make health-care accessible, affordable, and adequate. On the supply-side, rules and regulations need to be altered at federal and state levels to encourage both growth in the number of health-care professionals and health-care providers. In particular, control of the market by large health-care systems should be curtailed. On the demand-side, patients' control of the market should be reinstated by handing over spending decisions to consumers. This can be done by converting federal health-care spending to household vouchers to be used for the purchase of portable health insurance policies.

Chapter 4 Endnotes

1. "Number of Heart Transplantations in the U.S. from 1975 to 2017," *Statista*.

2. Mullin, "A Simple Artificial Heart Could Permanently Replace a Failing Human One."

3. Kaiser Family Foundation, "Peterson-Kaiser Health Tracker System."

4. Centers for Medicare and Medicaid Services, "Data on 2019 Individual Health Insurance Market Conditions."

5. "U.S. National Health Expenditure as a Percent of GDP from 1960 to 2019," *Statista*.

6. U.S. Bureau of Economic Analysis, "Gross Domestic Product by State." Health care spending includes spending from both private sources and public (government) sources.

7. United Health Foundation, *America's Health Rankings, 2016 Annual Report*.

8. Atlas, "Single Payer's Misleading Statistics."

9. Ho and and Preston, "US Mortality in an International Context: Age Variations."

10. U.S. Bureau of Labor Statistics, "Consumer Price Index," *op. cit.*

11. "U.S. Average Hourly Wages," *Trading Economics*.

12. Mislinski, "U.S. Household Incomes: A 51 Year Perspective."

13. Calabresi and Bobbitt, *Tragic Choices: The Conflicts Society Confronts in the Allocation of Tragically Scarce Resources*. Furthers the discussion on the difficult tradeoffs we face for spending.

14. Leatherby, "Medical Spending among the U.S. Elderly."

15. "Share of Old Age Population (65 Years and Older) in the Total U.S. Population from 1950 to 2050," *Statista*.

16. "Total Number or Doctors of Medicine in the U.S., 1949-2015," *Statista*.

17. "U.S. Population," *Trading Economics*.

18. "Demographic Characteristics of the Population Age 65 and Over," *Proximity*.

19. HIS Markit, "The Complexities of Physician Supply and Demand: Projections from 2015 to 2030."

20. D'Antonio and Whelan, "Counting Nurses: The Power of Historical Census Data."

21. "Number of Hospital Beds in the U.S. from 1975 to 2016," *Statista*.

22. Centers for Disease Control and Prevention, "Health, U.S., 2016—Individual Charts and Tables."

23. Silver and Hyman, *Overcharged: Why Americans Pay too Much for Health Care*, p. 33.

24. Scherer, "The F.T.C, Oligopoly, and Shared Monopoly"; U.S. Departments of Health and Human Services, Treasury, and Labor, *Reforming America's Healthcare System through Choice and Competition*.

25. Zweig and Blum, "When Does the Law Against Kickbacks Not Apply? Your Hospital."

26. Gaynor, "Examining the Impact of Health Care Consolidation."

27. Gibson, "Duke Outpaces Other Hospitals in Market Share."

28. "5 Forces Driving Hospital Consolidation," *Stratasan.*

29. Rubb and Sumner, Economic Principles, pp. 231-239.

30. Biery and Sageworks Stats, "These are the 10 Most Profitable Industries in 2017."

31. Seibold, "Impact of Commercial Over-Reimbursement on Hospitals: The Curious Case of Central Indiana."

32. Rosenthal, *An American Sickness*, p. 53.

33. Capps and Dranove, "Hospital Consolidation and Negotiated PPO Prices"; Dafny, "Are Health Insurance Markets Competitive?"; Diez, Leigh, and Tambunlertchai, "Global Market Power and its Macroeconomic Implications"; Gaynor and Vogt, "Competition among Hospitals"; Gowrisankaran, Nevo, and Town, "Mergers When Prices are Negotiated: Evidence from the Hospital Industry"; Haas-Wilson and Garmon, "Hospital Mergers and Competitive Effects: Two Retrospective Analyses"; Town and Vistnes, "Hospital Competition in HMO Networks"; and Vita and Sacher, "The Competitive Effects of Not-for-Profit Hospital Mergers: A Case Study."

34. Matthews and Evans, "Hospitals Push Doctors to Keep Referrals In-House."

35. Lanfear, "How Big Pharma Suppresses 'Biosimilars.'"

36. Thimou, "When Paying Cash for Prescriptions Beats Using Insurance."

37. Jaffe, "No More Secrets: Congress Bans Pharmacist 'Gag Orders' on Drug Prices."

38. Kantarjian and Rajkumar, "Why are Cancer Drugs so Expensive in the United States and What are the Solutions?"

39. Torjesen, "Drug Development: The Journey of a Medicine from Lab to Shelf"; and "Costs to Bring a Drug to Market Remains in Dispute," *Managed Care.*

40. *Managed Care, op. cit.*

41. Hooper, "Pharmaceuticals: Economics and Regulation."

42. "Why the FDA has an Incentive to Delay the Introduction of New Drugs," *The Independent Institute.*

43. "Trump Signs 'Right to Try' Allowing Gravely Ill Patients to Bypass FDA fir Experimental Medicine," *CNBC.*

44. U.S. Food and Drug Administration, "Fast Track, Breakthrough Therapy, Accelerated Approval, Priority Review."

45. Kiplinger, "How Can the Approval Process for New Drugs Be Speeded Up?"

46. Upcounsel, "How Long Does a Drug Patent Last?"

47. U.S. Government Accounting Office, "Savings from Generic Drug Use."

48. Silver and Hyman, *op. cit.*, p. 39.

49. *Ibid.*, pp. 86-87.

50. Silver and Hyman, *op. cit.*, pp. 86-87.

51. Silver and Hyman, op. cit., p. 227.

52. *Ibid.*, p. 40.

53. *Ibid.*, p. 41. There is litigation pending regarding whether such settlements are legal.

54. Laugesen, *Fixing Medical Prices.*

55. American Immigration Council, "Foreign-Trained Doctors are Critical to Serving Many U.S. Communities."

56. *Ibid.*

57. Center for Insurance Policy and Research, "The Relevance of the McCarran-Ferguson Act."

58. New, "The Effect of State Regulations on Health Insurance Premiums: A Preliminary Analysis."

59. Japsen, "States Ease More Restrictions to Physician Assistants as Team Care Takes Hold."

60. Timmons, "Healthcare License Turf Wars."

61. Nunn, "Occupational Licensing and American Workers."

62. Johnson and Kleiner, "Is Occupational Licensing a Barrier to Interstate Migration?"

63. National Conference of State Legislatures, "Con – Certificate of Need State Laws."

64. Mitchell, "Certificate of Need Laws: Are They Achieving their Goals?"

65. Zweig and Blum, *op. cit.*

66. Silver and Hyman, *op. cit.*, p. 144.

67. Cochrane, John, "The Tax and Spend Healthcare Solution."

68. Quincy and Hunt, "Revealing the Truth about Healthcare Price Transparency."

69. Centers for Medicare and Medicaid, NHE Fact Sheet. Data are for 2017.

70. Gneezy, Haruvy, and Yafe, "The Inefficiency of Splitting the Bill."

71. Silver and Hyman, op. cit., pp. 157-159, 171-172.

72. *Ibid,* p. 154.

73. *Ibid,* p. 271.

74. Abutaleb, "U.S. Healthcare Spending to Climb 5.3% in 2018: Agency."

75. Anand, "Health Insurance Costs and Employee Compensation: Evidence from the National Compensation Survey."

76. Dickow, "A Dysfunctional Market: What the Foundation is doing to Control Healthcare Costs."

77. Kliff and Scott, "We Read Democrats' 9 Plans for Expanding Health Care. Here's How They Work"; Sanders, "The Medicare for All Act of 2019"; Sitaraman and Alstott, *The Public Option.*

78. Pollin, Heintz, Arno, Wicks-Lim, and Ash, "Economic Analysis of Medicare for All."

79. Book, "Medicare Administrative Costs are Higher, Not Lower, than for Private Insurance."

80. Woolhandler and Himmelstein, "Single Payer Reform: The Only Way to Fulfil the President's Pledge of More Coverage, Better Benefits, and Lower Costs."

81. *Ibid.*

82. Kaiser Family Foundation, "10 Essential Facts about Medicare Prescription Drug Spending"; Anderson-Cook, Maeda, and Nelson, "Prices for and Spending on Specialty Drugs in Medicare Part D and Medicaid."

83. Davis, Schoen, and Bandeali, "Medicare: 50 Years of Ensuring Coverage and Care."

84. Laugesen, *op. cit.*

85. Silverstein, "This Is Why Your Drug Prescriptions Cost so Damn Much."

86. Conover, "Why Bernie Sanders' Health Care Plan Will Cost at Least 40% More than Advertised."

87. Abutaleb, *op. cit.*

88. Pryde, "A National Sales Tax to Pay for Health Care?"

89. Congressional Budget Office, *Analysis of the Long-Term Costs of the Administration's Goals for the Military*; U.S. Bureau of Labor Statistics, "Employment, Hours, and Earnings from the Current Employment Statistics Survey, op. cit.

90. U.S. Postal Service, *U.S. Postal Service FY2018 Annual Report to Congress.*

91. Smith, "$37 Screws, a $7622 Coffee Maker, $640 Toilet Seats: Suppliers to our Military Just Wont' be Oversold."; Dillard, "Customers Upset with Area Post Office for Unpredictable Midday Closures."

92. NHS, "Guide to Waiting Times in England."

93. Yeginsu, "N.H.S. Overwhelmed in Britain, Leafing Patients to Wait."

94. Canadian Institute for Health Insurance, "How Canada Compares: Results from the Commonwealth Fund's 2017 International Health Policy Survey of Seniors."

95. Cullis, Jones, and Proper, "Waiting Lists and Medical Treatment: Analysis and Policies."

96. Cohn, "The Big New Idea for Reducing Health Care Costs Is Actually Really Old."

97. Eby and Cohodes, "What Do We Know about Rate Setting?"; McDonough, "Tracking the Demise of State Hospital Rate Setting."

98. Kaiser Family Foundation, "Summary of the Affordable Care Act."

99. Amadeo, "What is Wrong with Obamacare?"

100. Mangan, "This Map Shows How Much of the United States Could See Zero or Few Obamacare Insurers Selling Health Coverage Next Year."

101. Panhans, "Adverse Selection in ACA Exchange Markets: Evidence from Colorado."

102. Goodman, "Six Problems with the ACA that Aren't Going Away."

103. Wogan, "No Cut in Premiums for Typical Family."

104. Goldman, Woolhandler, Himmelstein, Bor, and McCormick, "Out-of-Pocket Spending and Premium Contributions after Implementation of the Affordable Care Act."

105. Duggan, Gupta, and Jackson, "The Impact of the Affordable Care Act: Evidence from California's Hospital Sector."

106. Badger and Haislmaier, "How Congress Can Reduce Obamacare Premiums."

107. Weinick, Burns, and Mehrotra, "How Many Emergency Department Visits Could Be Managed at Urgent Care and Retail Clinics?"

108. Atlas, *Restoring Quality Health Care.*

109. Shi, "The Impact of Primary Care: A Focused Review."

110. Schencker, "More Doctors Embrace Membership Fees, Shunning Health Insurance."

111. Gavura, "What Does a New Drug Cost?"

112. Rosenthal, *op. cit.*, p. 312.

113. Sullivan, "Defensive Medicine Adds $45 Billion to the Cost of Healthcare."

114. Frakes and Gruber, "Defensive Medicine: Evidence from Military Immunity."

115. Keith, "Federal Judge Strikes Down Entire ACA." At the time this book was published, appeals of the ruling had no yet been decided.

116. Simler and Hanson, *The Elephant in the Brain*; Finkelstein, Hendren, and Luttmer, "The Value of Medicaid: Interpreting Results from the Oregon Health Insurance Experiment"; Brook, Robert H., Emmett B. Keeler, Kathleen N. Lohr, Joseph P. Newhouse, John E. Ware, William H. Rogers, Allyson Ross Davies, Cathy D. Sherbourne, George A. Goldberg, Patricia Camp, Caren Kamberg, Arleen Leibowitz, Joan Keesey, and David Reboussin, "The Health Insurance Experiment: A Classic RAND Study Speaks to the Current Health Care Reform Debate."

117. Brill, *America's Bitter Pill*. The deductibility of employer-provided health insurance originated in the 1940s World War II period as an alternative to pay raises for workers.

118. Fontenot, Semega, and Kollar, *Income and Poverty in the United States, 2017*.

119. Kasier Family Foundation, *Employer Health Benefits 2018 Annual Survey*.

120. Keckley, "Medical Necessity and Unnecessary Care."

121. Bai and Anderson, "Extreme Markup: The Fifty US Hospitals with the Highest Charge-to-Cost Ratios."

122. Wachter, *The Digital Doctor*; and Topol, *Deep Medicine*. Discussion of the potential benefits and issues related to technological developments in health care.

123. Kaiser Family Foundation, *Employer Health Benefits, 2018*; Anand, *op. cit.*

124. Kaier Family Foundation, *State Health Care Facts, Health Coverage of the Total Population, 2017*.

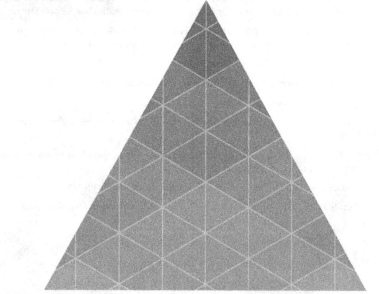

CHAPTER FIVE

CREATING MORE HOUSING WITH LOWER PRICES

THE IRON LAW OF REAL ESTATE

Early in our marriage, my wife and I were ready to buy a house. Both of us liked our jobs and the city, and we had saved enough for a down payment. With my relatively new Ph.D. in economics, I thought I would use the home-buying occasion to "educate" my wife about the real estate market. I told her local real estate prices exhibit a distinct pattern; homes located closer to jobs, shopping, and entertainment options cost more per square foot because they give the owners easy access to those activities. Homes in more remote areas and farther away from jobs, restaurants, and stores cost less per square foot, but owners will have longer commutes to reach those activities.

In my best professorial manner, I told my wife this tradeoff between distance and real estate prices was called the "iron law of real estate." I continued by saying that with a fixed amount of money to spend on a house, she had two choices: buy a smaller house close to the city center with the benefit of shorter commutes, or buy a larger house farther from the city center with the disadvantage of longer commutes. Looking at her like one of my students, I asked her which one would she choose.

Perfectly understanding what I told her about the real estate market, but not liking the way I presented the information in a "professor to student" manner, my wife's answer was a forceful, "I want a large home in the heart of the city."

Of course, my wife knew she couldn't have that, but she wanted to make the point that she was not to be treated like a student in my classroom. I quickly realized my mistake and apologized, and, in case you're wondering, we bought a small home close to the city center. Still, I don't know how many times I have heard homebuyers on the various real estate reality television programs say, "If only we could move this house closer to the city, then it would be perfect." The agent usually then patiently explains the iron law of real estate. The buyers walk away frustrated, but at least knowledgeable.

A decade ago, no one talked about the iron law of real estate because home-buying was almost dead. The Great Recession of 2007-2009 was prompted by an unprecedented crash in home prices that took years to recover. Potential buyers kept away from purchasing houses because they considered them a losing investment, and while house prices did decline and were flat for several years, they have since come back.

Today, home-buying is again alive and well—indeed, some say it is too alive and well! This is because—particularly in metropolitan areas adding jobs at rapid paces[1]- home prices have been on a steep rise. For example, according to the S&P/Case-Shiller Home Price

Index, average home prices in the twenty largest urban areas rose 46% from 2012 to 2018, more than wiping out all the loses from the Great Recession.[2] This works out to be an average annual gain of 6.5%, easily beating what savers could earn on safe financial investments like insured bank certificates of deposit and money market funds during the same period. The gain in urban home prices has also beaten gains in both suburban and rural areas.[3]

△ THE NEW AFFORDABLE HOUSING CRISIS

These geographic differences in home prices have revived the recognition of the iron law of real estate. But it's now going under the new name of the "affordable housing crisis." Increasingly, to afford homes or even apartments close to jobs in cities and urban areas, a person has to earn significantly more than the median salary.[4] Lower-paid workers and also some middle-paid teachers and public safety (police and fire) workers often can't afford to live where they work; their only option is to live far from their job and endure the long and congested drives.

It wasn't always like this! In the past, big cities often had sections of older and sometimes dilapidated neighborhoods that were affordable to households at the lower end of the economic ladder. Granted, these parts of town were often referred to as "slums," and while not necessarily pretty and often plagued by crime and other social issues, they did serve the purpose of giving people a place to live that was affordable and convenient.

But the slums are being "gentrified." This means they are being bulldozed and rebuilt, or renovated and upgraded, for much high-er-income residents who want to live in the city and walk to work, restaurants, bars, and sporting events.[5] While good for cities' images, tax revenues, and tourism, the losers are the original residents who have three choices: move somewhere else, afford the higher rents by doubling or tripling-up with other households, or become homeless. Several studies have documented measurable rates of displacement of original residents in gentrified neighborhoods,[6] although those forced to move sometimes have an improvement in their living standards.[7]

Here's an example. I grew up in Cincinnati in the 1950s. There's a historic neighborhood just north of the city's central business district called "Over the Rhine," so named because it developed near a former canal and was initially populated by German immigrants in the 19th century. When I was a youngster, Over-the-Rhine was a rough place, and one which most people avoided unless they lived there, but today it's one of the hottest areas in the city. Nine-teenth-century brick buildings have been repaired and rebuilt and turned into fashionable condos. Light-rail transit now services the neighborhood, and a stadium for a major league soccer franchise is being constructed just blocks away. Over-the-Rhine is "the place to live" for young professionals working in the city, and the area's transformation has received national attention.[8] But not everyone has benefitted, as hundreds of homes of previous low-income resi-dencies have been remodeled or destroyed and rebuilt for the new urban pioneers.[9]

△ ZONING OUT ANSWERS

My wife doesn't like to be told what to do, or what not to do for that matter. On reflection, who does? But in my wife's case, her aversion to orders has had an impact on where we live in our city (Raleigh, North Carolina). There is a historic neighborhood in Raleigh that we have considered moving to several times; once we were just a signature short of buying a beautiful 100-year-old home in this inner-city gem. What deterred my wife were rules in the neighborhood about what residents were allowed to do to the exteriors of their homes, yards and gardens. Since my wife is passionate about design and gardening, and has distinct ideas about both, she decided she couldn't stomach allowing other people to possibly overrule her paint selections for the house and plant choices for the yard.

While it's uncommon for all but historic neighborhoods to operate under these kinds of restrictions, most neighborhoods—especially in cities—do have rules about what kind of construction is allowed. These rules are grouped under a bureaucratic heading called *zoning*. The original purpose of zoning was to keep incompatible land uses separate. For example, zoning rules usually meant housing developments weren't permitted to be adjacent to industrial developments, the reasoning being that noise, traffic, and potentially smoke and smells from factories distract from the peace, quiet, and family atmosphere of residential areas. Zoning also often keeps owner-occupied, single-unit developments separate from rental, multi-unit developments under the assumption that homeowners and renters have different interests and lifestyles.

At the same time, there are concerns that some cities have used zoning to restrict or eliminate affordable housing or even any kind of housing at all.[10] Take San Francisco as an example: San Francisco is a modern growing city with limited land availability for new construction. In such situations, the solution to building more housing is to build up, but if you look at the zoning map of San Francisco, you see most of the city is zoned to prevent buildings higher than four stories.[11] It is little wonder then that the city's housing supply is rising at an anemic rate compared to its job growth.[12]

Or consider the boarding-room house common in most of the 20th century. This was a type of living arrangement where individuals and families rented only one or two rooms for sleeping and then shared common areas like the dining room, living room, and bathroom with other tenants. Often breakfast and dinner were provided as part of the daily fee. Rents were much lower than when households lived in their own individual functioning units.

But boarding houses and similar accommodations have largely been prohibited in most cities. Cities have used zoning to set minimum square footage sizes for residential space and maximum numbers of unrelated individuals living in the same structure.[13] Cities have also used zoning to limit the use of manufactured housing ("trailers") within their boundaries and to set standards for the building of residential structures that effectively eliminates the use of lower-cost, factory homes constructed off-site.[14]

Each of these standards and regulations has pros and cons that can be debated. Boarding-room houses were prohibited in part because some groups thought that they were not considered decent living arrangements. Of course, viewpoints are different today; strict limitations on the use of manufactured housing in cities are based on a worry these housing units would lower the economic value of nearby traditional "site-built" housing. Nonetheless, there does appear to be agreement among economists that strict city zoning regulations have three results: housing prices are higher, housing becomes more unaffordable, and housing supply expands more slowly.[15]

△ FAKE SOLUTIONS

There has not been a lack of suggestions for solving the new affordable housing crisis. Unfortunately, many of them would actually make the problem worse, or would only address a tiny portion of the problem.

One of the most widely offered solutions, and usually the first to be touted, is price controls.[16] If home prices and apartment rents are going up too fast, just make it a law that they can't go up that much. Problem solved, right?

Wrong. Price controls—mainly on rental units so they end up being called rent controls—have been used in many cities and they flat-out don't work. They're a good example of the "law of unintended consequences," which is a fancy term for something sounding good, but which turns out to have bad after-effects. Rent controls hurt in two ways. First, the controls reduce the investment earnings received by the owners of the units. While you may not be sympathetic (unless you own rental property), the reaction of owners is to say—"OK, I'll simply reduce my investment in the property until the earnings, as a percentage of the property's investment value, rise back to where they were." But how can rental property owners do this if the units are already there? Simple: the owners reduce maintenance and upkeep, which means the quality of the units deteriorate, and so does the investment value. The second "unintended consequence" of rent controls is they discourage investors from building new rental housing. Investors are always looking for the highest returns they can make on their money, and if those returns are limited or decreased for rental housing, then investors will take their money and put it somewhere else.

So, rent controls reduce both the quality and quantity of rental housing. As I have mentioned, economists are known for disagreeing. Indeed, it's reported that President Truman, frustrated because his economic advisors often wouldn't give him direct recommendations, once said, "Give me a one-handed economist. All my economists say, on the one hand this, on the other that."[17] But on the matter of rent controls, President Truman would be happy. A survey of economists published in 2001 found the adverse impacts of rent controls were one of the top 40 issues receiving widespread agreement among this normally disagreeable bunch.[18] A big reason is that there is significant research confirming the adverse impacts of rent controls.[19] Ironically, then, rent controls work against improving the affordability of housing.

Although not as common as rent controls, controls on home prices have the same impact. Homeowners aren't as motivated to spend money to keep their home in good shape because they won't necessarily get that money back through a higher sales price. Similarly, builders of new homes then take their money to cities without price controls or look at other investments in the economy.

Other approaches to increasing affordable housing, while also well-intentioned, simply don't have enough resources behind them to make much of a dent in the problem. For decades, governments and private organizations have used several programs to subsidize the rents or home payments of renters and owners. Still, in 2017 it is estimated only 35% of the households who needed to live in affordable housing were able to do so using the programs.[20] This means there is still a shortage of over 7 million affordable housing units in the country. Other estimates paint an even gloomier picture, with close to 40 million households being burdened by their housing costs. This means they are paying more than 30% of their income for shelter.[21]

Private organizations like Habitat for Humanity do good work in building affordable housing, but in its fifty years of its existence, it has only built 800,000 homes worldwide.[22] It's estimated my home city of Raleigh has an affordable housing shortage of over 26,000 units.[23] Yet the City of Raleigh's latest plan commits to creating only 570 units of affordable housing a year for the next ten years.[24] Therefore, after a decade, Raleigh will reduce its current affordable housing shortage by about 20%, but in ten years it will likely be much less than that because the total shortage will almost certainly have grown.

The point is that we're not helping the majority of households facing a housing affordability problem, but to do so using public and private programs would require substantially more money—as much as $100 billion annually![25] Isn't there a better way?

△ REAL SOLUTIONS

The real solution to the lack of affordable housing, particularly in cities, has three components: expand the supply of housing, allow alternative living arrangements for households, and reconsider restrictions on housing types and materials.

A major part of economics, as I've mentioned, is about demand. So, to recap: as young college-educated graduates and some empty-nester retirees have flocked to cities for jobs and living, the demand for housing in cities has increased relative to the supply of housing, and thus real estate prices have jumped.

Logically, then, one major way to contain the rise in housing prices— both rents and home prices—is to make sure there are not unreasonable limits to expanding the construction of new housing units. In other words, make sure local zoning ordinances don't make it impossible or very costly to build more apartments and homes.

A common way to discourage affordable housing is to zone neighborhoods for large lots. For example, zoning that states only one housing unit can be built per acre makes it much more expensive to construct new housing than if the zoning allowed for two, four, or twenty units per acre. Therefore, something as simple as increasing the number of housing units that can be built per acre can go a long way to improving affordability.

However, I want to be honest here. City zoning officials and elected leaders should take baby steps in changing zoning. Those who bought homes in neighborhoods with low housing densities per acre probably did so, in part, because they wanted that kind of space and were willing to pay for it. Existing residents could become upset if the zoning changed to increase a neighborhood's allowable density from, for example, something like two units per acre to four units per acre.

Consider the zoning change Minneapolis recently made. By 2040, the city plans to prohibit zoning requiring single-family homes anywhere in the city. Single-family homes can be built; they just can't be built exclusively in any neighborhood. Many residents think such a plan goes too far, and as a result the plan has prompted considerable pushback.[26] Hence, changing zoning rules must be done cautiously, carefully, and with much communication.

When new housing has to be constructed at less central or outer fringes of the urban area, but job growth is in the urban core, then transportation options should also be part of the plan. In only a few areas of the country does fixed-route (usually rail based) transportation make practical or economic sense. New York City is probably the best example. In other metropolitan areas, rail-based mass transit takes too long to construct, is too costly, and may become obsolete as growth patterns change. The best option is for buses to be used to transport people from residential developments to large employment areas using major roads, perhaps with a dedicated bus lane. The buses can either be publicly funded using a Pumfee or privately funded by large employers.

Housing structures with private rooms but shared public areas, like boarding-room homes in earlier times, and housing units constructed using low-cost materials and methods, such as trailers, are an important part of the affordable housing solution. Boarding-room structures—now called "co-living" by some—need to be brought back, and in some cities, they have. New York City, perhaps the most expensive housing market in the country, now has 250 square foot "co-living" units with a bed, table, kitchenette, and bathroom for half the rent of a one-bedroom apartment. There are shared public areas for lounging, eating, and doing laundry.[27] While households with children would need more space, the concept is the same: private space is limited to sleeping and bathing, with public space devoted to relaxing, eating, and entertainment.

Most states and localities have relaxed restrictions on using factory-built modular housing components, and entire housing units are now being constructed this way.[28] Housing units built in factories don't have to deal with weather issues, can make use of more machinery and technology, and can therefore be an answer to lowering costs in the construction industry, an industry which has struggled to improve efficiency in recent decades.[29] Pre-made housing units can also be assembled very rapidly: a 22-unit, four story building for graduate students at UC Berkeley went up in four days.[30]

It may also be time to go further and legally authorize the ultimate in low-cost single-unit homes—the trailer, now termed "manufactured housing." Owners of traditional homes worry the proximity of manufactured housing will lower their own property values, and this is a reasonable concern. One option is for cities to again use zoning to separate locations where traditional housing and manufactured housing are permitted. Still, cities should consider low-cost trailer parks as part of the solution for affordable housing.[31]

Let me close with a broader benefit of increasing the supply of affordable housing. Let's say Lois Lane has found the perfect job at the newspaper *The Daily Planet* in the city of Metropolis. She wants the job, and *The Daily Planet* considers her the best qualified candidate for the job. There's just one problem; Lois can't afford to live in Metropolis due to its super-high housing costs. As a result, Lois doesn't take the job and misses out on a great career. Likewise, *The Daily Planet* loses by hiring someone much less capable than Lois. In fact, because this perfect employee-employer match wasn't made, the entire economy loses.

Economic researchers estimate that the lack of affordable housing in many regions has cost the job market millions of lucrative matches. According to these numbers, economic growth in the country is one-third slower because workers cannot take the most suitable jobs for their skillset.[32] This translates to a loss of $200 billion each year for the economy! The affordable housing issue doesn't just hurt renters and homeowners; it hurts everyone by making the economic pie smaller. Affordable housing is therefore a winner—if done the right way.

▲ SUMMING UP

With the crash in real estate prices during the Great Recession long past, affordable housing has re-emerged as an issue, especially in fast-growing and popular metropolitan areas. The issue has a three-part solution. First, where possible, remove zoning barriers to increasing housing supply. If new housing cannot be built close to job markets, then make sure publicly or privately funded transportation is available from housing to major job centers. Second, encourage the availability of boarding room (also called "co-living") structures where occupants have private sleeping and personal care space but share dining, laundry, and relaxing spaces. Third, change local ordinances and zoning to permit lower-cost manufactured housing structures.

Chapter 5 Endnotes

1. Kolko, "Where the Fast-Growing Jobs Are."

2. Federal Reserve Bank of St. Louis, "S&P/Case Schiller National Home Price Index."

3. Florida, "The Incredible Rise of Urban Real Estate."

4. "The Salary You Must Earn to Buy a Home in the Largest 50 Metros," HSH.com.

5. Su, "The Rising Value of Time and the Origin of Urban Gentrification."

6. Zuk, Bierbaum, Chapple, Gorska, Loukaitou-Sideris, Ong, and Thomas, "Gentrification, Displacement and the Role of Public Investment: A Literature Review," pp. 27-33. For a contrary view that gentrification has not resulted in higher rates of displacement of poorer households, see Freeman and Braconi, "Gentrification and Displacement: New York City in the 1990s."

7. Brummet and Reed, "The Effects of Gentrification on the Well-Being and Opportunity of Original Resident Adults and Children."

8. Mahtani, "From Ailing to Artisanal: The Transformation of a Cincinnati Neighborhood."

9. Jackson, "The Rise and Fall of the African-American Community in OTR Cincinnati."

10. Metcalf, "Sand Castles Before the Tide? Affordable Housing in Expensive Cities."

11. Chanowitz, "Do San Francisco Zoning Laws Prevent Neighborhoods from Building Tall Buildings for More People Live in Hurt Its Residents and Drive up Rents?"

12. Brinlow, "SF Built One New Home for Every 10.4 New Jobs Last Year."

13. Badger, "Is It Time to Bring Back the Boarding House?"

14. Mandelker, "Zoning Barriers to Manufactured Housing."

15. Furman, "Barriers to Shared Growth: The Case of Land Use Regulation and Economic Rents"; Glaeser and Gyourko, "The Impact of Zoning on Housing Affordability"; Aastveit, Albuquerque, and Anundsen, "Time-Varying Housing Supply Elasticities and US Housing Cycles."

16. Parker and Vielkind, "New York Passes Overhaul of Rent Laws, Buoying Wider Movement to Tackle Housing Crunch."

17. "Harry S Truman on Economy and Economics," *Quotationsbook.com*.

18. Alston, Kearl, and Vaughan, "Is there Consensus among Economists in the 1990s?"

19. Block, Walter, "Rent Control." For recent evidence, see Diamond, McQuade, and Qian, "The Effects of Rent Control on Tenants, Landlords, and Inequality: Evidence from San Francisco."

20. Aurand, et al., *The Gap: A Shortage of Affordable Housing.*

21. Joint Study for Housing Studies at Harvard University, *The State of the Nation's Housing, 2017.*

22. Habitat for Humanity, *Habitat for Humanity's Milestones in History.*

23. Aurand, *et al.*, Emmanuel, Yentel, and Errico, *op. cit.*

24. City of Raleigh, *Affordable Housing in Raleigh.*

25. Joint Center for Housing Studies at Harvard University, *op. cit.* Using Harvard's estimates of the number of households needing assistance to avoid paying more than 30% of monthly income for rent.

26. Buhayar, "To Fix Its Housing Crunch, One US City Takes Aim at the Single-Family Home."

27. Durbin, "As Rents Soar, Co-Living a More Appealing Option."

28. Dougherty, "A Factory-Made Answer to a Crisis."

29. Barbosa, Woetzel, Mischke, Ribeirnbo, Sridhar, Parsons, Bertram and Brown, "Reinventing Construction: A Route to Higher Productivity."

30. Rauch, "Prefab Housing Complex for UC Berkeley Students Goes Up in Four Days."

31. Semuels, "The Case for Trailer Parks."

32. Hsieh and Moretti, "Housing Constraints and Spatial Misallocation."

CHAPTER SIX

CLOSING THE INCOME INEQUALITY GAP

A FAILURE TO COMMUNICATE

One of my favorite actors is the late Paul Newman, and one of my favorite Paul Newman movies is *Cool Hand Luke*. In the movie, Newman plays a likeable convict sentenced to prison in the rural South. Newman's character, Luke, tries to escape several times, and after one attempt he is severely beaten. As he lies helpless on the ground, the warden then utters one of the more memorable lines in movie history—"What we've got here, is failure to communicate"—suggesting the warden has been unable to convince Luke to conform to the rules of the prison, especially the rule of not attempting to escape.

Income inequality has become a popular economic phrase cited by newscasters, politicians, and policymakers as perhaps *the* economic issue of our time. But the issue isn't about income inequality *per se*. Most people accept that all individuals won't earn the same amount of income. While there may be a few on the extreme of the political/economic spectrum who want to mandate equal incomes for all (thus, by definition, eliminating income inequality), most of us know this isn't likely. We also realize there's actually a societal benefit from income inequality if it motivates people to work hard and acquire skills that the workplace needs.

Instead, the real issue is about *increasing* income inequality; it is claimed the gap between the rich and the poor has become wider in the 21st century. This is actually true, but with one correction. As I'll show, the gap between the income earned by the rich and the income earned by the poor started to expand in the 1980s. Thus, for almost four decades, the difference between incomes of the rich and the poor has been getting wider.

Unfortunately, at this point some people have gone off the rails. They think—or they have been told to think—that the gains of the rich have come at the expense of the poor. In other words, today's increase in income inequality is often interpreted as a "reverse Robin Hood," where income from the poor has been transferred to the rich. Increasing income inequality means the "rich are getting richer while the poor are getting poorer."

Yet this is *not* what has happened, and therein lies the failure to communicate. Look at Figure 6-1. It shows average (mean) incomes for five income groups for each year from 1967 to 2017. The incomes have all been adjusted for general inflation and are expressed in 2017 purchasing power dollars. The incomes only include what households have earned or received and importantly exclude the value of any non-cash government support programs like Medicaid, Medicare, and Food Stamps. The incomes are also before taxes are subtracted. The five income groups are based on dividing the income distribution into five equal pieces: the 20% of households

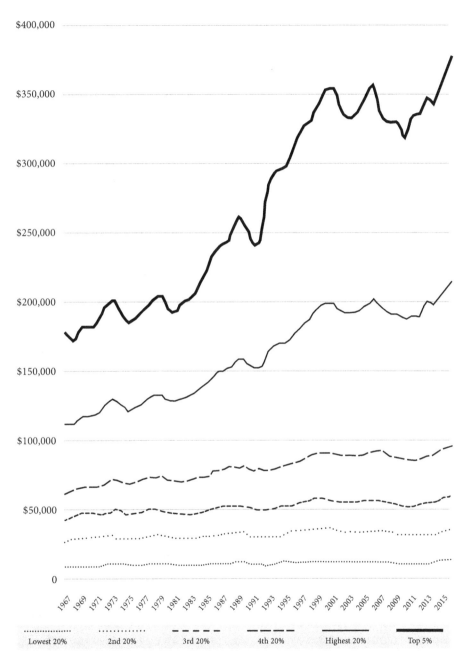

Figure 6-1. Average Household Income by Income Group, 1980-2017 (2017 $).
Source: Semega, Fontenot, and Kollar, U.S. Bureau of the Census.

with the lowest average income, the next 20% of households with the second lowest average income, the third 20% of households by average income, the fourth 20% of households by average income, and the 20% of households with the highest average income. There is also a sixth group shown—the 5% of households with the top average income.[1]

There are two big takeaways from Figure 6-1. First, average incomes for each of the five groups were all higher in 2017 than in 1967. Even the 20% of households with the lowest average income had an almost $3,000 gain in annual income over the fifty years, which works out to be a 30% jump. But the second takeaway is that the income gains for the richest households have been much, much larger. The average incomes for the top 5% jumped almost $200,000, which is more than a 20% boost. In fact, you can clearly see that as the 20% groups move up the income ladder, the income gains increase.

There are several amendments to these two takeaways. Even though the 20% of households with the lowest average income gained money between 1967 and 2017, their peak income year was 1999, and they lost $1,300 in annual income between that year and 2017. This is certainly not enough of a loss to account for the gains of rich households, but it does suggest something may have happened to the labor market at the dawn of the 21st century. More on this later.

Remember Figure 6-1 does not account for taxes and the value of non-cash government programs. Despite what many think, the rich do pay significant taxes, whereas most lower-income households pay taxes, especially income taxes, at a reduced rate. Furthermore, some lower-income households do not pay any income taxes and then receive additional money from the IRS (this is discussed in more detail in the next chapter). Programs like Medicaid and food stamps also help pay for health-care and food for many lower-income households. When taxes and government programs are included, several studies show the increase in income inequality since the 1960s has been much lower by as much as 80%.[2] This is a big reason why the gap between how much high-income households spend and how much low-income households spend has not diverged nearly as much as their incomes.[3] Taxes and government programs have helped level the playing field between the rich and not-so-rich.

It's also important to realize that the households depicted in Figure 6-1 don't necessarily remain in their 20% income bracket forever. In fact, researchers have found the ability of low-income households to move up the income ladder hasn't changed much in decades, although there are significant differences for racial groups.[4] Almost two-thirds of people born in the poorest 20% income category will move up and out of that income level in their lifetime.[5]

The numbers in Figure 6-1 also don't account for cost-of-living differences based on where richer and poorer households live. It turns out richer households disproportionally live in higher cost regions, so when these cost differences are added, the recent expansion in income inequality shrinks a bit.[6] Furthermore, expanding income inequality isn't solely a U.S. trend; it's also happening worldwide, although to varying degrees.[7]

Finally, Figure 6-1 doesn't distinguish between female and male workers. Studies indicate income inequality has actually increased more among female earners than among male earners.[8]

Before moving on, I should distinguish between income inequality and wealth inequality. Income inequality looks at the differences between what households earn each year, mostly from a job, whereas wealth inequality compares the wealth, or net worth of households— that is, the difference between the value of their investments and the value of their debt. Changes in wealth inequality have tracked changes in income inequality with one difference: wealth inequality has been more pronounced.[9] This should make sense because higher-income households have more money to invest, and the value of those investments can grow and become even larger over time.

△ SO, WHAT'S THE PROBLEM?

If all income groups have experienced positive trends in their incomes over the past five decades, then what's the problem? Why is increasing income inequality even an issue?

There are several possible good answers. Sociologists worry the widening income distance between the rich and the poor reduces cohesiveness in our society as the lifestyles of the groups become increasingly different, even though both lifestyles may have improved.[10] Yes, the poor now have modern electronics, indoor plumbing, and even air conditioning, but the rich live in gated communities with multiple vehicles, pools, tennis courts, and vacation homes. The two groups can't relate to each other, and some argue that's not good for the health of our shared society.[11]

Political analysts focus on the increased public power the rich can wield when their income rises faster than the incomes of the non-rich.[12] Millionaires and billionaires finance their own campaigns for office, while the non-rich have to beg and cajole others for political funds. Even if they don't run for office, the rich can use their money to directly or indirectly lobby office holders for legislation favorable to their interests.

Economists bring another perspective to the table, and it's based on the old adage of "keeping up with the Joneses." This phrase was actually the title of a comic strip that ran in newspapers during the first half of the 20th century. It followed the McGinis family, who struggled socially and economically to make their lifestyle comparable to the neighboring Jones family.[13] The comic demonstrated that people and families don't only judge their progress by comparing where they were yesterday to where they are today, but also by comparing their living standards to the living standards of others. Instead of being happy that they could afford a vacation this year, the McGinis family was disappointed when they compared themselves to the Joneses, who took a vacation both last year *and* this year!

Economists call this the difference between an *actual* comparison where you judge your situation now versus your situation previously, and a *relative* comparison where you judge your improvement against the improvements made by others.[14] Some people may view increasing income inequality as an issue if the gains of lower and middle-income households are positive, but still less than the gains of rich households, meaning that the rich are becoming even farther out-of-reach to others. Some economists worry middle and lower-income households may overuse their credit cards and take on too much debt in an "arms race" to keep up the spending of the standard-setting upper class.[15] And we all know that "living beyond our means" eventually catches up with us and doesn't usually end well.

Last, some economists have found evidence that rising income inequality has slowed overall economic growth,[16] while others have found greater income inequality has reduced the ability of lower-income households to move up the income ladder.[17] Non-economists have also worried that increases in relative income inequality may increase stress, mental illnesses, drug and alcohol abuse, and even gambling problems among those trying to catch up.[18] There's also been a proposed linkage between rising income inequality and recent decreased levels of happiness expressed by many households.[19]

△ WHAT'S HAPPENED TO INCREASE INCOME INEQUALITY?

My late father was a high school dropout, and my 92-year-old uncle (my father's brother) only finished eighth grade. Yet both men married, had families, worked as carpenters, occasionally took vacations, and retired with a pension in addition to Social Security. Looking back on the lives of my father and uncle, I'd say they both lived solidly in the middle class.

It's hard today to repeat the stories of my father and uncle; there certainly are exceptions, but most people today without a high school degree have a very tough way making it in the current economy. The average unemployment rate for those individuals is almost twice as high as for the general workforce, and individuals without a high school degree make a fourth less than those with a high school diploma and almost 60% less than workers with a college (bachelor's) degree.[20]

One reason for these changes is simple: today's economy is not my father's economy. Machines do much of the hard, physical labor my father and uncle did. For example, nail guns have replaced hand-driven nailing. And that's a good thing, because as my father told me countless times after a hard day of back-breaking work, "You don't want to do what I'm doing for a living." It's the same for factory work, which traditionally paid good, middle-class wages to workers. Manufacturing jobs in the country are down 35% since their peak in 1978,[21] and despite a recent rebound, forecasts suggest more of the same.[22] It's not that we're manufacturing less; in fact, in 2017 the nation's factories and manufacturing companies produced almost 300% more total output than was produced in 1978.[23] It's simply that manufacturing has changed and now requires more machinery and technology and fewer workers.

In the past four decades, there has been a major shift in the kinds of skills needed for the economy. There's less need for physical and manual skills requiring strength and precision because those skills can now be accomplished by machines.[24] There's even less need for basic skills in reading, math, and communication (termed *basic cognitive skills*) because technology can increasingly perform those too! Instead, what's wanted by companies more and more are higher quantitative and statistical skills, the ability to interpret complex information, and advanced programming, data analysis, and technology development and maintenance skills.[25] Most of these skills require at least some training beyond high school.[26]

Technology has also increased income inequality in another way.[27] Think about highly-paid professional athletes and top entertainers.

Modern technology allows games, movies, and concerts to be broadcast both nationwide and worldwide, making audiences and fan bases almost limitless. The sky is the limit for revenues from live and rebroadcast games and performances, as well as from endorsements and products. Technology has thus enhanced the ability of the rich to become even richer.[28]

The result of these forces has been a transformation to a "hollowed-out" labor force,[29] which is to say that traditional middle-paying jobs, such as in manufacturing, have been disappearing. High-paying jobs using technical skills and usually requiring a college degree have been expanding. This is good. But workers without training in those skills—many of whom would have taken manufacturing jobs in the past—have been relegated to low-paying service jobs in fields like food service, personal services, and retail. These low-paying jobs have also been expanding as the service sector has grown. Also, these jobs have not yet (with the emphasis on "yet") been threatened by technology.

We used to have a "thick middle" society. Although having a thick middle isn't good for one's health (my "middle" is thicker than it should be—I just tell people it's all muscle!), for society it's considered good because it means the middle class is the largest group. Using an annual income of between $35,000 and $75,000 (in 2016 purchasing power dollars) as the definition of middle class, in 1967 the middle class constituted 42% of households, the lower class 38%, and the upper class 20%.[30]

Since then, our society has "bulked up," meaning the upper class has grown relative to the middle and lower classes. The upper class has doubled its share of households to 40%, while the middle class has "slimmed down" from 42% to 30% of households, and the lower class has also dropped in size from 38% to 30% in 2016.[31]

On the surface, these changes sound positive, right? The middle class has shrunk largely because the upper class has expanded. My situation is a good example of this! My father earned middle-class income as a carpenter. Following his strong advice to go to college (I was the first in my family to do so), I've ended up earning an upper-class income as a university professor. But this hasn't happened to everyone exiting the middle class. The federal government studied workers who lost their jobs in middle-class occupations such as construction, manufacturing, and transportation, and unfortu-nately, the results showed that the number of people finding new jobs paying over 20% *less* than their old job was 70% greater than those finding new work paying over 20% *more* than their old job.[32]

These changes have also had a geographic component. High-paying jobs in the new economy have typically been located in big cities where firms can more easily access college trained workers with the skills the businesses want.[33] In contrast, rural areas traditionally have been dependent on agriculture and low-wage manufacturing. These are industries which increasingly have incorporated auto-mation and have lost jobs to even lower-wage foreign countries. This has led to diminishing employment opportunities and greater social issues in many rural regions.[34] The result has been a deep economic divide between the rich urban areas and the poor rural areas, a divide which has even reshaped our national politics.[35]

The good news about changes in our income distribution is that more workers have moved into the upper class, and these workers have also, on average, gotten good pay raises. The bad news is that the glue in our country—the middle class—has shrunk, and a significant number of former middle-class workers have backtracked into lower paying jobs, which also happen to be the jobs receiving the slowest pay raises. The big question is, what to do about these trends?

△ FAKE SOLUTIONS

There have been numerous solutions offered for reducing income inequality and rebuilding the middle class. Several of them I categorize as "fake" because they have serious unintended consequences that would ultimately undermine the goal of a more equal distribution of income. Six examples are: limiting CEO pay, instituting a "maximum wage," significantly increasing the "minimum wage," taxing businesses for government benefits received by their workers, bringing back worker unions, and establishing a social investment fund. Let's look at what's wrong with each of these ideas.

CEOs are chief executive officers of corporations. Translated, they make the big decisions of a corporation. Many people think CEOs own the corporation, but they don't; they're a hired hand just like most workers. The difference is, they get paid really big bucks, usually in the millions of dollars per year.

CEO pay has been rising. A favorite statistic calculates how many times bigger the average CEO salary is to the average worker salary, technically called the "CEO-to-worker compensation ratio." Based on the CEO and average worker salaries at the top 350 U.S. firms, this ratio rose from 20 in 1965 to 260 in 2017 (again, using inflation-adjusted dollars).[36] If it's any consolation, there's been a decline since 2000 when the ratio peaked at 376. Many think a straightforward simple solution to income inequality would be to limit CEO pay to be no more than some fixed multiple of a worker's pay.[37]

However, there are two problems with this idea. First, CEO salaries make up a tiny fraction—only 0.06%—of all wages and salaries in the country.[38] And second, there is a valid reason CEO pay has risen so much. Corporations today are bigger because they operate in a national and increasingly international marketplace.[39] They also have more competition from other domestic and international companies and from a rapidly changing technical world that can quickly eliminate a product or an entire industry. Corporations are willing to pay gigantic salaries to have a qualified person guide the company through these never-ending challenges.

Every decision a CEO makes is worth millions, maybe billions, of dollars to the corporation's bottom line, yet not every decision a CEO makes is profitable for the company. But, as the saying goes, hindsight is always 20-20. Certainly, some corporations make mistakes paying their CEOs big salaries. However, this is the same in other industries, such as professional sports. How many teams have made a mistake paying a player a large guaranteed salary expecting their performance to continue, and then it doesn't? When CEOs don't deliver, they are fired.

What about a "maximum wage?" If we have a minimum wage, which sets a floor for what workers are paid per hour, shouldn't we also have a maximum wage which establishes a ceiling? Sounds logical, right? But who would determine the maximum wage? What would a maximum wage do to incentives to take risks, sacrifice, and work hard today for a potential big payoff later? Moreover, making a lot of money doesn't mean you keep it all yourself. Taxes take a big chunk, as I discuss in Chapter 15. Also, high-income earners are big donors to charity.[40] While a maximum wage has been discussed many times in our and other countries, it has never been implemented. In my opinion, wiser heads have prevailed.

Yet many countries do have a minimum wage. Ours was implemented in 1938. Recently, there's been a nationwide move to significantly increase the minimum wage to $15 an hour from its current $7.25, part of the reason being that the minimum wage hasn't kept up with inflation. Indeed, after adjusting for inflation, the current minimum wage of $7.25 per hour is the lowest since 2009 and is almost $4 under its inflation-adjusted peak in 1968.[41]

Hence, a case can be made for significantly increasing the minimum wage. But there's a big disadvantage from doing this; some minimum wage workers would lose their jobs, and others would keep their jobs but have their work hours reduced. Some companies may decide it's cheaper to hire a single higher-paid worker to do the jobs of several minimum wage workers. Still other companies would consider substituting automation for minimum wage workers. Indeed, McDonald's has already begun replacing workers who take customers' orders with kiosks.[42] In fact, the conclusion from 70 years of economic studies is that a higher minimum wage is a job killer, specifically for the workers the minimum wage is supposed to help.[43] There is a better alternative, which I will discuss in the next chapter.

An alternative proposal is to tax companies for the public assistance any of their employees receive.[44] Proponents argue companies not paying their employees enough to avoid having them qualify for poverty-based programs like food stamps and Medicaid should reimburse the government for the costs of those programs. Supporters of the idea expect it would motivate companies to increase worker pay in order to avoid the new tax.

But the company could go in the opposite direction. Just like with a higher minimum wage, the company might decide the work done by the employees isn't worth their wage plus the tax, so over time the company replaces the workers with machinery, technology, or more skilled workers. Alternatively, the company could raise the prices of their products to cover the tax, but this move would likely reduce sales and lead to some of the workers who were intended to be helped by the plan ultimately being fired.

Could a revival of labor unions help decrease income inequality? I have to admit, I have a soft spot in my heart for labor unions. My father was a long-time member of a labor union (carpenters) for over fifty years. One of his proudest moments was receiving his fifty-year membership watch. When he returned from World War II, he joined the union and learned the skills of his trade. Every month until a year before his death, he looked forward to the Thursday night meetings of his union's "local"—another name for a chapter.

Unions have fallen on hard times in recent decades. The decline in employment in traditional union-strong industries like manufacturing, the movement of many unionized companies to non-union states in the South, the loss of union jobs to foreign competitors, and the growth of the service sector where labor unions have been weak, have combined to reduce the strength of unions from their peak representation of one-third of workers in the early 1950s to only 10% today.[45]

Unions helped my father earn good wages by using the backing of the government to control who was allowed to work and the conditions under which the work was done. Research shows that this successfully increased wages of the members and kept a lid on rising income inequality.[46]

Yet the reality is that these union tactics are harder to successfully employ in today's open and highly internationalized economy. Plus, there's the additional problem that unions often slow the pace of change in work that allows companies to adapt to today's fast-paced economy. Futurists see technological advances continually forcing companies to re-define and re-bundle jobs and job tasks in order to stay competitive and continue employing workers.[47] Union rules and regulations impede this kind of swift action by companies; they're just not a viable solution for today's work world.

The last fake solution attempts to reduce income inequality by tapping into one of the reasons that supposedly helped create it—investments. The argument goes like this: since the rich have more money to invest, they've increased their income and wealth even more by reaping the rewards of those investments. Why not let those who aren't rich do the same by establishing a social investment fund that can pay investment returns to the non-rich? The fund can be established and financed through taxes paid from the income and wealth held by the rich.[48] In other words, if it's good enough for the rich, then it should be good enough for those who aren't rich.

Yet who will run the social investment fund and establish its rules? If tax dollars are used, then you know it will be the government, and you know what that means. The government (Congress and the President) will be influenced by their financial contributors to direct investments (especially investments in the stock market where the real money can be made) to the companies of their buddies and cronies. Also, if the social investment fund became sizeable, it could influence the direction of the entire stock market. Do we really want political forces doing that? This a big reason why the creators of Social Security prohibited it from investing in the stock market; the tradeoff is Social Security earns relatively puny returns by being restricted to investing in super-safe government bonds. But this is not what the social wealth fund promoters want.

△ REAL SOLUTIONS

Seven decades ago, a famous economist named Joseph Schumpeter coined my favorite economics phrase, "creative destruction."[49] At first glance, the phrase appears to be meaningless because it's composed of two words with opposite origins. The origin of creative, "create," means to build or establish, while the origins of destruction, "destruct," implies tearing down or destroying. What was Schumpeter thinking when he paired the two words, and, maybe more importantly or more worrying to you, why is this puzzling phrase my favorite?

I like "creative destruction" for two reasons: it's a clever use of words, and it has profound meaning. Creative destruction means the economy is constantly changing by adding some new parts while simultaneously destroying other parts. Economies do *not* change with all pieces advancing; some pieces move forward, while others drop back. This is a big reason why economic forecasting is so difficult.

Creative destruction is easily seen in the job numbers. While manufacturing shed 7 million jobs since 1978, professional and business services added 4 million, health-care and education increased by 10 million, and leisure and hospitality gained 17 million jobs.[50] So any solution for decreasing income inequality must contend with the fact we never really know where the good jobs will come from. Therefore—reinforcing something I said in Chapter 2 about higher education—our colleges and universities must constantly remain informed about where jobs are being created, and they must be flexible to move funds to fields and majors where the largest job expansions are occurring.

But is there anything that can be done to specifically create more middle-income jobs? Yes, there are three things we can and should do. First, we must communicate to job seekers, and especially to young people who are still in high school, that there are many good paying jobs that don't require a four-year college degree. The Center on Education and the Workforce at Georgetown University has identified 16 million jobs that pay over $55,000 annually, 8 million jobs that pay between $45,000 and $55,000 annually, and another 6 million jobs paying between $35,000 and $45,000 a year—with all of them *not* requiring a bachelor's degree.[51]

Our society has become so focused on pushing young people to attend four-year colleges that many students are unaware there are other options. Indeed, one-third of those who enter college do not leave with a degree. I remember a student not doing well in one of my classes coming to me in tears. She said she needed a good grade so she could graduate, otherwise—and this is what stunned me—she said she would end up poor! She saw only two options: a bachelor's degree or poverty.

The second change we need to make is to refocus our two-year community and technical colleges on their original mission of educating individuals for technical and skilled jobs. Labor market experts say we face a shortage of people qualified to do skilled trade jobs, like carpentry, plumbing, electric, and HVAC (heating, ventilation, and air conditioning), as well as truck driving, nursing, and other technical health jobs. They say the shortage will only get worse as existing workers retire.[52] The construction trades alone are expected to add 600,000 jobs between 2016 and 2026 and experience a job-growth rate almost 50% faster than other jobs.[53]

Yet many students at community and technical colleges appear not to be interested in these craft and trade jobs. A survey showed 80% of students entering community and technical colleges say they were only there to get a good GPA (grade point average) in basics like English and math so they can then transfer to a four-year college. [54]They also usually save money since two-year colleges are cheaper, and they can transfer their two-year college credits to many four-year colleges, especially if the colleges are state supported.[55]

Changes need to be made to eliminate community and technical colleges from simply serving as a "warm up" for four-year colleges and universities. If a young person wants a four-year college degree, they should go to a four-year college. Plus, if the changes I recommended for colleges in Chapter 2 are adopted, then affordability shouldn't be the issue it is today for four-year schools. Community and technical colleges are training students for respectable, valuable, and needed occupations, and this should be both the attending students' and colleges' shared mission. Additionally, community and technical colleges are affordable, with tuitions only one-third the amount of four-year colleges.[56] Occupations obtained through community and technical college degrees can lead to good paying jobs, particularly for those losing jobs from the churning in the economy.

One reason why today's young people are shunning jobs like plumbing, carpentry, and even technical health-care jobs is because they have no exposure to them. This is where my third recommendation comes in, which is reintroduce apprenticeships and joint programs between community/technical colleges and high schools.

Psychologists say there are seven different kinds of intelligences displayed by humans (physical, musical, interpersonal, intrapersonal, spatial, logical-mathematical, and linguistic).[57] Unfortunately, only two (logical-mathematical and linguistic) receive most of the attention in high schools, and they both lead to four-year colleges. We need to expose high school students to the other types of intelligences and to the job opportunities for each type, then we need to allow students to explore the opportunities for applying those intelligences by spending time with companies that have those types of jobs. This can be done with the use of apprenticeships, where students actually study and work with companies. Apprenticeship programs have enjoyed a revival; for example, South Carolina has doubled the number of apprenticeships in recent years and used them to expand their transformative auto manufacturing sector. [58]Where high school apprenticeship programs are not feasible, the high schools could form linkages to the programs of nearby community/technical colleges.

Now, let me be clear, I am not talking about tracking or forcing selected students away from the four-year college academic path. This has long been a criticism of the German system, which specifically selects students who will attend college-preparatory high schools and alternative vocational high schools.[59] Instead, I'm recommending high school students be given broader options for finding their passion.

These three initiatives won't necessarily stem the erosion of middle-income jobs and reverse the expansion of income inequality. Some speculate that even craft jobs like carpentry, plumbing, and bricklaying will be taken over by machines, robots, or off-site manufacturing; indeed, an automated bricklaying machine has already been developed![60] These same innovations could even replace employment in lower-paying personal service jobs. For example, restaurant meals may be delivered by robots with ordering and payment done through tablets on the table, which are already available in some restaurants. Yet there are contrary forecasts suggesting a consumer rebellion against "machine-made" and a return to hand-crafted production—at least in part.[61]

Either way, we can address income inequality by expanding employment options and occupational pursuits.

▲ SUMMING UP

The term "increasing income inequality" does not mean the "rich are getting richer and the poor are getting poorer." Instead, for the last four decades it has meant the "rich are getting richer faster than the poor are getting richer." Advances in technology and automation and the movement of human work from brawn to brain have been behind the changes in earnings from work. To boost middle-income jobs, we must convince students that there are good-paying alternatives to those from four-year college degrees. This means restoring the original purpose of community and technical colleges and exposing high school students to the wide opportunities of work in the trades and crafts.

Chapter 6 Endnotes

1. Semega, Fontenot, and Kollar, *Income and Poverty in the United States: 2016*.

2. Auten and Splinter, "Income Inequality in the United States: Using Tax Data to Measure Long-Term Trends"; Burtless, "Income Growth and Income Inequality: The Facts May Surprise You"; Congressional Budget Office, *The Distribution of Household Income, 2014*; Armour, Burkhauser, and Larrimore, "Deconstructing Income Inequality Measures: A Cross-Walk from Market Income to Comprehensive Income."

3. Meyer and Sullivan, "Consumption and Income Inequality in the U.S. Since the 1960s."

4. Zarroli, "Study: Upward Mobility No Tougher in US than Two Decades Ago"; and Chetty, Hendren, Kline, Saez, and Turner, "Is the United States Still a Land of Opportunity? Recent Trends in Intergenerational Mobility."

5. Stossel, "Debunking Popular Nonsense about Income Mobility in America." However, research has found that a smaller proportion of children born in the late 20th century ultimately exceeded the incomes of their parents as compared to earlier decades. Only 50% of children born in the 1980s were found to have earned more than their parents, compared to 90% born in 1940 (Chetty, Grusky, Hell, Hendren, Manduca, and Narang, "The Fading Dream: Trends in Absolute Income Mobility Since 1940"). However, one explanation for the finding may be a much higher proportion of college educated children having parents with a high school or less education in 1940 compared to the 1980s. Thus, it was easier for children in 1940 to exceed the income of less educated parents.

6. Geloso and Msaid, "Adjusting Inequalities for Regional Price Parities: Importance and Implications"; Moretti, "Real Wage Inequality."

7. Bughin, Hazan, Allas, Hjartar, Manyika, Sjatil, and Shigina, *Tech for Good*; Organization for Economic Cooperation and Development, *Under Pressure: The Squeezed Middle Class*.

8. Gordon and Dew-Becker, "Controversies about the Rise of American Inequality: A Survey."

9. Kuhn, Schularick and Steins, "Income and Wealth Inequality in America, 1949-2016"; Wolff, *A Century of Wealth in America*.

10. Frey and Taylor, "The Rise of Residential Segregation by Income."

11. Sorkin, "Economic Inequality: A Matter of Trust."

12. Porter, "The Politics of Income Inequality."

13. Markstein, "Keeping Up with the Joneses."

14. Frank, *Luxury Fever*.

15. Frank, *Falling Behind: How Rising Inequality Harms the Middle Class*.

16. Partridge and Weinstein, "Rising Income Inequality in an Era of Austerity: The Case of the US."

17. Corak, "Income Inequality, Equality of Opportunity, and Intergenerational Mobility."

18. Wilkinson and Pickett. *The Inner Level: How More Equal Societies Reduce Stress, Restore Sanity and Improve Everyone's Well-being*.

19. Graham, *Happiness for All?*

20. U.S. Bureau of Labor Statistics, "Unemployment Rates and Earnings by Educational Attainment, 2017."

21. U.S. Bureau of Labor Statistics, "Employment, Hours, and Earnings from the Current Employment Statistics Survey."

22. Lacey, Toossi, Dubina, and Gensler, "Projections Overview and Highlights, 2016-2026."

23. U.S. Bureau of Economic Analysis, "Real Gross Domestic Product by Major Type of Product, Quantity Indexes."

24. Koru, "Automation and Top Income Inequality."

25. Bughin, Hazan, Lund, Dahlstrom, Wiesinger, and Subramaniam, *Skill Shift: Automation and the Future of the Workforce.*

26. Piketty, *Capital in the 21st Century*, 2013. A French economist, Piketty makes an argument for broader impact of technology. Technology is a type of capital investment that includes physical and other non-human investments. Piketty claims investments in capital will grow faster than growth in the general economy, thereby insuring that investors in capital – who are often higher income persons – will automatically have faster income growth than those not investing in capital, thereby resulting in widening income equality. However, Piketty's work has been widely criticized and debunked in Delsol, Lecaussin, and Martin, *Anti-Piketty*.

27. Frank and Cook, *The Winner-Take-All Society*

28. Kaplan and Rauh, "It's the Market: The Broad-Based Rise in the Return to Top Talent."

29. Autor, "Work of the Past, Work of the Future"; Walden, "Labor Market Hollowing-Out in North Carolina: Measurement and Causes"; Bughin, *et. al, op. cit.*; Organization for Economic Cooperation and Development, *Under Pressure: The Squeezed Middle Class.*

30. Semega, Fontenot, and Kollar, *op. cit.*

31. *Ibid.* Other research defining "middle class" in different ways have reached the same conclusions, such as in Pew Research Center, *The American Middle Class is Losing Ground.*

32. U.S. Bureau of Labor Statistics, "Worker Displacement: 2013-2015."

33. Berger and Frey, "Did the Computer Revolution Shift the Fortunes of U.S. Cities? Technology Shocks the Geography of New Jobs."

34. Coile and Duggan, "When Labor's Lost: Health, Family Life, Incarceration, and Education in a Time of Declining Economic Opportunities for Low-Skilled Men."

35. Rodden, *Why Cities Lose.*

36. Mishel and Schieder, *CEO Pay Remains High Relative to the Pay of Typical Workers and High-Wage Earners.*

37. Johnston, "Efforts to Regulate CEO Pay Gain Traction."

38. Mishel and Schieder, *op. cit.*; U.S. Bureau of Economic Analysis, "Wages and Salaries by Industry."

39. Gabaix and Landier, "Why Has CEO Pay Increased So Much?"

40. Maxwell, Locke, and Ritter, "Do the Rich Give the Most to Charity?"

41. Oregon State University, "Minimum Wage History."

42. Whitten, "McDonald's to Add Self-Order Kiosks to 1000 Stores Each Quarter." However, McDonald's says it will "redistribute" workers from the counter to table service, as seen in Peterson, "McDonald's Shoots Down Fears It Is Planning to Replace Cashiers with Kiosks."

43. Neumark and Wascher, *Minimum Wages*; Clemens, "Making Sense of the Minimum Wage"; Congressional Budget Office, *The Effects on Employment and Family Income of Increasing the Federal Minimum Wage*; Harasztosi and Lindner, "Who Pays the Minimum Wage?"

44. Goldstein, "Sanders Rolls Out 'Bezos Act' that Would Tax Companies for Welfare their Employees Receive."

45. Dunn and Walker, "Union Membership in the U.S."

46. Faber, Herbst, Kuziemko, and Naidu, "Unions and Inequality over the Twentieth Century: New Evidence from Survey Data."

47. Bughin, Hazan, Lund, Dahlstrom, Wiesinger, and Subramaniam, *op. cit.*

48. Banres, *With Liberty and Dividends for All*, Bruenig, "Social Wealth Fund for America."

49. Schumpeter, *Capitalism, Socialism, and Democracy*

50. U.S. Bureau of Labor Statistics, "Employment, Hours, and Earnings from the Current Employment Statistics Survey."

51. Carnevale, Stohl, Cheah, and Ridley, *Good Jobs that Pay without a BA.*

52. Wright, "America's Skilled Trades Dilemma: Shortages Loom as Most-In-Demand Group of Workers Retire."

53. U.S. Bureau of Labor Statistics, "Employment Projections: Employment by Detailed Occupation."

54. Robson, "For Many Students, Community College is the End of the Academic Road."

55. Eneriz, "Benefits of Attending Community College for Two Years to Save Money."

56. National Center for Education Statistics, *op. cit.*, Table 330.10.

57. Gardner, *Frames of Mind: The Theory of Multiple Intelligences.*

58. Ashford, "South Carolina Puts Its Support behind Apprenticeships."

59. Carapezza and Noe-Payne, "Stopping German Students in their Tracks."

60. Castle, "This Brick Laying Robot Can Build an Entire House in Two Days Flat."

61. Alpert, "5 Reasons Craftsmanship in Making a Return."

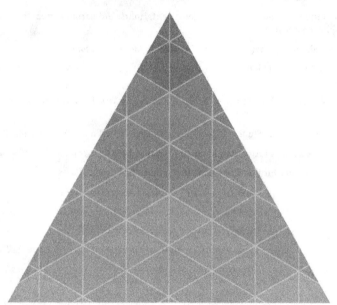

CHAPTER SEVEN

WINNING THE FINAL BATTLE OF THE WAR ON POVERTY

A WIN OR A LOSS?

Are we winning or losing the "war on poverty?" Liberals and conservatives don't agree on much, but on the question of the war on poverty, they agree but for different reasons. Liberals say the war has not been won because we don't understand the challenges poor people face. Conservatives say we've spent trillions of dollars to end poverty but still have lost the war, therefore suggesting we need a new strategy to motivate people to escape poverty.

I both disagree and agree with each of these positions: I disagree with liberals and conservatives because the evidence shows we've actually won most of the war on poverty, if winning is defined as providing households with enough resources that they aren't defined as "poor." But I support conservatives in the need for a new strategy to ultimately claim final victory in the war. Also, I back liberals who say we need to recognize incentives and circumstances that might lead some people to poverty.

The confusion about whether we've mostly won or mostly lost the war on poverty depends on how poverty is measured (stay with me, I'm not wandering into the weeds of statistics). If poverty is measured by comparing the financial resources a household earns from its own efforts (working and investing) plus cash from various government programs (like Social Security, unemployment compensation, and disability payments) against the resources needed to escape poverty, then it's true that the fight against poverty has stalled in recent decades. In 1959, the poverty rate was 23%, and by 1974 it had fallen to 11%. But since the mid-1970s, the poverty rate has changed very little, with a reading of 12.3% in 2017.[1]

Yet there's a big hitch with this official poverty measure. It's based on what households needed to spend in 1955 for healthy meals. And then, to obtain total needed spending, the meal expenditures are simply multiplied by 3! Now, don't worry, the 1955 prices are updated for inflation, but there's no specific accounting of spending for other basic necessities like transportation, shelter, and clothing. And even for food, much has changed in how and what we eat since 1955.

Fortunately, the federal government has recognized these shortcomings in their official poverty measure. That rate is still published each year, but it is now joined by a new rate, the *Supplemental Poverty Measure*. This measure is based on specific observed spending data and is not estimated using a multiple of 3 applied to food spending in order to derive needed spending for shelter, clothing, utilities, transportation, child expenses, etc. On the resource side, the measure adds to money income the monetary value of non-cash benefits like rent assistance and food stamps. The Supplemental Poverty Measure in 2016 was 13.9%, slightly higher than the official measure.[2]

Yet some researchers think more adjustments must be made to get an accurate reading on poverty. For example, the Supplemental Poverty Measure doesn't include the value of Medicaid benefits received by low-income households. This is a big deal today, especially with the rising cost of medical care. Also, many economists think the inflation rate used in both the official poverty rate and the Supplemental Poverty Measure is inadequate because it doesn't completely account for how people change their spending patterns over time.[3]

Scott Winship of the think tank, The Manhattan Institute, has developed an alternative poverty rate incorporating the value of all federal anti-poverty programs—including cash and non-cash programs—as well as using the measure of inflation most favored by economists. He finds the poverty rate among children has continued to drop in recent years and is now at an all-time low. In 1995, Winship estimates child poverty stood at 10%. In 2014, it was half, at 5%.[4]

Another way to track poverty is to look at a household's spending rather than income. If households classified as poor can afford a wider array of consumer products and services after receiving the benefits of poverty programs, then the programs must be working to lower their level of need.

Using this spending measure, the results are also encouraging. Meyer and Sullivan tracked the spending (economists refer to it as "consumption") of single-parent households, who make up a large part of the poverty population. The researchers found that the poverty rate, now measured by the spending of households rather than their income, dropped from 13% in 1980 to 2.8% in 2017. [5]Consistent with these findings, another study shows that high percentages of poor households have access to modern conveniences, appliances, and electronics: 99% use a TV and refrigerator; over 90% use a stove, phone, and microwave; 80% use air-conditioning; and 67% use cable or satellite TV.[6]

But "wait, wait" you say. "How can poverty be so low and spending by low-income households be so high if so many children go hungry every day?" Indeed, I've seen billboards along roads in my state stating that 2 out of 10 children are hungry.[7] If true, then certainly the numbers presented above showing how relatively low the poverty rate is can't be accurate.

The answer to this apparent puzzle is that the statistics purporting to show high percentages of hungry children are based on a new definition of hunger developed by the federal government in 2006. Rather than hunger being defined as not having enough to eat, the new definition of hunger includes adults and children not eating a balanced diet—for example, a diet low in fruits and vegetables. In other words, hunger has been expanded to include the *quality* of the food, not just the *quantity*.[8] If the definition of hunger is simply not getting enough *quantity* of food to eat, then government statistics show about 1% of children are hungry.[9] Rather than the billboards meaning 2 in 10 children don't get enough calories daily, they really mean 2 out of 10 kids aren't eating enough nutritious calories.[10]

Should we be happy with these results showing an improved picture of poverty? Not necessarily. We certainly should be happy that government programs are keeping the vast majority of poor households living much better than they would be if they relied only on their own resources. And for 21% of poor households who are either elderly (over age 65) or disabled, this is perhaps all we can accomplish.[11] We shouldn't necessarily expect elderly and disabled households to be self-supporting.

But for the other 79% of poor households, wouldn't we ultimately like them to be earning enough to support a decent existence? This is especially important for children. Research has linked an upbringing in poverty to lower earnings, poorer health, and greater exposure to crime in adulthood. The lost economic output and higher public costs total hundreds of billions of dollars annually. [12]Wouldn't moving poor households to self-supporting economic status represent the ultimate victory in the war on poverty?

If the answer is "yes," then what's stopping us from achieving this goal? You may be surprised to learn that a big impediment is the current anti-poverty programs themselves.

△ THE PUBLIC ASSISTANCE TAX CLIFF

Taxes are always a controversial topic, and the tax rate that different households pay is one of the top issues. Don't worry—we'll address this and other tax issues in a later chapter. But if I told you that people participating in various kinds of public assistance programs actually pay the highest tax rates, would you believe me? You should!

I don't mean tax rates as most of us think of them; when someone talks about a tax rate they usually mean the percentage of their income they pay in taxes. So, if Jerome earns $50,000 from his job, and if he pays $10,000 in taxes, then his tax rate is 20% ($10,000 is 20% of

$50,000). Instead, for poor households participating in public assistance programs, the tax rate is hidden. Economists call it an *implicit tax*, and it comes in the form of the dollar value of public assistance that is *reduced* when the household earns more from working.

Let's say Martha is receiving $4,500 worth of food stamps a year. She is working a minimum wage job earning only $14,000 annually. She finds a job paying $20,000 and immediately takes it. She's jumping up and down with joy. But only later does she realize that, due to her higher income, her food stamp assistance has been cut to $2,500, resulting in a loss of $2,000 in food stamps. In terms of Martha's buying power, she needs to subtract $2,000 from the extra $6,000 in earnings. This $2,000 in lost food stamps resulting from a $6,000 increase in her income is an implicit tax, with a rate of 33% ($2,000 is 33% of $6,000).

It can get worse. For example, let's say Martha is also receiving $1,000 annually for help with her winter heating bill and another $4,000 a year to help pay her rent. Now based on her new $20,000 salary rather than her previous $14,000 salary, Martha finds the help with her heating bills is cut by $250, and her subsidy for rent is reduced by $1,000.

To summarize, because of her extra $6,000 in earnings, Martha has lost $2,000 in food stamps, $250 in heating assistance, and $1,000 in rental assistance, for a total loss of $3,250. This is a whopping 54% of her extra $6,000, meaning her implicit tax rate on the additional income from her better job is 54%.

Many of you are saying, "Surely this can't be how the public assistance programs work." Unfortunately, it is the way they work!

Numerous studies have found poor households often face implicit tax rates above 50%, and in some cases almost 100%![13] A big reason is that the programs aren't coordinated; each program is run by a different government agency, and the agencies don't talk to each other. Therefore, when a recipient household earns more money, each program thinks the household doesn't need as much government help, so each program cuts its assistance. But when the cuts are combined, implicit tax rates can go through the roof!

These high implicit tax rates impact the incentives of poor households to work and earn more. In fact, a summary of numerous studies for the U.S. suggests every 10% increase in the implicit tax rate reduces hours worked by an individual by about 2%.[14] This is one reason why welfare spending reduces investments in the economy.[15]

Yet before you think you've heard it all, with high implicit tax rates on poor people discouraging them from working more and becoming financially self-sufficient, the situation actually gets worse. To see how, read on.

△ HAVE POVERTY PROGAMS DESTROYED FAMILIES?

As discussed in Chapter 1, single-parent households, especially headed by mothers, have been on the rise. The percentage of births to unmarried mothers has risen from 3% in 1950 to over 40% today.[16] While single mothers raising children can do an extraordinary job, child rearing is often easier with two parents present. Monetary resources are usually greater, and two parents can split the child rearing duties. It takes tremendous skill and stamina for one person to balance work, children, and a personal life.

Unfortunately, and amazingly, government public assistance programs can discourage two-parent households. How, you ask? First is when a high implicit tax rate is paid on the extra income earned by the second parent. The second occurs when the extra expenses (food, clothing, transportation, etc.) of the second parent are also considered. Combining these two factors can discourage the parents from remaining together.

Here's an example: let's say Jack and Jill have two children but are not married. If Jack and Jill marry, Jack can bring $10,000 of additional income to Jill and their two children. But now the $10,000 will be added to Jill's income in determining financial assistance from the government. Assume 60% of the $10,000 is implicitly taxed away through reduced public assistance benefits. Further, if Jack's expenditures for food and other necessities are $7,000 a year, then from Jill's point of view Jack can be considered a financial net loss. Here's the math: Jack adds $10,000 in earnings, but $6,000 is lost in reduced government benefits to Jill, and Jack will add $7,000 in new costs to the household. In pure money terms, Jill sees Jack as a net loss ($10,000 - $6,000 - $7,000 = -$3,000), and, financially speaking, Jill and her children see themselves better off without Jack.

An excellent analysis published by the American Enterprise Institute confirmed the adverse effects on married families of government anti-poverty programs in two ways. First, the authors did number crunching comparing the extra income provided by the second parent versus benefits lost through implicit taxation as well as new expenses. And guess what? The analysts easily showed how a second parent can result in a financial loss for the other parent receiving the government benefits. Second, the authors also conducted a survey and found that one-third of those interviewed knew a couple who had not married for fear of losing too many government program benefits.[17]

There is some solace in knowing that the anti-family impact of public assistance programs used to be worse. Until 1968, the government's main cash welfare program, Aid to Families with Dependent Children (AFDC), allowed states to prohibit any financial assistance if there was an adult male in the household, even if the male was the husband. Fortunately, this rule was overturned, and today's AFDC successor, TANF (Temporary Aid to Needy Families), prohibits such a restriction.[18] Still, some scholars, most notably Daniel Patrick Moynihan (former Harvard professor, White House aide, and U.S. Senator), argued as early as in the 1960s that the AFDC "no-male-present" rule was still responsible for the breakup of many poor families.[19]

△ FAKE SOLUTIONS

There are several solutions to poverty offered today, with some from the left and others from the right side of the political spectrum. While the proposed solutions may be popular with each side's supporters, they still have problems, so I label them as "fake."

Many left-of-center activists support a universal guaranteed income (UGI). This is not a new idea; it was actually proposed over 200 years ago,[20] and even President Richard Nixon considered backing a version of the concept in 1969.[21] Recently, the idea has been revived by several prominent people, including Facebook founder Mark Zuckerberg, Tesla inventor Elon Musk, and Virgin Airline founder Richard Branson. [22]Some propose replacing existing poverty programs with the UGI, whereas others want to add the UGI on top of current programs.[23]

With a UGI, the government simply guarantees and provides every person a certain amount of money each year. Nothing, including working, is required in exchange for the money. Under the simplest proposal everyone would receive the income no matter the size of their earnings, and the universal income amount wouldn't change as the individual's earnings changed. The amount would be enough to provide each person with some socially acceptable standard of living. Recent proposals have recommended annual amounts between $6,000 and $18,000 per person.[24] Some proposals would make the payments to households rather than individuals, with the amount varying based on the numbers of adults and children in the household.[25]

The political scientist Charles Murray has outlined a detailed plan for a UGI. Murray can't be labeled as left-of-center or right-of-center in his political orientation. He is best described as a libertarian, meaning he believes in limited government and maximum individual freedom. In Murray's plan, every adult would receive $13,000 per year, with the amount increased by inflation over time. The only stipulation is that $3,000 of the amount must be used to buy catastrophic health insurance. Persons making over $30,000 would gradually have their UGI reduced as their income rose until it reached $60,000. Those making $60,000 or more would receive a UGI of $6,500.[26] The plan would be paid for by taking all the money now spent addressing various aspects of poverty—including food stamps, TANF, Social Security, Medicare, and Medicaid and totaling over $2 trillion annually—and converting the funds to the UGI.

No country today uses a UGI, but several have had experimental versions. Finland is one of those countries.[27] Finland limited payments to unemployed persons and experimented for a couple of years with regular, "no-strings attached" payments to a sample of jobless individuals. The Finns concluded the UGI wasn't a good idea, and in 2019 they decided to end the three-year program.[28] Why? Because to achieve broad political support, UGI programs must often promise (and then follow through on that promise) that participants will use the income to support their own schooling and training that ultimately leads to self-sufficiency. Most people don't want a universal income program allowing able-bodied people to survive without working. Stated bluntly, the body politic doesn't want to support lazy people.

Finland ended their UGI experiment after finding the program had negligible impact on increasing employment.[29] The U.S. also ran several pilot programs during the 1960s and 1970s that provided guaranteed cash payments to low-income households. Again, the programs weren't exactly UGIs because all households, regardless of income, didn't receive the money. But academics who studied the programs found one clear result: the programs *reduced* employment among the participants by as much as 20% for the most generous plans.[30] The fact that the UGI does not seem to result in an increase in work by recipients appears to be its "Achilles heel."

Right-of-center advocates have an opposite way of solving poverty, and that is to just make every able-bodied, non-elderly person work, and if a person can't find work on their own, then the government will provide them with a job. The claim is there is plenty of valuable work the government can pay people to do, like helping teachers, cleaning up neighborhoods, or even building affordable homes for low-income households. The logic is to make people work for their benefits. In 2018, the U.S. House of Representatives passed such a proposal requiring individuals to work in order to receive food stamps.[31]

What's wrong with a work requirement in order to receive government help? First, won't people need to be trained in order to do the work? And if so, who provides the training, and how long does it take? The track record of the largest government job training program—the Job Corps—shows the gains to earnings received by trainees eventually disappear.[32] Further, if people are to be trained, why not motivate them to get trained for jobs the private sector wants? If the government is hiring the individuals to do valuable work, then isn't this just taking jobs away from private workers and private companies?[33] Additionally, individuals put in "make-work" jobs create resentment in those forced to supervise the work. The situation often leads to frivolous activities that everyone knows is a waste of time. Supervisors and workers alike realize the program is mostly a game, which is not the attitude we want instilled in those trying to move to self-sufficiency.

The biggest problem with work requirements is that they don't accomplish their goal! TANF (Temporary Aid to Needy Families), the nation's main "cash" welfare program, instituted work requirements in the 1990s when the program was overhauled. Research has shown that either the requirement has had no impact on work—meaning those who work would have done so without the requirement—or any employment increases were modest and decreased over time.[34]

Another fake idea mandates a four-day workweek. The goal is to create more jobs for low-income people so as to increase their income. However, there's no reason to think poverty-level individuals will have the skills for those new jobs. Furthermore, advocates of the four-day workweek think it will increase worker productivity enough so the same work is done in four days as in five.[35] But if the same amount of work is now accomplished in a four-day workweek, then why would any new jobs be created?

It honestly pains me to label the next solution as "fake." This is because the solution has been proposed from someone I greatly admire, Nobel Prize-winning economist Edmund Phelps. His idea is called a *wage subsidy*.[36] The notion is simple: people who are impoverished because of their low income receive a government subsidy. This subsidy raises the wage rate to a level that allows the individual to achieve a minimal acceptable standard of living.

Because Phelps is an economist he understands the importance of incentives. He knows the incentive to work will not increase if the wage subsidy is reduced cent for cent with an increase in the worker's earnings. Instead, he would make sure earning more is not totally penalized by a reduced wage subsidy. For example, if Bob earns $8/hour and the wage subsidy is $7/hour, Bob's total hourly earnings is $15/hour. Now, if Bob gets a $2/hour raise from his company, Phelps would reduce the subsidy, but by less than $2/hour. So, if Bob is now making $10/hour from the company, Phelps might make the subsidy

$6.50/hour, bringing Bob's total hourly earnings $16.50/hour, still considerably more than the original $15/hour.

I like the intent and recognition of incentives in Phelps' wage subsidy proposal. Then why do I label it "fake"? I have three reasons.

First, the wage subsidy ignores the complication of children. Workers don't just support themselves; they also often support spouses, children, and perhaps elderly parents and other family members. Thus, a wage subsidy adequate for a worker with no dependents is not enough for a worker with dependents. Conceivably, this could be handled with different wage subsidies for workers with different numbers of dependents, but such a system has the real possibility of creating resentment and friction among workers when they realize they are being paid different rates for the same job.

The second problem is the possibility that companies will attempt to "game the system" by lowering the wage rate they pay and expecting the government to make up the difference with a higher subsidy. Sure, a regulation could be imposed to prevent this, but regulations have to be enforced, so such a regulation would require more bureaucracy. Also, how would this "system-gaming" wage drop be distinguished from a wage reduction that was motivated by market conditions, such as a recession? As you can see, things could easily get messy and complicated.

Third, I think there could be strong political pushback on a wage subsidy. Recognize the wage subsidy comes from public (that is, tax) money. Taxpayers are paying for the wage subsidy, yet there are no controls on how the wage subsidy is spent. Also consider this fact: almost two-thirds of people favor restrictions on how public assistance dollars are spent by recipients.[37] Any poverty program must take this reality into account.

△ REAL SOLUTIONS

I think individuals of every political stripe can agree that government poverty programs need to be consolidated and managed by one agency. At the federal level, where most public assistance programs originate and are funded, there are 92 individual poverty programs operated by 27 separate agencies.[38] For example, the U.S. Department of Agriculture manages food stamps (now called SNAP, or "supplemental nutrition assistance program," but I'll still call them food stamps) and rural housing programs. HUD (U.S. Department of Housing and Urban Development) runs urban housing programs, the Energy Department handles household energy assistance programs, HHS (Health and Human Services) operates Medicaid, and even the U.S. Treasury Department has a hand in poverty programs by supervising the Earned Income Tax Credit, which is a program providing cash to needy households. Usually, each program has its own rules regarding who qualifies, income limits, and implicit tax rates when earnings of the recipients change.

This is madness! All these programs should be under the control of one department or agency, with the possible exception of the Earned Income Tax Credit that is run through the individual tax system of the IRS (an agency within the Treasury Department). Also, if the various programs are each kept, they should all use the same consistent rules about eligibility and phasing out of assistance as recipients (hopefully) move toward self-sufficiency.

Economists like me tend to prefer simplicity and transparency. We also think people should be left to make their own decisions, sometimes with nudges from government. This is why many economists have favored the idea of a "negative income tax," or NIT, as the major anti-poverty program. Popularized by the Nobel Prize-winning economist Milton Friedman in the 1960s, the NIT would collapse all poverty programs into one program administered by the IRS.

The proposed program operates very simply: when households submit their income tax forms, the IRS checks their income against spending needed by that household (based on the number of adults and children in the household) to be above the poverty level. If there is a shortfall, the household would first be returned some or all of their tax withholding, and, if after that is done there is still a shortfall, additional money would be sent to them. And, very importantly, as the household earns more income on their own, the public financial support would gradually be reduced in a way to preserve the incentive to earn more.

A big advantage of the NIT is its low administrative costs. Current poverty programs have an estimated average administrative cost of between 15% and 20%, with some as high as 40%.[39] In contrast, the Earned Income Tax Credit, which is similar to the NIT by providing money to working households through the income tax system, has an administrative cost of only 1.5%.[40]

The NIT could transfer a lot of money to the poor. Using a compilation of poverty-specific programs (but excluding programs like Social Security, Medicare, Medicaid, the children's health insurance program (CHIP), and unemployment assistance), a NIT would result in $8,800 being available for every poor person (adults and children) in 2017, and this is after subtracting a 1.5% administrative cost.[41]

The researchers Wiederspan, Rhodes, and Shaefer (WRS for short) have outlined an NIT program using current and new poverty funds to bring all households above the poverty level.[42] The implicit tax rate in their calculations is 50%. This means poverty support is reduced only 50 cents for every dollar increase in the household's earnings from working. Since this implicit tax rate is lower than current rates in existing poverty programs, and because lowering the rate extends financial assistance to more households, WRS' NIT program would require an additional $265 billion in 2018. If the implicit tax rate was reduced to 33%, the additional bill rises to $407 billion in 2018.

Remember that with an implicit tax rate lower than 100%, the NIT program would extend assistance to households outside the poverty level. The plan outlined by WRS provides money to households who are already living at twice the poverty level.[43] This is necessary to prevent a tax cliff of 100% at the cutoff point between those below the poverty rate and those above, and so the plan encourages more work and moves recipients toward self-sufficiency. An alternative solution might increase the implicit tax rate to 75% for households higher than the poverty level, which frees up more funds for those below the poverty level.

With an NIT, the household makes all the decisions about how to spend their funds, including those they have earned plus those received from the government. Food stamps, housing vouchers, TANF, and all the other anti-poverty programs would be eliminated.

The NIT, like the UGI (universal guaranteed income, in case you forgot), gives the decision-making about spending to recipients with no-strings attached.

But this is exactly what likely doomed the Finland UGI experiment and caused President Nixon to drop his version of the NIT. Taxpayers want regulations to ensure that, in their view, public money goes for "necessary spending," such as food, shelter, medical care, and transportation. They worry people receiving the NIT will spend the money on frivolous things and not use it to keep them and their families intact while striving to improve their lives. Political reality therefore means the NIT is out and strings-attached programs are in. Therefore, my "real solution" keeps the WRS proposal using a 50% implicit tax rate, except I add some strings.

Remember I have already dealt with financing health-care in Chapter 4 by recommending poor and many middle-income households be provided funds to purchase private-market health insurance. As a result, the ideas I present here will not include any of the health-care programs for the poor, the most important being Medicaid, but the poverty assistance program I recommend will follow the concept of the health insurance vouchers.

My plan collapses the funds from the non-health-care individual poverty programs into four spending groups. Three of the groups are strings-attached programs to assist low-income households pay for the necessities of food, shelter, and transportation. The fourth is a cash group. Each of these groups would be implemented with a debit card electronically replenished every month. The three strings-attached debit cards would each be programmed to only accept purchases related to their category, and the fourth cash debit card would accept payments for anything. The amounts on all four cards are calibrated for the number of people in the household.

I've used data on spending patterns of households to split the total monetary value of the assistance among the four categories. Using the spending patterns for the 20% of households with the lowest incomes and excluding health-care, I recommend splits of 17% for food, 44% for shelter, 17% for transportation, and 22% for cash.[44] Of course, the individual preferences of all households won't fit this spending split, but this is a concession for garnering political support.

I call my poverty plan SSS: *Simplicity* in structure, *Supportive* of those needing help, but providing incentives to move poor households to *Self-sufficiency*.

However, there are two important adjustments needed for my plan. One is to consider the household's assets. There are certainly situations where households are "cash-poor"—meaning their annual income is low—but are asset-rich—meaning they have investments worth large amounts of money. We don't want households with little annual income but large financial assets qualifying for public assistance. I suspect that's certainly not the intent of most taxpayers.

Current poverty programs have asset tests, and many require a household to spend down their assets before they can qualify for assistance.[45] But such a strict requirement can motivate poor households to avoid saving and building up assets,[46] which is not good because it discourages thrift and planning for the future.

I recommend substituting a much less restrictive asset test by "amortizing" the household's assets over their lifetime and taking this value into account when considering their income shortfall. Amortizing is a fancy financial term meaning to divide the asset value over future years, but also taking into account expected interest earnings.

Here's an example of how my asset rule is much less onerous than the current rule. Let's say Jamie and Roderick have $3,000 in savings. Under current rules in many states, Jamie and Roderick would have to spend the $3,000 before they could qualify for many public assistance programs. But if Jamie and Roderick have a remaining 50-year life expectancy, and assuming they earn 3% annually on their money, then using my recommendation, only $116 from the $3,000 would be added to their other annual income when calculating the amount of public financial help they qualify for.

The second adjustment modifies payments to account for cost-of-living differences based on where people live. Calculations by the federal government show there is a 38% difference between the highest cost-of-living state (Hawaii) and the lowest (Mississippi). This means a dollar of public assistance will go much further in Mississippi than in Hawaii. There's an even bigger 60% difference between the highest cost area of the country (San Jose, California) and the lowest cost area (rural Alabama).[47] These cost-of-living differences should be used to adjust public assistance payments so they are the same in purchasing power in different geographic regions. A program at the Massachusetts Institute of Technology (MIT) has, in fact, developed a methodology to do just this.[48]

Last, one public social-support program needs special attention and reform: Social Security Disability Insurance, or SSDI for short. Funded by the Social Security system, SSDI is a companion program to Social Security retirement that pays a monthly amount to individuals who have become disabled and cannot work. Originally, the requirement was that individuals were so disabled that they could not do any work of any kind.[49] This is in contrast to many private disability policies that pay as long as the individual's disability prevents them from doing the work they were trained to do. However, SSDI has gradually been relaxing its "can't be gainfully employed" requirement, and this is one of the problems; with the more lenient work requirement, more individuals have qualified for SSDI and costs have risen.[50]

Another change has been SSDI's definition of disability. When the program began in the 1930s, disability was primarily defined in physical terms. Physical disabilities are obvious and subject to little disagreement, but in recent decades SSDI has expanded the definition of disability to include psychological disorders. These disorders are less obvious and based more on subjective evaluation. Greater weight is now given to the evaluation by individuals' personal physicians. As a result of the expanded definition of disability and the evaluations by personal physicians, the number of individuals qualifying for and receiving SSDI has skyrocketed. Since 1970, the number of SSDI recipients has increased almost 500%, over 8 times faster than general population growth.[51] Since judges in each state make the determination of SSDI eligibility, there are now states known to have sympathetic judges.[52] Almost 10% of the working age population (age 18-64) receives SSDI in several states.[53]

Some claim SSDI has become a form of poverty assistance in some states, unrelated to whether the recipient is disabled or not.[54] The broader issue is that SSDI is rapidly running out of money and will ultimately require support from general tax revenues to continue. [55]Some economists say the easing of SSDI rules is one reason why labor-force participation among persons (particularly men) in their prime working years has plunged in recent decades.[56] In short, SSDI has become an alternative to work for a significant number of people.

SSDI needs to be reformed, and several promising ideas have been offered. Better medical screening is one, perhaps accomplished by limiting the role of the individual's physician as well as independent (and often elected) judges. The alternative is to entrust the decision about disability to SSDI-paid evaluators. Another solution replaces public SSDI with private disability insurance policies paid for by both employers and employees. The advantage is employers and employees would be motivated to keep claims honest and valid. [57]If not, they'll end up paying more for premiums on the insurance policies. Other ideas include requiring a "back to work" plan to be developed when a worker is considered to be disabled, or allowing for a condition of partial disability, meaning the worker continues to work part-time while receiving treatment and partial disability payments.[58]

▲ SUMMING UP

When considering only a household's earnings, the poverty rate hasn't improved in the last three decades. However, when the ability of households to spend on goods and services is considered, only 3% of households today live in poor conditions. Still, if the goal is to move households to self-sufficiency, then major changes need to be made to poverty programs, including reducing the rate at which assistance is removed when the household earns more, and removing features of programs that discourage two-parent households. Poverty programs need to be combined and coordinated with simple cash payments supporting expenditures on key necessities. Implementing these reforms will initially add more spending to our poverty programs, but hopefully over time, these changes—together with those recommended for both K-12 and college education—will enable more poor households to move into self-supporting situations. Our poverty programs need a strong dose of SSS: Simplicity, Support, and moving people to Self-Sufficiency.

Chapter 7 Endnotes

1.   Fontenot, Semega, and Kollar, op. cit.

2.   Fox, *The Supplemental Poverty Measure, 2017.*

3.   McCully, Moyer, and Stewart, "Comparing the Consumer Price Index and the Personal Consumption Expenditures Price Index."

4.   Winship, *Poverty after Welfare Reform.* Similar improvements are found for another measure of poverty termed "extreme poverty," which calibrates the number of people living on less than $2 a day. When the value of benefits from various poverty programs are included, 90% of the people are removed from extreme poverty; Meyer, Wu, Mooers, and Medalia, "The Use and Misuse of Income Data and Extreme Poverty in the United States."

5.   Meyer and Sullivan, "Annual Report on U.S. Consumption Poverty: 2017." The rates are based on the percentages of households who didn't consume the typical market basket of goods and services from 1980.

6.   Sheffield and Rector, *Understanding Poverty in the US: Surprising Facts about America's Poor.*

7.   Annie Casey Foundation, "Hunger a Harsh Reality for 14 Million Children Nationwide."

8.   Carter, "The Government Isn't Being Honest About Hunger in America."

9.   U.S. Department of Agriculture, "Food Security Status of Households with Children in 2016."

10. Allcott, Diamond, and Dube, "The Geography of Poverty and Nutrition Food Deserts and Food Choices across the U.S." The problem does not appear to be access to nutritious foods, but simply choosing not to select them.

11. Fontenot, Semega, and Kollar, *op. cit.*

12. Holzer, Schanzenbach, Duncan, and Ludwig, "The Economic Costs of Childhood Poverty in the United States."

13. Maag, Steuerle, Chakravarti, and Quakenbush, "How Marginal Tax Rates Affect Families at Various Levels of Poverty"; Congressional Budget Office, *Effective Marginal Tax Rates for Low- and Moderate-Income Workers in 2016.*

14. McClelland and Mok, *A Review of Recent Research on Labor Supply Elasticities.*

15. McDonald and Miller, "Welfare Programs and the State Economy."

16. Badger, "The Unbelievable Rise of Single Motherhood in America over the Last 50 Years."

17. Wilcox, Price, and Rachidi, Marriage, Penalized. Studies with similar findings include Besharov and Gilbert, *Marriage Penalties in the Modern Social-Welfare State; Rachidi, The Earned Income Tax Credit and Marriage Penalties: Does a Childless Worker Expansion Make them Worse?*"; and Rector, *How Welfare Undermines Marriage and What to Do About It."*

18. Gordon and Batlan, "AFDC: The Legal History."

19. Moynihan, *The Negro Family: The Case for National Action.*

20. Van Parijs and Vanderborght, *Basic Income.*

21. Bregman, "Nixon's Basic Income Plan."

22. Ryan, "Richard Branson is the Latest Entrepreneur to Show Support for Universal Basic Income."

23. Lowrey, *Give People Money.* Annie Lowrey is an example of the second group—adding the UGI to existing poverty programs.

24. *Ibid.*

25. Van Parijs and Vanderborght, *op. cit.*, pp. 133-169.

26. Murray, *In Our Hands: A Plan to Replace the Welfare State.*

27. Shingler, "Quebec's New Basic Income Plan has Proponents Dreaming Big, Others Skeptical." Quebec is another region embarking on a guaranteed income experiment.

28. Crisp, "Finland Ends Universal Basic Income."

29. Reuters, "Finland's Basic Income Trial Boosts Happiness, Not Employment."

30. Munnel, *Lessons from the Income Maintenance Experiments.*

31. Dewey, "GOP Proposes Stricter Work Requirement for Food Stamp Recipients, a Step toward a Major Overhaul of the Social Safety Net."

32. Schochet, Burghardt, and McConnell, "Does Job Crops Work? Impact Findings from the National Job Corps Study."

33. Ip, "The Problem with a Federal Jobs Guarantee (Hint: It's Not the Price Tag)"; Gulker, "The job Guarantee: A Critical Analysis."

34. Musumeci and Zur, "Medicaid Enrollees and Work Requirements: Lessons from the TANF Experience"; Hahn, Pratt, Allen, Kenney, Levy, and Waxman, "Work Requirements in Social Safety Net Programs"; Hamilton, Freedman, Gennetian, Michalopoulos, Walter, Adams-Ciardullo, and Gassman-Pines, "National Evaluation of Welfare-to-Work Strategies."

35. Lucas, "Benefits and Drawbacks of a Four-Day Workweek."

36. Phelps, *Rewarding Work.*

37. Cohen, "Majority of American Support Welfare Spending Restrictions."

38. U.S. House Budget Committee, *The War on Poverty: 50 Years Later.*

39. Isaacs, "The Costs of Benefit Delivery in the Federal Food Stamp Program: Lessons from Cross-Program Analysis."

40. *Ibid.*

41. Federal Safety Net, *Safety Net Programs.*

42. Wiederspan, Rhodes, and Shaefer, "Expanding the Discourse on Antipoverty Policy: Reconsidering a Negative Income Tax." The authors do not include Medicaid funds in the NIT plan.

43. *Ibid.*

44. U.S. Bureau of Labor Statistics, "Consumer Expenditure Surveys."

45. Prosperity Now, "Asset Limits in Public Benefit Programs."

46. Vallas and Valenti, "Asset Limits are a Barrier to Economic Security and Mobility."

47. U.S. Bureau of Economic Analysis, "Real Personal Income for States and Metropolitan Areas, 2017."

48. Nadeau, "Living Wage Calculator."

49. Kearney, "Social Security and the 'D' in OASDI: The History of a Federal Program Insuring Earners against Disability."

50. Burkhauser and Daly, *The Declining Work and Welfare of People with Disabilities.*

51. Pradhan and Capretta, *Disability Insurance Needs Reform.*

52. Ohlemacher, "House Investigators: Social Security Disability Judges Too Lax."

53. Office of Retirement and Disability Policy, *Annual Statistical Report on the SSDI Program.*

54. Raab, "Has Disability Become a 'de facto welfare program'?"

55. Autor and Duggan, "The Growth in Social Security Disability Rolls: A Fiscal Crisis Unfolding."

56. Autor and Duggan, "The Rise in the Disability Rolls and the Decline in Unemployment."

57. Autor and Duggan, *A Proposal for Modernizing the U.S. Disability Insurance System.*

58. Autor, "The Unsustainable Rise of the Disability Rolls in the United States: Causes, Consequences, and Policy Options," in Scholz, John, Hyunpyo Moon, and Sang-Hyop Lee (eds.), *Social Policies in the Age of Austerity: A Comparative Analysis of the U.S. and Korea.*

CHAPTER EIGHT

RECONCILING THE REALITIES OF PAY DIFFERENCES

IT'S NOT RUDE TO ASK ABOUT THESE PAY DIFFERENCES

It's natural we like to compare ourselves to others. We make comparisons of our appearance, kinds of vehicles we drive, how our children and grandchildren are doing with their jobs and families, and, at least in my circle of friends, what books we're reading. These comparisons don't have to be based on envy or pride; instead they can simply be sources of conversation, or, so to speak, a comparison of notes.

Of course, an excellent example of our curiosity is differences in what people are paid. When I was growing up in the 1950s and 60s, my parents told me I could wonder about someone's salary but never ask. Asking what someone made was simply rude! I perceive this standard still exists today, although in a more relaxed fashion. Plus, there are ways of using the internet to discover a person's salary, and people can also give hints about their paycheck through the possessions they own.

There are two big pay differences that we, as a society, have made our business to worry about out of a sense of fairness. These are differences in pay based on gender (woman vs. man), and based on race (mainly Black vs. White). In each case, there's a sense that one party has been unfairly underpaid. Indeed, there has been legislation already enacted, and other legislation proposed, to remedy these pay differences.[1]

In this chapter, I'll look at the status of the gender and race pay gaps, review the reasons for the gaps, and then consider both fake and real solutions for resolving the pay differences.

△ THE GENDER PAY GAP: COMPARING APPLES TO APPLES AND NOT TO ORANGES

Each year, both national and local media update the gender pay gap. In 2017, it was announced the gap was 82%, meaning women working full-time earned 82 cents for every dollar earned by men working full-time. Although the gap was better than in 2000 (77%) and much better than in 1980 (64%), it doesn't seem fair that a woman would be paid less than a man for doing the same job.[2] But that's *not* what the statistic measures. There's no comparison of men and women in the exact same jobs. Instead, the statistic was derived by taking the average weekly salary of all women working full-time and comparing it to the average weekly salary of all men working full-time. The problem is, this is clearly an apples-to-oranges comparison.

This statistic assumes that the characteristics of the women and men being compared are the same, except for their gender. Clearly, this isn't the case. As groups, women and men have traditionally differed on important features like education, experience, occupation, and industries where they work. Each of these factors affects a worker's salary. For example, any worker—female or male—with more education and more experience is typically more valuable to businesses and therefore is paid more than those with less education and less experience.[3] This isn't discrimination; it's common sense.

What happens when we do an "apples-to-apples" comparison for the pay of men versus women? The good news is, most of the pay gap disappears. Indeed, for the last twenty years, the gap has been 92%. This means that after accounting for workers' education, occupation, experience, industry, and several other work-related factors, the average female worker earns 92% of the average male worker. By comparison, in 1980 the gap by this measure was 79%.[4]

I know some of you are saying: "Still, there's a gap, it's just smaller, but it's a gap nevertheless, which is evidence there's continuing discrimination against female workers in favor of male workers." I understand this response, and I'll address it, but first I need to detour slightly into how females have been able to raise their pay from 79% of male pay in 1980 to 92% today.

The explanation starts with education, a big determining factor in worker productivity. For most of the 20th century, women had much lower educational attainment than men. As recently as 1980, the percentage of men age 25 and older with bachelor's degrees or higher (21%) was one-half greater than for women the same age (14%). Even among young people aged 25-29 in 1980, the percentage of men with college degrees outpaced women with college degrees by 24% to 21%.[5]

Today, women have caught up to and actually surpassed men in education; in 2017, 35% of women over age 25 were college graduates, compared to 34% of men. More telling, among the 25-29 age group, the percentage of women with a college degree hold an edge to the percentage of men with a college degree by 39% to 32%.[6] In fact, the number of women in college has outnumbered men every year since 1979.[7]

And with more women having a college degree, job doors have opened to them that were previously closed. Importantly, many of these doors opened to higher paying salaries, and as a result, women's overall work experience has increased.[8] Women are CEOs, heads of companies, doctors, lawyers, presidents of universities and colleges, and likely—in my remaining lifetime—presidents of the United States. A recent study even showed that young (under age 30), unmarried women living in the nation's biggest cities out-earn comparably aged men due to their better education.[9]

Why has all this happened? Certainly, Title IX, the federal legislation passed in 1972 prohibiting gender discrimination at colleges and universities, has had some impact.[10] Yet there have also been factors working outside laws and rules that have allowed and motivated females to seek more formal education and training.

In the late 20th and early 21st centuries, the nature of work changed, moving away from physical jobs requiring strength and more suited for males, to jobs needing knowledge and cognitive decision-making that gave no particular advantage to males or females. As farm life retreated and urban life grew, the rural division of labor and task stereotypes between males and females disappeared. Modern home conveniences (refrigerators, vacuums, washers and dryers, and indoor plumbing) also reduced the time needed to manage homes and families, a task traditionally performed by females.[11] Finally, the development of easy and reliable contraceptives (the "pill") to better control child bearing made it easier for women to plan education paths and work careers.[12] The result was that women now had the time, ability, and opportunity to pursue advanced education and new kinds of jobs.

△ EXPLAINING THE LAST 8%

Now what about that last 8%? This is the current difference between male pay and female pay after accounting for differences in work-related personal characteristics (education and experience) and in the occupations and industries in which females and males work. Why should there be any gap at all between female and male pay if men and women are now treated by the same standards with no discrimination?

First, not everyone agrees the gap is only 8%; there's an argument the real gap is higher. The reasoning is that, while education levels of females have improved and, by some measures, now exceed those of men, discrimination still keeps some women out of many high-paying occupations and also prevents many qualified women from being promoted. This barrier has been dubbed as the "glass ceiling" for women.[13]

The glass ceiling is a valid concern that cannot be disproved. I can only point to statistics indicating that, if such discrimination exists, it appears to have diminished. In high-paying professions like doctors, lawyers, and computer scientists, the percentages of women holding those jobs have increased significantly, even in the last dozen years. For example, comparing 2004 to 2016, the percentage of doctors and surgeons who are women rose from 29% to 38%, the percentage of female lawyers rose from 29% to 36%, the female share of computer systems analysts jumped from 29% to 36%, and female dentists spiked from 22% to 34%.[14]

Alternatively, the real gap could be less than 8% because there are many characteristics of workers important for jobs that can't be easily measured. In several high-paying business fields, traits of risk-taking, tenacity, and sometimes combativeness are preferred, particularly when high-stakes negotiations are involved. Traditionally, for good or for bad, proportionally more men have been perceived to possess these traits than have women.[15] Therefore, the reasoning goes that some companies will hire a man rather than a woman—even if both have the same education and experience—because they are looking for particular work-related personal characteristics that can't easily be put on a resume.[16]

Some research suggests women often choose to be paid less than men? Uh, how would this happen? Well, one answer is if women are less willing to work overtime, or if women avoid jobs with uncertain hours yet which pay more. Indeed, a detailed study of bus and train operators in Massachusetts found women were less willing than men to take the less desirable shifts and routes even though they paid more, and this was a big determinant in the gender pay differences of those occupations.[17]

Why would women shy away from better paying jobs with unpredictable times? The authors of the Massachusetts study speculated it may be because women have less flexible time schedules than men. And why might that be? Yes, you've correctly guessed it: it's because women, more so than men, have daily time commitments to children and to the home. These commitments originate from one continuing difference between women and men, which is the fact that women bear children, and men don't. Indeed, research strongly points to this fact as a continuing challenge for women in narrowing the pay gap with men.[18]

"Now, wait," some of you are saying. "How can child-bearing be a detriment for women in earning good pay? Women giving birth to children should be rewarded, not penalized. Society would eventually vanish if women didn't give us children."

Of course, child-bearing is vital for our society, and we should applaud women who take on this important role. But for some businesses, child-bearing can entail costs. Some women who are pregnant may not perform at their peak levels for the simple reason that pregnancy is demanding and exhausting. This is particularly the case for physically oriented jobs. Other women become ill or need bedrest during pregnancy, which adversely affects occupations where schedules and deadlines are important. Pregnant women who continue working may need to take frequent breaks for rest or nourishment that can delay the completion of job tasks. And once the birth occurs, the mother may also medically need extended time away from work, or the mother may desire a period of bonding with the newborn.

One solution is for a woman to take unpaid leave from work while pregnant and for some time after the child's birth, and then return to the job. If the employer doesn't pay the woman while she's away from work, why should the company care if a female employee becomes pregnant?

While this may work for some companies, it doesn't work for all. Firms with jobs requiring specialized skills will have to incur costs of training a new worker or reassigning work while the pregnant employee is absent. Additionally, for some firms it may not be easy to find a replacement, especially a temporary replacement, particularly when the labor market is tight. The company may have to pay more for a replacement worker than for the pregnant worker or mother who is taking leave.

Pregnancy is most costly to employers for jobs where personal relationships with clients and customers are highly important. Take a law firm as an example. Cases are assigned to a specific lawyer, and it is not unusual for cases to span months or years. During that time, the client interacts personally with the attorney, and the attorney develops detailed knowledge specific to the case. The attorney would be difficult to replace if she took an absence due to a pregnancy and birth. It's likely the case would be delayed, and as is often said, time is money. There are also similar "client-professional" bonds for architects, engineers, doctors, and top-level salespersons.

And even after children are beyond the toddler stage and are in school with their own schedules, a mother's pay may still suffer because women continue to be the dominant parent in their children's lives, even if a devoted father is present. Surveys show mothers devote almost twice as much time to their children than fathers do.[19] This makes many women reluctant to work longer or uncertain hours and commit to long-term projects—decisions which can particularly hurt them in high-paying professional work.[20]

The hit that child-bearing and motherhood make to a woman's paycheck is called the "mommy discount," which many studies have tracked. For example, one looked at a sample of law firms and followed a selection of lawyers through several years of their careers. Initially, male and female lawyers with the same training earned the same salaries. But a decade later, when many of the females had gone through extended absences due to pregnancies, child-births, and child-rearing, the male lawyers earned 50% more than the female lawyers.[21] A similar study found the same results for MBA graduates.[22] But on a good-news note, these pay disparities may not persist. Some research has found that the mommy discount for young women ultimately disappears by middle-age.[23]

The mommy discount may be the last major hurtle woman face in achieving pay equality with men. What are the real solutions available to address it? I'll discuss them, but first let's turn to the other glaring pay gap in our society: the one between races.

△ WHAT'S LEFT TO OVERCOME?

Black workers, on average, earn less than White workers. Using data for 2016 from the federal government, the average weekly earnings of full-time Black workers was 73% of the average weekly earnings of full-time White workers. For full-time working Black women compared to full-time working White women, the gap was some-what better at 79%.[24] However, the current gaps are much improved than they were in the past; for example, in 1970 the racial pay gap for men was 68%.[25]

But, again, this is an apples-to-oranges comparison, not an apples-to-apples comparison. As with the commonly-touted gender gap percentage, the Black-White earnings comparison doesn't account for differences in education, experience, occupation, industry and other important traits. And like the gender pay gap, when these characteristics are recognized, the racial pay gap shrinks.

Although there is variation from numerous studies, the adjusted racial pay gap for males is around 90%, meaning the average Black male earns 90 cents for every dollar of earnings by White males, after accounting for differences between races in education, expe-rience, occupation, industry, etc. Interestingly, research has found the gap is almost nonexistent for highly educated, highly skilled men, but it is wider for less educated, less skilled men. Also, Black women are closer in pay to White women than Black men are to White men.[26]

Better education for Blacks is the major reason for the improved racial pay gap. In 1960, only about one-third of young (age 25-29) Black adults had a high school degree, compared to two-thirds for young White adults. By 2016, over 90% of both young Black and White adults were high school graduates. Also, between 1960 and 2016, the percentage of young White adults with a college degree rose a whopping 264%, but the percentage of young Black adults who were college graduates jumped 320%.[27]

Last, the "gold standard" of measuring learning at the elementary school level—the National Assessment of Educational Progress (NAEP)—shows Black student achievement moving closer to scores for Whites. For example, in 4th grade reading, Black student scores were 86% of White student scores in 1992; in 2017, Black scores were 89% of White scores. There have been similar gains for 4th grade math, where Black student scores climbed from 85% of White student scores in 1992 to 90% in 2017.[28]

Besides the racial pay gap, there is a corollary racial employment gap, particularly for men. Black men have higher unemployment rates and are employed for shorter periods of time than White men, even after accounting for differences in education.[29]

Just as with the gender pay gap, the big question is why there should be any racial pay and employment gaps at all, unless it is a result of pure discrimination. Although various measures of racial attitudes and harmony have improved in recent decades,[30] there is no way to completely eliminate discrimination as a reason for some or all of racial labor market differences.

The most logical alternative explanation for the racial pay gap is based on employers' assessments of the qualifications of applicants. If it is more difficult for employers to evaluate the capabilities, skills, and work attitudes of (particularly male) Blacks as compared to Whites, then this uncertainty will cause employers to offer lower rates of pay and shorter employment periods to Black applicants. Furthermore, if it is easier for employers to judge the qualifications of college graduates than of non-college graduates, then this explanation can also explain why little or no adjusted racial pay gap is observed for workers with college or advanced degrees.

Why might employers question the work characteristics of Black males who have only attended high school more than of White males? There may be several reasons. Although Black high school academic performance has improved relative to White high school academic performance, Black scores are still lower than Whites scores. Blacks, especially males, are also disciplined in high school at a higher rate, and if employers know this, they may decide Black males make less reliable and trustworthy workers.[31] Even more problematic, the Black male incarceration rate is five times higher than for Whites.[32] Since incarcerated prisoners have a higher proportion of individuals with a high school degree or less,[33] employers may use this information to conclude Blacks are "riskier" hires than Whites.

I know what you're thinking: it isn't fair to attribute the statistics for a group (here Black males) to any individual. I agree. But if potential employers don't have records, such as high school disciplinary records, for individuals, then companies' natural recourse may be to substitute the group information.

△ FAKE SOLUTIONS

The traditional remedy for concerns about discrimination in pay is simply legislation outlawing it. Over fifty years ago, Congress passed the Equal Pay Act of 1963 that prohibited companies from paying workers differently based on their gender if the workers do the same job and have the same training, skills, and productivity. An update and expansion of the Act was proposed, but not passed, in 2017.[34] Several states have also implemented their own laws prohibiting pay differences based only on gender.[35]

Since the Equal Pay Act was implemented, both the unadjusted and adjusted gender pay gaps have narrowed, so an argument can be made that the law had its intended impact. But earlier I showed key factors that improve the productivity and pay of workers—in particular, education—have increased significantly for women in recent decades and are also a logical reason why the gender pay gap has improved.

There are three big problems with relying on laws to eliminate any observed differences in pay between men and women. First, the laws may motivate some firms to just reduce their hiring of women if the company determines the wage paid to a woman required by the law exceeds her economic value to them. Second, the law mandates records and data be provided on job tasks, worker characteristics, and work output. Besides being time-consuming to the company, some of the data require subjective evaluations that inevitably would prompt disagreements and possible court cases.

Third, and maybe most important, the laws don't address what today may be the key difference impacting the relative pay of women and men: the role that only women play in child-bearing and child-rearing. It is this role I will address in the "real solutions" section.

A proposed direct solution to the economic loss suffered by mothers and families from the pregnancy and birth of a child is requiring businesses to provide paid leave, as is done in many foreign countries. Wouldn't this be "proper payback" to businesses who pay women less just because they're mothers?

Requiring paid family leave could exacerbate the mommy discount rather than reduce it. "How so?" you ask. Family leave means a business loses the employee for a period of time. It also means that the business must pay the non-working employee. This is a double whammy against the pay of females who might give birth after being hired. To compensate, businesses might offer potential mothers lower pay.[36]

Most proposed family leave plans also limit the time away from the job to weeks; however, research indicates significant benefits from stay-at-home-parents to older children.[37] If our objective is to support parents (mothers or fathers) who want to be present during the formative years of a child's life, then required paid family leave plans don't do it.

Last, family leave imposes all the costs on businesses. Yet if we believe providing children with appropriate financial resources and emotional and behavioral guidance from their parents ultimately makes them positive contributors to society, then everyone benefits. If true, shouldn't society help fund these efforts through government?

For racial pay differences, the solution often offered is "affirmative action." Affirmative action means reserving slots or giving preferential treatment to the hiring of minorities, particularly Blacks. The method has been used to some degree in government hiring and in the hiring by private companies using government contracts.[38] In a related and controversial use, affirmative action has also been used in some university admissions by giving preferential consideration to minorities for acceptance in order to diversify enrollment.[39]

The use of affirmative action is noble. The idea is that members of particular groups have been wronged in the past by not being hired or not being admitted into educational institutions despite having equal credentials except for one: their race. Affirmative action is used to "right those wrongs" by making up for the past mistakes in giving advantages to current members of the discriminated group.

Still, affirmative action as a remedy has three obstacles to overcome. First, various court decisions have raised questions about the legality of governments and educational institutions to use the tactic.[40] Second, the policy is unpopular, with many believing it is unfair to favor an entire group simply because of the group's characteristic.[41] And third, affirmative action doesn't necessarily help those who were aggrieved in the past; it confers benefits on the current members of a group to compensate for the wrongs inflicted on earlier group members.

A solution to racial economic differences receiving greater attention in recent years is reparations. A reparation is a payment to compensate for past grievances. In this case, the original grievance is enslavement of ancestors of current Black persons. Actually, however, after the Civil War, the federal government promised to compensate former slaves by providing each with a land grant of 40 acres. Therefore, according to economists Darity and Mullen, the real basis for reparations is the failure of the federal government to follow through on their promise. Using an estimate of current land values, Darity and Mullen estimate each qualified individual would be owed between $40,000 and $60,000. The total amount of reparations would be between $1.5 and $2 trillion. To qualify for the funds, individuals would have to demonstrate a direct ancestral connection to an enslaved person in the country prior to the end of the Civil War.[42]

Darity and Mullen see reparations as a way to narrow the wealth gap between Black and White households. With their wealth increased, Black households would have a greater ability to access funds for education, business development, and homeownership, all activities that should improve their standard of living over time.

I am sympathetic to the justification for and implementation of reparations proposed by Darity and Mullen. It would follow in the tradition of the reparations paid to Japanese-Americans interned during World War II, in which each former internee received $20,000. If legislation modeled on Darity and Mullen's plan reached Congress, I would support it. But politically I think we may be years or decades away from this idea receiving broad approval. In the meantime, we need real solutions that can be implemented now. The next section will provide those.

△ REAL SOLUTIONS

In considering real solutions for the gender pay gap, I'll separate women into two groups, because the two groups are impacted differently by the decisions related to the mommy discount.

The first group is women in low to low-middle income households, which I will call "income-constrained." If the mother works, it is usually out of necessity to simply keep food on the table and a roof over the family's head, and if a husband is present and employed, his earnings are also modest. The birth of a child presents a real economic challenge for the family; added expenditures are needed to support the new member of the family. While federal child care credits are available (discussed later), they usually aren't enough to cover the costs of the new child. The mothers in these households therefore can't afford to stop working for long time periods. Sometimes child care is provided by relatives or friends.[43]

The second group is women in higher-income households, from upper-middle to high income. Now I need to tread carefully here, because I have no intent of criticizing any decisions parents in this happy situation have made about careers, and I don't want to imply their decisions about work, career, children, and child-rearing are any less important or stressful than those confronted by the income-constrained group. But the reality is, in these households where there are often two parents and both are employed, the decision to work is, at least in part, based on the personal fulfillment derived from a career and is less about money. Stated another way, having a child does not have the same financial challenges as experienced by the income-constrained households. Research shows women in high-income careers often don't face as large of a mommy discount.[44] I call this second group "career-constrained."

Due to their different circumstances, I have different proposals for the two household groups. For the income-constrained group, remember my poverty solution expands assistance to households with up to twice the poverty level in earnings. I consider this range to cover income-constrained households. My plan also allows for a gradual phase-out of assistance, specifically a reduction of 50 cents in benefits for every dollar increase in earnings. This help will reach an estimated 52 million households with earnings of up to almost $40,000. Further, recall I provide the financial help through the four debit cards (Chapter 7). The amounts on the cards increase with an increase in the number of children in the household. Each additional child raises the total amount on the debit cards by approximately 15% annually.[45] So, my poverty program already provides additional assistance to income-constrained households having an additional child.

Currently, there are two federal programs helping households with children. First is the *child tax credit*, or CTC. Here, households earning up to a fairly substantial amount of money ($400,000 for married couples filing jointly, $200,000 for single households) with children under age 17 can receive tax credits worth $2,000 per child when they file their income taxes each year. A tax credit means your tax bill is reduced by this amount. Even if your tax bill isn't $2,000, up to $1,400 can be paid back to you in cash.[46]

The second is the *child and dependent care tax credit* (CDCTC), which is available for parents (or guardians) who pay for care of children under the age of 13. The "dependent" part of the title means that the credit can also be used by households who pay for the care of adults, like older parents or disabled individuals. The credit is worth between 20% and 35% of allowable expenses (as defined by the IRS), where the percentage is higher for lower-income households and lower for higher-income households. The maximum credit is $3,000 for one child (or dependent) and $6,000 for two or more children (or dependents).[47]

These two programs are costly. In terms of lost revenue to the federal government, the annual bill is approximately $130 billion annually, after excluding the portion for dependent adults.[48] While I don't question the value of the funds in helping families raise children, I think the programs have two major shortcomings.

First, the programs are not narrow enough in their financial scope: they help more than income-constrained households. I suspect this was done to gather broad political support for the programs, but this means the money is dribbled out in relatively small amounts to large numbers of households (many of whom are not financially strapped) rather than giving a much smaller number of households a large and meaningful dose of help.

Second, while the CTC is independent of the decision made by parents (particularly the mother) to work or not to work, the CTCDC only helps parents who have chosen paid child care. This obviously tips the important decision of a parent (again, usually the mother) to work or not work after the birth of a child in favor of working. I don't think this is a wise public policy. In my opinion, public policy should, at the least, remain neutral for such a crucial life choice for parents. As much as possible, I want parents to make this important decision between time at work and time with children independent of government programs.

Therefore, I recommend eliminating both the CTC and CTCDC and using those funds to institute a new public program called CHILD: Child Help In Loving Dollars. All parents, whether working or not, would be able to apply for CHILD. Therefore, parents can decide to use CHILD to pay for day care costs or to substitute for some of the lost earnings when a parent decides to temporarily reduce or stop working in order to care for children at home. It's important for parents to make this choice, as some evidence suggests having parents work and earn additional income can aid successful child development.[49] Other research finds parental time spent with a young child is pivotal to a child's successful start in life, especially if the alternative is day care with strangers.[50] It should be parents who choose between these two.

Like the other financial assistance programs outlined earlier, I would make CHILD available with a debit card, but with expenditures limited to necessities like food, mortgage or rent, electricity, and fuel. Also like the other assistance programs, it uses an implicit tax rate of 50%, which I judge to be in the neutral area of neither encouraging nor discouraging paid work. Using this rate, CHILD provides funds for households with children up to 200% of the poverty level. So, the financial help for children, whether taken to pay for child care costs or to replace foregone earnings, would be consistent with the other financial assistance programs for resource-limited households.

CHILD would only be available for children under age 6; that is, before they begin attending school full-time. At age 6, children are in school, and therefore parents who decide to forego working can return to the workforce. Also, research shows the early years of a child's life, particularly from birth to age 3, are the most crucial for parents to be involved in their child's development.[51] For children in school who have no parental supervision after school, the after-school programs I recommended in Chapter 1 would provide that attention as well as additional education.

Money already allocated by the federal government for the two-child related tax credit programs will completely finance CHILD. The two child related tax programs now have a budget of $130 billion. This gives my plan about $14,000 annually per child for the current number of children under age 6 in qualifying households (those with earnings of up to 200% of the poverty level).[52] The amount of $14,000 is enough to afford most high-quality child care programs[53] or to replace a high proportion of the earnings of most lower-wage workers (96% for minimum wage workers), as well as covering other costs of raising a child outside of child care.[54] Combined with the financial assistance from the poverty-based debit cards outlined in Chapter 7 that automatically increases with a new child, CHILD should go a long way in helping income-constrained households choose their best way for successfully raising young children.

I do have one flashing-light caution about CHILD to throw into the mix. Economics is all about demand and supply. Pushing on one usually pulls on the other. Research shows the current child care tax credits have increased the use of child care. However, the same research shows the availability of new child care centers hasn't kept up with the increased use. As a result, approximately half of the value of the child tax credits have been absorbed by higher child-care prices, ironically, therefore reducing the affordability of child care.[55]

Consequently, any policy resulting in the use of more paid child care (which CHILD likely would) should be accompanied by policies encouraging a greater supply of good quality child-care centers. Studies of early childhood development suggest the education and training of the child-care providers are much more important than the size of the child groups in achieving quality child care. So, perhaps regula-tions should be focused on the caregivers' education while relaxing requirements on group sizes.[56]

Career-constrained mothers can confront a bigger "mommy dis-count" than do income- constrained mothers. The foregone income of bearing and rearing children is greater for career-constrained mothers earning large salaries. In many cases, these women face a deep psychological struggle between their commitment to career or home.[57] Yet in terms of the financial resources needed to provide basic care to children, most career-constrained mothers do not have the same pressure as their income-constrained counterparts.

Put another way, I suspect there is very little public sympathy for a six-figure paid lawyer who takes time away from her job and salary to raise a child. Recommending CHILD financial support for these mothers would significantly increase costs of the program and would likely not be a winning political strategy.

Therefore, for career-constrained mothers defined here as those with earnings above 200% of the poverty level, I offer nothing. Higher-income households will just have to compare the relative benefits and costs of having children versus continuing to pursue a career. For many this is a tough decision; for others, it is not. We shouldn't expect government and public policy to make every decision easy and costless, and this is one of those cases.

Now what about the racial pay gap? For the answer, I can simply say see Chapter 1 on improving the results for K-12 schooling. Although Black children have raised their academic performance relative to Whites, they still trail, and therefore they have the most to gain from the investments I outlined to lift the academic performance in K-12. Increased teacher ability, smaller class sizes to provide more individual attention, Pre-K programs, after-school activities, neighborhood and family counseling and support, and dormitory schools are methods to help all students, including Black students, achieve their full capabilities and ultimately successfully compete for good-paying jobs.

There is one other recommendation I have that will actually cost no money: it is to give young people, especially those seeking work after high school, the ability to have their grade and disciplinary transcripts released to prospective employers. This would provide those youths with good records a way to communicate those records to employers, thereby avoiding employers applying a "group average" to the individual.

▲ SUMMING UP

After adjusting for differences in education, experience, occupation, and industry, the pay gap between women and men and between Blacks and Whites is around 8% to 10%. The gaps may even be smaller if we could better measure the talents and abilities of workers. The best explanation for any remaining pay gap for women is the "mommy discount"—the fact that time away from work due to childbearing can reduce a woman's value to an employer, especially for a high-profile occupation. The best explanation for any remaining pay gap for Blacks is linked to the higher proportion of Black men, in particular, who have faced discipline at school or incarceration in life.

While the "mommy discount" may never be eliminated, a CHILD (Child Help In Loving Dollars) payment targeted to lower and lower-middle income households can help working mothers manage child-care costs, or can help replace some of the lost earnings for mothers who choose to be their own child care giver. CHILD can be completely funded by refocusing existing child and child care tax credits. Continued improvements in the educational attainment of Blacks should work to close the racial pay gap. In addition, making individual school disciplinary records available to potential employers can help close the information gap for young Black workers.

Chapter 8 Endnotes

1. Becker, "Kamala Harris Proposes Equal Pay Measure to Close Gender Gap."

2. Hegewisch and Williams-Brown, *The Gender Wage Gap: 2017.*

3. Wilkie, "Why Two Workers Doing the Same Job Earn Different Pay."

4. Blau and Kahn, "The Gender Wage Gap: Extent, Trends, and Explanations."

5. National Center for Education Statistics, op. cit., Tables 104.10 and 104.20.

6. *Ibid.*

7. National Center for Education Statistics, *op. cit.*, Table 303.10.

8. Blau and Kahn, *op. cit.*

9. Luscombe, "Workplace Salaries: At Last, Women on Top."

10. U.S. Department of Justice, *Equal Access to Education: Forty Years of Title IX.*

11. Greenwood, Seshadri, and Yorukoglu, "Engines of Liberation."

12. Bailey, Hershbein, and Miller, "The Opt-In Revolution? Contraception and the Gender Gap in Wages."

13. Bertrand, "The Glass Ceiling."

14. U.S. Bureau of Labor Statistics, *Women in the Labor Force: A Databook, 2004, 2016*

15. Sundheim, "Do Women Tsk as Many Risks as Men?" One difficulty in making this assessment is defining the traits, which are, by nature, subjectively judged. Still, the important point is that there is a perception of the differences between women and men.

16. Bertrand, "New Perspectives on Gender," in Orley Ashenfelter and David Card's, *Handbook of Labor Economics.*

17. Bolotnyy and Emanuel, "Why Do Women Earn Less than Men?"

18. Miller, "The Gender Pay Gap Is Largely Because of Motherhood."

19. Varathan, "Modern Parents Spend More Time with their Kids than their Parents Spent with Them."

20. Hersch and Stratton, "Housework and Wages."

21. Noonan, Corcoran, and Courant, "Pay Differences among the Highly Trained: Cohort Differences in the Sex Gap in Lawyer's Earnings."

22. Bertrand, Goldin, and Katz, "Dynamics of the Gender Gap for Young Professionals in the Financial and Corporate Sectors."

23. Kahn, Garcia-Manglano, and Bianchi, "The Motherhood Penalty at Midlife: Long-Term Effects of Children on Women's Careers."

24. U.S. Bureau of Labor Statistics, "Usual Weekly Earnings of Wage and Salary Workers."

25. Lang and Lehmann, "Racial Discrimination in the Labor Market: Theory and Empirics."

26. *Ibid.*

27. National Center for Education Statistics, *op. cit.*, Table 104.20.

28. National Center for Education Statistics, *op. cit.*, Table 222.10.

29. Lang and Lehmann, *op. cit.*

30. *Ibid.*

31. U.S. Government Accounting Office, *Discipline Disparities for Black Students, Boys, and Students with Disabilities.*

32. Gramlich, *The Gap between the Number of Blacks and Whites in Prison in Shrinking.*

33. Ewert and Wildhagen, "Educational Characteristics of Prisoners: Data from the ACS."

34. Govtrack, "H.R. 2095: Fair Pay Act of 2017."

35. Brainerd, *"State Equal Pay Laws."*

36. Richman, "Mandated Paid Family Leave Harms Its Intended Beneficiaries"; Timpe, "The Long-Run Effects of America's First Paid Maternity Leave Policy."

37. Bettinger, Haegeland, and Rege, "Home with Mom: The Effects of Stay-at-Home Parents on Children's Long-Run Educational Outcomes."

38. Kellough, "Affirmative Action in Government Employment."

39. Jaschik, "Closing Arguments in the Harvard Case."

40. National Conference of State Legislatures, "Affirmative Action: Court Decisions."

41. Bouie, "Where Do Americans Stand on Affirmative Action?"

42. Darity and Mullen, "How Reparations for American Descendants of Slavery Could Narrow the Racial Wealth Divide."

43. Layzer and Burstein, *National Study of* Child Care for Low-Income Families: Patterns of Child Care Use among Low-Income Families.

44. Anderson, Binder, and Krause, "The Motherhood Wage Penalty Revisited: Experience, Heterogeneity, Work Effort, and Work-Schedule Flexibility"; Amuedo-Dorantes and Kimmel, "The Motherhood Wage Gap in the United States: The Importance of College and Fertility Delay"; Lubin, "When Pregnancies and Bigger Jobs Go Hand in Hand."

45. U.S. Bureau of the Census, "Poverty Thresholds."

46. Frankel, "The 2018 Child Tax Credit: What You Need to Know."

47. Josephson, "All About Child Tax Credits."

48. Committee for a Responsible Federal Budget, "The Tax Break-Down: Child Tax Credit"; Rohaly, "Reforming the Child and Dependent Care Tax Credit." The cost includes the expansion of the CTC beginning in 2018.

49. Goldberg, Prause, Lucas-Thompson, and Himsel, "Maternal Employment and Children's Achievement in Context: A Meta-Analysis of Four Decades of Research."

50. Bouffard, *The Most Important Year*; Baker, Gruber, and Milligan, "The Long-Run Impacts of a Universal Child Care Program."

51. Komisar, *Being There: Why Prioritizing Motherhood in the First Three Years Matters.*

52. Semega, Fontenot, and Kollar, *op. cit.* and Wiederspan, Rhodes, and Shafer, *op. cit.*

53. Gould and Cooke, "High Quality Child Care is out of Reach for Working Families."

54. Lino, Kuczynski, Rodriguez, and Schap, *Expenditures on Children, 2015.*

55. Rodgers, "Give Credit Where? The Incidence of Child Care Tax Credits."

56. Thomas and Gorry, Regulation and the Cost of Child Care.

57. Rubin and Wooten, "Highly Educated Stay-at-Home Mothers: A Study of Commitment and Conflict."

CHAPTER NINE

MAKING THE TRANSITION FROM DOMESTIC TO INTERNATIONAL TRADE

TRASHING TRADE

The 2016 election of Donald Trump as President of the United States is the biggest political upset that I have witnessed. To win, Donald Trump worked the key issues of international trade and its potential adverse impacts on the U.S. workforce to his advantage. He claimed that international trade deals put the U.S. in a financial hole with the rest of the world, hurt the American economy, and decimated the workforce. As President, Trump continued this line of attack and used it as the basis for renegotiating trade agreements between the U.S. and several countries. President Trump's ideological opposite, Senator Bernie Sanders, has made similar arguments.

Do President Trump and Senator Sanders have a point? Does international trade inevitably hurt the American economy and its workers? We're a big country; why do we need to trade with foreign countries at all? Or perhaps it's just the particular trade agreements negotiated in the last quarter-century that have done the damage?

To see where trade may have gone wrong and how to fix it, we have to start at the beginning and address some key questions: why do people and countries trade, how is international trade measured, and how are foreign investments and foreign trade linked?

△ WHAT IF "ANYTHING YOU CAN DO, I CAN DO BETTER"?

There's a song I remember from my childhood in the 1950s with the catchy title, "Anything You Can Do (I Can Do Better)." It was from the Broadway play "Annie Get Your Gun," which debuted right after World War II. Many would consider it a silly song today, but it's actually perfect for illustrating the benefits of trade; that is, trade makes sense when another person can do something better than you, and you can do something better than them, but it even makes sense when you can do anything better!

My father was a carpenter and he built the house where I lived as a child. The house was constructed on a hill, so tons of dirt had to be excavated and moved, but my dad did not own a bulldozer. Even if he did, he didn't have the skills for the tricky kind of earth moving that was needed. So, he traded some of his carpentry skills to a friend who was an expert excavator and owned a dozer. My dad built some roof trusses for his friend, and in turn, the dozer-owner turned a portion of the hill into a nice flat lot for our home.

My dad traded his time and carpentry knowledge for his friend's time and earth-moving ability. Economists call this *bartering*, and centuries ago it was the way most people traded. Alternatively, my dad could have simply hired and paid an excavating company to do the work. But this would still have been a trade, because the source of the money my father would have paid the company was his earnings as a carpenter.

Now, suspend reality and assume there really is someone who fits the song and can do everything better than anyone else. Would they still trade? Yes, they would, and here's the example I use in my classes to understand why.

In the 1980s and 90s, Michael Jordan was considered the top athlete in the world. During those years, my wife and I frequently vacationed at Wrightsville Beach off the North Carolina coast, and we would pass by Jordan's beach house on our morning walks. Often, we would see a landscaping crew mowing his lawn and trimming the shrubs. Several of the workers struggled to maintain their stamina in the hot Carolina summer sun.

As the best conditioned athlete in the world at the time, Michael Jordan ("MJ") could have run rings around the workers and finished the landscaping jobs faster than any three-man crew. MJ was clearly better as a basketball player, but he certainly had the physical conditioning to do landscaping. So why didn't MJ do his own landscaping? Because that would take time away from his "best" talent—being a pro ball player. Every minute he devoted to landscaping was a minute he could use practicing his jump shot, studying film, developing plays, or making commercials.

Even if someone is better at everything, they're motivated to focus on their best talents and trade for everything else. Indeed, this is one of the challenges of education: helping individuals find their best talents and nurturing them. Should your best talent coincide with something you enjoy, then your work life is set.

Countries also differ in their talents; some have plentiful natural resources such as oil, natural gas, and timber. Some have an abundance of high-skilled and high-paid workers, others have many low-skilled and cheap workers. Countries with great beaches, resorts, or historical sites attract tourists. Countries with lower costs-of-living can become retirement havens. Therefore countries, like people, trade. In reality, it's companies and individuals in those countries who are engaged in trading, but usually we find patterns in their exchanges so we lump them together and talk about the "country" doing the trading. Since many Middle Eastern countries have large reservoirs of cheap oil, yet, at the same time, live on millions of acres of arid land unsuitable for food production, it makes sense that they trade oil for food. In contrast, Japan has no oil and not much land for large scale food production. Japan has survived by using skilled laborers and modern technology to manufacture vehicles and electronics which they trade for oil and food.

I know what you're thinking: this all makes sense, but still, shouldn't trade between countries be on an "equal for equal" basis? That is, like when my dad bartered his carpentry skills for dirt-moving services, they both agreed they were exchanging equal values. But isn't the U.S. "in the hole" on international trade, meaning we buy much more from foreign countries than they sell to us? Isn't this the problem, and if it is, then isn't international trade (at least from the perspective of the U.S.) unfair? Let's see.

△ FUNNY NUMBERS

My wife and I have a friend who makes pottery. She's actually been quite successful at it and makes enough to earn a good profit each year. She sells her pottery at numerous stores and outlets in the city, and the stores make a commission on the sale (usually at least 33%), leaving the rest for our friend. She doesn't mind the stores' cut, because the stores reach many more customers than she could reach alone. In business management lingo, the store has "added value" to our friend's pottery by displaying and advertising her pieces.

Let's say one of our friend's pieces sells for $100. With a 33% commission, the store keeps $33, and our friend pockets $67. But if this was an international trade transaction, guess what? Official government statistics would count the full $100 of pottery as being created by the store. Nothing would be counted as being created by the potter!

When politicians, business persons, and others complain about how international trade has damaged the American economy, they use as support the official numbers on U.S. trade transactions. There are four key concepts in these numbers. *Exports* are what U.S. companies sell to foreign buyers, and *imports* are what U.S. consumers and businesses buy from foreign sellers. If exports exceed imports, then the U.S. runs a *trade surplus*. But if imports exceed exports, the U.S. has a *trade deficit*. For all but one of the last fifty years, the U.S. has run a trade deficit.[1] In 2017, this deficit was $566 billion.[2] This is the number that is referenced to supposedly expose how bad international trade is for the U.S.

Let's zero in on the biggest alleged villain in the trade-deficit drama: China. In 2017, the U.S. had an official $375 billion trade deficit with China, most of which had developed since China joined the World Trade Organization (WTO) in 2001.[3] How was this number determined? It was calculated by totaling all the products (and services) bought by U.S. companies and individuals from China and then subtracting all the products (and services) bought by Chinese companies and individuals from the U.S.

But just because a product—say, an iPhone—is shipped from China doesn't mean all its value was created there. In fact, China's main contribution to the iPhone is only assembling the phone's parts, but most of the parts are actually made in Korea and Taiwan. Also, the operating system of the iPhone, which is actually the heart of the phone, was developed in the U.S. by Apple. Therefore, a detailed analysis of costs shows that only $8.46 of the value of every iPhone exported from China is due to value created in that country, mostly in assembly. Yet the full factory cost of $238 is what is counted in the international trade statistics as the export value from China. The biggest cost component to the buyer is the $283 of profit Apple makes when it sells an iPhone in the U.S.[4] This $283 of profit goes to the shareholders of Apple, most of whom are in the U.S.

The iPhone is just one example of these crazy trade statistics. If the iPhone example is applied to everything sold from China, the U.S. trade deficit with China in 2017 shrinks from the official $375 billion to $238 billion, a 37% reduction. This $137 billion reduction would have actually exceeded President Trump's stated goal of a $100 billion trade deficit curtailment with China.[5] Moreover, if a careful accounting of where parts (including intellectual property) are made and applied to all of U.S. international trade, then the "true" trade deficit is roughly half of the official number. [6]This puts the U.S. trade deficit in 2017 at $238 billion, or 1.5% of the total national income in that year.

So yes, the U.S. runs a trade deficit, meaning U.S.-based companies and consumers buy more from producers in foreign countries than we sell to those countries. Yet talk about fake news—or better, fake statistics! The real deficit numbers are much, much smaller than the reported ones.

△ BOOMERANG MONEY

My dad was in Australia during World War II, and one of the cleverest things he saw was a boomerang. In case you don't know, a boomerang is a curved wooden object which, when thrown, moves through the air in a circular fashion and ultimately returns to the thrower. It's based on an early form of air dynamics developed by indigenous Australian tribes. What if I told you that the dollars accumulated by foreign countries when they sell more to us than we sell to them ultimately act like a boomerang? It's true!

When China accumulates dollars from its trade surplus with the U.S., they don't use those dollars internally. China has its own currency, the yuan. If China lets those dollars sit in the vault, they earn nothing; in fact, they would actually *lose* money with dollars locked away, because inflation would erode their value to purchase now higher-priced products and services. Instead, China ultimately uses those dollars to acquire U.S. assets like stocks, bonds, land, buildings, or companies.

For a long time, China put their dollars in relatively safe U.S. government bonds, an investment which helps fund the annual U.S. budget deficits. Recently, China has shifted more of its dollars to non-financial assets, like companies. For example, in my state of North Carolina, China bought the giant pork producer, Smithfield Farms.[7] They are also building an 800-worker tire factory in eastern North Carolina.[8] And in South Carolina, they recently expanded an appliance factory that its investors have operated for almost twenty years.[9]

The bottom line is this: the dollars accumulated by Chinese companies as a result of running a trade surplus with the U.S. eventually return to our country through Chinese investments that fund governments, buy or establish companies, and create jobs. The same is true of all other countries that sell more to us than we sell to them! To see this, look at the numbers from 2010 to 2016. The annual total trade deficit, properly measured, averaged $252 billion.[10] But yearly foreign investment in the U.S. over the same period averaged $283 billion.[11] Accounting for measurement and estimation error, these numbers are essentially the same!

There's more. It's estimated that these foreign investments support over 12 million jobs in the U.S.,[12] and many of them pay more than their domestic counterparts.[13] Furthermore, this job total is more than twice as high as estimates of net job losses due to competition from imports.[14]

Here's the correct way to look at a trade deficit: when the U.S. buys more goods and services from other countries than it sells to them, that deficit is not a debt like your home mortgage or auto loan.[15] The country doesn't have to ultimately pay that debt back with cash. Instead, the debt is paid for with U.S. investments and assets. So, our country is buying foreign-made cars, electronics, shirts and pants, and paying for them with U.S. stocks, bonds, land, and companies.[16] And, in the transaction, we lose some jobs by buying imports, but we gain jobs by having foreigners putting their money here. Is there anything wrong with this trade? Maybe so.

△ TAKE THE BENEFITS AND RUN

I've thrown cold water on the hysteria expressed by some about trade deficits. First, I've shown the real trade deficit isn't nearly as large as it is reported to be. And second, I've shown foreigners don't hoard the dollars they accumulate from a U.S. trade deficit. Instead, they use the money to buy investments in the U.S. and create jobs here.

Are trade deficits bad? Actually, most economists answer no. A big part of the problem is the language: *trade deficit* implies something the country owes and has to repay at some point, which is incorrect. As I've explained, the country ultimately pays for extra foreign products and services by selling assets. It's like you paying for a new car by selling some property you own.

Plus, we're buying many foreign products and services because they're cheaper. The largest part of our international trade deficit is in consumer products like clothing, furniture, appliances, and electronics. Since foreign trade took a huge upswing beginning in 2000, the prices of each of these items have plunged: clothing is down 4%, appliances by 12%, furniture by 18%, and TVs have dropped in price by a whopping 95%! In comparison, the prices of all consumer products and services rose 42% between 2000 and 2017.[17]

Buying cheaper-made foreign products makes sense; it improves our standard of living and frees-up money for purchasing other things. One study showed that access to lower-priced products due to foreign trade has improved the purchasing power of lower-income households by 62%, has boosted the purchasing power of middle-income households by 29%, and has made little difference in the purchasing power of higher-income households.[18] Lower-income folks benefit the most because a larger part of their spending is devoted to the consumer products most affected by prices reductions from foreign trade.

Yet there is a cost. Although almost all the studies done by economists show foreign trade increases income, adds employment, and raises wages in our country,[19] it doesn't necessarily do these great things for everyone. These are "net" numbers, meaning there are winners and losers, but the winners win more than the losers lose. Still, we'd like to know how many losers there are, and what happens to them.

Unfortunately, there are problems in tracking these numbers. Let's say a worker leaves a job at a clothing factory. There could be several reasons for this, and trade is certainly one possible reason. Maybe the factory is downsizing because consumers are now buying cheaper clothing from Asia. But another reason could be that the factory is replacing workers with machines, which could (or could not) be related to trade. Or, perhaps the worker left the clothing factory job for a better job, or maybe the worker decided to move to another town or state for reasons totally unrelated to trade.

Taking all of these issues into account, the best current number for U.S. job losses due to trade—using a combination of private sector and public sector (government) estimates—is between 3 million and 5 million workers.[20] Again, to make sure I am clear, this isn't a *net* number; it doesn't mean the total number of jobs has dropped by that amount. Instead, this is the number of jobs cut as a result of foreign trade. If the economic studies of trade are to be believed, then many more jobs were *gained* from trade (indeed, 12 million as cited above) than the 3 to 5 million jobs *lost* from foreign trade. But here's the rub: those 3 to 5 million workers who lost their jobs due to trade often don't have the skills needed to take the new jobs that were created from foreign trade.

Let me stop here just a minute and take a sidetrack into manufacturing. Manufacturing has been used as the "poster boy" for the bad results from international trade. But I bet you would never guess this fact: today, U.S. factories produce more output than at any time in our nation's history.[21] We produce different things now than in the past—more technology, advanced machinery and aircraft, and less clothing, steel, and TVs. We also make these things using less labor and more machinery. But the labor reductions in manufacturing which began in the early 70s have been due more to automation than to foreign trade.[22]

Now back to our story! We have made trade agreements that have helped consumers, widened the array of products and services available for everyone to buy, and, in fact, have improved overall economic growth.[23] But we have often forgotten the workers who lost their jobs as a result. It is true that the country has a program to help workers displaced by trade; it's called the TAA—the Trade Adjustment Act—but many argue it has been inadequate. Tough restrictions on who can qualify have resulted in less than half of the estimated number of workers who have lost their jobs due to trade since 2000 being helped.[24] Furthermore, several studies have found that workers being re-trained by TAA ended up earning *less* than similar workers not using the program.[25] Therefore, although numerous sources have estimated the gains from trade for the country resulting from lower prices, greater variety, and more competition have far exceeded the cost—by over a trillion dollars annually[26]—not enough has been done to assist the losers. This is the big problem with international trade; the winners have taken the benefits and run!

△ FAKE SOLUTIONS

When people corner me to talk about international trade, I hear two common comments. One says, "Hey, we're a big country with lots of smart people and resources. Why don't we just make everything we need and stop trading with other countries?" The other comment is, "I believe in international trade, but it has to be 'fair' trade."

Here are my reasons why these aren't real solutions. It is true that our country could go the self-sufficiency route, but this is like saying to each person, "Do everything yourself! Raise your own food, knit your own clothes after growing the cotton, cut down trees and build your own house, and use a horse as transportation." In essence, go back to living like most of our ancestors did 250 years ago. And actually, there was a PBS series called *Frontier House* where people did this! And guess what? Most of them didn't like it at all. While there's nothing preventing people from "going back to nature" to live, I think probably 99.9% of people (if they experienced the life of self-sufficiency) wouldn't do it.

The reason we trade with other countries is because we can purchase certain products cheaper from them than we can make ourselves, and other countries buy things from us for the same reason. If we gave up trading, the prices of many, many items would rise.

The problem with supporting only "fair trade" is knowing what that means. There is no clear definition for it. Does it mean countries can't have tariffs? A *tariff* is a tax placed on an imported product or service. Although tariffs have dropped tremendously in the last three decades, they do vary from country to country and product to product. But what if U.S. tariffs are lower than the tariffs of most other countries, and yet we still benefit from the trade? We'd still lose if the trade stopped.

Some interpret fair trade as meaning all costs, importantly labor costs, have to be the same between trading partners. This is absurd. The main reason any trade occurs, domestic or international, is because production costs vary. Countries with plentiful and easily-accessible oil, like Saudi Arabia, have a cost advantage for selling oil on the world market. And, incidentally, the U.S.'s costs of oil production have been falling with the use of hydraulic fracturing technology, which is one reason why our country is on the verge of being a net oil exporter.[27]

People who have studied computer technology for years have a big advantage over me in repairing my laptop. I'd have to devote time and money studying computer science just to begin. It doesn't matter if the worker is domestic or foreign. Complaints that it's not fair that foreign workers are paid less than domestic workers ignore lower costs of living and limited alternative job opportunities often prevailing in other countries. Then there's the complaint that foreign countries don't have the same working conditions and environmental standards as the U.S. This is true, although many of those countries have been making strides to correct such situations.[28] If this is very important to you—like it is to my wife—then one option is simply not to buy products made in those countries. For most things, there's a domestically-made substitute, although usually more expensive. If the government prevented trade with foreign countries as is suggested with the self-sufficiency idea, this would eliminate the buying options of lower-priced, foreign-made goods—which is not ideal for those on a budget.

△ REAL SOLUTIONS

Fortunately, in my opinion, international trade is embraced in our country. Polls now show that the majority of Americans support open trade, exactly the opposite of sentiments twenty years ago. [29]Consequently, I don't think the "economic self-sufficiency" movement will ever be very large.

Yet we always want trade agreements to give as much net economic benefit to the U.S. as possible. This was the goal of the Trump Administration when, from 2017 to 2019, it battled our trading partners—Mexico, Canada, China, and the European Union—over restructuring trade regulations, conventions, and policies. In the process, the U.S. levied higher tariffs on some of those countries (particularly China) as a way of getting their attention and convincing them we meant business. Previous administrations had also complained about China impeding U.S. companies from selling in their country.[30]

We are unlikely to ever have trade agreements unimpeded by tariffs or restrictions, but we can try negotiating the best deals. For example, two big issues with China have been the country's use of internal laws to limit access of U.S. companies to the growing Chinese market, while at the same time allowing China to have almost unfettered access to the U.S. market. China has also had particularly onerous rules affecting U.S. companies building factories there; one rule required U.S. companies to accept Chinese partners who will have access to the companies' intellectual property, such as private technology and processes. Most countries trading with China have long complained about this requirement.[31]

That being said, it is perfectly proper and reasonable for trade disputes between countries to be negotiated, with the threat of temporarily making trade more expensive. However, the ultimate goal should always be trade that results in countries being able to access the lowest cost products and services anywhere.

Perhaps most importantly, the U.S. needs a real solution that helps workers who have been harmed by international trade. Trade creates jobs in two ways: by expanding industries, and by generating new income spent by U.S. consumers. But there is not necessarily a correspondence between the skills of workers displaced by trade and the skills needed in the newly generated jobs. We need to remedy this.

Fortunately, there is a logical solution. If trade creates benefits for some people, and if those benefits are greater than the losses imposed on other people, then a simple solution is to use some, but not all, of the benefits to help those who have suffered from trade; in other words, transfer some of the monetary benefits from those who win to those who lose, but still leave the winners better-off than without trade.

To accomplish this, I propose a TAT: a *trade assistance tax*. A TAT of only one-tenth of a cent (hardly perceptible) applied to 2017's total import value of $2.9 trillion would raise $2.9 billion—more than three times what is currently spent annually by the Trade Adjustment Act.[32] This should be enough to revamp the program and make it more effective for trade-displaced workers. This amount should also be sufficient enough to help communities, such as the hollowed-out textile towns in the South or factory cities in the North, rebuild and make themselves attractive once again for families, entrepreneurs, and businesses.

International trade is a double-edged sword; the favorable side brings us new products we may never have experienced, as well as lower prices for common products, however, the unfavorable side creates labor competition, lower wages, and often lost jobs. In fact, some see foreign competition heating up in the future, with "tele-migrants" (people who live in a foreign country but work U.S. jobs by using the internet) competing with domestic workers without even leaving their home country.[33] So we need to be ready to enjoy the good but deal with the bad of international competition.

▲ SUMMING UP

Just like you and I benefit from domestic trade, we also benefit from international trade. Some products and services can be obtained at lower cost if produced in other countries. Likewise, foreign buyers benefit from purchasing U.S. made products and services that we are efficient in making.

The negatives from international trade have been exaggerated. When a country only gets credit for the value it adds to an export, the latest data show the U.S. only buys $238 billion annually more from other countries than we sell to them. This is just 1.5% of our total annual national income. Also, the dollars foreign countries accumulate from selling products in the U.S. don't just float away; instead, they are invested in U.S. assets like bonds, stocks, companies, or property, and these investments create jobs in the U.S. In fact, it is estimated that foreign investments have created 12 million U.S. jobs, far exceeding the number lost due to imports.

The problem is that those who have lost jobs from foreign trade are not always able, due to lack of training, to take the jobs created by foreign investments. Therefore, we need a TAT—Trade Adjustment Tax—on the retail sale of foreign imports to provide financial support and retraining of trade-displaced workers. A TAT of only one-tenth of a penny applied to the purchase of foreign imports would provide these necessary funds.

Chapter 9 Endnotes

1. McBride, "The U.S. Trade Deficit: How Much Does It Matter?"

2. Amadeo, "The U.S. Trade Deficit and How It Hurts the Economy."

3. Hoffman and Lundh, "'Huge' Trade Deficits are Smaller than You Think."

4. Dedrick, Linden, and Kraemer, "We Estimate China Only Makes $8.46 from an iPhone – and that's Why Trump's Trade War is Futile."

5. Sink and Mayeda, "Trump Asks China for Plan to Cut $100 Billion Off U.S. Trade Gap."

6. Bailey and Looney, "The True Trade Deficit."

7. Woodruff, "Who's Behind the Chinese Takeover of World's Largest Pork Producer?"

8. Dalesio, "Chinese Tiremaker Picks NC Site for Major Plant."

9. Burris, "Haier America to Expand Kershaw County Appliance Plant, Add 400 jobs."

10. U.S. Bureau of the Census, *U.S. Trade in Goods and Services—Balance of Payments Basis.*

11. Jackson, *Foreign Direct Investment in the United States: An Economic Analysis.*

12. Richards and Schaefer, *Jobs Attributable to Direct Foreign Investment in the U.S.*

13. Maynard, *The Selling of the American Economy.*

14. Acemoglu, Autor, Dorn, Hanson, and Price, "Import Competition and the Great U.S. Employment Sag of the 2000s."

15. Gayou, "A Trade Deficit Isn't a Mortgage."

16. Adinolfi, "How Much of America Do Foreigners Really Own?" As of 2016, foreigners owned an estimated 24% of all U.S. assets, based on $32 trillion of foreign asset ownership from a total of $124 of national net worth.

17. U.S. Bureau of Labor Statistics, "Consumer Price Index."

18. Fajgelbaum and Khandelwal, "Measuring the Unequal Gains from Trade."

19. Khachaturian and Riker, *Economic Impact of Trade Agreements Implemented Under Trade Authorities Procedures.*

20. Acemoglu, Autor, Dorn, Hanson, and Price, *op. cit.*; Kessler, "The Trump Administration's Claim that the U.S. Government Certified 700,000 Jobs Lost by NAFTA"; DiChristopher, "Sizing up the Trade Adjustment Assistance Act"; Scott and Mokhiber, "The China Toll Deepens."

21. U.S. Bureau of Economic Analysis, "Real Gross Domestic Product, Chained Dollars."

22. Cocco, "Most U.S. Manufacturing Jobs Lost to Technology, Not Trade."

23. Irwin, "Does Trade Reform Promote Economic Growth? A Review of Recent Evidence."

24. Vijya, "Broken Fever: How Trade Adjustment Assistance Fails American Workers."

25. Dolfin and Schochet, *The Benefits and Costs of the Trade Adjustment Assistance (TAA) Program Under the 2002 Amendments*; Reynolds and Palatucci, "Does Trade Adjustment Assistance Make a Difference?"

26. Office of the United States Trade Representative, "Economy and Trade."

27. *The Guardian*, "U.S. Will Become a Net Oil Exporter within 10 Years, Says IEA."

28. Song, Sha, "Here's How China Is Going Green."

29. Jones, "In U.S., Positive Attitudes toward Foreign Trade Stay High."

30. Swanson, "American Presidents Have a Long History of Walking Back Tough Talk on China."

31. Mendenhall, "WTO Panel Report on Consistency of China Intellectual Property Standards."

32. Employment and Training Administration, *Trade Adjustment Assistance for Workers Program*.

33. Baldwin, The Globotics Upheaval.

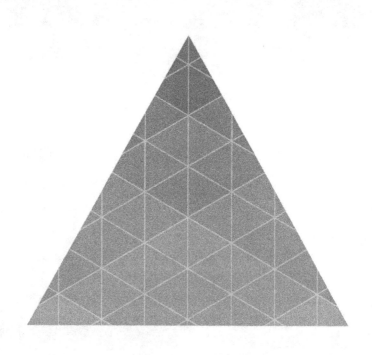

CHAPTER TEN

BENEFITING FROM BYTES AND BOTS

ECONOMIC ROCK STARS

Economics is not known for creating rock stars like other disciplines. In physics, there was Albert Einstein, Carl Sagan and now Neil deGrasse Tyson, all brilliant in their fields and, in the case of the latter two, academics who can explain complex subjects. In law, there is Alan Dershowitz, famous for the O.J. Simpson case and frequent TV guest on legal matters. And in anthropology stands Jane Goodall, known for her research and passion for animals in Africa, particularly chimpanzees. Perhaps the closest economist to attain rock star status in recent decades has been Milton Friedman, who had a regular column in the magazine Newsweek and several informational series on *PBS*.

But two English economists came close to rock star status in 2013, albeit fleetingly, with their research about the impact of technology on the job market. Carl Frey and Michael Osborne published a paper at the University of Oxford stating that almost half (specifically, 47%) of current occupations were vulnerable to elimination by technological advances in coming decades.[1] In short, robots and machines could be taking all kinds of jobs from humans, poten-tially pushing jobless rates into double-digit levels forever.[2]

The term for this "machine over woman and man" takeover is *tech-nological unemployment*, and it's not new. Just in the last 100 years, there have been two major technological transformations in our economy. One was on the farm, and the other was in the factory. While not all economists agree with Fry and Osborne's 47% predic-tion, the economic rock star duo did get the discussion started on how rapidly advancing technology could impact the labor market.

But before we go there, let's see what we can learn from past tech-nological changes.

△ TECHNO REVOLUTIONS

The first technological revolution in the last century took place on the farm. A century ago, the biggest source of employment was farm work,[3] and although there were big cities like New York, Boston, and Chicago, America was still a rural nation. The largest economic sector was farming, accounting for over one-third of national production.[4] Farming was labor-intensive and back-break-ing; plowing was done by having a horse or mule pull at the same time that someone pushed the plow, turning over the soil so seeds could be planted and moisture could reach them. Harvesting was also done by hand and sometimes, depending on the crop, aided by a cutting blade called a sickle or scythe. Harvested crops had to be hand-loaded into a wagon and taken to market, powered again by the indispensable horse or mule.

Both of my grandfathers were farmers for a time, and you could see it in their weather-beaten faces and tired walks. Farm women carried water from outdoor wells several times a day, hand-washed clothes, made all meals from scratch, and usually helped in the fields at harvest time. Both farming and farm life were tedious and physically taxing.

Then a technological revolution came to the farm: the development of the internal combustion engine resulted in trucks and cars replacing wagons and buggies. It became much easier and faster to get from farm to town and back. But the most important change was the tractor. The tractor plowed faster, more efficiently, and in much tougher terrains than any plow guided by a man and pulled by an animal could do. Later came combines which harvested crops, irrigation systems that watered plants during droughts, and many other kinds of machinery which literally replaced the personal blood, sweat, and tears of both farm men and women. The result was that fewer farmers were now needed as machines substituted human labor. Between 1925 and 1970, the farm population fell 70%, yet farm production doubled.[5]

Where did these technological-displaced farmers go, and what did they do? They moved to the cities to work in the relatively new industry of manufacturing, where employment jumped 350% between 1914 and 1970.[6] During the same period, when the farm population was plunging, the share of the population living in cities rose from 46% to 74%.[7] Former farm workers—both male and female—were now employed in the steel and textile mills, the vehicle and clothing factories, and machine and lighting shops. The transition wasn't easy! Rural people had to adjust to living in close quarters, and factory workers had to learn how to read in public schools. But the transition did take place.

The second great shift was technology coming to the factory. New machines and processes accelerated work through tools like assembly lines, mechanized drills, and laser cutting machines. Workers were still needed, but with the improvement in what each worker could accomplish in a day, not as many were. As a result, factory employment peaked in 1978, and even as manufacturing output continued to rise, factory employment did not.[8]

The decline in manufacturing jobs and the displacement of millions of factory workers occurred at the same time as the growth of a new kind of work: services. The rise of post-World War II prosperity led to many households paying for tasks rather than performing those tasks themselves. Employment surged in the repair of the growing number of household appliances. Increased driving led to new jobs in servicing vehicles. Women in the paid workplace had limited time for traditional household chores. Eating-out, once reserved for special occasions, became a regular family outing and set off an explosion of jobs in the restaurant sector. Add to these the millions of new jobs related to the expanding importance of education, the enhanced abilities of health-care, and the development of the entertainment industry, and you will see that the service sector exploded. At the dawn of World War II, service jobs accounted for about half of all work; today, almost 9 out of 10 jobs are classified as being in service industries.[9]

△ AUTOMATIC RE-SET?

Conventional economic thinking holds that technology will recon-figure job patterns but will not result in widespread and permanent unemployment. This is because the economy will automatically re-adjust itself.[10]

The re-adjustment happens in several ways. Changes prompted by technology in one area of a company's operations may create job opportunities in another. Retailing is a good example of this. Amazon and other cyber sellers have certainly caused some traditional "brick and mortar" sellers, like Sears and Macy's, to downsize by closing stores and eliminating jobs. But at the same time, the online retailers have created thousands of new jobs at their warehouses (which Amazon calls "fulfillment centers"). Other regular retailers have reduced in-store clerks but have added positions devoted to packaging and loading for buyers who placed online orders and then came to the store for pick-up.[11] Some companies retrain exist-ing workers they no longer need in one area for new tasks at the same factory or store.[12] In fact, one study by the Federal Reserve showed that even though cyber sellers have eliminated thousands of traditional retailing jobs, the new retailers have generated enough new jobs to almost offset the losses.[13]

Jobs can also be added if technology reduces the cost of making products. Here's an example: when bar codes were introduced in the 1980s by retailers, notably supermarkets, it was thought that this would lead to massive reductions in the number of cashiers, yet the opposite happened. Supermarkets become more efficient, and they passed their savings on to customers; Lower prices boosted sales, resulting in the number of cashiers rising over the next two decades.[14]

The same may occur for kiosks being introduced into fast-food restaurants for ordering. The kiosks will reduce the number of human order-takers at the restaurants (incidentally, my first paid job). But if the kiosks also lower restaurant expenses, then those reduced costs mean lower prices for hamburgers, fries, and shakes. Therefore, when prices fall, consumers can buy more. Consequently, the adoption of kiosks may cause fast-food companies to expand existing outlets and/or open new restaurants, both of which would result in more total employment, although the percentage devoted to order-taking would drop.

Lower prices allow dollars to buy more—it's the same as giving consumers a pay increase. If companies across the economy adopt cost-cutting technologies, then consumer prices will drop and consumers will feel as if they have more income. When consumers have more income, they spend most of it, and the new spending creates new jobs.

Last, new automation and technology create jobs even as they eliminate others.[15] If restaurants make widespread use of kiosks, some workers will be needed to manufacture the kiosks, others will be needed to install them, and still more workers will be hired to train others in the use and maintenance of the kiosks after installation. Using the lingo of economists, although kiosks will be substitutes for some jobs (order-takers), they will be complements for other jobs (manufacturers, installers, trainers, and maintenance workers).

Therefore, many economists pooh-pooh the idea of new technological developments being big job-killers. A 2017 report updating the Frey/Osborne 2013 blockbuster, and including Osborne as a co-author, estimated only 20% of today's occupations could face significant downsizing by technology.[16] Later reports have come in with even lower numbers—one at 10%. Hence, the fear of massive unemployment resulting from robots and machines may be overplayed.[17] Sure, there will be some reshuffling of jobs in the economy, but as far as 20%, 30% or more unemployment becoming the norm, forget about it.

Or, maybe not!

△ IS THIS TIME DIFFERENT?

We will continue to see new versions of automation applied in the workplace over time. For example, 3D printing is expected to be widely deployed in factories in the future. These printing techniques make products such as appliances, furniture, and even vehicles in one continuous process by layering materials to form them. The process allows almost unlimited possibilities for customization to meet buyers' unique specifications. Computers direct the production with little need for human workers, and therefore, experts think factories of the future will have fewer people working there. 3D manufacturing perpetuates the modern trend of substituting machinery for people; any task that is routine and repeatable will ultimately be performed by machines and technology.[18] So 3D manufacturing isn't a game-changer, it's just the latest version of the new way manufacturing occurs.

But there is something on the horizon that could be a game-changer for the labor market. *Artificial intelligence* (or AI for short) could be what makes the current technological transformation different from earlier ones. AI developed only because information (data) on a variety of products and activities is more available than ever before. For example, in my field of economics, researchers now have access to millions of records on consumer spending, investment transactions, household mobility, business spending and production decisions, and travel, to name a few. One project directed by MIT and Harvard regularly tracks *billions* of prices.[19] Economists study this information for patterns which can then be used to make predictions. In one application, analysts working for an airline might use their research results to predict how many more people will fly on a weekend if ticket prices were lowered on Tuesday versus lowered on Wednesday, and then use the answer to recommend a pricing strategy to boost the airline company's profits.

Here's an even better example: driverless vehicles operate using AI.[20] As the vehicle moves, hundreds of sensors collect information on the location and speed of nearby vehicles as well as the positions of curbs, lanes, intersections, and pedestrians. When a close vehicle changes speeds or lanes, the AI system uses its database of similar changes to predict where that vehicle will be in the coming seconds. This prediction makes adjustments to the vehicle's speed and position so as to avoid collision and continue traveling to the destination.

AI will have broader applications as its technology advances. Indeed, AI technologies might tutor school children, diagnose medical problems, make investments, and even cook meals (I would certainly be happy with the last one). Science fiction writers and film producers have even depicted futures where machines rule and people obey; however, this is far-fetched. I think a more reasonable (albeit less exciting) forecast for AI always includes human control. AI is no better than its data and its analytical models, which are products of human design.

The most popular way to visualize AI is through robots. I think this is because many robots, particularly those depicted on TV and in the movies, are made to look like mechanical people, with heads, arms, feet, and bodies. This is why we feel threatened by them—because they look like us. Yet my automated vacuum cleaner is a form of a robot and looks nothing like me; only our cats seem threatened by it.

The key for expanding the use of robots is to increase their dexterity. Most of us rarely think about how marvelous our hands are in their abilities to grasp and manipulate numerous objects of a variety of shapes and sizes. This takes the coordination of many, many muscles, tendons, ligaments, and nerves—it's an incredibly complex operation that futurists think robots will achieve.[21]

The range of human tasks robots will be able to replicate will likely multiply many times over: most of the jobs in restaurants could be done by robots, same for construction, manufacturing, and maybe even retailing. However, the impact on jobs doesn't stop there. Research shows the development of advanced robots could significantly expand the types of jobs and occupations these robots could perform.[22] Some say even STEM (science, technology, engineering, and math) jobs have been, and will continue to be, vulnerable to displacement by technology.[23]

This is why many observers think "this time is different," meaning the current technological revolution, which will inevitably destroy many jobs, will not be accompanied by enough growth in new industries and new occupations to replace those jobs. Some say it's already happening.[24] Although it may sound like a stretch, there are futurists who call today's technological transformations the "beginning of the end" of work as we know it.[25] Others have speculated that while AI and its most recognizable representative, the robot, are only doing what humans can do, the key difference is AI can usually do those tasks more rapidly and with fewer mistakes than humans. And so, the big question becomes whether we will gradually turn over more decisions to AI.[26]

In the 1930s, an English economist named John Maynard Keynes, who was adviser to presidents, prime ministers, and architect of post-World War II financial institutions, predicted that most human work would ultimately be done by machines.[27] The "economic problem" of people having enough resources to survive would be solved. He thought this would be a positive development because it would eliminate the great worry of survival and would give humans time to contemplate big philosophical questions. Humans would be freed from the need to work and could concentrate on widening their knowledge and pursuing their interests. It would be like being on a permanent vacation. A modern thinker, Yuval Harari, echoes Keynes' sentiments, arguing many jobs today are difficult, boring, and unfulfilling. He sees a reduction in employment as allowing us more time to fully achieve our potential as humans.[28]

Although I admire Keynes as a great economist and thinker and

Harari as a current prominent historian and philosopher, I think both have failed to recognize that most people need purpose in their lives, and for many, work gives them that purpose.[29] I'm also dubious that without work and with all our financial needs somehow met (Keynes was never clear on how people would live without working), people would devote their time to "intellectual pursuits." I could just as easily see people frittering away their time on video games, mindless TV programs, and even non-social behavior. Consequently, I don't think life without work is something to look forward to.

More importantly, I also don't think it will happen. Humans have the advantage over machines, as machines can only make decisions based on data and programs that humans have installed. Only humans can create and think "outside the box." Machines, by design, can only "think" inside the box created for them. Also, all decisions aren't just about data and calculations; subjectivity, judgement, and emotion are factors in decisions that only humans can provide.

In general, jobs with predictable and therefore programmable tasks with little need for human interaction or management are most likely to be taken over by machines. However, in contrast, jobs that entail unpredictable tasks, unique decisions, and considerable human interaction are likely the safest from being taken over by AI.[30]

Still, people want to know which specific occupations will be performed by technology, as well as those that will thrive even with expansion of technology. There have been many attempts to provide these answers. For example, the most recent study looking at the interaction between jobs and technology shows that the top ten occupations most threatened by technology include woodworkers, printers, metal and plastic workers, financial clerks, energy plant operators, fabricators, food processing workers, loggers, miners, and financial specialists, while the top ten occupations expected to expand include teachers, animal care workers, lawyers, engineers, stylists, counselors, librarians, entertainers, managers, and media workers.[31] Of course, it's much more difficult—if not impossible—to predict new occupations.

△ FAKE SOLUTIONS

The threat of job loss and the prediction of less work due to technology has prompted many "fake solutions" in order to address the imminent dislocations and dilemmas.

Bill Gates has proposed a "technology tax."[32] The tax would be levied on new technology that eliminates jobs, and the funds would be used to retrain displaced workers and support them and their families until they find new work. On the surface, a technology tax makes sense because it's a form of the winners compensating the losers. If new technology makes businesses more efficient and profitable but also cuts some jobs, then isn't it only fair that those who develop and use the technology pay for the job losses? Isn't this just like my proposed tax on imports to help workers who lost their jobs?

But there are more questions about technology and jobs than about imports and jobs. For most imports there are domestic substitutes, or near substitutes, so it's easier to see a one-to-one relationship between more foreign produced imports and fewer domestically produced alternatives. The link is less clear with technology. As I already discussed, all new technology does not necessarily eliminate jobs. I've already mentioned the example of retailing; despite the development of online buying, there are 3 million more people working in retailing today than at the dawn of the computer age in 1990.[33]

I also fear politics would impact decisions about what constitutes "job-killing" technology. Individual companies and entire industries will send armies of lobbyists to Washington to argue for exemptions of their machines and devices from the technology tax, leaving the politically weak to bear the full cost.

The strongest argument against the technology tax is that it would likely stymie technological innovation. Developing new technology is risky, and innovators have no assurance their ideas and plans will find interested buyers. Higher costs mean fewer investors. One cost factor is taxes, and economic research clearly shows innovation drops as taxes on innovation rise. [34]While new technology creates issues for the economy and the job market, few of us would want to give up all the good things it promises.

An extreme version of dealing with technology is preventing it in the first place. The Luddites in 18th century England tried this when they broke into textile mills at night and destroyed the looms that were replacing workers. Can you imagine a movement today to outlaw the next iPhone or iPad? I certainly can't. As a society, we are too linked to technology and the constant improvement of that technology. A modern version of stifling new technology comes from farming, where in the past (and even in some cases today) highly productive farmers were paid to not plant crops because plentiful supplies were depressing prices.[35] Most of this would consider this tactic silly and wasteful.

A related idea is to simply pay people not to work, thereby moving them out of the labor force and reducing competition for the dwindling number of jobs. But what would those people without work do? Keynes might say they would read the classics, engage in literary discussions, and appreciate the fine arts. I suspect people would lose their pride and self-worth.

A compromise might be "make-work" jobs. The government could create things for people to do and pay them. Presumably, these would be jobs the private sector doesn't find profitable. They would not be jobs the government already needs and pays for, such as those in public safety, education, and public recreation. While some say the government could always use more people in these fields, many of the unemployed may not be qualified for these occupations until they obtained extensive training and education. "Make-work" jobs could end up being like those from the movie (yes, again) *Cool Hand Luke*, where Luke is told to dig a hole, fill the hole, dig it again, fill it again, and so on, just to punish him with useless work! People might eventually catch on that the jobs they are given are worthless, raising questions of what this would do to their well-being and attitudes about work and the government.

△ REAL SOLUTIONS

Although I am asked countless times each year to predict where new jobs and occupations will be in the future, I'm honest by answering that I don't really know. I have hunches, and I refer to predictions from other economists and studies. For example, some economists predict new occupations related to producing, installing, and maintaining new types of technologies, in addition to new opportunities in personal health, nutrition, and aging.[36] But the economy is simply too fluid and unpredictable to make any job forecast ironclad. I also have history to contend with. Few economists saw the vast development of information technology (IT)—including computers, tablets, and smart phones—and the kinds of jobs and occupations that would be created from it. There is likely work going on right now in labs and research centers that, if successful, will create a wave of new businesses and employment decades in the future.

Should we throw up our hands and say, whatever happens, happens? No. Although we may not be able to precisely *predict* jobs, we can *monitor* what's happening to jobs, specifically which occupations are expanding and which ones are declining. This type of monitoring, if done on a continuous basis, can then be used to inform job seekers as well as educational institutions about available future occupations and the training needed to obtain them.

The *real* solution to successfully coping with the on-going impact of technology on the job market has four parts. First, each state should develop a process and plan to monitor actual occupational changes occurring in the labor market, which is information that has been sorely lacking.[37] Fortunately, there are federal data published each year for each state showing trends in over 700 occupations.[38] Online job services like LinkedIn can also be used to provide details about what employers are looking for in new hires.

Second, states should establish a formal process whereby the occupational tracking from the monitoring is made available to educational institutions, including high schools, community and technical colleges, and universities. This will allow the institutions to realign their training and educational programs in light of the real-time reality of the job market. As discussed in Chapter 2, states should expect community colleges and universities to periodically reallocate resources to reflect what's needed in the dynamic job market.

Third, higher education institutions (community and technical colleges, universities) should develop training programs targeted at adult students who need to change their career to a different occupation. I know I said this in Chapter 2, but it bears repeating: these programs should be quick, tailored to a specific occupation, and very affordable.

Fourth, the unemployment compensation (UC) system should be revised to assist in retraining. Currently, UC pays workers dismissed from their job a weekly amount for a limited number of weeks, with the funds used for living expenses. I recommend the UC be expanded to include additional funds for re-training. UC is jointly funded by both the state and federal governments, but I suggest that additional funding be provided from other federal sources as well. Assuming that 20% of the workforce will need to be retrained between now and 2030, and using average tuition costs at public 2-year and 4-year institutions, and then paying for two years of re-training, results in a cost of $360 billion spread over several years.[39] Using ten years as an example, the new spending would be $36 billion annually.

My plan should not detract from the likelihood that private companies will also step up and add their own retraining efforts,[40] which they would do for three reasons. First, they know the skills they need, and they know public educational institutions often move slowly. Second, by providing their own re-training, firms can more easily phase out old tasks at the same time that they are introducing new tasks. Third, companies can use the option of in-house re-training as a recruiting tool for workers worried about the impacts of new technology in the workplace.

▲ SUMMING UP

Continued advancement in the capabilities of technology will likely result in major changes in the job market. Some forecasts suggest as much as 20% of all occupations or more will lose significant employment as a result of technology and modern machines/devices taking the place of humans in performing certain tasks. But technology can also create new jobs and occupations, just as it has done in the past. So, while the outlook may be uncertain about how many jobs will actually be lost and created by technology, it is almost a certainty that technology will remake the labor market.

To successfully address this remaking of jobs, technological advances shouldn't be stopped—in fact, these changes can't be stopped! Instead, what is needed is a system that monitors labor market changes, communicates those changes to educational and training institutions, and motivates these institutions to offer rapid and affordable programs for workers needing to be reskilled for new occupations and tasks. An expansion and re-focusing of the existing unemployment compensation insurance program to help fund worker re-training is recommended.

Chapter 10 Endnotes

1. Frey and Osborne, *op. cit.*

2. Yang, "Silicon Valley is Right – Our Jobs are Already Disappearing."

3. U.S. Bureau of the Census, *Historical Statistics of the U.S.: Colonial Times to 1970*, Chapter K, Agriculture.

4. *Ibid.*

5. *Ibid*, and President's Council of Economic Advisors, *Economic Report of the President, 1975.*

6. U.S. Bureau of the Census, *Historical Statistics of the U.S.: Colonial Times to 1970*, Chapter P, Manufactures.

7. U.S. Bureau of the Census, *United States Summary: 2010, Population and Housing Unit Counts.*

8. U.S. Bureau of Labor Statistics, "All Employees, Thousands, Manufacturing, Seasonally Adjusted."

9. U.S. Bureau of Labor Statistics, "Current Employment Statistics." Service employment is all employment outside of farming, manufacturing, construction, mining, and oil and gas extraction.

10. Trilling, "Robots are Taking Jobs but also Creating Them: Research Review."

11. Corkery, Michael, "Hard Lessons Breathe New Life into Retail Stores."

12. Illanes, Lund, Mourshed, Rutherford, and Tyreman, "Retraining and Reskilling Workers in the Age of Automation."

13. Bram and Gorton, "How Is Online Shopping Affecting Retail Employment?"

14. Chui, Manyika and Miremadi, "Where Machines Could Replace Humans – and Where They Can't (Yet)."

15. Acemoglu and Restrepo, "Implications of Technology for Growth, Factor Shares, and Employment."

16. Bakhshi, Downing, Osborne, and Schneider, *The Future of Skills: Employment in 2030.*

17. Arntz, Gregory, and Zierahn, *The Rise of Automation for Jobs in OECD Countries.*

18. D'Aveni, *The Pan-Industrial Revolution.* D'Aveni also thinks manufacturing worldwide will eventually be dominated by a handful of international firms using 3D and 4D techniques.

19. Massachusetts Institute of Technology and Harvard University, "The Billion Prices Project."

20. Frey, *The Technology Trap.*

21. Knight, "Exclusive: This is the Most Dexterous Robot Ever Created."

22. Acemoglu and Restrepo, "Robots and Jobs: Evidence for U.S. Labor Markets."

23. Deming and Noray, "STEM Careers and Technological Change"; Berg, Buffie, and Zanna, "Should We Fear the Robot Revolution? (The Correct Answer is Yes)."

24. Acemoglu and Restrepo, "Automation and New Tasks: How Technology Displaces and Reinstates Labor."

25. Ford, *Rise of the Robots.*

26. Harari, *21 Lessons for the 21st Century.*

27. Keynes, "Economic Possibilities for Our Grandchildren."

28. Harari, *op. cit.*

29. Shell, *The Job.*

30. Chui, Manyika and Miremadi, *op. cit.*

31. Bakhshi, Downing, Osborne, and Schneider, *op. cit.*

32. Delaney, "The Robot that Takes Your Job Should Pay Taxes, Says Bill Gates."

33. U.S. Bureau of Labor Statistics, "All Employees, Thousands, Retail Trade, Seasonally Adjusted."

34. Akcigit, Grigsby, Nicholas, and Stantcheva, "Taxation and Innovation in the 20th Century."

35. Frank, "Why Does the Government Pay Farmers Not to Grow Crops?"

36. Autor and Salomons, "New Frontier: The Evolving Content and Geography of New Work in the 20th Century."

37. Council of Economic Advisers, *Addressing America's Reskilling Challenge.*

38. U.S. Bureau of Labor Statistics, "Occupational Employment Statistics."

39. National Center for Education Statistics, *Digest of Education Statistics*, 2017, Table 102.10.

40. Cutter, "Amazon to Retain a Third of Its Workforce." Amazon has already announced a retraining effort.

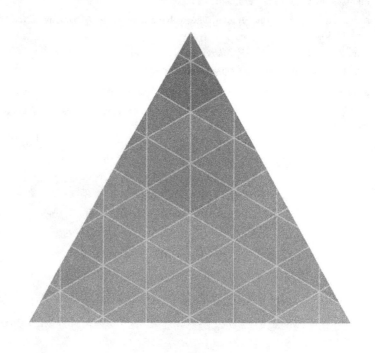

CHAPTER ELEVEN

PROTECTING THE ENVIRONMENT FOR TODAY AND TOMORROW

THE AWAKENING

A book was published in 1962 with the pleasing title, *Silent Spring*.[1] The author was a 50-something-year-old government bureaucrat who did research on fisheries. Who knew at the time that her book would set off a revolution in how we think about the world around us, resulting in new government agencies, new regulations, and the creation of a new term—"green"—as a permanent part of our culture?

The woman was Rachel Carson. For almost two decades she worked for the U.S. Bureau of Fisheries, and in the late 1950s she was one of many scientists who began documenting the harmful effects of pesticides on nature, leading to the publication of her work, *Silent Spring*. Almost immediately, the book became the rallying point not only for worries about pesticides, but for the broader issue of humans' adverse effects on the environment. Today, Carson's birthday is widely celebrated, and she has structures and statues honored with her name all around the world.

Many people may applaud Rachel Carson but also ask, "What took so long?" Haven't humans been doing bad things to the environment for a long time, maybe forever? Why is it that in only the last half-century we have been trying to do something about our bad behavior? The simple answer is: priorities. It takes a certain level of economic affluence and security to be concerned with matters beyond basic necessities like food, clothing, shelter, and safety. It may be hard for many people today to believe, but it wasn't until the late 19th century that these necessities were achieved for a large proportion of the population, and even this was only in "developed" countries in Western Europe and the U.S.[2] If your main concern is freezing in the winter, and the most attainable source of fuel is coal, then you are likely not worried about the pollutants coal spews into the atmosphere.

Plus, there's the matter of scale. Nature has a way of cleansing itself, meaning that a certain level of environmental damage can be absorbed without long-term harm.[3] Even though 150 years ago trains were emitting coal smoke into the air, and trash and chemicals were being dumped into rivers and streams, the quantities of the pollutants were relatively small, so there was no major harm. But as countries like ours developed economically and new forms of pollution were added from cars, planes, and factories, the levels of pollution rose exponentially to the point where cities were engulfed in smog and rivers literally caught on fire.[4]

Thus, there is a direct link between a country's economic success and its concerns for matters beyond basic survival, like environmental quality. We're seeing this linkage today with China; few countries in history have experienced the kind of economic growth as China has in the last two decades. Where it was an impoverished country on the verge of starvation only fifty years ago, China is now an economic superstar on par with—or maybe larger than—the U.S. economy.[5] For years, the environment was ignored during China's rapid economic assent. Wearing face masks became common in China. Indeed, prior to the 2008 Olympics, Chinese meteorologists used several methods to try to dissipate the smog engulfing the Olympic sites in Beijing to avoid embarrassment before an international audience.[6]

Yet with over half its urban population now achieving middle class status or above, the Chinese government has made environmental improvement a priority.[7] The country has quickly been developing its solar power industry, which is now the largest in the world. Moreover, anti-smog rules in cities have been implemented together with a public relations campaign promoting anti-polluting behavior.[8]

Other countries that have moved beyond subsistence levels are also beginning to address pollution. One study found a 10% increase in income is associated with a 1% to 2% increase for low-income households and a 6% to 7% increase for high-income households in their willingness to pay for a reduction in pollution.[9]

△ GAINING OR LOSING?

It's one thing to be concerned about the environment; it's another thing to act on those concerns. Concern is cheap—action is expensive. For over fifty years, we've been worried about the environment, but have we done anything about those worries? Has the environment improved, or does it continue to deteriorate?

Measurement is a key issue in answering these questions. A standard way to evaluate our impact on the environment is to measure pollutants emitted per dollar of economic production. Using this metric shows tremendous progress in reducing major pollutants. For example, carbon dioxide (CO_2) emissions released into the air are considered by most experts to be a major cause behind global warming.[10] As the world industrialized and expanded, CO_2 emissions per dollar of total income doubled from the mid-19th century to the mid-20th century. Yet since the mid-20th century, which corresponds to the beginning of the environment movement, world CO_2 emissions per dollar have dropped back to the levels of 1900. U.S. CO_2 emissions have fallen even more, but the prize for reductions goes to China, which has cut its CO_2 emissions per dollar by 75%.[11] There have been similar improvements for other air pollutants and water pollutants.[12]

This looks like progress, but is it? Even though we have been reducing pollution relative to the size of our economy, the U.S. and the world economies are much, much bigger than they were in the past. So, in a way, yes, our environmental footprint per dollar of our economy has been cut. But it is the total footprint that matters.

In fact, the numbers for our total environmental impact are not as good. Total world CO_2 emissions rose by an average of 1.3% per year between 2006 and 2016, although annual U.S. emissions fell slightly over the same time period.[13] There's also evidence indicating that total water pollution may be getting worse in water bodies with the highest concentration of pollutants.[14]

Are we therefore frauds for claiming to be environmentalists when the record shows otherwise? Not necessarily. Most people pollute, not because they want to harm the environment, but because pollution is a byproduct of something they value. For example, most of us pollute the air when we drive. (And as an aside, yes, I'm including even those who drive electric vehicles, because unless the electricity is generated from some renewable source like solar, wind, or hydro, the production of electricity for electric vehicles generates pollution[15]). Yet driving creates enormous benefits for us: driving gets us to work, school, shopping, and activities for our children and grandchildren. Some of us will try to justify the pollution by thinking our relatively little amount won't harm the planet. But when we aggregate all the little amounts, they become a big amount!

Reducing pollution is hard because, in most cases, it involves a tradeoff between the bad and the good. In order to reduce a bad (pollution), we also have to reduce a good (such as driving). Or, we can continue to drive the same miles, but in order to lower our pollution we have to buy a more expensive hybrid or electric vehicle, and even then, if the electricity is generated from conventional sources, our total pollution may not drop!

So here we are today, still facing an environmental problem with severe outcomes. Many link air pollution to a whole host of health problems such as asthma, stroke, lung cancer, and even heart disease.[16] Water pollution can cause rashes and liver illness.[17] Even more alarming is the association many scientists have made between air pollutants like CO_2 and global warming.[18] Average temperatures have been rising, and there are warnings of adverse consequences for sea levels, and the destruction of coastal property, farming and food production, wildlife, and habitats in some regions.[19] Total costs of these consequences have been estimated to be in the multiples of trillions of dollars worldwide.[20] The most pessimistic see Earth becoming uninhabitable.[21] How do we change the behaviors leading to pollution before it is too late?

△ CONTROL VS. CAJOLE

Pollution is a public policy issue that can be addressed in two different ways. One is a top-down, or control, method where the government establishes rules and regulations designed, in this case, to reduce pollution. This method appeals to politicians because it puts them in charge and allows them to take credit for any positive results. The costs of the approach are often hidden because they occur through increases in product prices, and companies such as vehicle manufacturers can say the higher prices are paid for by the mandated better fuel economy. Also, the control approach appeals to many people because it indicates action by the government. It is supported by those who think, if something is bad, just stop or control it.

The alternative approach is the bottom-up, or as I call it, the cajole method. This approach works via incentives. For a negative outcome like pollution, people are not simply told to cease polluting or to pollute less, instead, they are given a motivation to do so. Often this motivation is financial, like paying a fee to pollute or receiving money if pollution is reduced.

Most of the efforts to reduce pollution and improve the environment have been of the top-down, control variety. For vehicles, the federal government has increased efficiency standards (miles driven per gallon of gas), regulated emissions, and issued health-related smog alerts. Power plants, particularly those using coal, have to comply with regulations about the amount of chemicals, such as CO_2, they release into the atmosphere. Other regulations prohibit dumping unwanted items into bodies of water, which was common a century ago when rivers and streams were used to carry away garbage, chemicals, and even animal parts! Some cities have municipal ordinances; in Raleigh, for example, it is illegal to park a vehicle in an unpaved area, such as on a lawn.[22] The purpose of this is to prevent oil and gasoline dripping into the ground water system.

It is easy to pass these top-down regulations, police them, and see the results (although, based on my observation, Raleigh's law targeting parking on yards and green space is not regularly enforced). Polls show that people think environmental regulations are needed and that they work.[23] But businesses often argue that the regulations add to costs and ultimately increase the prices charged to consumers.[24] During the Trump Administration, the business community mobilized to have some existing as well as planned environmental rules rolled back.[25] Yet for the most part, the top-down, control approach of rules to improve the environment has been the go-to method.

Still, there have been some applications of the bottom-up cajole approach. A popular one has been financial incentives for purchasing environmentally-friendly vehicles, like hybrids and electric-powered vehicles. Here the federal government and sometimes state governments offer tax reductions to buyers of these vehicles that don't use the conventional gasoline-powered internal combustion engine. One version of this plan was the "cash for clunkers" program in 2009 that paid people to trade in their older, less fuel-efficient vehicles for newer, more fuel-efficient ones.[26] (It is important to add that the "cash for clunkers" program had an additional purpose of stimulating car buying to help the economy recover from the Great Recession, which studies show was actually not successful.[27])

Programs to cajole people into voluntarily reducing pollution come in two varieties. One is straightforward: put a price on pollution, and make people or industries who pollute pay the price. Conceptually, the pollution price is set high enough to entice people to reduce pollution to acceptable levels, or to raise enough revenue to pay for the costs resulting from pollution.

The second cajole program sets up a market for pollution and allows trading of pollution permits. In popular lingo, it's called "cap-and-trade," and it works like this: first, scientists determine the aggregate amount of pollution that is safe and acceptable during a given time period, such as a year. Second, this total is divided into individual units, and "pollution permits" are attached to each unit. Third, for any entity (individual, business, etc.) to pollute a certain amount, they must purchase permits totaling that amount, and if they pollute more than what they paid for, they are fined. If they pollute less than they paid for, they can sell their excess permits to someone else who has gone over their pollution limit. Importantly, the price of the permits is based on interactions of those buying and those selling permits, just as prices are determined in any other marketplace.

Both cajole methods—pricing pollution and cap-and-trade—are expected to spur innovation in pollution-reducing technologies and methods. Both methods create incentives for users paying pollution fees or for pollution permits to avoid those costs. In turn, this incentivizes companies to develop new ways of doing the same thing, such as driving vehicles or powering our homes, which generate less pollution.

There have been several cap-and-trade systems established both in the U.S. and around the world, including a new system in China and an existing one in California.[28] One problem is that some politicians lump pollution related fees and permits in with taxes, and use opposition to the "t-word" (taxes) as a way of heading off cap-and-trade or pollution fee ideas. In the noise of political campaigns, logical, reasonable solutions can be drowned out.

Economists generally prefer cajole approaches to top-down plans, as top-down approaches rely on government politicians and bureaucrats knowing what's best, even though those people don't have their own money on the line. In contrast, cajole methods put decision-making directly in the hands of those impacted and who are best able to weigh the tradeoffs implied by paying for polluting. Research conducted by economists show the benefit/cost ratios ("bang for the buck") are significantly higher for cajole methods than for government commands.[29]

While the rules, regulations, financial incentives, and pollution markets can be credited with reducing pollution, especially measured on a per-dollar of income basis, there's reason to think we need to go further. Although our air and water are, on average, cleaner than in the past, there's still the major worry about atmospheric warming caused by continuing emissions of CO_2. Also, all of our waters still aren't as clean as we want them to be. These are the next challenges in protecting our environment.

△ FAKE SOLUTIONS

Fake solutions for reducing environmental damage give simplistic answers implemented by top-down edicts. They also leave little room for alternative approaches, so they stifle innovation and outside-the-box thinking as ways of addressing the problem; they are grounded in a one-size-fits-all thinking.

One of the best examples of a fake solution to pollution was California's 2018 law mandating that by 2045, energy in the state will only be derived from renewable sources, like solar, wind, and ocean wave power, etc.[30] The state will completely stop using energy from coal, natural gas, oil, and nuclear sources. Therefore, the thinking goes, California will do its part to reduce air pollution, curtail global warming, and achieve harmony with nature.

Will it happen? I doubt it, and for four reasons. First, while coal, natural gas, and oil are all non-renewable sources derived from decayed extinct animals from millions of years ago, and while these sources do emit varying amounts of pollution-creating CO_2, nuclear is a safe power source. The problem with nuclear power is bad publicity based on meltdowns at three generators (Three-Mile Island, Pennsylvania in 1979; Chernobyl, Ukraine in 1986;

and Fukushima, Japan in 2011). While these meltdowns grabbed worldwide headlines, the fact that nuclear power has a very low accident rate compared to other power sources is ignored.[31] Three-fourths of electric power in France is generated from nuclear power, and incidents have been minor.[32] Sweden produces almost 40% of its electricity from nuclear power.[33] Consequently, nuclear power should be part of any future energy plan.

Second, the renewable energy sources each have their own problems. Wave power is still significantly more expensive than conventional sources to deliver the same amount of energy.[34] Solar and wind power are intermittent, meaning they only generate power when the sun is shining or the wind is blowing. To increase renewable energy production, large scale storage facilities (in other words, "big batteries") would have to be developed.

Third, the two most-used renewables, solar and wind, take space—lots of space. To supply all the country's electricity by wind power would require a land area equal to Nebraska covered by turbines. And to generate enough solar power for everyone, an area the size of the state of Maryland would have to be totally covered by solar panels.[35] Of course, these are conventional estimates; research from Harvard suggests the land demands for solar or wind power could be five to twenty times greater than previously thought.[36]

Fourth, the decree to eliminate non-renewables and go full-force with renewable energy sources by a specific year significantly reduces incentives for innovation and removes the consideration of tradeoffs. If non-renewable energy producers know they are being phased out, they have absolutely no motivation to look for ways to reduce their adverse environmental impact. Already in recent years (2005-2017), the quantity of CO_2 released through electricity generation is down 25%, mainly by moving away from coal and turning to natural gas generation.[37] You can bet this would stop if a California-type plan is adopted.

I'm not convinced California's all-renewables plan will ever be implemented. Some economists predict that once the plan begins, there will be a reduction in the reliability of power combined with an increase in its price.[38] If this happens, public support will fade rapidly.

The proposed "Green New Deal" offered by some national politicians goes even further than the California plan.[39] It would apply nationally rather than in a single state. Like California's goal, it wants a future of renewable energy replacing carbon-based ones. But it goes beyond state climate plans and attaches goals such as reducing income inequality, promoting unions, guaranteeing a living wage, guaranteeing quality health-care to all, and much more. Using tax revenues and borrowed funds, the Green New Deal would retrofit all dwellings for energy efficiency, expand funding of higher education, and create several new federal "investment" initiatives. It's as if all the nation's problems and solutions could be wrapped into one package centered on the environment.

Similar to California's all-renewables-by-2050 plan, the Green New Deal's energy plan will suffer from the same problems. On the non-energy side, the solutions are vague, simplistic, and, compared to my real solutions, counterproductive. Hence, I give the Green New Deal a double "fake" designation.

Another common fake solution dictates where we live. It's argued that living in dense cities is much "greener" for the planet than living in suburbs, exurbs, and rural areas because of reduced commuting.[40] Since jobs and residents are packed closely to one another, there is less need for transportation-based energies. But a comprehensive consideration of all energy uses casts doubt on this assertion. Factories and power-generating facilities that supply the products, conveniences, and lifestyles that city dwellers enjoy, as well as the energy that cools them in the summer, warms them in the winter, and keeps the lights and computers on all the time, are typically located outside of city boundaries. So while cities ultimately cause the pollution, they're not shown to be responsible for them.[41] When these environmental costs are factored in, as they should be, the "greenness" of cities disappears.[42]

And one more thing: low-rise dwellings outside of big cities offer some options for temperature control, especially cooling, that the high-rises typical of urban living can't.[43] Tall ceilings and attic venting, which high-rises typically don't have, allow hot air to escape in the summer. Also, opening windows on opposite sides of a home at night can allow cross breezes that reduce the need for air conditioning, and, in many high-rises, windows can't even be opened!

A popular fake solution involves our eating habits. I have a niece and nephew who are vegans, meaning they eat no animal products of any kind. They live this way for health and ethical reasons, and I respect their choices. But some environmentalists want all of us to become vegans or at least vegetarians by prohibiting the consumption of meat, particularly beef.[44] Their reasoning is that cattle emit large amounts of methane gas each day, and methane has the same effect on the atmosphere as CO_2. In fact, the same quantity of methane gas has a larger negative impact on the atmosphere than CO_2.[45] The U.S. Environmental Protection Agency estimates almost 10% of greenhouse gases—the creator of global warming—is due to methane gas.[46]

Would the only losers from such a policy be people who like a good steak or hamburger? Clearly, cattle ranchers would also be losers in this situation, and they would have to find other employment—maybe, as the vegans suggest, growing the additional fruits, vegetables, and nuts for a vegan diet. Yet there may also be some health downsides; while the increased consumption of salads and fruit bowls would have health benefits for many people, some research indicates that the complete elimination of animal protein from a diet can have negative consequences for some individuals.[47]

The last fake solution requires another dramatic change to our lifestyle; in this case, to live more simply and reduce our consumption and ownership of material things. Once again, I can understand the idea. As a society, we do use a lot of "stuff," and as globalization and automation have reduced the cost of this "stuff," we're consuming more of it. In fact, today in our country there is just shy of 1 vehicle per person (specifically 0.8 per person), which is double the rate of fifty years ago.[48] The number of TVs per household doubled even faster; it took only 35 years between 1975 and 2010 for this to happen. The only reason the number of TVs per household has dropped slightly in recent years is that more people are watching TV on their phones, tablets, and laptops.[49] And, one more—the number of individual pieces of clothing the average person has in their closet has increased by two-thirds from 1991 to 2015, despite the two reces- sions during the time period.[50] Maybe a reason why those clothes don't overwhelm us is that we throw 80 billion items of clothing, which translates to 70 pounds per person, into landfills each year.[51]

While some people will live a simpler and less gadget-oriented life, most won't, so this is a proposal that isn't likely to gain traction. Plus, like the requirements to live in cities and eat as a vegan or vegetarian, it restricts the freedom of people to live the way they choose. Now, I hear some of you saying: "But what if the way we live is destroying the planet? Is there a way to preserve our freedom of choice yet still make us pay for the harm we create with pollution?"

Fortunately, there is, so keep reading.

△ REAL SOLUTIONS

I'm in favor of free choice and also stand against pollution. Can I have both? The answer is yes, and the solution is either of the two cajole approaches: direct pollution pricing or cap-and-trade.

There has been a lively debate among economists as to which of these approaches is best. Mathematically, with the same information, ben- efits, and costs of polluting, the two cajole approaches will ultimately give the same results.[52] Practically speaking, pollution pricing is easier to administrate by simply applying a fee for the amount of pollution emitted. Cap-and-trade is more involved; after deciding on the allowable aggregate amount of pollution, permits must be issued and sold, the amount of pollution emitted must be monitored, and the market for trading permits must be operated. International coordination of pollution control is also easier with pollution pricing since the level of the fees can be directly compared.[53]

However, politically the nod goes to cap-and-trade. A pollution fee is clear for people to see, and many will interpret it as a tax and argue against it on those grounds. Cap-and-trade is subtler, and somehow paying for a permit to pollute seems acceptable to more people.[54]

But if I'm going to choose (and I get to do that since I'm writing the book), I would pick a pollution fee over cap-and-trade. A pollution fee is far easier to establish and administer, clearer to understand, and can be quickly adjusted over time as the conditions warrant. Here I'll outline a plan for a fee applied to CO_2 emissions, which get the most blame for global warming.[55]

A pollution fee applied to CO_2 has commonly been called a carbon tax. I'll stick with carbon fee because the word "tax" implies a cost to support the general activities of government, where the taxpayer really doesn't know exactly what they're getting in return. However, a "fee" means you're paying to get a specific outcome. Here, the carbon fee allows you to emit a certain amount of polluting CO_2.

Several groups have recommended a carbon fee of $40 per ton of emitted CO_2.[56] I'll adopt this fee amount and apply it to the three sectors that emit 80% of CO_2—transportation fuel, electricity generation, and manufacturing.[57] This means oil refineries making gasoline and jet fuel that emit CO_2, utilities generating electricity using CO_2-emitting coal, oil, and natural gas, and factories pumping CO_2 into the atmosphere during their production processes mainly due to using coal or oil would be subject to the carbon fee.[58]

Of course, don't think these producers won't pass some or all of the carbon fees they're charged on to consumers in the form of higher prices—they will. Using the $40 per ton of CO_2 fee, estimates suggest the cost of driving would rise almost 13%, electricity bills could jump 30%, and the price of other household products we buy would rise about 2%.[59]

There is an important concern about how carbons fees could impact foreign imports of products and services. Virtually all of U.S. fuel refining and electricity generation are done within the country.[60] But this is not the case with manufacturing, where almost $2.6 trillion of manufactured products are imported annually into the U.S. from other countries.[61] Imposing a carbon fee on U.S. manufacturers without competing countries placing a similar fee on their manufacturers (especially the ones that sell products in the U.S.) would put our manufacturers at a competitive disadvantage. The problem would best be solved by foreign countries also instituting a carbon fee for their factories. If this can't be negotiated, then the next best solution is placing a special carbon fee tariff on the imported products, or—as a last resort—providing some special compensation to U.S. manufacturers.[62]

There are three big advantages from the cajole method of a carbon fee. First, raising consumer prices for products with high CO_2 emissions gives people a direct financial incentive to use those products frugally. Drivers will reduce trips, increase carpooling, and purchase hybrid and electric vehicle options—all things that environmentalists encourage us to do, but now people will see a financial payoff.

Second, people paying higher prices due to carbon fees will naturally prefer not to, and as a result, they will be motivated to look at options and products that pollute less and therefore are more affordable. In turn, companies will have a strong motivation to make products as well as use inputs in their production process that pollute less. Thus, carbon fees are a great way to harness the inventive skills of our entrepreneurs and workforce to strive to provide what we consumers want, and at the same time reducing our harm to the planet.

The third payoff comes in the form of savings. With pollution being addressed through cajoling, the top-down control approach apparatus can be dismantled. We will no longer need the complicated rules and regulations issued by politicians and bureaucrats in the name of reducing pollution, especially when there's no assurance they even know *how* to reduce pollution. Wouldn't you like these decisions made by smart scientists and engineers working in company labs? Won't these experts be motivated by the big payoffs they could earn making commonly bought products with reduced pollution impacts?

A majority of economists think the cajole approach to pollution makes sense.[63] Some top public and private leaders, both Republicans and Democrats, have endorsed the idea of carbon fees.[64] Even the oil giant Exxon backs a carbon fee,[65] and the Trump Administration considered a carbon fee as part of their tax overhaul package in 2017.[66]

Does the cajole approach to pollution control work? So far, the answer is yes. There have been some experiments with carbon fees in Europe and Canada, and the results have shown that the fees can result in measurable reductions of CO_2 emissions.[67] Estimates of what would happen with a carbon fee in the U.S. show similar results.[68] But I have to be honest—while most economists believe a carbon fee will reduce CO_2 emissions, they don't agree on how much. Some researchers have calculated the carbon fee must be $600 per ton of CO_2 emissions, or fifteen times higher than I recommended, to achieve a significant (60%) reduction in emissions.[69] One approach would be to start small and increase the fee as needed.

So why aren't we dumping the long arm of the EPA (Environmental Protection Agency) and going with a simple, logical, and effective carbon fee? One reason is the success of opponents framing the carbon fee as just another tax. Another reason is based on the realization that the payoff to reducing air pollution (CO_2 emissions) isn't that we will reduce global warming and return to some earlier, pristine, environment; the payoff is we will avoid the potentially worst, catastrophic effects of continuing to warm the planet at the rate we are now.[70] This is a tough argument to make: that if I pay this fee, things will only be *less* bad in the future, and not necessarily better! Plus, it's always difficult to compare possible future benefits to actual costs today.

Then there's the question of the impact from carbon fees raising consumer prices. Won't this be a big financial burden, especially on low-income households? Any price increase on essentials such as gasoline and electricity will hit lower-income people more than higher-income people. This is because lower-income folks tend to spend a higher *percentage* of their income on these essentials than others.[71] So, measured by the price increase as a portion of their income, the percentage increase would be higher for lower-income individuals. Indeed, research done by economists at Colorado State and Duke Universities confirms this: the price increases from a carbon fee cost lower-income households a much higher percentage of their income than it would richer households.[72]

Yet there is a solution. It's a carbon fee with a "chaser," where the "chaser" is a rebate of the collected revenues back to consumers. This is commonly known as a "carbon dividend." Perhaps you are thinking: "You're a nutty economist! You want to charge someone to reduce pollution, but then give them money back! That's absolutely stupid. How will that change anyone's behavior? You're simply taking money from one hand and then giving it back to them in the other hand."

I'll let you vent because I totally understand this reaction. I've heard it countless times in my classes. But I have convinced thousands of students that the carbon dividend is logical, so let's see if I can convince you, too.

There are two main economic factors affecting how much of a product we buy, like gasoline for our car. One is the price of gas, and the other is our income. Drivers buy less gas when the price (per gallon) goes up, but they buy more gas when their income rises. Many economic studies have confirmed this.[73]

The average household spends about $2,000 a year on gas.[74] Let's say the carbon fee hikes the price of gasoline by 40 cents per gallon. Using a $3 gas-gallon price before the tax increase, and implementing the research findings on how many fewer gallons drivers buy when prices rise, the 40-cent price increase will cost each driver about $250 more in spending on gasoline.[75] Now, here's the important question: what will drivers do with the $250 that is returned to them?

Ultimately, the $250 check from the government does not cause gas purchases to return to levels prior to the imposition of the carbon fee. With the boost in gas prices, gas is now relatively more expensive compared to other products and services. Economic logic motivates drivers to be more frugal in buying gas and to shift their spending to comparatively cheaper products and services. Drivers will spend most of the $250 on things other than gas, which detailed studies by economists have shown.[76]

Would there be "winners and losers" from a carbon dividend plan? Yes, there likely would. Consider the results from a plan developed by a prestigious collection of former public and private leaders who formed a group called the Climate Leadership Council (CLC). [77]The CLC suggests sending each household a "carbon dividend" of equal dollar amount, regardless of income. The U.S. Treasury Department estimates the 30% of households with the highest incomes would actually lose from this plan—meaning the dividends received would fall short of the carbon fee they implicitly pay—while the other 70% of households would gain. And the lower the household income, the bigger the gain.[78] So most households would be protected from the higher consumer prices resulting from a carbon fee.

The idea of a carbon fee can be applied to other types of pollution as well. For example, nutrient runoff is a common type of water pollution where excessive nitrogen and phosphorous from fertilizers, animal waste, and household and industrial wastewater can lead to excessive algae growth that kills fish and contaminates water supplies.[79] A pollution fee applied to fertilizers, both household and industrial wastewater, and even to animal farms, would be complementary approaches to carbon fees for air pollution. The pollution fee would motivate innovations like recycling wastewater and developing alternatives to traditional fertilizers for improving the yields of farm fields. Alternatively, if it is decided that the bigger problem is the lack of sufficient wastewater treatment plants and facilities for animal waste control and treatment, then the revenues from the pollution fees could be diverted to spending on the needed infrastructure. There have also been examples of successful "cap-and-trade" systems for water regions, including the Chesapeake Bay.[80]

Since Rachel Carson opened our eyes, we've made great strides in reducing and containing pollution, but we're not done. Many say the challenge of our day is global warming. I won't settle the debate over how much of global warming is caused by us versus how much is based on natural climate cycles—greater minds than that of a mere economist will have to decide. I do know that as standards of living improve, concerns about pollution rise. Economists predict that worldwide standards of living will increase significantly in coming decades,[81] and maybe this will motivate us to act.

▲ SUMMING UP

Nations generally don't begin worrying about pollution until they have reached a certain level of economic development and have satisfied the basic needs of their citizens. Traditional pollution policies have followed a top-down, or control, approach, by directly restricting amounts of pollution or dictating the performance of pollution-generating products. Some groups want to expand these restrictions into lifestyle choices. A better approach that preserves both individual choice while simultaneously addressing pollution is the implementation of a pollution (mainly carbon) fee system with return of the collected revenues to households. This approach reduces pollution, incentivizes the development of non-polluting options, and shelters most households from any resulting price increases.

Chapter 11 Endnotes

1. Carson, *Silent Spring*.

2. Deaton, *The Great Escape: Health, Wealth, and the Origins of Inequality*.

3. Nagayach, "Do Polluted Rivers Play Any Role in Cleaning Themselves?"

4. Ohio History Central, "Cuyahoga River Fire." The Cuyahoga River in Cleveland caught on fire in 1969 from years of being used as a dumping area for discarded industrial chemicals.

5. Smith, "Who Has the World's No. 1 Economy? Not the U.S."

6. Ramsey, "Beijing's Olympic War on Smog."

7. Iskyan, "China's Middle Class is Exploding."

8. Gardiner, "China's Surprising Solutions to Clear Killer Air."

9. Barbier, Czajkowski, and Hanley, "Is the Income Elasticity of the Willingness to Pay for Pollution Control Constant?"

10. Pachauri and Meyer, Climate Change 2014 Synthesis Report.

11. Pinker, *Enlightment Now*, Figure 10-7, p. 143.

12. *Ibid*, Figure 10-3; Mason, "EPA Releases Report on Progress Made to Reduce Water Pollution from Non-Point Sources."

13. "BP Statistical Review of World Energy 2018," *British Petroleum*.

14. U.S. Environmental Protection Agency, *National Water Quality Inventory: Report to Congress*.

15. National Academy of Sciences, *Hidden Costs of Energy: Unpriced Consequences of Energy Production and Use*.

16. World Health Organization, "Ambient (Outdoor) Air Quality and Health."

17. U.S. Environmental Protections Agency, "Nutrient Pollution—The Effects: Human Health."

18. "Is Human Activity Primarily Responsible for Global Climate Change?" *ProCon.org*. An excellent summary of the debate over the effect of humans on climate change.

19. Lindsey, "Climate Change: Global Sea Level."

20. Nordhaus, *A Question of Balance*.

21. Wallace-Wells, *The Uninhabitable Earth*.

22. "Raleigh Leaders Approve Front-Yard Parking Ban," *WRAL-TV*.

23. Bialik, "Most Americans Favor Stricter Environmental Laws and Regulations."

24. Minter, "Why Business is Worried about EPA."

25. Popovich, Albeck-Ripka, and Pierre-Lovis, "76 Environmental Rules on the Way out under Trump."

26. Carty and *USA Today*, "Cash-for-Clunkers Bill Passes, Offers up to $4500 for a New Car."

27. Guilford, "The Obama Administration Accidentally Accelerated the Corolla Conquest of American Roads."

28. Center for Climate and Energy Solutions, "Cap and Trade Basics."

29. Nordhaus, *The Climate Casino*.

30. Rogers and Murphy, "California Mandates 100% Clean Energy by 2045." In 2019, New Mexico, New York, Hawaii, and the District of Columbia had passed similar legislation; Coren, "New Mexico is the Third State to Legally Require 100% Carbon-free Electricity;" Barnard, "Demise of Gasoline Cars? What We Know about N.Y.'s Ambitious Climate Goals."

31. Nuclear Energy Agency, "Comparing Nuclear Accident Risks with those from other Energy Sources."

32. World Nuclear Association, "Nuclear Power in France."

33. Goldstein and Qvist, *A Bright Future*.

34. Astariz, Vazquez, and Iglesias, "Evaluation and Comparison of the Levelized Cost of Tidal, Wave, and Offshore Wind Energy."

35. Jenkins, "How Much Land Does Solar, Wind, and Nuclear Energy Require?"

36. Burrows, "Large-Scale Wind Power Would Require More Land and Cause More Environmental Impact than Previously Thought."

37. Ramseur, *U.S. Carbon Dioxide Emissions Trends and Projections: Role of the Clean Power Plan and Other Factors*.

38. Nikolewski, "Can California Really Hit a 100% Renewable Energy Target?"

39. U.S. Government Printing Office, "Recognizing the Duty of the Federal Government to Create a Green New Deal."

40. Glaeser, *Triumph of the City*.

41. Day and Hall, "The Myth of the Sustainable City."

42. Drum, "Raw data: How Green are Our Cities?"; Oliveira, Andrada, Jr., and Makse, "Large Cities are Less Green"; and Day and Hall, *America's Most Sustainable Cities and Regions*.

43. Sisson, "How Air Conditioning Shaped Modern Architecture—and Changed our Climate."

44. Loria, "You Can't Eat Meat and Be an Environmentalist. Period."

45. U.S. Environmental Protection Agency, *Overview of Greenhouse Gases*.

46. *Ibid*.

47. Craig, "Health Effects of Vegan Diets."

48. U.S. Environmental Protection Agency, *Fact 962: Vehicles per Capita*.

49. "U.S. Homes Add Even More TV Sets in 2010," *Newswire*; Nededog, "The Number of U.S. Homes without a TV Doubled in just Six Years."

50. Bain, "American have Stopped Trying to Stuff More Clothes into their Closets."

51. Confino, "We Buy a Staggering Amount of Clothing, and Most of It Ends Up in Landfills."

52. Goulder and Schein, "Carbon Taxes vs. Cap and Trade: A Critical Review."

53. Hsu, *The Case for a Carbon Tax*.

54. Frank, "Pricing Carbon: A Carbon Tax or Cap-and-Trade?"

55. U.S. Environmental Protection Agency, "Greenhouse Gas Emissions."

56. Climate Leadership Council, "The Conservative Case for Carbon Dividends," and Nordhaus, "Projections and Uncertainties about Climate Change in an Era of Minimal Climate Policies."

57. *Ibid.*

58. Hollingsworth, Copeland, and Johnson, "Are E-Scooters Polluters? The Environmental Impacts of Shared Dockless Electric Scooters." Even electric scooters, used in part to reduce the rider's adverse impact on the environment, are associated with CO_2 emissions when they are manufactured.

59. Nordhaus, *The Climate Casino. op. cit.* Nordhaus' estimates are based on a tax of $25 per ton of CO_2. To estimate the results for a $40 per ton of CO_2 tax, Nordhaus' estimates were increased by 60%, the percentage amount by which $40 is higher than $25.

60. U.S. Energy Information Administration, "Weekly U.S. Product Supplied of Finished Gasoline," and "Weekly U.S. Imports of Total Gasoline." The U.S. imports less than 10% of its gasoline consumption; U.S. Energy Information Administration, "What Is the U.S. Electricity Generation by Energy Source?" The U.S. imports less than 1% of its electricity usage.

61. U.S. Bureau of Economic Analysis, "International Transactions." Data are for 2017.

62. Marron and Toder, "Tax Policy Issues in Designing a Carbon Tax."

63. "Do Economists All Favor a Carbon Tax?" *The Economist.*

64. Schwartz, "A Conservative Climate Solution: Republican Group Calls for Carbon Tax."

65. Dlouhy and Flavelle, "Exxon Puts $1 Million into Quest for Carbon Tax and Rebate."

66. Paletta and Ehrenfreund, "Trump Considers Value Added, Carbon Taxes as Part of Tax Code Overhaul."

67. Sumner, Bird, and Smith, *Carbon Taxes: A Review of Experience and Policy Design Considerations*; Pretis, "Does a Carbon Tax Reduce CO_2 Emissions? Evidence from British Columbia."

68. Davis and Kilian, "Estimating the Effect of a Gasoline Tax on Carbon Emissions"; Hafstead, "The Year of the Carbon Pricing Proposal."

69. Heal and Schlenker, "Coase, Hotelling, and Piguo: The Incidence of a Carbon Tax and CO_2 Emissions."

70. Global Climate Change, "Responding to Climate Change."

71. U.S. Bureau of Labor Statistics, "Average Expenditure, Share, and Standard Error Tables, 2017."

72. Fremstad and Paul, "A Short-Run Distributional Analysis of a Carbon Tax in the United States."

73. Bento, Goulder, Jacobsen and von Haefen, "Distributional and Efficiency Impacts of Increased US Gasoline Taxes."

74. U.S Bureau of Labor Statistics, "Databases, Tables and Calculators by Subject."

75. Bento, Goulder, Jacobsen and von Haefen, *op. cit.*

76. *Ibid.*

77. Climate Leadership Council, "The Conservative Case for Carbon Dividends."

78. Horowitz, Cronin, Hawkins, Konda, and Yuskavage, "Methodology for Analyzing a Carbon Tax."

79. U.S. Environmental Protection Agency, "Nutrient Pollution: The Problem."

80. Quinlan, Paul, "Cap-and-Trade for Water Pollution—Trendy, Hip, Glitzy, and Controversial."

81. Organization for Economic Cooperation and Development, *Looking to 2060: Long-Term Global Growth Prospects.*

CHAPTER TWELVE

SECURING SOCIAL SECURITY'S SOLVENCY

IN THE BEGINNING

A month doesn't go by that my wife doesn't ask me about Social Security. As I've already shared, she's a retired school teacher. In our home state of North Carolina, public school teachers are considered state employees, so she receives a state pension check each month. She could also be taking Social Security, but she hasn't done so yet on my advice. Based on substantial analysis, 70 is the best age to begin receiving checks from Uncle Sam, as long as a person expects to live at least the average life span.[1] And, without giving away any secrets, my wife is not yet 70!

My wife is a smart person. Even though math isn't her specialty, she understands the advantages of waiting to receive her Social Security checks. However, she still worries that if she waits until age 70, Social Security won't be there. Or that even if Social Security survives, payments will be cut way back. So, her attitude is, take as much as you can while the taking is good!

My wife is not alone in her worry over Social Security. A recent poll found almost two-thirds (63%) of those who had retired within the last ten years believe Social Security is running out of money. And an even greater percentage (78%) of those over 50 who have not yet retired think the same thing.[2] Perhaps even more concerning is that already half of Millennials, many of whom are just beginning their work career, think Social Security won't exist by the time they retire.[3]

How did we get to this level of concern in a program begun over 80 years ago with such hope and fanfare? The introduction of Social Security reflected the changing times of the health and the economy of America in the 1930s. Farm living was often multi-generational, with older grandparents living with their children and grandchildren and contributing in any way they physically could. It was considered the responsibility of the children to take care of their parents. But then manufacturing replaced farming as the major industry, and with technology in the form of tractors taking over the work of people, displaced farm families moved to the cities to be employed in the expanding factories. This was a different kind of work that older folks didn't know and often couldn't do. There was also nothing for them to do in the crowded tenements of big cities, whereas on the farm, there were always at least some chores older men and women could perform.[4]

Plus, people were living longer. Although the average lifespan in the 1930s seems short compared to today (60 for males and 65 for females,[5] compared to 76 for males and 81 for females in 2018[6]), living to 65 at that time was 20 years longer than the average lifespan had been in 1900.[7] And then, of course, the Great Depression hit in the 1930s. The country had never experienced such an economic collapse, with the nation's aggregate production falling 40% and unemployment hitting 25%.[8] Older people who had outlived their working lives disproportionately made up the destitute population.[9] Many were confined to "poorhouses."[10]

But weren't there company pensions to help older people? There were a few, but private pensions covering a significant number of workers came later.[11] Still, why weren't people farsighted enough to save for their own retirement? The answer is that most people were poor, barely earning enough to put food on the table, clothes on their body, and a roof over their head; saving was a luxury only the rich could afford.

The crash of the economy and the new activism of the federal government in trying to revive it made both the economics and politics of passing Social Security possible in the 1930s. But the system was not as generous as many might think. First, Social Security was never designed to be the only financial support for an elderly individual. It was meant to be a *supplement* to other support from family or work, and that intention remains true today. Social Security is designed to replace a portion of earnings, with the size of the pension based on earnings from a lifetime of work.[12]

Additionally, the initial age for receiving a full Social Security pension was 65—higher than the average lifespan at the time. As a result, in 1940, five years after Social Security's passage in 1935, only half of men and 60% of women lived to that age. This could be viewed as a diabolic plan by the government to limit pay-outs. However, those who reached age 65 typically lived for another 10 to 15 years. Additionally, the actuaries of Social Security knew that lifespans were increasing and that pay-outs would consequently increase.[13]

Over time, Social Security expanded. Initially, only 55% of the work-force in selected industries participated in Social Security, but today, 95% of the workforce participates, with the non-participants mainly being some teachers and federal government employees.[14] New groups were added for coverage, such as disabled workers in 1957.[15] Also, the generosity of Social Security was increased several times, mainly as a way of preventing checks from being eroded by inflation.

Yet Social Security kept its financial solvency by gradually increas-ing tax rates and raising the maximum earnings subject to the tax. As a result, it maintained a financial cushion, technically termed the Social Security Trust Fund, of several billion dollars. The Trust Fund declined in only five of the years between 1941 and 1974.[16]

After three decades of operation (1940s, 1950s, and 1960s), Social Security seemed to be in good shape. It had expanded to include more of the population, it had accommodated retirees living lon-ger, and it had even been able to afford periodic increases to allow pensions to keep pace with a rising cost-of-living.[17] Could anything go wrong? Unfortunately, the answer is yes.

△ WITH REGRETS, THE GIFT OF 1972

Inflation took off in the mid-1960s and early 1970s. Fueled by the increased military and social spending of the Johnson Administra-tion and the generous printing of money during the Nixon Admin-istration, the annual inflation rate more than doubled between 1964 and 1971. Periodic increases of Social Security pensions at the discretion of Congress were no longer acceptable. Retirees wanted automatic cost-of-living adjustments to protect them from the ravages of inflation.

Negotiations between the Nixon Administration and Congress produced this result in 1972, but with a bonus: not only would Social Security recipients see their future monthly checks automatically increase each year because of inflation, but all recipients would also receive a one-time *20%* jump in their pension. Presumably, this was included to make up for the past failures of pensions keeping pace with inflation. It's important to note that 1972 was also an election year, so the legislation boosted the re-election efforts of President Nixon and members of Congress. As a result of the bill's passage, the average Social Security recipient check was 22% higher in 1974 than in 1970.[18]

These moves, plus an underperforming economy in the 1970s and early 80s, imploded Social Security's budget. For eight of the next nine years (1975-1983), the program paid out more than it brought in. The Social Security Trust Fund was almost cut in half over that period, and it was headed for financial disaster. The situation was so dire that one estimate suggested pensions couldn't be paid on time beginning in 1983.[19]

The National Commission on Social Security Reform was appointed by President Reagan in 1981 to save the program. It was headed by Alan Greenspan, who later led the Federal Reserve for nineteen years.[20] Composed of members from business, labor, academia, as well as politicians from both parties, the Commission's recommendations were released in 1983 and were largely adopted by Congress and the President that same year. The most prominent 1983 reforms included increasing Social Security tax rates, gradually increasing the age for receiving full benefits from 65 to 67, taxing a portion of pensions when recipients had earnings from work, and adjusting the cost-of-living index to making it slightly less generous.[21]

These changes moved Social Security closer to a typical savings plan and were supposed to put the system in good shape until the middle of the 21st century (2050). In fact, a huge multi-trillion-dollar surplus in the Social Security Trust Fund was built up to help fund pensions for multiple decades.

But it didn't happen. The 2018 Trustee's Report predicted the Social Security Trust Fund hitting a zero balance by 2034.[22] Consequently, starting at 2034, Social Security will only be able to make payments based on revenues coming into the system from current workers. It's estimated that those payments will be 21% less than promised by Social Security.[23]

△ WHERE DID SOCIAL SECURITY GO WRONG?

So the Greenspan Commission was off by 16 years. Instead of Social Security being able to pay its promises until 2050, the Trust Fund will be broke by 2034. Some may say this isn't bad for government work, but for the 50 million people receiving Social Security, this is no laughing matter. To be fair, making long-run projections over long periods of time and involving many factors is not easy; I know because I've been involved in many projects attempting to forecast the far future. A big problem is how small errors in early years can grow to be much larger errors later on due to the power of compounding.

Also, to be fair, Social Security makes three sets of projections based on optimistic, intermediate, and pessimistic assumptions for determining factors. For example, consider assumptions for average wage increases, which is a key factor in Social Security's solvency. An optimistic assumption would be for fast wage growth because that puts more money into Social Security's coffers and extends its solvency. In contrast, a pessimistic assumption would be slow wage growth as that supplies less money to Social Security's Trust Fund and thereby shortens its solvency. An intermediate assumption about wage growth would be somewhere in the middle.

Most who track Social Security use the projections from the intermediate assumptions. However, examining the long run projections after the adoption of the Greenspan Commission recommendations show that the projections from the pessimistic assumptions were almost on-target with what has actually happened. They show Social Security's Trust Fund being depleted in 2030.[24]

The intermediate assumptions from the Greenspan Commission were wrong in several areas. They over-estimated general economic growth and, in specific, they over-estimated wage growth. One culprit was the Great Recession, which most economists didn't forecast, or, if they did, they missed its severity. A second culprit was the slow economic recovery for several years after the Great Recession. The intermediate assumptions also over-estimated the percentage of total wage growth that was subject to Social Security taxation; this is because a greater share of recent wage growth has gone to high earners who benefit from a cap on the total earnings subject to Social Security taxation.

However, the biggest misses were in regard to demographics. Fertility rates were overestimated. This is important because fewer children turn into fewer workers a couple decades later, and fewer workers lead to lower revenues for Social Security. The intermediate assumptions predicted a growing number of people reaching age 65, but the assumptions underestimated how many. But the Social Security demographers' biggest miss was the number of years those individuals would live past age 65.[25] Obviously, a retiree living longer past age 65 draws more from Social Security and thereby adds to the drain of the Trust Fund. The underestimate of the longevity of seniors is likely due to the inability to predict all the medical advances that are now keeping people alive longer.

I, for one, am not as hard as others on Social Security forecasters for missing the mark on the system's solvency. But my compassion doesn't do any good for my wife who is worried about not getting what she expected in her pension checks. Hence, what should we do to get Social Security back on a solvent path for another 50 years? As usual, there are fake solutions and real solutions.

△ FAKE SOLUTIONS

The fake solutions for Social Security span the extremes—from eliminating Social Security altogether and replacing it with private saving, to making it just another government program funded by general tax revenues. There are also claims that there would be enough money if the federal government didn't steal some of it for other purposes. Let's dig in to these fake claims and fake solutions as well as others.

Let's start with the argument that Social Security is solvent and that the government is simply taking some of its revenues and spending them on other things. The idea, then, is that if Social Security revenues were kept in a safe place away from the hands of politicians, everything would be fine. This is the idea of putting Social Security revenues in a "lockbox."[26]

This is a silly idea, and those who support it simply don't understand how Social Security really works. We don't want revenues collected from workers today—but not scheduled to be spent on their pension until years later—to sit idle. We want them to collect some interest, and so did the originators of Social Security. The original Social Security Act requires unspent Social Security revenues to be invested in U.S. Treasury securities.[27] Similar to a CD (certificate of deposit) at a local bank, Treasury investments (usually called securities) pay interest to investors until the investment (security) is sold or redeemed. It's a way for the Social Security Trust Fund, which stood at almost $3 trillion in 2018, to earn money for the system.

Doubters claim that U.S. Treasury securities are just pieces of paper because the money used to purchase securities are immediately spent by the government. It is true that the federal government spends the funds in Treasury securities. Indeed, this is how the annual federal budget deficits are funded. But it's not true that this makes the Treasury securities worthless. Except in very rare and unusual circumstances, the federal government has always made timely interest payments on Treasury securities and fully redeemed the original investment amount when it came due.[28] Most observers think this excellent track record will continue because a failure to make timely payments would make it difficult to sell future Treasury securities. This is why U.S. Treasury securities are generally considered the safest investment in the world.[29] Many of you probably own them as a safe part of your investment portfolio.

The discussion about Social Security's investments does open up the question of whether they should be confined to Treasury securities. With Treasury securities' low risk also comes a low amount of interest paid on the investment to owner of Treasury securities. Some have called for allowing Social Security to also invest in alternative investments, including stocks.[30]

I don't think this is a good idea for two reasons. Allowing Social Security to make investments other than Treasury securities raises the questions of which specific investments to add, and whether political pressure would be used to include certain investments. The issue of political pressure was a major worry debated when Social Security was originated in the 1930s.[31] Second, reducing the use of the super low-risk Treasury securities would automatically increase the risk level of the Social Security Trust Fund. I don't think this is something we want to do, especially for funds many are relying upon to pay a major part of their retirement expenses.

Another fake solution is to eliminate the requirement that Social Security be self-financing. So, if Social Security has a problem fulfilling its payments, as it is expected to do beginning in 2034, there's no problem. Simply have government funds from other sources, such as the federal income tax, make up the difference.[32]

This is a bad idea because it would change the entire purpose of

Social Security. It would move Social Security from being a self-financing program to another welfare program, where some people pay for others' benefits. The framers of Social Security, including President Franklin Roosevelt, didn't want this because they believed it would create resentment and undercut popular support for Social Security,[33] and I agree.

A popular recommendation is to eliminate the Social Security earnings cap.[34] First, let me explain what the earnings cap is: it is the earned income level for a person after which no additional Social Security taxes must be paid. In 2018, the earnings cap was $128,400. This means workers paid Social Security taxes on earnings up to $128,400, but for anything higher than that, no additional taxes were paid. The earnings cap is increased by the inflation rate each year, just as are Social Security payments.

The reason there is an earnings cap is because there is a tie-in to Social Security payments received by retirees; the formula determining Security Security's pension amount results in the pension payment being higher for retirees who had higher earnings while working. But there is a stopping point for this increase, and that stopping point is the same as the earnings cap. In other words, in 2018, someone earning more than $128,400 doesn't pay additional Social Security taxes because, once they retire, their pension amount will never go above the pension amount based on $128,400 in annual earnings. Thus, the earnings cap and the pay-out cap correspond.

So, if the earnings cap was eliminated but the pay-out cap was kept—as is the case in most of the proposals—Social Security would be moving partially to a welfare-type program. Higher-income workers would be paying more to Social Security without getting anything in return. Again, I don't think such a change helps the long-run support and acceptance of the Social Security program.

The last fake solution would eliminate some or all of Social Security and replace the discarded part with a form of private saving. After being re-elected in 2004, President George Bush proposed allowing workers to divert part of their Social Security tax payments to a private 401K-type retirement account, which would be used to augment the worker's Social Security pension in retirement.[35] He argued that individuals know better how to invest their own money, and their investment savvy would more than make up for what was lost in Social Security by diverting the money. Bush toured the country promoting the idea, saying he was willing to spend some of his "political capital" to get the plan passed. It ultimately didn't, and Bush failed with the idea.

There have also been proposals to go further, for example, completely scrapping Social Security and instead using tax incentives and other government help for people to direct their own private retirement planning.[36]

The political reality, as Bush and others have found, is that Social Security is still popular, and people are skeptical about the government getting rid of it. While investment experts may be able to show that individuals, on average, could end up with higher retirement pensions by investing their own tax money compared to turning it over to Social Security, there's no guarantee all would. Retirees seem to like Social Security, and for decades it has seemed to work. It just needs to be tweaked periodically.

△ REAL SOLUTIONS

What is needed is a new commission similar to the Greenspan Commission to hammer out a fix for Social Security for the next 50 to 60 years. President Obama actually tried this; in 2010, he appointed a commission headed by former U.S. Senator Alan Simpson and former Presidential Chief-of-Staff Erskine Bowles to examine the federal government's fiscal affairs. A big part of the work involved looking at Social Security. Like the Greenspan Commission a generation earlier, it included elected politicians of both parties and representatives of business and labor.

The Commission issued a report and was virtually never heard from again,[37] and even the Obama Administration ignored the report.[38] I think the problem was timing; during the Greenspan Commission, we were looking into the abyss. Social Security deficits had already been occurring for a decade, and no one needed convincing that the system was about to fall over a cliff. Now is different. We still have more than a decade before Social Security checks will have to be cut.

So, I predict that somewhere around 2030 it will be more obvious something has to be done, and that will be the time to form a new Social Security Commission to preserve its solvency for decades to come.

The big question is, what should that commission do? Many groups, commissions (such as the Simpson-Bowles Commission), and prominent individuals and thinkers have made recommendations. Many of these ideas are presented and analyzed in a fabulous publication by the non-partisan Congressional Budget Office, a federal office charged with tracking and studying all issues related to the federal budget. This publication, *Social Security Budget Options*, analyzes 35 alternative changes to Social Security and what each will do to improve the system's solvency through 2075.[39] The options include changes such as increasing Social Security tax rates, raising the retirement age, changing the measure of inflation, changing the Social Security pensions received by retirees (especially high-income retirees), and changing the earnings cap used for Social Security payroll taxes.

Each option will have its supporters and opponents, and each of us will evaluate these in different ways. From my perspective, I think increasing the Social Security tax rate and raising the retirement age are non-starters. Anti-tax groups will strongly oppose a tax rate hike, as will those who worry about income inequality because the Social Security tax rate is a flat rate paid by the poor and rich alike. Increasing the retirement age can be easily opposed as a stealth way of reducing Social Security's support of the elderly. I also think increasing or entirely eliminating the earnings cap without any corresponding increase in benefits for higher-income retirees will significantly lessen this important group's support for Social Security.

My preference is to focus on two changes which, according to the Congressional Budget Office, would together extend Social Security's solvency through 2075. The first would change the formula used to calculate a retiree's Social Security pension. This would be done by reducing the rate at which the pension increases with increases in the retirees' work earnings until the earnings cap is reached. In other words, higher-income retirees would receive a somewhat smaller Social Security check under this new formula. The change would be justified by the fact that higher-income households have been receiving a larger share of aggregate earnings in recent decades compared to when Social Security began. Therefore, richer retirees will still get a Social Security check, but just not as much. Social Security retirees with the highest incomes would see their monthly check reduced by around 20%.[40]

The second change I'd make is in how a worker's earnings history is used to calculate the individual's initial pension. Social Security recognizes that earnings in past years need to be adjusted by some inflation index to make them comparable to current earnings when developing an average annual-earnings amount. Currently, Social Security uses the inflation in average wage rates to do this. I recommend using the inflation rate in average consumer prices instead. If the intent is to put earnings in different years on a common footing for purchasing power, then the change in consumer prices does this. Making this change will improve Social Security's solvency because typically wages increase at a faster rate than prices. So, yes, this change will mean a retiree will begin with a slightly lower inflation-adjusted average-earnings amount. But the new calculation will be fairer.

So that's it. With these two adjustments, we can put Social Security on smooth sailing for decades ahead. My wife and the Millennials will be able to rest assured they will get a Social Security pension. Of course, like the Greenspan Commission, despite the best of intentions and use of the best brainpower, forecasts of key factors like demographics, wages, and the ups-and-downs of the economy are subject to errors over such a long period of time. So, at some future point—say around 2050 or 2055—we might have to pull Social Security back into the garage for another tune-up.

There is one more recommendation I have unrelated to Social Security's finances. It is to take Social Security out of the general federal budget and make it a stand-alone program with its own accounting. Of course, this is exactly what Social Security is and can continue to be with the changes I have suggested. In fact, Social Security was a stand-alone program outside of the federal budget until President Johnson combined it with the rest of federal spending in the 1960s. President Johnson didn't do this for logical reasons, he did it because Social Security was running large budget surpluses at the time while the rest of the federal budget was facing growing deficits. Adding Social Security's surpluses helped mask (at least temporarily) the growing red ink in other federal programs. Social Security is, and should continue to be, a self-financing separate program. It deserves to stand out on its own.

▲ SUMMING UP

Social Security has actually performed rather well for eight decades since its beginning in the 1930s. Payments were consistently made from revenues until the unexpected 20% jump in payments ordered by Congress and President Nixon in the early 1970s. The Greenspan Commission rescued Social Security from insolvency, but errors in forecasting key factors, such as longevity and economic growth, have put the system back in trouble. It is now predicted that Social Security will not be able to meet its promises to retirees beginning in 2034. However, two relatively simple alterations to Social Security's financial model—modestly reducing the rate at which the pension is increased for higher earnings, and changing the inflation rate used in the calculation of the initial pension amount—can put Social Security on the path to fiscal soundness for several decades.

Chapter 12 Endnotes

1. Konish, "If You Can't Wait Until 70, this is the Next Best Age to Claim Social Security Benefits."

2. Vernon, "Americans Fear Social Security Will Go Broke, Poll Shows."

3. "Half of Millennials Don't Think Social Security Will Exist when They Retire: Poll," *HuffPost*.

4. Altman, *The Battle for Social Security*, p.7.

5. "Life Expectancy in the USA, 1900-1998."

6. "Average Life Expectancy in North America for those Born in 2018, by Gender and Region," *Statista*.

7. "Life Expectancy in the USA, 1900-1998," *op. cit.*

8. National Bureau of Economic Research, "U.S. Business Cycle Expansions and Contractions;" and United States History, "Unemployment during the Great Depression."

9. "Senior Living History, 1930-1939," *Seniorliving.org*.

10. Altman, *op. cit.* p. 23.

11. Tehrani, "The History of Retirement Pensions."

12. Social Security Administration, *Understanding the Benefits*. There's also a question of whether Social Security redistributes income from richer workers to poorer workers. While the formula for determining Social Security benefits does replace a higher percentage of earnings for lower income workers than for higher income workers, since higher income workers tend to live longer, and because there is a cap on taxation of earnings, analysis shows there is no redistribution from rich to poor. Indeed, the redistribution may go from poor to rich according to Coronado, Fullerton, and Glass, "The Progressivity of Social Security."

13. Social Security Administration, "Life Expectancy for Social Security."

14. Martin and Weaver, "Social Security: A Program and Policy History."

15. *Ibid.*

16. Social Security Administration, "OASI Trust Fund, a Social Security Fund."

17. *Ibid.* Author's analysis of the average Social Security pension adjusted for inflation.

18. Social Security Administration, *op. cit.* Differences in the earnings profiles of those individuals receiving Social Security in 1974 compared to those receiving Social Security in 1970 can account for the difference between 20% and 22%.

19. Martin and Weaver, *op. cit.*

20. Social Security Administration, "Report of the National Commission on Social Security Reform."

21. Social Security Administration, "Summary of Social Security Amendments of 1983- Signed on April 20, 1983."

22. Board of Trustees, Federal Old-Age and Survivors Insurance and Federal Disability Insurance Trust Funds, *The 2018 Annual Report*, Washington, D.C., June 5, 2018.

23. *Ibid.*

24. Board of Trustees, Federal Old-Age and Survivors Insurance and Federal Disability Insurance Trust Funds, *The 1985 Annual Report*.

25. *Ibid.* This and the other comparisons were derived from comparing intermediate assumptions in the 1985 Trustees' Report with the actual results from the 2018 Trustees' Report.

26. Hilzik, "Disproving the Notion of the Social Security 'Lockbox.'"

27. Center on Budget and Policy Priorities, "Policy Basics: Understanding the Social Security Trust Funds."

28. Austin, "Has the U.S. Government Ever 'Defaulted'?" The exceptions were in 1812, 1933, and 1979.

29. Conley, "Treasuries are the Safest Investment."

30. Munnell and Tanner, "Should the Social Security Fund be Invested in the Stock Market? It's Complicated."

31. *Ibid.*

32. Brown, "Why Do We Fund Social Security Differently from Other Government Programs?"

33. Altman, *The Battle for Social Security, op. cit.*, pp. 21-35.

34. Bauer, "So Hey, Why Not Just Remove the Social Security Earnings Cap?"

35. Sahadi, "Bush's Plan for Social Security."

36. Bosworth and Burtless, "Privatizing Social Security: The Troubling Trade-offs."

37. National Commission on Fiscal Responsibility and Reform, *The Moment of Truth.*

38. Pethokoukis, "Not Only Did Obama Ignore Simpson-Bowles, but now He's Doing the Opposite of What They Recommended."

39. Congressional Budget Office, *Social Security Policy Options.*

40. *Ibid.*

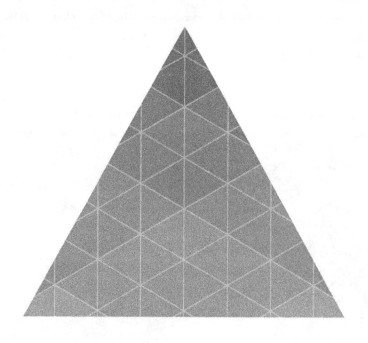

CHAPTER THIRTEEN

CONTAINING THE NATIONAL DEBT

WILL THEY COME FOR YOUR MONEY?

There's an old and all-purpose phrase in sports about star players, and it goes like this: "'name of player' can't be controlled; he can only be contained." This means the player is so good he will get his points or hits, so the best the opposing team can do is try to limit his scoring.

Many feel this way about the national debt. They're not confident we'll pay off the debt in any of our lifetimes. Maybe the best we can expect is to limit the growth of the debt and keep its size manageable.

These words aren't very reassuring to those who see the national debt as a major threat. When I do public talks around North Carolina, I get numerous pointed questions about the debt. Some of the questions include: will the debt bankrupt our children and grandchildren; will foreign owners of the debt suddenly one day want their money back; and perhaps the scariest question of all, will a government agent ultimately knock on my door and want me to pay my share of the national debt? The answers I give are often received with mixed looks!

Still, if you've gotten this far in the book and have actually learned a few useful things, hopefully you'll give me a chance to explain my views on the national debt. In this chapter, I'll address the questions mentioned above as well as others, including what the national debt is, how it differs from private debt you and I might have, and how to best measure the debt. I'll show (and please don't throw the book across the room when you read these words) that there is both "good" debt and "bad" debt, and how one of our goals should be to only borrow for the "good" debt and avoid borrowing for the "bad" debt. The discussion in this chapter will then directly lead to the topics of the next two chapters, spending and taxes, which are the ultimate creators of the national debt.

So, let's think of the color red (for red ink) and talk about debt.

△ A USEFUL BUT SOMETIMES MIS-USED TOOL

The development of financial institutions offering credit to users was one of the most significant economic creations of all time. Consider the situation of a farmer: he plants crops in the spring, raises them throughout the summer, and then harvests the crops in the fall. This means he goes more than half the year without earning any revenue. The payoff to farming all comes in the fall. So how can the farmer live while raising the crops? And where does the farmer obtain the money for equipment, irrigation, labor, and other essentials for farming?

The answer comes in the form of credit. Financial firms, such as banks, loan money to farmers in the spring and then receive the money back with a profit in the fall once the farmer's crops are sold.

Of course, many things can go wrong, such as widespread drought, losses to pests, and even severe summer storms. But banks know this, and with enough experience these risks can be priced into the cost of the loans. The point is, credit solves the farmer's problem, and loaning funds to farmers provides a nice profit to banks, even factoring in the inevitable losses due to uncontrollable events.

Here's another example. Caitlin and Matt are a couple planning for a family. They want to move out of their small apartment and buy a house, which will provide more room for them and their children. Owning a house will give them the security of knowing they can't be forced to leave a rental unit when their lease is up. Plus, buying the house will allow Caitlin and Matt to make the structural changes to the dwelling needed over time as their family grows and ages. The problem is, they don't have the money for the home purchase.

One solution is for Caitlin and Matt to wait until they've saved enough money to purchase the house. But with most home prices today easily taking several hundreds of thousands of dollars, this isn't an option for a young couple, no matter how frugal they are. Plus, if a big part of the reason for purchasing a house is for them to raise their children in it, then waiting years, maybe even decades, to save the money defeats that purpose.

The answer, once again, is credit. A bank, credit union, or similar financial institution loans Caitlin and Matt the money to buy the house. In banking lingo, such a loan is called a mortgage. Caitlin and Matt then make monthly payments—which are often not much different in amount than rent payments—until they repay the loan or sell the house.

Again, as with the farmer, there is always the possibility of a bad ending. Caitlin and Matt could lose their jobs, not be able to make their mortgage payments, and then be forced to forfeit the house to the lender. Or, there could be a crash in the housing market, such as during the Great Recession of 2007-2009, that reduces the value of their home to less than the value of the mortgage. This is called being "underwater" with your home mortgage. Many homeowners who were in this situation during the Great Recession simply walked away from both their payments and their house.

Yet while these bad outcomes of buying a home are possible, they are relatively rare. The default rate on mortgages is very low, usually between 2.5% and 3%.[1] And several respected economists consider the Great Recession to have resulted from special circumstances unlikely to be repeated.[2]

Here's the essential benefit of credit and borrowing. First, it allows businesses and people to move resources from the future to the present, and to spend those resources today when they are more valuable. Second, it aligns the payment of the debt with the benefits from the debt. By borrowing, the farmer matches growing his crops while paying for them. Caitlin and Matt will enjoy raising their family in their home for years to come. At the same time they are receiving these benefits, they will be paying for the cost of the house via their monthly mortgage payments.

But like most good things, people can misuse credit and thereby give it a bad name. While most households have credit payments they can comfortably afford, around one-quarter of households have too much debt or have related credit problems.[3] These are the

314

folks who receive the media attention. Lenders have a self-interest to evaluate borrowers' ability to repay loans for the simple reason that they lose too if payments are missed or never made. But psychology can get in the way of this logic, especially when everyone is optimistic about the economic future. A general belief that the housing price boom of the early 2000s would continue, and bail out any borrower no matter how reckless they had been with debt, was certainly a big factor leading to the ultimate crash of the housing market during the Great Recession.[4]

△ IS GOVERNMENT DEBT DIFFERENT?

It's often easy to understand issues in the larger economy by expressing them in personal terms. Many people like to think about government debt as they would their own personal debt. Most of us who have debt, whether from a home, vehicle, or college costs, want to eventually re-pay it. In fact, we're forced to repay it because most debts have a term (I like to call it a "fuse") at which time we must make the last payment and retire the debt.

Indeed, there's a typical pattern of debt over the lifetime of a household. Let's pick up with Caitlin and Matt again. When the couple is young and just beginning their careers and families, they have many needs (home, vehicles, appliances, furniture) but little money. In order to meet their needs, they borrow. Those needs have their highest value now as Caitlin and Matt are raising their children and building their careers. As Caitlin and Matt age, become more prosperous in their careers and earnings, and as their children grow and ultimately become self-sufficient (so they hope!), more resources can be devoted to paying off debts with the goal of being debt-free in retirement. The statistics clearly show this pattern: debt is highest for 20-35 year-olds, more modest for 35-55 year-olds, and lowest for those over 55 years of age.[5]

However, the government can't be equated to a household. Government does not go through a life cycle of youth, middle-age, and old-age. There is not a death of government unless there's a political revolution or overthrow of the government by a foreign power. Government is multi-generational with an unlimited lifespan. Since there is not an end to government—just as there is not an end to our country and society—government does not have to pay all its debts and become debt-free.

Does this mean government can just borrow, borrow, and borrow with no worry of the consequences? How do we know when the amount of government debt is too high? What is the best way to measure the real cost of the debt? Read on!

△ THE REAL COST OF DEBT

When we hear the debt of the U.S. government, usually referred to as the "national debt," is $21 trillion, most of us let out a gasp.[6] We can't conceive of that amount of money. Most of us can't even comprehend $1 trillion, $1 billion, or even $1 million. So, with $21 trillion in government debt, our brains tell us that amount certainly has to bankrupt us soon.

Yet here's the story I tell my students to convince them that the dollar amount of the debt isn't the best measure. Say you make a new friend—we'll call him Tom. You and Tom have lunch one day, and the conversation turns to personal finances. You tell Tom that you've been working hard to pay off your home mortgage by making double payments each month. And, with a smile, you add that within five years you'll be debt free.

Tom congratulates you and then lets it drop that his personal debt is currently $1 million. Your mouth opens in amazement, and you immediately think you need to pick up the tab for lunch. Tom notices your dismay, and then quickly adds that his annual income averages around $5 million. Now you're thinking two things: lunch is on Tom, and you want to keep him as a friend.

What changed your attitude about Tom's debt? Easy. You did a simple calculation that Tom's debt is only 20% ($1 million/$5 million) of his annual income. Even with your hard work at reducing debt, your debt is still 33% of your annual income. In fact, for the average U.S. household, the debt-to-income ratio is close to 89%.[7]

Let's therefore look at the ratio of government debt to national income (the income earned by everyone in the country for a year, also known as GDP, or *gross domestic product*) for the U.S. I call this ratio the "relative debt load," because it measures the debt relative to national income. Currently, the relative debt load stands at 105%. This is not an all-time high either, which actually occurred the year after World War II ended, peaking at 119%. But since hitting a record low of 32% in 1981, the relative debt load has steadily crept upward.[8]

We're not alone with relatively high government debt loads. Italy, Portugal, and Singapore all have debt loads larger than ours, and

Belgium, France, and Spain are in our neighborhood.[9] The prize for the highest debt load goes to Japan, where the national debt as a percentage of GDP is 253%![10] Of course, these ratios don't justify our relative levels of debt, but they do put our debt into perspective and suggest that government debt is not an issue confined to the U.S.

The dollar value of the U.S. national debt doubled between 2008 and 2016, and the relative debt load also jumped from 68% to 105%. [11]Did you hear much about these trends during the 2012 and 2016 presidential elections? No, there was barely a mention. That's because what matters most to anyone in debt, whether they're a person, business, or government, is the relative "carrying cost" of the debt, which is the periodic payment on the debt as a percent of the debtor's income. The carrying cost is determined not only by the amount of debt, but also by the interest rate charged on the debt.

Think again about Caitlin and Matt buying a house. If they borrow $200,000 and the interest rate is 5% and the borrowing term is 30 years, their monthly payments are $1,073. But if the interest rate is 3%, the same payment will allow them to borrow $255,000. Lower interest rates make debt more affordable.

Between 2008 and 2016, and while the national debt was doubling, interest rates were plunging like a rock. In 2008, it cost the federal government 4% to borrow money; in 2016 the interest rate was only 1.4%.[12] Here's the amazing result: the federal government's interest charges on the national debt as a percent of national income (GDP) actually dropped from 1.7% in 2008 and 1.3% in 2016! In fact, the interest charges relative to GDP were lower in 2016 than they were in 1981 when the debt-to-GDP ratio hit an all-time low.[13] This is why there was no hue and cry about the doubling of the debt amount between 2008 and 2016. And, in case you're wondering, the federal government doesn't set the interest rate it pays on the debt. That rate is set from the interaction between borrowers and savers.

But that was then. We were in an unusual interest rate environment due to the Great Recession and relatively slow economic recovery. When economic times are weak, interest rates are usually low. The Federal Reserve, which has some degree of control over rates, keeps rates low during bad times in an effort to stimulate borrowing and spending. In fact, the Federal Reserve's key interest rate was kept near 0% from 2009 through 2015.[14] Borrowing money during that time was essentially free!

By 2018, however, interest rates had begun returning to more normal levels, and as they continue to do so, the cost of financing the national debt will increase. Plus, if federal borrowing continues as it is now, there will be the double whammy of more borrowing financed at higher rates. The non-partisan Congressional Budget Office predicts that interest payments on the national debt as a percentage of national income will steadily rise to 6% of GDP by mid-century, which is double the previous high level in 1990.[15] Even more troubling, interest payments will take 21 cents out of each dollar of federal spending in 2048, compared to only 6 cents in 2018.[16]

This, then, is the real cost of a rising national debt. It takes away resources that could be spent in other parts of the federal budget or in other private uses.

There is a possible second cost of the debt, which is the impact of increases in federal borrowing on the level of interest rates. There's a worry that government borrowing will ultimately increase interest rates, thereby making it more difficult for everyone to borrow. The reasoning is simple economics: the more borrowers there are for a given amount of loanable funds, the higher lenders can charge for that borrowing. When it's a "seller's market" for borrowing, meaning the desire to borrow is increasing faster than the funds are available for borrowing, the price of borrowing—the interest rate—rises. It's the same reason home prices rise when there are more buyers than there are homes for sale.

This potential impact of government borrowing on interest rates has been a concern for a long time. Recent studies cited by none other than the Federal Reserve show that more government borrowing is linked to higher interest rates. The problem is that the results of the studies are not consistent; some show interest rates rising a lot, and others show them increasing very little.[17]

△ PHONY THREATS FROM DEBT

There are many concerns about the government debt, which I know because I usually hear them at many of the presentations I give each year on the economy. Here I'll discuss three of the main concerns and see if they're myths or not.

The first fear is that at some point in the future the government will require each of us to pay our share of the national debt. Today, that would translate to over $36,000 for every person, including children. I've had people tell me they are just bracing themselves for getting a "pay-up" letter in the mail someday.

Let's see, how can I respond and leave no doubt about what I mean? Let's try this: THIS IS NOT GOING TO HAPPEN! The federal government will not liquidate the national debt by sending each of us a bill for our part. If something calamitous were to happen such that the federal government couldn't pay interest on the debt and couldn't redeem debt issues when they came due, it would be the holders of the debt who would lose. And, incidentally, the majority of the U.S. debt is held by government agencies such as the Federal Reserve, state and local government pensions, and investors like you and me.[18] So many of us do want the federal government to continue paying its bills.

A related worry is that the debt will get so big as to financially overwhelm our children and grandchildren. Technically, this is actually possible. The annual interest costs of the debt, which are similar to the interest costs on a home mortgage or car loan, could become so large as to prompt a big tax increase or cause large reductions in other government spending. To me, this is the main reason we need to logically think about the debt and the expenditures we finance with the debt. Rest assured, I'll do this later in the chapter.

Then there's distress that foreign holders of our debt can potentially harm our country by threatening to demand full payment on the loans they have made to the U.S. For example, China currently (2018) holds $1.1 trillion dollars of the total $21 trillion U.S. government debt.[19] The worry is, if China wants the U.S. to do something in foreign affairs and we balk, can't China demand the U.S. immediately pay back the $1.1 trillion we've borrowed from them?

The answer again is a big NO. Consumer loans, such as an auto loan or a home mortgage, have a stated term, at which time the loan must be repaid. U.S. Treasury securities, which are the investments the federal government uses to borrow money, also have a stated term. Hence, any foreign or domestic holder of Treasury securities can't just say, "I want my money back." They have to abide by the term stated on the security.

Foreign owners, as well as domestic ones, do have an alternative; they can always sell the Treasury securities before the end of their term. What would prevent China from trying to hurt the U.S. by selling their $1.1trillion of Treasury securities?

While China could certainly do this, it wouldn't necessarily hurt the U.S. Actually, if China were to dump all their U.S. Treasury securities in the open market, it would hurt them! There are many willing foreign and domestic buyers for U.S. Treasury securities because they have always been considered to be the safest investment in the world. So, the U.S. would still keep the money it borrowed. But China would lose because they would sell the securities at a loss. This is because, with more Treasury securities being sold in the financial marketplace, the price of the now amply available Treasury securities would drop, and China—not the U.S.—would suffer the loss from the price fall.

△ WILL THE REAL SIZE OF THE NATIONAL DEBT PLEASE STAND UP?

Before I talk about both fake and real solutions to the national debt, there's a fundamental question that must be answered: how big is the debt? Any number is big, but is the real number big, or is it really, really, really big?

The official size of the national debt—a.k.a., the outstanding amount of money owed by the federal government—was just shy of $21 trillion in 2018.[20] However, about $6 trillion of this debt was held by government agencies, mainly Social Security, so some people don't count this part because they claim it is the government owing itself.[21] I disagree for two reasons, the major reason being that Social Security has been instructed to invest any surpluses it has into U.S. Treasury Securities (as a reminder, these are the financial instruments used to fund the national debt). Because they are considered the safest investments in the world, investors know they will receive their initial money back plus interest, so we certainly want to count this debt as an obligation of the federal government.

And secondly, if you recall in the last chapter, I want to pull Social Security out of the federal budget and treat it as a stand-alone pension program, which was the original intent of Social Security's founders in the 1930s. Therefore, from an accounting approach, the federal government's debt obligations to Social Security should be treated just like their debt obligations to other investors, like you, me, or China!

There are other people who want to go in the opposite direction on the national debt and argue it is much, much bigger than the $21 trillion in 2018. Again, remember that the Social Security System has made promises of payments to recipients based on their income and years in retirement. I discussed how, with no changes, Social Security won't be able to meet these obligations from their projected revenues. These unmet obligations are called *unfunded liabilities*, and there are examples of this from other programs, such as Medicare. Some analysts want to include the total of these projected unfunded liabilities over the next several years (75 years is often used) as money the federal government will have to borrow, and this is added to the national debt.

When these calculations are done, the increase in the national debt is staggering, rising to close to $100 trillion or even $200 trillion.[22] Although I understand the methodology, I disagree with the logic; while the $21 million is money the feds have already borrowed and promised to repay, the so-called unfunded liabilities are estimates of *potential* future borrowing. The federal government can make changes to eliminate these unfunded liabilities, as I have shown with Social Security. Or, the federal government could simply ignore the liabilities and not fund them.

Either way, the $21 trillion "official" national debt is a legally binding commitment, while the unfunded liabilities amount is not. They are not equivalent and should never be combined, period![23]

△ FAKE SOLUTIONS

The most popular fake solution to federal borrowing is implementing a requirement, possibly in the form of a constitutional amendment, that the federal budget be balanced each year. Spending in any year is never to exceed revenues in the same year. Borrowing to fund the federal government would be prohibited.

Certainly, the idea has a nice ring to it. After all, 49 states have the same requirement (Vermont is the hold-out), so if it's good enough for the states, shouldn't it be good enough for the feds? If politicians can't refrain from borrowing and plunging the country into debt, then let's simply make it impossible for them to do it. If the requirement is in the form of a constitutional amendment, then it would have to go through the process of having enough states support it, which may take years, but it's been done before, and wouldn't it be worth it?

There are some forms of the balanced budget amendment allowing exceptions to the requirement that spending can never exceed government revenues. The two most common are in the case of war and when an economic recession occurs.[24] Pandemics, such as the coronavirus pandemic of 2020, will likely be added as a third exception in future proposals. Wars, recessions, and pandemics are considered extraordinary events requiring additional spending by the government. Past proposals with the war and recession exceptions usually include conditions that must be met to indicate a recession is occurring or a war has been authorized.

There are two big problems with the balanced budget amendment or requirement. First is the assertion that states (again, except for Vermont) require a balanced budget and therefore never borrow money. States do require a balanced budget for a portion of their spending, but not for *all* spending. I'll talk about this in more depth later.

Second, the balanced budget amendment or requirement ignores the positives from borrowing, specifically the benefit of building a long-lasting project today which will produce benefits for the borrower over many years in the future. The requirement assumes that all borrowing and all debt are bad, which, as I've already illustrated, is simply not true.

A second fake solution indirectly controls federal borrowing by controlling federal spending. One popular plan limits annual increases in federal spending to the previous year's inflation rate plus population growth rate.[25] So, for example, if inflation in 2018 was 3% and the nation's population that year grew by 1%, then total federal spending in 2019 could not rise by more than 4%. Supporters say when such as formula for spending has been tried, it not only eliminates borrowing but usually results in governments running a budget surplus.

Yet what is not revealed is the reason why spending is controlled and surpluses occur. It's because, relative to the size of the economy, the formula by definition will shrink the size of government. This is because the third element in the total growth of an economy, the growth in productivity per person, is ignored in the formula. Productivity growth occurs when workers do their job better, perhaps as a result of more training or by using better machinery or technology. And this is a big factor in determining our use of government services and programs. So, if you want to eventually starve the government of its resources, the inflation plus population growth limit is a way of accomplishing it. I don't think most people want the government running up big debts, but I also don't think most people want the government chopped down to nothing. There has to be a middle ground.

Last is a fake solution that says no solution to the national debt is actually needed. Huh? A new viewpoint with some popularity states that the solution to the national debt is to realize it's not actually a problem. In fact, this viewpoint says not only is the national debt a non-problem, but it can be the solution to many other problems, and therefore, it should be used more!

This viewpoint goes under the title of *modern monetary theory*, or MMT, and here's its reasoning. If the federal government issues debt and sells it to the Federal Reserve (the "Fed"), the Fed will effectively pay for that debt by printing more money. The federal government can then use that money to do good things, like pay teachers more, build affordable housing, develop more mass transit, etc. In the minds of the MMTers, these good things will generate jobs, higher incomes, and economic growth. And with a more prosperous economy, tax revenue will rise and the government will have no problem paying the interest on the new debt. In fact, the MMT promoters say this positive chain of events even works if money is borrowed from foreigners.[26]

Remember the saying, "If it sounds too good to be true, it probably is?" Well, MMT is an example of this. MMT backers are missing a big potential downside—inflation.[27] One of the strongest economic relationships found by researchers is between a nation's money supply and its inflation rate.[28] If the amount of paper money increases faster than the nation's economic growth rate, then the excess money will be sopped up by higher prices.

Granted, the MMT folks expect their money-backed spending binge to increase the nation's economic growth rate. If they're correct and they achieve growth that uses the new money, then no additional inflation will occur. But that's a very big "if."

I do have to thank the MMT movement for one contribution: their emphasis on government spending generating faster economic growth. This is a key point in differentiating "good" uses of government debt from "bad" uses, and it is an important part of my "real" solution revealed next.

△ REAL SOLUTIONS

There is a middle ground. The real solution to government borrowing is to do what the states, as well as most businesses, actually do, which is to have two budgets. One is called a "current budget," which includes spending for services and projects whose benefits occur in the current year, such as the salaries of government employees, payments to support the health and living standards of households, and expenditures on government operations. The current budget would always be balanced with one exception—in the cases of war or recession, both life-threatening and economy-threatening events.

The second budget is called the "capital budget." This budget funds projects that are long-lasting and which provide benefits over time. It's also essential to match the benefits from the project to payments for it. Examples are highway construction and maintenance, construction of military hardware and equipment, basic research, and education.

Are these examples just phony justification to continue government borrowing and debt? Absolutely not. For example, what sense does it make for current taxpayers to pay the full cost of a new highway that will likely last decades and benefit future taxpayers as well? Borrowing and then spreading the payments over time will allow all taxpayers who use the road to pay for it. The same logic applies to military equipment like aircraft carriers, tanks, and fighter air-craft, or support to households and businesses during a recession.

Arguments ensue over whether a particular expenditure belongs in the current or capital budget. Education is a good example. School buildings are certainly long-lasting investments that properly belong in a capital budget. But the argument can also be made that instruc-tion by teachers helps create skills, knowledge, and talents in students that are investments with a long pay-off. If you agree, then teacher salaries should also be considered a capital spending item. Lines will have to be drawn between current and capital expenditures, and dif-ferent people may draw the lines differently. Using my own logic, I make these delineations in the next chapter on government spending.

There's one more piece in my plan to contain deficits and restrict them to reasonable purposes, which is the creation of a "Rainy Day Fund" as an element of the current budget. While economists can't predict the precise timing of economy-wide downturns like reces-sions, whether caused by economic factors or pandemics, we do know they periodically happen. When recessions do occur, they cause big problems for government finances.

Recessions have predictable impacts on government budgets. They increase government spending, particularly for programs that financially support households. They also decrease government revenues as both business profits and worker incomes fall. Both these effects usually lead to much bigger federal budget deficits.

The Rainy Day Fund saves government revenues during good times in the economy and then draws on those saved revenues during recessions. Such a system would allow the federal government to avoid raising taxes and/or cutting spending (both of which can aggravate the severity of a recession) or, as is often the case, borrowing more. For example, during the three years of the Great Recession, federal government borrowing averaged $1.3 trillion annually, up from an average of $290 billion for the three prior years. That extra $3 trillion was borrowed.[29] If there had been an ample Rainy Day Fund in place, the extra borrowing during the recession could have been avoided.

This chapter conceptualized a federal budget that allows borrowing, but for logical purposes. The next chapter puts the concept to work by creating a new federal spending plan.

▲ SUMMING UP

Borrowing is not always bad for people, businesses, or government. Borrowing allows resources to be shifted over time to where they will be most beneficial, and is particularly useful for purchasing long-lasting investments that allow the investment to be repaid while the benefits are occurring. A household buying a home is a good example.

Of course, borrowing can be overdone, even if used for good purposes. The problem with federal government borrowing is that no distinction is made between borrowing for short-term purposes and borrowing for long-term purposes. The first step in containing federal government borrowing is separating government spending into two budgets: a balanced current budget for short-term programs and a capital budget for long-term borrowing.

Chapter 13 Endnotes

1. Federal Reserve Bank of St. Louis, "Delinquency Rate on Single Family Residential Mortgages."

2. Ferguson, "Can the Great Recession Happen Again?"

3. Board of Governors of the Federal Reserve, *Report on the Economic Well-Being of U.S. Households in 2017.* Based on the percentage of adults who are turned down for credit.

4. Blinder, *After the Music Stopped: The Financial Crisis, the Response, and the Work Ahead.*

5. Fiorillo, "Average Net Worth by Age: Mean, Median, and How to Calculate."

6. Federal Reserve Bank of St. Louis, "Federal Debt: Total Public Debt." Shows the national debt as of June 2018.

7. U.S. Bureau of Economic Analysis, "National Income and Product Accounts."

8. "United State Gross Federal Debt to GDP," *Trading Economics.*

9. "Country List Government Debt to GDP," *Trading Economics.*

10. *Ibid.*

11. Federal Reserve Bank of St. Louis, "Federal Debt: Total Public Debt."

12. "U.S. 10 Year Treasury," *CNBC.* The rates are for 10-year Treasury securities.

13. Federal Reserve Bank of St. Louis, "Federal Outlays: Interest as a Percent of GDP."

14. Federal Reserve Bank of St. Louis, "Effective Federal Funds Rate."

15. Congressional Budget Office, *The 2018 Long-Term Budget Outlook.*

16. *Ibid.*

17. Nelson and Buol, "Budget Deficits and Interest Rates: What Is the Link?"

18. Amadeo, "Who Owns the US National Debt?"

19. U.S. Department of the Treasury and Federal Reserve Board, "Major Foreign Holders of Treasury Securities."

20. U.S. Treasury Department, "The Debt to the Penny and Who Holds It."

21. Committee for a Responsible Government, "Q and A: Gross Debt vs. Debt Held by the Public."

22. De Rugy, "A Comprehensive Look at U.S. Debt."

23. Thompson, "Is Our Debt Burden Really $100 Trillion?"

24. National Conference of State Legislators, "Background on Federal Balanced Budget Amendment Proposals."

25. Mitchell, "If You Want to Control Fiscal Policy, Forget the Balanced Budget Amendment and Pursue Spending Caps."

26. Kelton, "How We Think about the Deficit is Mostly Wrong."

27. Shiller, "Modern Monetary Theory Makes Sense, Up to a Point."

28. Friedman and Schwartz, *Monetary Trends in the United States and the United Kingdom.*

29. Office of Management and Budget, *Historical Tables.*

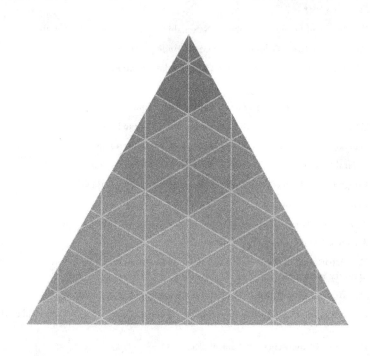

CHAPTER FOURTEEN

SETTING OUR SPENDING PRIORITIES

YOU CAN'T PLEASE EVERYONE, BUT CAN YOU PLEASE ANYONE?

There are many ideas from people and groups about changing federal government spending. The problem is, they often go in opposite directions. Some want to reduce entitlements like Medicaid and food stamps; others say to expand entitlements. Many groups argue for more military spending; on the other side, there are groups wanting to slash the spending. It's the same with education. Should the federal government spend more on education, or should education be left to the states and parents? The only consistent recommendation is to cut waste. Unfortunately, there is no agreed upon definition of waste. One person's wasteful program is another person's necessary expenditure.[1]

It's almost a certainty I won't please everyone with my federal spending recommendations in this chapter, but hopefully I will please some of you! Maybe more importantly, I'll provide a logic for examining federal spending that anyone can use to make their own preferred adjustments.

I do promise to produce a balanced federal current budget over the course of this chapter and the next. Of course, the federal capital budget introduced in Chapter 13, is, by definition, based on borrowing. And here's another promise: in the next chapter, I'll present a logical, easy, fair, and simple tax system to fund my proposed spending plan. I bet you never thought you'd see "logical, easy, fair, and simple" in the same sentence as "tax system."

△ MAKING SENSE OF FEDERAL GOVERNMENT SPENDING

When the nation was young and government was small, the main function of the national as well as state and local governments was to provide services that people or businesses couldn't easily or practically provide for themselves. These government provided services are termed *public goods* by economists. (I know what you're thinking. Why are they called "goods" if they are services? It's because "goods" is the all-purpose economics term for products or services that benefit its users. In comparison, "bads" are products or services taking away benefits or imposing costs. Pollution is an example of a "bad." Non-economists—meaning most people—simply refer to anything the government does as a *government service*. I'll stick with most people and use that term.)

National defense is one example of a government service. Once the armed forces are established, everyone in the country is automatically protected, whether they want to be or not. Plus, it would be impossibly expensive for any rich person or group of people to fund our national defense, which costs over $600 billion annually.[2]

Another traditional type of government service is roads. Originally, roads were tolled, meaning that in order to use a stretch of highway, drivers would first need to stop and pay a fee, or, using the Old English word, a toll. As driving became more common, this constant stopping and starting on different sections of roads became inefficient in terms of time used. Consequently, we evolved to a system of publicly funding roads through a gas tax.

However, toll roads have made a comeback as road sensors have replaced toll booths. When technology is developed to target those who benefit most from the government service, then funding can be done through fees. In this case, private companies could take over the service. Such a change from public to private funding is called "privatization." Its possibilities will be examined when I consider specific government funded services.

The era of small government prior to the 1930s grew into an era of larger government with the emergence of the second function of modern government, *income transfers*. Here, the government is used as a giant money re-distributor. By collecting money through taxes and then disbursing the funds through various government programs, the federal government moves money from some people to other people. Usually this involves shifting money from richer to poorer households. Excluding Social Security, which is self-funded and should be kept apart from the federal budget, the biggest federal household income transfer programs are Medicare, Medicaid, veteran's support, cash assistance, and food stamps, now known as the Supplemental Nutrition Assistance Program (SNAP). As income inequality has widened and certain services, such as medical care, have become relatively more expensive, household income transfers are now the dominant part of federal spending.

I've combed through the latest federal budget numbers and placed all spending into one of the two categories of government services or income transfers.[3] The results of my efforts are in Table 14-1, where the programs are ranked in each category by the size of their spending.

Government Services	$ billions	Income Transfers	$ billions
Military	$631	Health-Care	$1,250
Federal Retirement	$140	Poverty Assistance	$348
Transportation	$93	Veterans' Support	$179
General Government	$45	Disaster Relief Insurance	$35
Other Education	$45	Unemployment Assistance	$32
Pre-K-12 Education	$39	College Student Financial Support	$25
Foreign Economic Aid	$38	Deposit Insurance	$24
Courts & Prisons	$37	Farm Price Supports	$18
Medical Research	$36	Home Mortgage Assistance	$6
Energy & Environment	$23		
Science Research	$17		
Foreign Military Aid	$15		
Job Training	$9		
Public Health	$4		
Total	$1,172	Total	$1,917
Interest	$522		
Tax Expenditures	$1,600		
Grand total, including tax expenditures: $1,172 + $1,917 + $522 + $1,600 = $5,211			

Table 14-1. Categories of Federal Spending, 2018 Budget (excluding Social Security).

Among the government services, military spending is clearly the largest, followed by payments to federal retirees, federal transportation spending, and running the three branches of the federal government. Federal retirement spending is not considered an income transfer because it is part of the retirees' compensation for working. Pre-K through 12 spending is primarily grants to local school districts. Medical research and science research spending are for ground-breaking studies in these areas. The notion is that such studies are too preliminary and uncertain to have any real commercial value, therefore, the private sector won't do it without government help. However, if the scientific research leads to successful and useful results, everyone can ultimately benefit. Foreign economic and military aid are categorized as services because their assumed purpose is to advance both the economic and military security of the U.S. There's also spending to run federal courts and prisons, energy and environmental regulatory and research programs, job training, and public health programs like vaccinations.

Within the income transfer programs, health-care includes the two, big federal medical compensation programs—Medicare for the elderly and Medicaid for those of limited income. These programs, by far, dominate other income transfers (remember, Social Security has been moved off-budget). Poverty assistance includes a variety of programs, such as cash assistance, food stamps, housing assistance, child nutrition assistance for low-income households, and smaller programs to help both children and the elderly. A large part of veteran's support is for medical treatment. Disaster relief are funds to help communities and people recover from storms like tornados and hurricanes. Unemployment assistance pays jobless workers a portion of their lost earnings for a limited time. Only recently has financial support for college students even appeared as a major spending item. Federal deposit insurance protects the deposits of investors in case financial institutions like banks fail. Farm price supports protect farmers from low prices, and home mortgage assistance helps households purchase homes.

Income transfer programs have only emerged during the last 80 years, yet they now dominate federal spending, with their total spending being over 60% larger than the total spending for government services ($1,917 billion compared to $1,172 billion in Table 14-1). Further, the spending of many of these programs is "locked-in" by the formulas and qualifications stated in the legislation establishing them. This means Congress can't change the programs' spending unless they re-write the programs' enabling rules. In budget lingo, the income transfer programs are often referred to as "mandatory." In contrast, the spending of most of the government services programs can be directly changed by Congress; therefore, they are often termed "discretionary" programs.

Interest on the national debt in 2018 was $522 billion. Here's a technical note that hopefully isn't too deep into the weeds. The $522 billion is called the *gross interest cost* because it is the total amount of interest paid by the government. A large part of this interest cost—almost $200 billion in 2018—is paid to the Social Security system because the retirement system holds U.S. Treasury securities as investments.[4] When Social Security's budget was merged with the rest of federal spending in the 1960s, a benefit was that interest spending on the debt instantly fell because the interest paid to Social Security was considered the government paying itself. You and I both know this is just an accounting trick; with my recommendation to put Social Security in a separate budget, the full amount of interest paid on government debt is exposed.

There's one more entry at the bottom of Table 14-1 that I'm sure has raised your eyebrows, which is the entry of $1,600 billion for something called *tax expenditures*. It's a term you won't find in the official federal budget, but that doesn't make it unimportant. Tax expenditures are give-backs from the federal income tax and are mainly in the form of tax deductions and tax credits. The give-backs occur if the taxpayer has done something, usually in the form of an expenditure, that the federal government approves of and wants to encourage. Tax deductions for interest paid on home mortgages, employer contributions to employee health insurance (discussed in Chapter 4), child care tax credits (discussed in Chapter 8), and tax credits for purchasing an energy efficient vehicle are four good examples of this.[5]

So why have I included tax expenditures in Table 14-1 if they aren't a line item in the federal budget? It's because they represent tax revenues the federal government doesn't collect due to favored treatment in the tax code. If you think about it, the same thing could have been accomplished by the government directly paying people to do certain things, such as helping homebuyers pay their monthly mortgage payment rather than giving them a tax deduction. In this way, tax expenditures are really government spending; it's just that they're hidden.

In 2018, the federal government ran a budget deficit of $779 billion, meaning it added to the total national debt by that amount. But how much of this could be justified as borrowing for long-lasting "capital projects?" Unfortunately, the budget doesn't say. This is something I'll correct in my re-making of the federal budget.

The grand total of federal spending in 2018, including tax expenditures, was $5,211 billion, or rounding off at $5.2 trillion!

△ FAKE SOLUTIONS

I'll identify three approaches to the federal budget as "fake solutions" because they are illogical and won't work: eliminating income transfer payments, the "Penny Plan," and cutting government waste.

Eliminating transfer payments to help balance the budget is based on the obvious and true conclusion that growth in federal spending is driven by transfer payments. Three of the five largest income transfer programs listed in Table 14-1 (Medicare, Medicaid, and food stamps) were introduced in the 1960s and 1970s, and they have grown at a breakneck pace ever since.[6] Spending on Medicare and Medicaid has been driven by our aging population, expanded coverage, and increases in medical care costs.[7] Legislation broadening the eligible population receiving food stamps is behind this program's growth.[8] The conclusion among these critics is that there's nothing to stop politicians from spreading the benefits of these programs to more people, thereby increasing the scope of the programs and the power of government.

As I discussed in Chapter 4, I think there are numerous problems in both Medicare and Medicaid centered on the lack of incentives and the economic and political power of the medical industry. I offered a "real solution" of converting existing federal spending on health-care to vouchers that households would use to directly purchase their own health insurance. The voucher amount would be scaled by the household's income and medical condition. I also recom-mended a total remake of poverty assistance programs to eliminate inefficiencies and the disincentives facing recipient households to move toward self-sufficiency. Clearly, with these recommendations, I think there is a role, albeit a different role, for a social safety net.

There's a corollary to the "cut transfers" approach to eliminating defi-cits, which is to balance the budget by severely shrinking military spending.[9] The defense budget is a large contributor to both current spending and capital spending, so paring it back would do double-duty to both budgets. Still, I don't think this approach is practical nor, if I can offer my opinion, advisable. Our country has foreign interests and foreign foes, and maintaining a strong military is an important way to protect our interests and keep these adversaries in check. Certainly, I don't profess to know how large of a defense budget is needed to accomplish these objectives, but I think relying on substantially less military spending to balance the budget is not the safest approach.

The "Penny Plan" is named after former U.S. Congressman, Tim Penny. The idea is to reduce federal spending by only 1 cent out of every dollar each year. Then, over time, as federal spending drops and federal revenues rise (if for no other reason than due to infla-tion), the budget would be balanced within five years.[10] This plan is appealing for its simplicity. What could be easier? Just cut a penny a year from each dollar of federal spending, and bingo, the budget is balanced in no time. Plus, who's going to miss a penny of spending?

However, the simplicity of the Penny Plan obscures its problems. Consider programs like Medicare and Medicaid, where total spending is driven, in part, by the number of people participating in the programs. As the number of elderly people increases, Medicare and Medicaid will spend more, even if the amount spent per person doesn't change. The Penny Plan guarantees less, ultimately much less, will be spent per person as the number of people using these programs rises.

Also, the cut in spending is more than a penny per dollar per year. This is because inflation isn't taken into account. For example, if inflation is 3% annually, this means 3 cents more per dollar is needed to be spent just to keep up with higher prices. In this case, by cutting one cent per dollar, the Penny Plan really means that government spending is reduced by 4 cents per dollar in constant purchasing power. Over five years, this is a cut of almost 22% (including compounding) in constant purchasing power spending. You can bet this would be noticed by people using government programs.

The last fake solution is containing federal government spending by eliminating wasteful spending. I've been following presidential elections since 1960 (I was alive for both the 1952 and 1956 elections, but my focus was on the Lone Ranger and Cisco Kid), and I'm not aware of any candidate from any party who didn't recommend cutting waste in government. After all, who can be against reducing wasteful spending of any kind?

There are several on-going efforts to identify wasteful federal government spending. The focus ranges from identifying dubious research projects, eliminating inaccurate payments, and reducing bureaucratic inefficiencies to serious policy questions over farm and energy subsidies, federal land ownership, and the federal role in local economic development. Projections for the total savings also vary, from a couple billion dollars annually ("chump change" for the federal government) to serious amounts between $300 billion and $400 billion per year.[11]

Although I am sympathetic to these efforts—again, who would be against eliminating waste?—I have two problems with this solution. One is trying to get 536 elected national officials (435 Congress persons, 100 Senators, and the President) to agree on the wasteful programs. Programs are in the federal budget because there's enough political force to put them there. Supporters will naturally fight harder to keep the programs than opponents will to remove them. It's a political fact of life.

Second, even if there was some consensus on wasteful programs and they were eliminated, it simply wouldn't be enough to solve the government spending and deficit problems. Let's take the high number estimated for government waste of $400 billion annually. If an agreement could be reached to reduce this amount by half, which would still require heavy political lifting, the total still falls well short of recent federal budget deficits.

I will adopt some of the recommendations for reducing waste in my real solutions, but there has to be more tough choices to create any real answer to government spending.

△ REAL SOLUTIONS

Using the 2018 budget, my recommendations for revising federal government spending are available in Table 14-2. I know it looks messy; I crossed out spending items I'm eliminating, and I put in **bold** the major spending changes. To create a government services capital budget, I rely on a Congressional Budget Office (CBO) report that split the 2018 government services budget into current spending and capital spending.[12] This has a major impact on the classification of military and transportation spending. Capital spending for medical research, energy/environment, and science research are also substantial. Notice CBO considers education and job training as investments, and I concur. To help fund my recommended multi-billion-dollar investment in Pre-K through 12 education, I eliminate the Other Education category and merge those dollars with Pre-K-12.

To fund expected job training requirements resulting from automation, I shift the $32 billion from unemployment insurance income transfers and add other funds to bring the total to $77 billion, enough to cover the re-training recommended in Chapter 10. Lastly, I budget a $200 billion annual contribution to a federal Rainy Day Fund. It is based on a cumulative shortfall of $1 trillion during a four-year recessionary and post-recessionary time period and five years between economic downturns. These funds would not be collected during recessions.

Government Services	$ billions	Income	Transfers	$ billions
	Current	Capital		
Military	$436	$195	Health-care Assistance	$1,250
Federal Retirement	$140		Poverty Assistance	$613
Transportation	$0	$93	Veterans' Support	$179
General Government	$16		CHILD	$130
~~Other Education~~	~~$45~~		Disaster Relief Insurance	$35
Pre-K-12 Education	$0	$415	~~Unemployment Insurance~~	~~$32~~
Foreign Economic Aid	$38		~~College Student Financial Support~~	~~$25~~
Courts and Prisons	$32		Deposit Insurance	$24
Medical Research	$0	$36	~~Farm Price Supports~~	~~$18~~
Energy & Environment	$11	$12	~~Home Mortgage Assistance~~	~~$6~~
Science Research	$0	$17		
Foreign Military Aid	$15			
Job Training	$0	$77[a]		
Public Health	$4			
Rainy Day Fund	$200			
Total	$892	$845	Total	$2,231
Interest on capital budget	$222			
Current budget debt retirement	$925			
~~Tax expenditures~~	~~$1,600~~			

Grand total including: $892 + $845 + $2,231 + $222 + $925 = $5,115

[a] $32 billion from unemployment insurance, $9 billion from existing job training, and an additional $36 billion for re-training (Chapter 10).

Table 14-2. Revised Federal Spending, 2018 Budget (excluding Social Security).

For income transfer expenditures, I collapse the financial programs helping households at poverty or near poverty income levels into the five categories of health care (vouchers), shelter, cash, food, and transportation assistance. As discussed in Chapter 4, the healthcare assistance uses existing expenditures. The other four categories use existing expenditures augmented by $265 billion in new spending to reduce the implicit tax rate in the programs (Chapter 7). I leave Veteran's Support unchanged but convert the medical component to health insurance vouchers. I fund the new CHILD program (Chapter 8) from existing tax expenditures in the budget. I keep federal disaster relief under the assumption massive storms such as hurricanes, tornadoes, and flooding can overwhelm the private insurance market and create unacceptable levels of suffering unless rapid responses are provided. As indicated in the previous paragraph, I merge unemployment assistance in the transfer section with job training in the services section.

Although a strong argument can be made to privatize deposit insurance for household accounts in banks and saving institutions, the system has worked reasonably well for over 70 years and is familiar to most people. However, I privatize college loans, farm income supports (mainly the support of farm prices), and mortgage credit support for a total savings of $49 billion. Financial support for these programs will be provided by fees and charges to the direct beneficiaries.[13]

Interest payments for the capital budget include funds for the 2018 capital budget ($222 billion) as well as funds for the capital borrowing component of the existing $22 trillion national debt. To calibrate previous capital budget borrowing, I use the CBO's estimate that 16% of federal spending between 1962 and 2018 was for capital projects.[14] The result is $3.5 trillion of the national debt has been for capital spending. It is economically logical to continue to carry this amount as debt.

However, the remaining $18.5 trillion is borrowing for past current spending, and it should be retired. To completely retire this $18.5 trillion debt over 30 years requires an annual payment of $925 billion.[15] Therefore, after 30 years debt payments would be based only on borrowing in the capital budget. I've chosen 30 years as a reasonable long-run repayment period, comparable to terms for home mortgages and U.S. government long-term borrowing instruments, like U.S. Treasury securities. However, this term is negotiable, although I wouldn't use a one longer than 50 years. The benefit of a longer term is it reduces the annual amount that must be budgeted to debt retirement.

Total spending in my revised 2018 budget (Table 14-2) is $5,115 billion compared to $5,211 billion in the actual 2018 budget (Table 14-1). Although the budgets are less than 2% apart, in my recommended budget there is a serious new investment in Pre-K-12 education, restructured poverty programs to provide incentives for work, a Rainy Day Fund for recessions, and a plan to retire that part of the existing federal debt related to past non-capital (current) spending. But notice my budget does not include an allocation for the "tax expenditures" that appear in the existing 2018 budget (Table 14-1). Why? For now, I'll let you think about the answer. I'll provide the explanation in the next chapter on federal taxes.

There's more good news. Under my plan there are several good reasons to predict federal spending could actually fall (in inflation-adjusted dollars) in the future. I expect the additional education spending to pay off with improved educational attainment, higher labor productivity, and reduced future expenditures for public assistance. Also, as an aside—if my recommendations for simplifying and reducing the expenses of higher education are adopted, publicly funded costs of higher education could also be substantially reduced.

Likewise, the restructured poverty assistance plan, which extends coverage to more households in order to gradually remove assistance as household income rises, should encourage work and self-dependency, ultimately reducing future spending for these programs. The development of a federal Rainy Day Fund will allow federal programs to continue during recessions without increasing tax rates.

Then, there is what could be considered my crowning achievement: elimination of over 80% of the national debt in 30 years. This means enormous savings in interest payments over time. You may now applaud!

Still, slightly over $5 trillion is a lot of money for the federal government to raise each year. Won't collecting this amount make federal tax rates sky-high and cause the federal tax code to be even more complicated and intrusive? Turn to Chapter 15 to get the answers.

▲ SUMMING UP

Reforming the federal budget to make it understandable, workable, and cost effective requires several changes. Social Security should be removed from the budget to stand alone, as it originally did. A current spending budget, which must be balanced, should be separate from a capital budget, where borrowing for projects can occur. Several programs in the budget should be removed from government control and be performed by the private sector. Spending on Pre-K through 12 education should be significantly increased, while spending on household "safety net" programs should be restructured and simplified. Lastly, a Rainy Day Fund should be established to save revenues during prosperous times and to fill shortfalls when the economy plunges into a recession.

Chapter 14 Endnotes

1. Congressional Budget Office, *Options for Reducing the Debt, 2019-2028.*

2. Congressional Budget Office, *The 2018 Long-Term Budget Outlook.*

3. Chantrill, "U.S. Government Spending."

4. *Ibid.*

5. Center on Budget and Policy Priorities, "Federal Tax Expenditures"; Joint Committee on Taxation, "Estimates of Federal Tax Expenditures for Fiscal Years 2017-2021."

6. Concord Coalition, "A Troubling Trend in Federal Investment Spending."

7. Cubanski and Newman, "The Facts on Medicare Spending and Financing," and Holan, Rowland, Feder, and Heslam, "Explaining the Recent Growth in Medicaid Spending."

8. De Rugy, "Food Stamp Spending and Enrollment Double in Five Years."

9. Friedman, "A Plan to Cut Military Spending."

10. Paul, "Chairman Paul's Penny Plan Budget: A Budget for Fiscal Year 2019."

11. Paul, "Senator Paul Highlights $1.8 billion in Wasteful Spending through Weekly Waste Reports"; Lankford, "Senator Lankford Releases Federal Fumbles, Vol. 3"; Citizens Against Government Waste, *Prime Cuts.*

12. Congressional Budget Office, *Federal Investment, 1962-2018.*

13. Edwards, "Agricultural Subsidies" and Goodwin and Smith, *The Economics of Crop Insurance and Disaster Aid.* These show arguments in favor of privatization and examples of how a privatized system would work for farmers.

14. Congressional Budget Office, *Federal Investment, 1962-2018, op.cit.*

15. U.S. Treasury Department, "Daily Treasury Yield Curve Rates."

CHAPTER FIFTEEN

MAKING TAXES SIMPLE, FAIR, AND ADEQUATE

A NECESSARY EVIL OR AN EVIL NECESSITY?

We've all heard the jokes about taxes: the only things certain in life are death and taxes. A fine is a tax for doing wrong, a tax is a fine for doing well. How do you know if you have a great tax accountant? He has a loophole named for him! And my personal favorite: the guy who said "truth never hurt" never had to fill out an IRS form 1040.[1]

Although these jokes may be funny, taxes are serious. All taxes—local, state, and federal—took 29 cents out of every dollar of income in 2017. Federal taxes (including Social Security) were the biggest part of this, taking 16 cents.[2] But it could be worse, as taxes consume 46 percent of total income in France, 45% in Denmark, and 42% in Italy.[3]

Most people understand they must pay taxes. How else are the functions of the government to be funded? So, while these people don't like it, they know the government has to take some of their money, and taxes are therefore a "necessary evil." Others have a different view; while they don't disagree that the government needs to be funded, they view the tax system as more than a way to raise revenues for government. Instead, they see the tax system as used to reward certain groups and punish others, provide "corporate welfare" to companies pulling political strings, and (through its complexity) to keep a cover over all these activities. In other words, taxes are an "evil necessity."

My goal in this chapter is to remove the "evil" from both perspectives and just leave taxes as a necessity we tolerate.

△ WORKING THE SYSTEM

As it has been throughout this book, my focus is on the federal government. At the federal level, by far the largest source of tax revenue is the income tax, which is applied to both households and corporations. In 2018, the federal income tax raised $1.9 trillion.[4] It has been said the Internal Revenue Service (IRS), which administers the federal income tax, has been the most successful tax-raising agency in history. Interestingly, before the income tax was adopted by a constitutional amendment in 1913, the federal government was mostly funded by tariffs on imports and other assorted fees, whereas import tariffs now account for only 1% of federal revenues.[5]

Taxing income seems like a simple concept, yet the U.S. income tax is far from simple. The IRS's federal income tax code runs 74,000 pages,[6] which is why thousands of accountants, lawyers, and finance experts earn good salaries selling their knowledge of the income tax rules.

Tax loopholes (or what was more politely called "tax expenditures" in Chapter 14) are the primary reason why the income tax is so complex. Tax loopholes come in three major varieties. *Tax deductions* are types of spending which can be used to reduce the income subject to the income tax. *Tax credits* are even better, because they are types of spending which can be used to directly reduce the amount of taxes owed. Last are *special lower tax rates*, which are usually applied to earnings from investments favored by the tax code.

While plenty of books have been written about how to use these concepts to reduce taxes, the loopholes do have five important consequences for the tax system. First, they are expensive. Remember in Chapter 14 how I showed that tax loopholes (a.k.a. tax expenditures) cost the federal government an amazing $1.6 trillion in lost tax revenue in 2018?[7] What this means is that, in order to make up for the lost revenue, taxes must be higher on other income not qualifying for tax loopholes.

Second, tax loopholes create an uneven playing field by picking winners and losers. How people live is a great example of this. If you live in a home you are purchasing with a mortgage loan—which is the way most people buy a home—the IRS allows you to reduce your taxable income by the amount of annual interest you pay on the loan. For most homebuyers, this loophole can amount to thousands of dollars in deductions. And more interesting, the loophole is even larger for people buying more expensive homes and borrowing more money. Yet renters are out of luck. There are no comparable loopholes for people who choose to rent rather than buy.

Third, loopholes can get in the way of sound economic decision-making. The own/rent decision is again a great example. You may want to rent because you don't like the responsibilities of homeownership and maybe you move frequently. But a real estate agent complicates your decision by showing how much you'll save in taxes by buying a home with a mortgage. The agent convinces you to buy. But then there's this possibility—suppose next year you're transferred and actually lose money by selling your house once all the special fees and costs of home-owning are included.

Fourth, tax loopholes favor higher-income taxpayers. Just shy of 62% of the $1.6 trillion annual tax expenditures go to the richest 20% of households.[8] While this result might be expected because higher-income households spend more and therefore have more opportunities to use tax loopholes, the loopholes are a hidden form of tax cuts for richer households. Consequently, the loopholes contribute to widespread suspicion that the tax code is rigged to favor the rich at the expense of the poor.

Fifth, and maybe most importantly, getting loopholes put into the tax code for special interests and keeping the ones that are already there is one of the main jobs of Washington lobbyists. The IRS doesn't decide what kinds of spending or economic behavior are deserving of tax loopholes; it is Washington politicians, including presidents, senators, and congress women and men who do. Frequently the loopholes making it into the tax code are the ones fought hardest for by special interests. Of course, these special interests and their hired lobbyists accomplish this by offering contributions to the campaign chests of politicians. In a cynical way, the federal income tax code is a bag of goodies bought and paid for by organized groups who want the benefits.

△ WHAT PEOPLE WANT

Although people may not like paying taxes, they are more likely to do so without complaining if the tax system meets their standards. What are these standards? What is it that people want in a tax system? I don't think the characteristics of a tax system desired by most people are that profound or complicated. I think they include five simple principles: fairness, low tax rates, easy to understand rules, transparency, and inclusiveness.

While fairness is often in the eyes of the beholder, people have a pretty good idea of what it means in taxes. Tax fairness means everyone is treated the same; there are no favorites. This means no tax loopholes! It also means the amount of taxes paid bears a relationship to the person's impact on the economy or ability to pay. Translated—poorer people pay less, and richer people pay more.

Economists like low tax rates because it means tax considerations are less likely to conflict with personal or business considerations. With low rates, people aren't as motivated to make a particular decision just to save taxes. Low rates tell people that, yes, they are paying taxes, but they don't have to devote a lot of time to worrying about them.

People also want taxes that are easy to understand. They don't want a tax code running 74,000 pages that only experts can decipher. They also want a transparent tax code that is out in the open and not buried in section 12, subsection C, paragraph 5. People want simple and understandable taxes.

Everyone has a stake in our government, so everyone should help pay for it; this is the principle of inclusiveness. Inclusiveness also protects citizens from having a government run by and for the few. If only a relatively small number of people, such as the rich, paid for the government, they would think the government worked only for them. Politicians and policies would be in the collective pocket of the tax paying-class. But if everyone shares in paying for the government, everyone rightly believes the government is working for them, and people therefore will be more motivated to follow the debates about government policies and, especially, more motivated to vote.

△ FAKE SOLUTIONS

There have been dozens of proposals to change the federal tax system in the 40+ years I have been a professional economist, and new ones are offered all the time. I'll review the popular ones here and tell you why I don't think they'll get the job done; that is, why they are fake.

A long-standing tax plan, mainly offered by those on the left side of the political spectrum, is to construct an income tax system with very high tax rates for the rich. I'll call this the "soak the rich" plan. For example, in early 2019 one member of Congress proposed a tax rate as high as 70% for the richest households.[9] Some professional economists who have studied tax policy have also made the case for high tax rates on high income earners.[10]

To be fair, the "soak the rich" proposals do not mean all earnings of a rich person would be taxed at the recommended rates. For example, Congresswoman Alexandria Ocasio-Cortez proposed the 60% or

70% tax rate to apply only to people with incomes above $10 million. In fact, the current federal income tax system already taxes higher levels of income at higher rates. It is an example of a "progressive tax system," where, rather than taxing all income at the same rate, a person's income is divided into ranges, with higher income ranges taxed at higher rates and lower-income ranges taxed at lower rates. The 2018 federal income tax had seven ranges, with tax rates for the ranges spanning a low of 10% to a high of 37%. For single taxpayers, the 37% rate applied to income above $500,000, and for married tax-payers the 37% applied to incomes above $600,000.

Thus, the big questions with a progressive income tax system are how fast the rates will rise and what the highest rate should be. Even though a very high rate, such as 70% on the richest taxpayers, seems like it would raise a lot of revenue for the government, it really wouldn't. For example, the Ocasio-Cortez plan would impact only the 16,000 income tax filers who have incomes above $10 million. This is a mere 0.5% of all income tax filers, and the extra annual revenue raised using the most optimistic calculations would be $72 billion.[11] Certainly $72 billion is a big number, but it's less than 4% of the amount currently raised by the federal income tax. If the purpose of the "soak the rich" super-high tax rates is to provide enough money to reduce the annual budget deficit or fund new programs, eventually the high rates will have to drift downward to incorporate "less rich" taxpayers.

We've had experience with "soak the rich" super-high tax rates, and they didn't seem to work. In the 1950s, the highest federal income tax rate was 90%. That rate was later reduced by the Kennedy and

Reagan administrations during the 1960s and 1980s. Why? Because super high tax rates motivate the rich to find more tax loopholes or possibly hide their money in foreign countries. In fact, the evidence shows that as the top tax rate is *reduced*, the share of total taxes paid by the richest taxpayers actually rises as they are now motivated to engage in more income-producing activities.[12]

What super-high tax rates can do to incentives and ultimately to tax revenues might be the biggest problem with "soak the rich" plans. Consider this simple example: if you earn an extra $1,000 and know 70% ($700) will be taken away from you in taxes, what's your incentive to work for that $1,000? I (and most economists) would answer—not much! Tons of economic research confirm the hunch that workers consider the tax bite when deciding how much to work.[13] Simply put, the higher the tax bite, the less motivation to work and create both income and tax revenues.

The disincentive to work as a result of very high tax rates can be so strong that pushing them up can actually *reduce* tax revenues, not increase them. This was the insight of economist Arthur Laffer and his famous (at least to economists!) "Laffer Curve." The Laffer Curve shows that as tax rates are raised from low levels to medium levels, tax revenues do increase, but as the rate is further pushed to very high levels, tax revenues actually decline. Studies in the U.S. as well as in several European countries show that "soak the rich" tax rates of 60%, 70%, or higher are really counterproductive because less, not more, tax revenues result. Research shows the highest government tax revenues are obtained from a rate between 30% and 35%.[14] There's also the added concern that very high tax rates decrease creativity and innovation in the economy.[15]

Another fake tax plan is the FairTax.[16] This plan replaces the federal income tax with a federal retail sales tax rate of 23% on non-necessities. To avoid taxing necessities, every household regardless of income would receive a cash transfer equal to the retail sales tax a poverty-level household would pay. Supporters say that by ditching the income tax, gone would be all the complications and tax loopholes that mainly benefit the rich. Gone also would be the expensive lobbying done on Capitol Hill to obtain tax favors for certain industries and companies. The FairTax would be paid by everyone and would be easy to understand. Although the 23% rate needed to replace the income tax is high, especially when piggy-backed on state and local sales taxes, advocates argue that it's still better than the complex combination of rates and loopholes inherent in the income tax. Plus, advocates claim there's an added bonus of the FairTax; by directly taxing spending (consumption), the tax would encourage people to save and invest, which they argue in the long run tends to grow the economy and make everyone better-off.[17]

The fact is, one major problem dooms the FairTax. Since the rich spend a much smaller portion of their income than do the poor, research shows the FairTax would take a larger percentage of a poor person's income than it would from the rich.[18] In tax lingo, this means the FairTax would be "regressive," even if the FairTax replaced all federal taxes, including the Social Security tax. Instead of richer people contributing relatively more of their income to taxes than poorer people, it would be the reverse. The FairTax could be labelled a "Robin Hood in reverse" scheme.

Another problem with the FairTax is the gigantic 23% rate. You know with this kind of rate, people will make a lot of effort to avoid the tax. I foresee airlines advertising shopping trips to countries with no or low retail sales taxes, and I'm willing to bet—probably by investing in the airlines—that such trips would be a big success if the FairTax were implemented.

Here's one more fake tax solution. What about keeping the income tax but simplifying it to one rate with limited loopholes? This is the proposal of "flat tax" advocates.[19] In this situation, everyone would pay the same rate on all of their income after deducting loopholes. Loopholes would also be constrained to very few which almost anyone could use. One of the loopholes, for example, would be a very large standard deduction, resulting in every household not paying tax on, say, their first $25,000 of income. Alternatively, the standard deduction could be based on the number of people (adults and children) in the household. Either way, a large standard deduction would shield the poor from much of the tax.

Once the household's taxable income is calculated, the tax rate on every dollar would be the same. There would be no more income ranges and brackets and progressive tax rates. Most flat tax plans propose a rate of around 20%.[20]

I am sympathetic to the flat tax idea. It is so simple that most people could calculate their taxes on a postcard. It's also easy to understand, and by using the same standard deduction amount for the rich and poor, the plan results in the rich paying a higher portion of their income for taxes than the poor and middle-class.

Yet three things don't work with the flat tax. First, limiting the number of tax loopholes is hard, as every group will say their loophole is essential. I would expect a big push to maintain popular deductions, such as for mortgage interest and charitable contributions. And once any deductions are allowed, the floodgates would be opened for others.[21] Second, most flat tax rates are still sizable and noticeable, usually at the double-digit level, which means there will continue to be a large motivation for tax avoidance. And third, the flat tax assumes income is the best economic source for raising taxes. As I will show in the next section, I think there are better ones.

△ REAL SOLUTIONS

There are three major economic aggregates that can be taxed: income, spending, and wealth. The federal government has relied primarily on income for generating revenue ever since the income tax was enacted a century ago. In my opinion, this reliance has been a disaster. Despite many efforts to change it, the federal income tax is still complicated, unfair, and intrusive. It is complicated because it takes a trained expert to understand the thousands of pages of IRS income tax code. It is unfair because it can treat two households or two businesses with the same income differently, depending on the number and size of tax loopholes available to them. It is intrusive because, in many cases, people base important life decisions like when to retire, how to invest, and what kind of estate to leave to descendants on such tax considerations. As one of my friends, Raymond, would say, "This is just wrong."

Therefore, I propose using the other two economic aggregates— spending and wealth—as the basis for raising revenue for the federal government. Here I outline a program that meets the five standards I set forth earlier for a tax system: fairness, low tax rates, easy to understand, transparency, and inclusiveness. I will utilize taxes on spending and wealth to generate enough revenue to cover the federal spending total presented in Table 14-2 ($5.1 trillion).

I dub my plan the "3.8% Tax Solution," because it will levy a simple 3.8% tax on all spending by households and businesses. It will also levy an annual 3.8% tax on all wealth (net worth) above the average (median) wealth level. There will be no federal estate tax.

My spending tax is different than the typical retail sales tax used in many states, which only applies to so-called "sales to final users." My spending tax would apply to any sale, including business-to-consumer sales, consumer-to-business sales, and business-to-business sales. The tax would be applied to the sales value at the time of purchase. Thus, when large durable goods are sold (such as buildings and vehicles), the tax would be applied to the total sales value. If the buyer borrows funds to finance the sale, the tax would be included in the amount borrowed, so payments (such as a monthly mortgage payment or a vehicle loan payment) would include a monthly amount for the tax.

In 2018, the total value of sales transactions in the making and selling of new products and services totaled $36 trillion.[22] I estimate that the resale value of durable products—again, mainly buildings and vehicles—to be $2 trillion.[23] With a total of $38 trillion of spending transactions in the country in 2018, a 3.8% tax would have raised $1.44 trillion that year.

Wealth includes the value of all types of investments, including financial (stocks, bonds, and interest-bearing accounts like CDs, whether they are held directly or are in mutual funds) as well as property investments (real estate, commodities, and precious metals). This is the definition of wealth tracked by agencies like the Federal Reserve. In 2018, total U.S. wealth stood at $109 trillion.[24] However, I wouldn't tax the entire amount; I would not tax each household on a wealth amount equal to the average (median) for all households. In 2018, this household average was $101,910.[25] I include this tax-free wealth amount to maintain a strong motivation for lower-wealth and lower-income households to save and accumulate wealth—an activity that is very important for improving standards of living over time.

After subtracting $13 trillion of aggregate median wealth, the wealth tax base in 2018 is $96 trillion. A 3.8% tax would generate $3.65 trillion, which, combined with the $1.44 trillion from the spending tax, totals $5.1 trillion—just enough to cover the $5.1 trillion of spending in Table 14-2.

How does the 3.8% Tax Solution stack up with my five characteristics of a preferred tax (fairness, low tax rates, easy to understand, transparency, and inclusiveness)? The plan is obviously inclusive with everyone paying a 3.8% federal tax on their spending. It is also simple because everyone understands spending; when money changes hands, a 3.8% tax is collected. Some education may be required to communicate the idea of wealth, but this is mainly to those with little or no wealth. Since the 3.8% Tax Solution is simple, there's no need for complicated rules and regulations buried in obscure tax documents; it's transparent. The two tax rates of 3.8% would be considered by most to be low, so the plan also passes for having low tax rates.

Now what about fairness? Data show the 40% of households with the lowest incomes now pay no federal income taxes.[26] These households would pay the 3.8% spending tax when they purchased products and services at the retail level, so this would be a change some could view as a step backward. I view it as a small price to pay to have all households involved in supporting the government and implementing a simple tax. Also, remember in Chapter 7 that I outlined a more generous social safety net for households needing a boost on the economic ladder.

The 3.8% wealth tax, which would fund almost three-quarters of federal revenue, is another matter. Revenues collected from this tax would be highly skewed to the highest income households, especially after including the deduction for median wealth. Indeed, using the deduction, 60% of households would pay no wealth tax, which is more than the 40% who currently pay no federal income tax. Also, over 80% (81%) of the wealth tax would be collected from the richest 20% of households,[27] higher than the share those households now pay of federal income taxes.[28]

Any tax plan will have critics, and mine is no exception. Some will argue my spending tax will result in something economists call "tax cascading."[29] This means that sales taxes paid at lower levels of the production process will be passed on in the form of higher prices later in the process. So, if there are four stages of production—for example, the farmer sells wheat to the flour miller, the miller sells flour to the baker, the baker sells bread to the grocer, and the grocer sells bread to the consumer—then 3.8 cents is charged at each sale, each 3.8 cent tax is added to the price at that point, and the total price for each $1 of bread sold to the consumer rises by 15.2 (3.8 x 4) cents.

Tax cascading certainly can happen, which is why some prefer a "value-added" spending tax instead. In this case, the cost of inputs (for example, the wheat and flour in the bread) are only taxed the first time they occur, and afterwards their costs are subtracted before the spending tax is applied. Canada and many European countries use a value-added sales tax. However, it adds paperwork and complications to the tax process. Plus, the value-added tax rate would need to be higher by a factor related to the number of production stages in order to raise the same revenue as my spending tax. Thus, the value-added tax doesn't meet my requirements of simplicity and a low tax rate.

In addition, tax cascading already occurs with income taxes; both businesses and workers consider taxes a cost, and so they will attempt to pass on those costs by trying to increase prices or wages. Indeed, this is the usual argument heard when tax hikes on businesses are proposed.[30]

There's a legitimate concern that taxing wealth will deter individuals from accumulating wealth. This is important to everyone because wealth is the source of investments that grow the economy. If wealth and investments decline, the economy grows slowly and everyone is hurt, including workers.

I have four responses to assuage this worry. First, a portion of wealth is already taxed by the IRS when investment earnings are included as part of taxable income.

Second, my wealth tax rate is low, at 3.8%. Over time, with a well-designed investment portfolio, investors should be able to easily exceed this rate and still build their wealth. Also recognize that with my plan to retire the current spending portion of the national debt over 30 years, once that payment is complete and $925 billion is removed from the annual federal budget, both the spending tax and the wealth tax can be reduced to 3.1%.

Third, with spending taxed instead of income, there is added incentive for individuals to earn income and save rather than spend. The additional income and added savings will boost wealth and be another way to grow wealth over time even with the new wealth tax. Estimates show the combination of adding a wealth and spending tax while eliminating the income tax would be a net plus for economic growth.[31]

Fourth, two policy changes I've recommended should also raise income and economic growth over time. One is my education plans for both Pre-K-12 and college that should elevate living standards and use education dollars more efficiently. The second is my plan to significantly reduce national debt levels which, in turn, should lower interest rates and induce faster economic growth.[32]

So, while by itself a wealth tax is bad for economic growth, this impact is more than offset by the elimination of the income tax, the addition of a spending tax, and the worker productivity and investment gains from the education and national debt reduction initiatives.

One problem with the wealth tax as compared to an income tax is that wealth is more volatile than income.[33] This means wealth tends to fluctuate more from year to year than does income. Studies show this greater up-and-down movement of wealth is mainly due to variations in real estate and stock values.[34] The greater volatility of wealth could make the revenues from the 3.8% Tax Solution more unstable and less reliable than the current system, particularly during a recession.

I see three ways of dealing with this problem. One is to devote more revenue during "boom" times to the Rainy Day Fund in anticipation of a bigger drop-off in revenues during "bust" times. The second is to suspend allocations to paying down the current spending portion of the national debt when revenues from the wealth tax plunge. A third option is to tax an average of several recent year wealth values rather than only taxing wealth from the most recent year. For example, for 2019, instead of taxing wealth from only that year, the average of wealth values for the last five years—2015, 2016, 2017, 2018, 2019— would be taxed after converting values from previous years to current year (in this example, 2019) purchasing power dollars. The idea is that the average of wealth over several years is less volatile.

There's one more related issue, and it's a legal one about the constitutionality of a national wealth tax. Legal scholars have argued on both sides of the issue.[35] Not having any training in the law, I leave this debate to the lawyers and law professors. However, I will say this: the federal income tax was initially declared unconstitutional, and it took a constitutional amendment (the 16th) to legalize it. The same could occur with a national wealth tax.

There are plenty of details which would need to be worked out to implement a national wealth tax. To do so, I recommend relying on existing wealth data as much as possible. Financial wealth data (stocks, bonds, mutual funds, bank deposits, etc.) are regularly sent to owners on yearly, quarterly, and sometimes monthly periods. Property and personal wealth are compiled and kept by local governments who rely on them for assessing local property taxes. One change I would make to the local property data is to subtract existing loan amounts (mortgages, vehicle loans) used to purchase the property, so that only *net worth* (another term for wealth) is taxed. These loan data are readily available from financial institutions.

Unless we're going to collect a year's worth of spending and wealth tax revenue a year ahead—something as likely as me scoring the next Super Bowl winning touchdown—then there will need to be monthly payments of the spending and wealth taxes to the federal government. For the spending tax, the feds could take a cue from state governments and require any company or individual on the receiving end of a transaction (meaning they receive the payment) to submit the associated spending tax revenue collected during each month to the federal government. Or, taking a cue from the current income tax, an estimated monthly spending tax could be collected directly from every household and business based on their spending patterns of the previous year, and any difference between what they owed and what they paid would be reconciled at the end of the year.

Similarly, the most efficient way for the government to collect monthly payments of the wealth tax would be directly from the institutions originating the wealth data, such as financial institutions and local governments. In today's world of high-speed data collection and transmission, there should be little cost to this method.

Since we are accustomed to taxes on spending at the retail level, it's only a short jump to getting comfortable with taxes on spending at all levels. While there has been some form of a wealth tax at the local and state levels (local taxes on property, and state and local taxes on estates), in modern times there has not been a comprehensive federal wealth tax. Yet a new federal wealth tax would actually be a return to the past, for in colonial times, taxing wealth was a major way of funding government.[36]

▲ SUMMING UP

The best taxes are simple and unobtrusive, yet today's federal taxes are the exact opposite. They are complicated, over-bearing, unfair, and disruptive to personal and business decision-making.

The best tax system has two main characteristics: they are applied to a large tax base, but they are applied with a very low tax rate. I recommend two taxes to fund the federal government: one is a tax on all spending, and the second is a tax on wealth above the average (median) level. Each tax would apply a rate of only 3.8%. They are simple, easy-to-understand without thousands of pages of explanations and exceptions, inclusive so that everyone contributes to supporting the government, and fair in terms of ability to pay. Indeed, the wealth component, which would fund almost three-fourths of total taxes, would result in 80% of the tax revenue being collected from the richest 20% of taxpayers, a proportion much higher than with the current income tax. Also, once the "current spending" component of the national debt is retired after 30 years, the spending/wealth tax rate could be reduced to 3.1%.

However, constant vigilance would have to be exercised to prevent the "3.8% Tax Solution" from being packed with special favors through deductions, credits, and exemptions.

Chapter 15 Endnotes

1. "Top Ten Jokes for Tax Season," *ATBS*.

2. Council of Economic Advisers, *Economic Report of the President, 2019*, Tables B-47.

3. Organization for Economic Cooperation and Development, "Tax Revenue."

4. Council of Economic Advisers, *Economic Report of the President, 2018*, Table B-20.

5. *Ibid.*

6. Russell, "Look How Many Pages are in the Federal Tax Code."

7. Joint Committee on Taxation, "Estimates of Federal Tax Expenditures for Fiscal Years 2017-2021."

8. *Ibid.*

9. Loudenback, Tanza, "Alexandria Ocasio-Cortex Has a Plan to Tax the Wealthiest Americans 60% to 70%, and it Highlights a Detail about Taxes Most People Get Wrong."

10. Diamond and Saez, "The Case for a Progressive Tax: From Basic Research to Policy Recommendations."

11. Tuttle, "Alexandria Ocasio-Cortez Suggested a 70% Tax Rate on the Rich. Here's How It Would Work." Other analysis of the 70% rate proposal estimates significantly lower revenues when potential adverse impacts on work and investing activity are included; Pomerleau and Li, "How Much Revenue would a 70% Top Tax Rate Raise? An Initial Analysis."

12. Saez, Slemrod, and Giertz, "The Elasticity of Taxable Income with Respect to Marginal Rates: A Critical Review."

13. Mertens and Ravn, "The Dynamic Effects of Personal and Corporate Income Tax Changes in the U.S."

14. Trabandt and Uhlig, "The Laffer Curve Revisited," and Hsing, "Estimating the Laffer Curve and Policy Implications."

15. Jones, Charles, "Taxing Top Incomes in the World of Ideas."

16. Americans for Fair Taxation, *The Fair Tax.*

17. Bhattarai, Haughton, and Tuerck, "The Economic Effects of the Fair Tax: Analysis of a Dynamic CGE Model of the U.S. Economy."

18. Tuerck, Haughton, Bachman, Sanchez-Penalver, and Ngo, "A Distributional Analysis of Adopting the FairTax: A Comparison of the Current Tax System and the FairTax Plan," and Burman, "The Trouble with the FairTax."

19. Hall and Rabushka, *The Flat Tax.*

20. *Ibid.*

21. Committee for a Responsible Federal Budget, "Senator Rand Paul Releases Flat Tax Plan."

22. U.S. Bureau of Economic Analysis, "Industry Data – Gross Output by Industry."

23. National Association of Realtors, "Existing Home Sales Statistics"; Edmunds, "Used Car Report 2018."

24. Board of Governors of the Federal Reserve System, *Financial Accounts of the United States, 3rd Quarter, 2018.*

25. Board of Governors of the Federal Reserve System, "Changes in U.S. Family Finances from 2013 to 2016: Evidence from the Survey of Consumer Finances." The wealth average is based on updating 2016 by the compound inflation rate (Consumer Price Index) between 2016 and 2018.

26. U.S. Bureau of Labor Statistics, "Consumer Expenditure Surveys." Income before taxes.

27. Wolff, *op. cit.*

28. York, "Summary of the Latest Federal Income Tax Data, 2017 Update."

29. Kagan, "Cascade Tax."

30. Walsh, "Businesses Don't Pay Taxes, Consumers Do."

31. Kotlikoff, "The Economic Impact of Replacing Federal Income Taxes with a Sales Tax"; Holtz-Eakin and Gray, "Wealth Taxes and Workers."

32. Grennes, Fan, and Caner, "New Evidence on Debt as an Obstacle to US Economic Growth."

33. Heathcote and Perri, "Wealth and Volatility."

34. D'Ambrosio, Menta, and Wolff, "Income and Wealth Volitality: Evidence from Italy and the U.S. in the Past Two Decades."

35. Johnsen and Dellinger, "The Constitutionality of a National Wealth Tax." The question boils down to whether the wealth tax is a "direct tax" on a person, or an "indirect tax" on an action. If it is considered a direct tax, it may have to meet the constitutional requirement of having the same amount per person collected from each state – something that is not likely. If it is deemed an indirect tax, then the wealth tax could go forward without a constitutional amendment; Barro, "Constitutional Concerns are a Major Risk for Federal Wealth Tax."

36. Rabushka, "The Colonial Roots of American Taxation: 1607-1700."

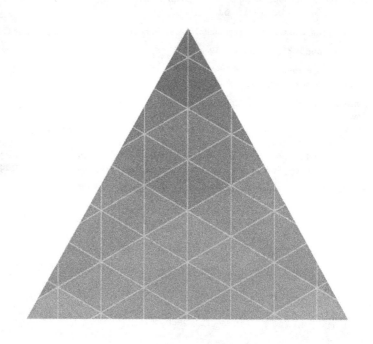

CHAPTER SIXTEEN

BALANCING THE BENEFITS AND COSTS OF IMMIGRATION

SHUTDOWNS AND CARAVANS

When I began writing the opening to this chapter, the federal government was operating under a partial shutdown, and a new migrant caravan was making its way to the U.S. border through Mexico. Both of these events were wrapped up in an intense debate about immigration. The government shutdown resulted from an impasse between President Trump and Congress over the logic and effectiveness of adding physical barriers, such as walls, along the southern border. Some say the large migrant caravans from Central America, which began to appear in 2018, have happened because migrants have been told it is relatively easy to enter the U.S.[1]

Hopefully by the time you read this chapter, these two immigration-related issues will have been settled, but maybe not. Immigration has become a cutting edge and divisive issue in current American politics. Of course, like most issues, there are the extremes. One extreme wants no immigration and is suspicious of all those who try to cross our borders. They say immigrants can bring crime and terrorism to the country and impose costs on taxpaying citizens for health care, schooling, etc. There are also some who worry how immigration changes the demographic and cultural composition of the country.[2]

At the other extreme are individuals who favor more immigrants and relatively open borders, because they claim immigrants actually boost the nation's economic growth and are especially needed as the nation's birth rate drops.[3] In their view, immigrants allow the nation to grow and prosper, and are, in other words, a net economic plus for the country.

In this chapter, I'll address the thorny issue of immigration and try to figure out who's right. Are immigrants a net gain for the economy, or do they simply saddle others with extra welfare costs? Alternatively, maybe reality is more complicated. Maybe there are "goldilocks" amounts of immigration—not too much, but not too small—that are optimal both for the immigrants and for the country. If so, where does the symbol of immigration for those both pro and con—the border wall—fit into an immigration solution?

But first, a short review of our history with immigration is useful to set the stage for today's debates. And guess what: most of today's issues are not new.

△ WE'VE SEEN THIS MOVIE BEFORE

Today is not the first time immigration has been debated in our country. In our nation's first century, immigration was encouraged. The reason is obvious—the land mass is huge, yet the population was small. For example, after the Mexican War in the 1840s resulted in the U.S. now spanning the Atlantic to the Pacific, the population was a mere 17 million, only 5% of today's total.[4] To develop the country as well as protect it from foreign enemies, more people were needed.

Between 1840 and 1920, over 22 million people emigrated to the U.S. from foreign countries, and this population combined with the natural population growth from existing citizens pushed the nation's total number to over 100 million.[5] The country was now a world power with an expanding role in international affairs.

The maturing of the nation also sparked the first major debate over immigration. Many worried the nation's identity was being eroded by immigrants. Some of these concerns were motivated by cultural and ethnic biases against the majority of new immigrants now coming from Eastern Europe. In earlier times, the bulk of immigrants to the U.S. were from Western Europe, especially Great Britain, Ireland, and Germany.[6]

The anti-immigration forces won the debate with the passage of the Immigration Act of 1924.[7] Immigration to the U.S. was dramatically reduced though the use of quotas. Immigrants from Western Europe, especially Great Britain, were favored, whereas immigrants from Asia were prohibited altogether. The number of "first generation immigrants"—those foreign-born persons living in the U.S.—dropped over 40% between 1910 and 1965.[8] Annual immigration rates plunged 98% between 1914 and 1933, from 1.2 million down to 23,000 immigrants.[9]

The tides turned again in 1965 when federal legislation began eliminating the 1924 quotas, thereby substantially increasing the total number of immigrants allowed each year. New laws also gave preference to immigrants who had family members living in the U.S.[10] As a result, the total number of first generation immigrants jumped to 39 million in 2015. As a percent of the nation's total population, there were three times more first-generation immigrants in 2015 than in 1965.[11] By the late 20th century, immigrants accounted for one-third of the nation's population growth, a rate not seen since the peak of immigration between 1840 and 1920.[12]

Today we have the next installment in the immigration debate; for a variety of reasons, including globalization, terrorism, drug and human trafficking, cultural identities, and the shrinking of the middle-class, immigration is a big part of many of our larger issues. Of course, there is also the fact that a substantial number of first-generation immigrants have not entered the country legally. Although the total number can only be an estimate, the number of illegal, or undocumented, individuals in the country is estimated to be between 11 and 22 million people.[13] Also, an increasing share of illegal immigrants in the country were initially allowed *legally* for a short period of time (in immigration lingo, they were given a temporary visa), but they have overstayed that period.[14] Last is the complex question of the status of children of illegal immigrants who, while born in another country, have been raised in the U.S. Should their status be considered differently?

△ BENEFITS OR COSTS, OR BOTH?

Before we can talk about alternative solutions to our immigration debate, we need to look at immigrants' impacts on our country, and particularly on our economy. Again, the extreme positions have been staked out. "Immigration pessimists," as I'll call them, focus on potential negative economic effects from immigrants. Pessimists claim that immigrants lower the wages of the domestic labor force by competing for jobs while unemployed immigrants increase public welfare expenses. If immigrants bring children with them or have children once here, they increase education costs.[15] Furthermore, some immigration pessimists believe the crime rate among immigrants is higher, which puts an economic burden on the criminal justice system.[16] And, to top it all off, some maintain that many immigrants, particularly those entering the country illegally, pay no or little taxes.[17]

Those in support of immigration, dubbed "immigration optimists," believe that it boosts economic growth by bringing new skills and capabilities to the country.[18] They argue that immigration is the key to the nation's success since the country's birth rate has dropped to levels leading to future depopulation and worker shortages.[19] In turn, immigrants require public services, like education. However, their paid taxes compensate for these public costs (and immigrants do pay taxes, according to optimists). Regarding crime, immigration optimists say that rates among immigrants are no higher—instead often lower—than for existing residents.

Who's correct, the immigration pessimists or the immigration optimists? What have the numerous studies on immigration determined? Do these studies say anything consistent and believable?

In fact, they do. The studies have been catalogued and summarized in a major report by the National Academies of Sciences, Engineering, and Medicine.[20] Sounds impressive, right? It should. The

National Academies of Sciences, Engineering, and Medicine include the top people from the academic world in their respective fields. It's a big deal in universities and colleges for any faculty member to be asked to join this group. For their study on immigration, the National Academies assembled respected economists, sociologists, and public policy experts to review the existing research that's been done on immigration.

What did they find? Fortunately, a lot, much of which makes sense, but with perhaps some surprises included. Here are the key findings:

- Immigrants have come to the U.S. mainly for work. Relative to the rest of the world, the U.S. is a rich country with a dynamic and expanding economy, so immigrants are able to find better jobs and economic opportunities here than in their home country.

- Immigrants tend to go to states with strong job growth.

- The average educational level of immigrants has improved over time and today is only one-half year of schooling lower than U.S. workers. Still, the proportion of immigrants with less than a high school education is higher than for U.S. residents.

- The average immigrant begins with earnings much lower than U.S. residents, however, over time this gap narrows considerably.

- Several studies show low-skilled immigrants have directly competed with domestic low-skilled workers, resulting in wages dropping for all.

- In contrast, high-skilled immigrants have a positive impact on wages paid to both domestic high-skilled and low-skilled workers by helping to increase overall innovation and economic growth.

- By expanding the work force, immigrants have had a dampening effect on consumer prices.

- In their initial years in the country, immigrants (especially young immigrants) impose net fiscal losses on government, meaning the cost of public services that immigrants use is larger than the taxes they pay.

- However, the longer immigrants stay—especially as young immigrants mature to middle-age—immigrants are a net fiscal benefit to government, meaning they pay more in taxes than they use in government costs. This pattern is found in the nation as well as in the majority of states.

- Immigrants have lowered the age profile of the country, thereby increasing the nation's population growth and helping to extend the solvency of programs like Social Security which rely on contributions from younger workers.

- Crime rates for immigrants are not higher than crimes rates for U.S. born persons of similar age groupings.

- Immigrants assimilate with the native population over time, but the pace of assimilation has slowed in recent years.

- Illegal immigration has been less in the second decade of the 21st century compared to the first decade.[21]

I'll let you decide if these findings are more in line with the immigration pessimists or optimists. I see a blend of both sides. The pessimists are correct that immigration can have adverse effects on some domestic workers, particularly low-skilled workers. They are also right in worrying about negative fiscal impacts on governments in the initial years of an immigrant's residence in the U.S. Last, the evidence backs their concern about the recent slower pace of assimilation of immigrants.

But the optimists have also had a number of their beliefs confirmed by the studies. Overall, immigrants have added to the nation's economic growth by augmenting the labor force. They have lowered the average age of the country and helped programs like Social Security. Higher skilled immigrants are often innovators and entrepreneurs. The optimists are also correct on crime; the average crime rate for immigrants is not higher than the crime rate for existing citizens.

△ HOT BUTTON ISSUES: WALLS, RULES, AND REALITY

Most fair-minded individuals agree that the response to immigration across the southern border is inadequate, but these fair-minded people can't agree on what it should be. Frustration comes in three forms: the first is over what should be done with undocumented immigrants already living in the country, some of them for decades. Mass deportation is not practical nor likely preferable. There's just no good way to remove between 11 and 22 million individuals from the country. Conversely, establishing a fast-track path to citizenship is seen by many as rewarding those who have not followed the legal procedures of becoming citizens. It's like rewarding people who cut in line.

The amount of time and effort required to deal with immigrants, especially those who are seeking asylum or have illegally entered the country, creates a second source of frustration. With a backlog of over 800,000 individuals awaiting their case in immigration court, most are ultimately released with a promise of later appearing in court.[22] This system has been called "catch and release." While a majority of released migrants do appear for their hearing, in recent years around 40% have not.[23] Critics argue more detention facilities are needed as well as judges and courts specifically devoted to immigration issues.[24]

Last is the issue that closed one-third of the federal government due to disagreements between the President and Congress in early 2019. This is the issue of border security. The government cannot determine what combination of technology, human guards, and physical barriers provides the most effective and cost-efficient method of deterring individuals from entering the country illegally in the first place.

Regarding border security, most studies agree additional patrol agents reduce illegal immigration. One study estimates 1,000 additional border patrol agents could deter around 1 million individuals annually from illegally crossing the border. Using this number and the salaries and benefits of the added agents, the cost of deterring one person works out to be $464 (2018 purchasing power dollars).[25]

A wall is often considered as the ultimate in border security, but walls come with problems; they are very expensive, they can be climbed or tunneled under, and they can't be built in all regions. And rather than deterring illegal crossings, they may just redirect those crossings to other parts of the border.[26] Studies in the U.S. based on comparing illegal border crossings and apprehensions before and after border wall and barrier construction in the 1990s and 2000s, have found very modest improvements to border security.[27]

For decades, Israel has used walls and fences as part of its border security with Gaza and Egypt. Has it worked, and if so, why?

Indeed, the data on the Israeli border barriers show a big success, with illegal crossings dropping 99% after completion of the barriers.[28] Yet Israel deters crossings with more than the barriers; their walls and fences are heavily patrolled, with guards posted every 1.2 miles (half the U.S. ratio) and numerous observation towers with high-tech equipment surveilling the nearby territory. There are clear sight lines at the southern Israeli border because the land is flat and barren, whereas, comparatively much of the southern U.S. border is hilly with vegetation. Plus, the southern Israeli border is only 150 miles, compared to 2,000 miles on the U.S.-Mexico border.[29]

Here's my conclusion: walls and barriers are useful in stopping and impairing illegal crossings, but not without help—mainly in the form of guards and technology. It takes the full-court press of these three tactics.

Yet is this really what we want to do to solve the immigration issue? Keep people out who want to come in? Wouldn't it be better to use motivations and incentives to act in ways where everyone benefits? We want solutions that maximize the benefits of immigration while minimizing the costs. Let's next look at solutions, both fake and real, and see how they stack up on creating a winning immigration policy.

△ FAKE SOLUTIONS

There's one fake solution that has a simple answer: let everyone in. In short, have open borders, not only in the U.S. but in every country in the world.

The supporters (I'll call them "OBs" for open-borderers) essentially consider national borders to be artificial and to stifle economic progress in the world. Limits on migration mean people can't move to other countries where their skills and talents could be put to better use. They can't move from countries where there may be no options for their capabilities to countries where their capabilities are in high demand. Some OBs even consider impeding immigration to be immoral and discriminatory because it limits a person's potential simply based on where they were born.[30]

In the OBs' view, restricting international immigration would be like limiting movement of people between U.S. states. Before he retired, my cousin in Ohio was a welder. He frequently moved to other states where the jobs for welders were sometimes more plentiful. We would never think of preventing welders from moving across state lines to take jobs. The OBs say we shouldn't prevent the same kind of movement between countries.

OBs use economics to support their idea. Most production requires two ingredients, workers (people) and capital, where capital is just a fancy word for money used to purchase machinery, technology, and buildings. OBs argue that there is already virtual free movement of capital all around the world. Allowing investors to put their money where it can earn the highest rate of return is smart because it achieves the "greatest bang for the buck." Why not use the same logic for workers?

In fact, the OBs claim permitting the free movement of labor would achieve a tremendous payoff for the world. OBs estimate total world economic production would increase between 50% and 200% with people moving to where their skills could be best used.[31]

But what about people already living illegally in countries, like the estimated 11 to 22 million undocumented individuals residing in the U.S.? Although OBs' proposal doesn't specifically address this question, presumably the answer would be: they stay. What sense would it be to deport them and then allow them to freely re-enter the country later.

There's one other idea that has gained some traction supporting open borders for specific populations, which is the idea is that open borders are a form of reparations for people who have been wronged.[32] In the case of the U.S., advocates say there are three wrongs that need to be righted. The first is U.S. settlers of mainly European descent taking land and resources that had legitimately been under Mexican control. It is argued the U.S.-Mexican War in the 1840s was largely a ruse to obtain Mexican land in today's western U.S., including California. Therefore, allowing Mexican immigrants into the U.S. is justifiable pay-back for that land grab.

The second wrong is past enslavement, mainly of individuals of

African origin. One way of compensating for that wrong is to allow current Africans to freely immigrate to the U.S.

Last is the idea that developed countries, including the U.S., are making life unbearable in many less developed countries by encouraging violence through the export of armaments and by being the main contributors to climate change and global warming. The notion is that developed countries owe a safe refuge and decent life to people adversely impacted by the wars and rising temperatures.

Clearly the idea of open borders is controversial on many levels and raises numerous questions. Would open borders imply anyone could move to a country and effectively become a citizen, thereby acquiring all the rights (voting, benefits, etc.) of a natural born citizen? What would this mean for the concept of a nation? Would nations effectively cease to exist? Would free movement of people be the first step toward a world government? Are we ready to end the concept of countries with shared backgrounds, cultures, and beliefs?

Strictly interpreted, the concept of open borders would mean having no control over who enters the nation. Presumably criminals, drug cartel operators, and possible terrorists could move to the U.S. at will. Even among law-abiding immigrants, there would be no limits on income level and education. Remember the evidence from the National Academy of Sciences comprehensive study suggesting low-skilled immigrants have had the effect of decreasing wages for domestic low skilled workers? A surge in low-skilled immigrants likely would economically harm similarly skilled current workers.

A wave of new immigrants, especially low-skilled ones, could also overwhelm public budgets, especially at the state and local levels. The National Academies of Sciences concluded immigrants create higher public service costs than they provide in public revenues in the initial years of their residence in the country. This situation could require significantly higher local and state tax rates or financial aid from the federal government, at least for a while.

So, I think the concept of open borders has practical problems related to who will enter the country and the immediate impacts of those entering. Yet more fundamentally, the belief has philosophical issues about the concept of a nation and the rights of nations to control their borders. While some may be willing to eliminate national boundaries, I'm not one of them. I believe nations are logical ways of organizing people with common backgrounds, core ideas, and goals. Therefore, I label the recommendation of open borders a fake solution.

If the open borders idea is, "if you want to come, come," it's conceptual opposite may be, "if you can pay to come, come." This is an immigration idea originally promoted by a Nobel Prize winning economist, Gary Becker, and refined by others since then,[33] which creates a "market" for immigration. Under current immigration policy, people perceive immigrating to the U.S. as a benefit, but without a price for doing so. Actually, some do by paying often unscrupulous individuals to smuggle them to the U.S. border under the promise they'll be able to cross and enter.[34] Some are able to enter—others aren't.

The immigration market would bring these transactions above board and create benefits to both parties—the immigrant as well as the receiving country, such as the U.S. The market would work like this: each year, the U.S. would set a number for the maximum number of immigrants the country would take. If desired, the number could be divided into categories, using, for example, education, occupation, or even age as groupings. At specific times during the year, a certain portion (maybe 10%) of the total would be advertised for bidding. Those making the highest bids would be granted entry to the country, which could be for a limited time period or forever.

The money for the immigrants' payment could come from several sources; some immigrants would pay themselves, others could be sponsored by U.S. companies who want to fill job openings. Immigrant families already in the U.S. could put up the money for relatives. Estimates suggest this plan could generate serious money, somewhere between $10 billion and $20 billion annually.[35] The funds could then be used for border security, to reimburse states and localities for the fiscal costs imposed by immigrants, or could be distributed to U.S. taxpayers.

A part of the plan would also deal with existing illegal immigrants living in the country. These individuals could legally remain in the country if they came forward and pleaded guilty to a misdemeanor for violating immigration laws. They would not serve jail time, but instead would pay a significant fine, perhaps between $1,000 and $5,000. Garnishment of a portion of wages would be an acceptable form of payment. Then individuals would either be granted permanent residency without citizenship or be put on a path to citizenship.

The economist side of me likes the Becker plan. It's a form of "pay to play," where the "play" is obtaining a legal right to be in the country. It's also a direct way of raising money to pay for the costs of controlling the border and immigration. Then why do I label it a fake solution?

I call it fake because I'm worried the plan could be "worked" or "scammed." What's to prevent drug cartel money or money from terrorist organizations from placing very high bids in order to have their agents legally cross the border? Money can be easily "laundered" and shifted in order to make it seem legitimate—for example, to make it seem as if the funds are coming from an established U.S. company or an existing immigrant family.

Then there's also the soft side of me which says part of the greatness of our nation is that we have taken the "huddled masses and the homeless." Sometimes there are things money can't measure, and maybe some of them are the hopes and desires of people who have little else.

△ REAL SOLUTIONS

There are four parts to a real solution to the immigration issue. Number one: we need a plan for the 11 to 22 million undocumented immigrants currently living in the country. While some who have committed crimes will be apprehended and deported, the vast majority won't. Indeed, the majority are employed and law-abiding. We need to give these individuals some form of status or certification for legally remaining in the country.

Number two: since I have labeled the open borders concept a fake solution, we need security for our borders. That is, we need to make our borders, and particularly the southern border, a true barrier for entering our country. Although we can't make borders airtight, to the extent possible we only want individuals to enter the country legally. The question is what methods and forms border security should take.

Number three: we need to decide the kinds of immigrants we want coming to our country based on characteristics such as family connections to existing U.S. citizens, work characteristics, or flight from political persecution.

Number four: we must decide on the allowable number of immigrants for each year. Also, we need a process for facilitating immigration. Some alternatives are first-in-line, a lottery, or those with the characteristics the country prefers. I have rejected as a fake solution allowing those to enter who offer to pay the most for that privilege.

I've reviewed numerous immigration plans, and the one that is most logical and covers all four solution parts has been developed by former Florida Governor Jeb Bush and his colleague Clint Bolick.[36] I'll refer to it as the BB (Bush-Bolick) plan. Here's what it would do.

For the first issue of illegal immigrants currently residing in the country, BB would allow those who present themselves to officials and plead guilty to illegally entering the country to pay a fine (perhaps in the $1,000 to $5,000 range) or accept community service. In exchange, they would be granted "permanent residence" status. But they would *not* be put on a path to citizenship. Ultimately, granting citizenship would condone the illegal entry committed by the immigrants and would be unfair to those who follow the legal steps to citizenship. However, children born to these illegal immigrants while in the U.S. are automatic citizens according to the Constitution.

What about individuals who were brought to the country as children by their parents? While they violated the law, the decision for them to cross the border was made by their parents and not by them. These children, many of whom are now be adults, are commonly referred to as "dreamers."[37] BB recommends the dreamers be treated differently; those who were illegally brought to the country while under the age of 18, who have resided in the country for at least five years, and who have not committed serious crimes, would be granted permanent legal status with a path to citizenship.

In 2019, a major national debate occurred over the second issue—border security—and what it really means. The debate was so intense that it caused a partial shutdown of the federal government for over a month. While the debate had political motives, there are also substantive differences about the best way to stop illegal border crossings. The U.S.-Mexico southern border is almost 2,000 miles long. Two-thirds of it has no walls or fencing.[38] Spanning the southern border with a high steel wall would cost around $25 billion.[39] But as Israel's experience has shown, border patrol personnel and technology to complement border walls are also important.

BB recommends (and I agree) leaving the form and type of border security to the experts in security, both inside and outside the government. This is not an issue that Congress or the President should attempt to micro-manage. Congress should seek recommendations from security experts about the best approaches to protection for the southern border when deliberating about the budget for immigration.

In terms of issue number three, the number and kinds of immigrants permitted to come to the U.S., BB thinks it is time to move away from the family-oriented policies enacted five decades ago. In the 1965 immigration legislation, preferences for immigrants were shifted from labor market characteristics to family characteristics.[40] Specifically, immigration preferences were established for relatives of existing U.S. citizens. Moreover, the preferences didn't stop at close relatives, such as spouses and children, but extended to grandparents, uncles, aunts, etc. Once one of these relatives enter the country, there is an automatic entitlement for their relatives to also be eligible. This led to the term *chain migration* where, similar to a chain letter, the connections expand exponentially once a new link is made. In recent years, two-thirds of legal immigrants have been relatives (often very distant relatives) of U.S. citizens.[41]

BB would not eliminate family member immigration, but instead would limit it to spouses and minor children of U.S. citizens, and they would only be one of four categories of immigrants. The other three would be those coming specifically for short-term work, those who are refugees or asylum seekers from politically dysfunctional countries, and finally "sponsored immigrants," who are individuals recommended by a U.S. citizen and could be a friend or extended family member.

For the fourth issue, BB rightly wants Congress (who represent the citizens of the nation) to ultimately designate the total number of immigrants as well as the number for each of the four categories. BB recommends an annual total of 1 million legal immigrants, which is very close to the annual average in the 21st century.[42] BB calls for percentage splits of 35% for immediate family (spouse and children) members, 27.5% for short-term work seekers, 10% for refugees and asylum applicants, and 27.5% for sponsored immigration. Adjustments could be made in both the total annual number as well as the percentage splits at the discretion of Congress.

Applications for entry to the country would be on a first-come, first-served basis for three of the categories—family member immigrants, refugee and asylum seekers, and sponsored immigration. For the short-term work category, immigration officials in consultation with other government agencies and the private sector would identify needed skills for the economy and give preferences for applicants with those skills. Foreign students studying in U.S. universities and colleges would be eligible to apply. Many see the competition for high-skilled foreign talent to be crucial for improving and growing our economy.[43] Also, for regular seasonal work, such as in agriculture, applicants could obtain a recurring work permit for multiple years.

I would make one addition to the BB immigration plan, which is to consider immigrants who are willing to move to economically-challenged regions of the country. Many of these regions are rural areas suffering from population loss. Potential immigrants in any of the four categories, and especially those with entrepreneurial skills, would receive extra consideration for admission to the country if they could help rebuild localities left behind by the new technologically-driven economy. Some have dubbed this idea a "heartland visa."[44]

It's very important to realize the BB plan would not eliminate our debates over immigration. In particular, I would expect on-going clashes about both the annual totals for allowable immigration as well as the proportions between the four immigration categories.

And even within those categories, there will be continuing strong differences of opinion, like those worried about adverse impacts on domestic wages, about fiscal costs from young immigrants, and about how assimilation may favor minimizing low-skilled immigrants and maximizing high-skilled newcomers to our country.[45]

The BB plan is a reasonable approach to the multi-faceted issues involved in immigration. It respects the law, respects individuals who have entered our country in a legal way, but also recognizes the realities, benefits, and compassion in our immigration history.

▲ SUMMING UP

Immigration has become a contentious issue as the number of undocumented individuals residing in our country has climbed to possibly as high as 22 million. Some want to open the borders to all desiring to enter. Others want the borders tightened and illegal immigrants deported. But the conclusion of the research on immigration suggests that it has been a net benefit to the country. A logical immigration policy would have four major parts. Existing illegal immigrants would pay a fine in order to receive permanent residency, but not citizenship. The southern border would be strengthened. Lawful immigration would be restructured to include immediate family members of U.S. citizens, individuals with needed work skills, a relatively small number of political refugees and asylum seekers, and other individuals sponsored by U.S. citizens. Total annual immigration would be decided by Congress, with 1 million annual immigrants being a logical number.

Chapter 16 Endnotes

1. Holpuch, "I Don't Want to Go Back: What's next for the Central American Migrant Caravan?"

2. Kaufman, *White Shift: Populism, Immigration, and the Future of White Majorities.*

3. See Bricker and Ibbitson, *Empty Planet,* for the implications of possible population decline.

4. "U.S. Population throughout History," *ThoughtCo.*

5. National Academies of Sciences, Engineering, and Medicine, *The Economic and Fiscal Consequences of Immigration.*

6. Goldberg, *Discontented America: The United States in the 1920s.*

7. Office of the Historian, U.S. Department of State, "The Immigration Act of 1924."

8. Migration Policy Institute, "Major US Immigration Laws, 1790-Present."

9. Migration Policy Institute, "Legal Immigration in the U.S., 1820-Present."

10. *Ibid.*

11. Radford, "Facts on U.S. Immigrants, 2016."

12. National Academies of Sciences, Engineering, and Medicine, *op. cit.*

13. Krogstad, Passe, and Cohn, "5 Facts about Illegal Immigration in the U.S."; Discusses the 11 million estimate. The 22 million estimate is found in Fazel-Zarandi, Feinstein, and Kaplan, "The Number of Undocumented Immigrants in the U.S.: Estimates Based on Demographic Modelling with Data from 1990-2016."

14. Del Real, "The Number of Undocumented Immigrants in the U.S. Has Dropped, a Study Says. Here are 5 Takeaways."

15. Salam, *Melting Pot or Civil War?*

16. Farley, "Is Illegal Immigration Linked to More or Less Crime?"

17. O'Dowd, "Stop U.S. Tax-Paying Law-Abiding Undocumented Immigrants Right Now."

18. Davies and Harrigan, "The Economic Case for Immigration."

19. Minarik and Ferguson, "Immigration is Best Solution for Shortage of Workers in America."

20. National Academies of Sciences, Engineering, and Medicine study, *The Integration of Immigrants into American Society.*

21. *Ibid.*

22. Lu and Watkins, "Court Backlog May Prove Bigger Barrier for Migrants than Any Wall."

23. Kruzel, "Majority of Undocumented Immigrants Show Up for Court, Data Show."

24. Cristobal and O'Shea, "Why Hiring More Judges Would Reduce Immigration Court Backlogs."

25. Muhlhausen, "Building a Better Border: What the Experts Say."

26. Bier, "Why the Wall Won't Work."

27. *Ibid*; and Allen, Dobbin, and Morton, "Border Walls."

28. U.S. Senate, "Securing Israel: Lessons Learned from a Nation under Constant Threat of Attack."

29. Valverde, "Border Fence in Israel Cut Illegal Immigration 99%, GOP Senator Says."

30. Pritchett, *Let Their People Come; Caplan, Open Borders.*

31. Clemens, "Economics and Emigration: Trillion-Dollar Bills on the Sidewalk"; Clemens and Pritchett, "The New Economic Case for Migration Restrictions: An Assessment"; Desmet, Nagy, and Rossi-Hansberg, "The Geography of Development."

32. Mehta, *This Land is Our Land.*

33. Becker and Becker, *The Economics of Life*; Vedder, "Immigration Reform: A Modest Proposal."

34. Kulish, "What It Costs to Be Smuggled Across the U.S. Border."

35. Vedder, *op.cit.*

36. Bush and Bolick, *Immigration Wars.*

37. "Immigration Case Management Blog: What Is the DREAM Act and Who are the DREAMers?" *LawLogix.* "Dreamers" refer to those immigrant children who would have been affected by the Development, Relief, and Education for Alien Minors Act, which was first voted on, but not passed, by the U.S. Congress in 2001.

38. Mark, Gould, and Kiersz, "As the Government Shutdown over Trump's Border Wall Rages, a Journey Along the Entire 1933 Mile US-Mexico Border Shows the Monumental Task of Securing It."

39. Frankel, "Build the Wall? It Could Take at Least 10 Years, Even with 10,000 Workers."

40. Migration Policy Institute, "Major US Immigration Laws, 1790-Present." *op. cit.*

41. Kandel, "U.S. Family-Based Immigration Policy."

42. Migration Policy Institute, "Legal Immigration in the U.S., 1820-Present," *op. cit.*

43. Kerr, *The Gift of Global Talent.*

44. Ozimek, Fikri, and Lettieri, "From Managing Decline to Building the Future: Could a Heartland Visa Help Struggling Regions?"

45. Salam, *op. cit.*

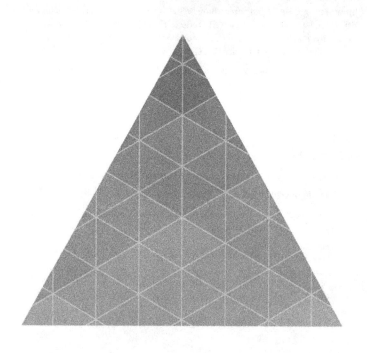

CHAPTER SEVENTEEN

CHOOSING THE BEST ECONOMIC SYSTEM

DEBATE OVER THE "ISM'S"

I smile when I hear some of my college students argue about the relative merits of capitalism and socialism. My reaction stems not only from thinking a discussion of how the country should organize its economic system is healthy, but also because I remember the same kinds of debates happening fifty years ago when I was a college undergraduate. The question of what is the best economic system has been argued frequently in our nation's history, with some of the fiercest clashes occurring during the Great Depression of the 1930s.

A similar fierce debate is occurring now, as concerns about our fundamental economic structure typically heighten during challenging economic times. The Great Depression, when the nation's economic output fell 25% and unemployment soared above 20% over several years, was the country's longest business plunge in the last 100-plus years.[1] Although statistics of the Great Recession of 2007-2009 were not nearly as bad, the near collapse of the financial and housing sectors rocked the confidence households had in important economic institutions. Then there was the short, but very deep, recession in 2020 associated with the coronavirus.

This has led many individuals, especially young people, to question the nation's economic system. Indeed, a poll in early 2019 showed the majority of individuals aged 18-29 supported socialism.[2] Perhaps even more telling, Senator Bernie Sanders, who espouses many socialist positions, almost won the Democratic Party's nomination for president in 2016 and came close again in 2020.

In this chapter, I'll review the major systems countries can use to organize their economies, specifically the "ism's" of capitalism, socialism, fascism, communism, and *authoritarian capitalism*. The front stage will be given to the first two ism's—capitalism and socialism—because they appear to be the two major contenders in the 21st century. The other three have either seen their day come and go, or are hybrids with little backing.

Unlike previous chapters, here I won't present "fake solutions" and "real solutions." Instead, in the last section I'll pick my preferred method, tell why I selected it, and offer modifications to make it better at providing the highest standard of living and the broadest prospects for economic opportunity.

△ CAPITALISM

The key feature of *capitalism* is private ownership. Specifically, it is private ownership of the factors used to make products and services (land, labor, and capital, where capital includes machinery and technology). The ownership can be by an individual (I own my labor), a couple of people (business partners), or by many people (shareholders of a corporation). The important point is that owners of these "factors of production" make all the key decisions about how their factors are used. Also, in purchasing or renting factors owned by others, mutual agreements are reached between the factor owners and the buyers or renters.

Often the private ownership and private interactions and trades of capitalism are referred to as "free enterprise." Within agreed-to limits, individuals have the freedom to use their factors of production as they wish and in the ways they wish. "Oh no," you're saying, "what are these 'agreed-to limits'?" They're simply rules and laws public bodies have developed to protect those engaged in capitalism, like laws against fraud and theft, rules about contracts and disclosures of information, and punishments for violations. The limits have been established to create a feeling of trust among the participants of capitalism and to ensure a level playing field in trades, interactions, and agreements.

Capitalism relies on both cooperation and competition. Cooperation is needed when various factor owners combine to make a final product or service. For example, the workers at points along an auto assembly line must cooperate in their individual tasks to complete putting together the vehicle. Likewise, companies delivering parts like engines and seats to the auto assembly plant must get them there on time so the plant can meet its production schedule.

At the same time, the capitalist system results in competition among alternative makers of the same product or service, which is good. Competition means no individual or company has a "lock" on sales.

Instead, capitalism encourages numerous buying options, which lets buyers evaluate the best fit for themselves. It also encourages companies to be efficient and frugal in their production so they can attract buyers with lower prices. Further, in facing competition, companies are motivated to invent and innovate to make better products and services that attract more buyers and earn higher revenues, even if only temporarily.

There are two threats to these positive outcomes from capitalism. First is the motivation for companies to replace competition with cronyism. What has been dubbed "crony capitalism" happens when one or a few companies in the same industry use the political system to buy influence and rig the rules to favor them and disfavor—or even better for them, eliminate—competitors.[3] An example of this is the discussion in Chapter 4 of pharmaceutical companies using political donations to influence rules and budgets affecting federal health-care agencies.

A second threat occurs when competition by many companies collapses to total control by one or a few companies. Control by one company is called a monopoly, while control by a few companies is called an oligopoly. We saw an example of an oligopoly with large health-care systems. The challenge for public policy is figuring out how to deal with these situations when they exist. For example, the information technology industry is now dominated by only four companies, the so-called "FANG" firms: Facebook, Amazon, Netflix, and Google. One line of thought suggests the FANGs should be broken up into many smaller companies.[4]

Critics of capitalism see four big problems with the system, which are greed, inequality, selfishness, and disposability. Critics say capitalism encourages companies to chase ever larger profits and ignore anything that doesn't contribute to those profits, such as a clean environment or the happiness of workers.[5] Because capitalism creates winners and losers, as well as owners and workers, unequal incomes are a natural result of the system.[6] The competitive nature of capitalism is said to make people self-centered and selfish, with a winner-take-all attitude.[7] With innovation and change necessary for companies to remain competitive and profitable, it's argued that capitalists have a "throw-away" attitude; if it doesn't help them now, critics worry capitalists have an incentive to get rid of "it," regardless of whether the "it" is a machine or a worker.[8]

There are counter arguments to the capitalist critics. In pure capitalism, competition keeps profits in line. In fact, the average profit rate for all companies is around 7%.[9] The response to unequal incomes is not to impose equality, but to have an educational system that offers equal opportunity. Furthermore, widening income equality doesn't imply the rich are taking income away from the poor, it usually means the rich are adding income at a faster rate than the poor.[10] Capitalists can be altruistic, with many examples of business owners being both wealthy and charitable.[11] Yet even without altruism, Adam Smith famously showed how those working in their own self-interest (like the farmer) provides benefits (food) to many strangers.[12]

When capitalist companies ignore broader public issues, such as pollution, there are methods and techniques that can be used to force them to recognize those issues (see Chapter 11). While innovation and progress often do have job casualties, having a broad and secure social safety net and re-training opportunities can treat those casualties and put them on the path to recovery.

△ SOCIALISM

The polar opposite of capitalism is *socialism*. A socialist economic system is one where the factors of production are owned by everyone. Usually "everyone" is represented by the government. The government therefore makes decisions about what to produce, how much to produce, prices charged, and payments made to workers, managers, and landlords. In capitalism, these decisions are decentralized to the interactions between buyers and sellers of both factors of production and final products. In socialism, economic decisions are centralized in the government. In capitalism, millions of people make economic decisions; in socialism, only a few do. When the government is elected by citizens of the country, the system is sometimes called "democratic socialism."[13]

Backers of socialism see big benefits from the system in the workplace.[14] In socialism there is no chasing of profits—instead, all participants in the economy are paid an "adequate" amount for their inputs, such as an adequate wage to workers and an adequate rent to providers of machinery. What is "adequate" is defined by the society through the government.

With government setting the payments, ideas of fairness among occupations and groups can be enacted. For example, in capitalist economics concerns have been expressed about how much more money that company managers (CEOs, or chief executive officers) make relative to average workers (see Chapter 6). Socialist economies can specifically set how much more a CEO makes relative to the average worker. Socialist systems can also dictate standards on pay equity between male and female workers.

Socialist supporters also tout attention to worker conditions as a benefit;[15] Rather than individual companies establishing rules like work hours, overtime, and vacation and sick leave, the government makes and enforces these rules in an expected "reasonable and fair" manner. Changes in production methods, like the introduction of labor-saving technology, can be introduced in a way and at a pace to minimize disruption to workers' lives.

Promoters say socialism can free companies and the economic system to pursue broader public goals like a clean environment, the elimination of discrimination, and healthy families.[16] Without worrying about making high enough profits or losing sales to an aggressive competitor, companies can switch to renewable energy, hire workers who deserve a break, and provide appropriate family leave time.

One of the key challenges for socialism is setting prices. Prices are actually a very important source of information for the economy. Most of us don't think of prices like this. If we're a buyer, we worry about prices being too high, and if we're a seller, we hope prices are high enough to cover our costs and leave a profit. However, in the economic system, prices are signals telling resources where to move. For example, consider what happened when Hurricane Fran hit Raleigh—where I live—in 1996. Anticipating the storm, people stripped the stores of food, water, tarps, and chain saws. For several days after Fran, no one could move. Yet when we could finally drive to stores, I was amazed—they were completely stocked, and prices were almost back to normal. How could his happen?

It was because the shortages after the storm caused prices for food, repair and construction tools, and materials to skyrocket. There were big profits to be made if companies could get products to the state. So, companies did that with an urgency, because they knew the high prices wouldn't last. This all happened without any central direction from the government.

I know what you're thinking: couldn't the government do the same thing just as fast? The government could try, but it couldn't order companies to move materials as fast as when the companies anticipated a large financial return from their efforts. When prices take a jump due to shortages, that's a large flashing light to companies to send supplies to end the shortage.

Here's an opposite example. A couple of decades ago, cassette tapes (which were bulky 5-inch by 3-inch holders of wound cellulite tape) were the common way to watch movies at home. But smaller and lighter diskettes and now streaming have killed off cassette tapes and the companies (Blockbuster was my favorite) that rented them. Companies making and renting the tapes saw their stock prices plunge and eventually closed down. The fall in stock prices was a clear signal for investors to sell and move their money (or what was left of it!) to other investments, like companies offering streaming.

Obviously, people working in the factories making the cassette tapes and the stores renting them lost their jobs and had to find other work. However, with consumers no longer interested in cassette tapes, it would have been wasteful to continue making them. Brutal as it may seem, a capitalist system immediately recognizes this. But the question is whether a socialist system would do the same, or at least do it as rapidly. Governments running the economy in socialist systems face a conflict of interest. Just like capitalist systems, they want a productive and modern economy, but sometimes that means making changes which temporarily hurt some workers, as the cassette tape example shows. In capitalist systems, businesses can be ruthless in making these changes, whereas in socialist systems, governments can receive backlash from workers at the ballot box that might give those governments pause in closing failing businesses and redirecting resources elsewhere. Capitalist businesses don't face a ballot box and so don't have this concern.

This is one big disadvantage of socialist economic systems; they often aren't willing to make the changes and allow the resource movements to keep an economy expanding, innovating, and producing. This is important because growth, innovation, and improved productivity lead to higher standards of living, and if socialist countries attempt to make these changes, they can sometimes be met by civil unrest, as witnessed by the worker riots in France in both 2018 and 2019.[17]

The sensitivity of socialist governments to voters often motivates them to set prices too low, thereby causing shortages.[18] Consumers want low prices, particularly for everyday items like gasoline, food, and clothing, but if prices are low, then so too will be the wages of workers making those products. Workers won't be motivated to work as hard, meaning production will suffer. Cheap prices do consumers little good if the shelves are bare! At the same time, shortages motivate bribery and favoritism for the well-connected and wealthy in securing access to limited supplies.[19]

There are two recent examples of socialist countries that moved toward capitalism and reaped the benefits with higher standards of living. The countries are the two largest in the world in population: China and India. After the communists took over China in 1949 (communism is a form of socialism, but more on that later), top-down control of the economy by the government was imposed. Every aspect of business was dictated and regulated by the government.

It was a disaster! Although China was already a poor country, poverty actually increased, and famine was widespread. It took the death of Mao Tse-tung in 1976, who had been the architect of the communist takeover, to make the new leadership realize that some capitalist principles—like private ownership and market-determined prices—would improve economic performance. And it has; in the last three decades, China's economic growth rate has been among the fastest in the world. China now has the largest middle-class population in the world, and although the government still manages a significant part of the economy, the benefits of capitalism are entrenched.[20]

India has gone through a similar transformation. After winning its independence from the British following World War II, India's government took control of several key sectors of the economy and also used central planning and heavy regulations to manage private businesses. Disappointed with its economic progress, the Indian government lessened its direct influence in the 1990s and allowed the capitalist component of the economy to expand.[21]

India is an example of a country which used what I call "stealth socialism." In stealth socialism, a government establishes broad and detailed rules for businesses to follow in their production and pricing rather than overtly owning and controlling the factors of production. Japan also employed stealth socialism through their powerful MITI (Ministry of International Trade and Industry). In fact, in the 1980s and early 1990s when Japan's economy was riding high, several prominent American economists advocated that the U.S. adopt a Japanese-style management of the economy.[22] Now that Japan has suffered through a multi-decadal period of economic stagnation, many are relieved that the U.S. did not go the MITI route.[23]

Speaking of the U.S., while most concede that our economy is primarily capitalist-driven because the majority of factors of pro- duction are privately owned, they also see elements of socialism. I'm not referring to government owned and run entities like the Postal Service, but to the large amounts of tax money the U.S. government uses to influence parts of the economy. Medicare and Medicaid, for example, have enormous impacts on the health-care system, as does the food stamp program on food production and delivery. Social Security has long been labelled a socialist program because, individual payments to the system are put into a large pool of money and then distributed by a formula. The U.S. economy has frequently been referred to as a "mixed economy" because it combines elements of capitalism and socialism.[24]

△ THE OTHER ISM'S

Although capitalism and socialism are the two dominant economic systems, there are three others I want to address because their names are frequently used, and often incorrectly.

Fascism is an economic system in which the economy is divided into major sectors—like farming, steel, vehicle manufacturing, health-care, etc.—and companies in each sector run that sector's economy under guidelines and directives from the government. Sector companies are told to cooperate, not compete, and the government guarantees profits.[25] In practice, however, usually the largest companies in each sector dominate decision-making.

One way to think of fascism is as crony capitalism but on steroids. However, unlike crony capitalism where companies usually try to keep their beneficial deals with the government out of the public eye, in fascism the dominance of the economy by big companies is expected. Simply because there is private ownership in both capitalism and fascism, some critics of capitalism refer to it as fascism,[26] but these critics are wrong. As I have emphasized, competition is essential to capitalism, whereas fascist economies don't include competition. Indeed, competition is outlawed in fascism. In its place is central control and central planning of the economy, albeit implemented by privately owned companies.

The most noted (maybe notorious is a better word) countries practicing fascism were Germany, Italy, and Spain in the mid-20th century. Several countries in South America have also flirted with fascism. Fascism's political component is associated with dictatorships and highly restricted human rights.

Communism, like socialism, is an economic system with no private ownership of the factors of production. However, in communism the factors of production are owned by workers; in socialism, the government owns the factors. While socialism allows differences in individual incomes based on education, training, and occupation, in communism everyone is economically equal; theoretically, there are no rich and poor. The phrase "from each according to his ability, to each according to his needs," popularized by the creator of communism, Karl Marx, summarizes the communist philosophy of the creation and distribution of products and services. People are to use the abilities they possess in the production of products and services. They then receive finished products and services based on their needs. Collective bodies called workers' councils make decisions about each person's abilities and needs.[27]

Communism reached its height in the second half of the 20th century when the Soviet Union, Eastern Europe, and China "officially" adopted the system. I say "officially" because the communist model as developed by Marx has never been fully implemented. Rather than workers running communist states, both political and economic control has eventually been seized by a small group headed by an all-powerful dictator. Members of the communist political party, not workers, are the dominant force making key decisions in the country.

Communism, at least in name, is past its peak. The Soviet Union is no more, and its main member, Russia, has adopted some capitalist principles, although with a large component of cronyism. Like China, communist Vietnam's economy has a strong competitive capitalist component. Vietnam is even moving beyond China by selling its state-owned companies.[28] Communist Cuba has tilted in a capitalist direction by recognizing private ownership.[29] It's speculated that even communist North Korea is slowly recognizing the economic benefits of capitalism.[30] However, with all these countries, tendencies toward capitalism have not been followed with tendencies to democracy. A small group of individuals, usually affiliated with the Communist Party, control political bodies and prohibit full democracy.

The last ism is authoritarian capitalism. Countries following this approach have a split personality between the economic system and the political system. The economic system is capitalist, with private ownership, profit motive, and competition. However, the political system is limited, with big restrictions on speech, religion, and opposition to those controlling the government.[31] Singapore, Turkey, and Hungary are current examples of this system. If China were to eliminate its state-owned companies, it would also be an example.

So, which economic system wins, at least in my view? You don't have to wait any longer for the answer than reading the next section.

△ THE BEST SYSTEM: "CAPITALISM-PLUS"

My selection for the best economic system is capitalism, but with some key additions. Hence, I call the system, *capitalism-plus*. In my evaluation, the only reasonable option to capitalism is socialism. So first, why do I pick capitalism over socialism? I have four reasons.

Number one is that capitalism harnesses humans' inherent nature to succeed when rewarded by success. I learned this lesson early in my life. My maternal grandfather's first occupation was farming. He took over his father's (my great grandfather's) small farm and made a living selling crops and livestock. When the Great Depression hit, farmers nationwide suffered from low prices and high debts. With a family to support, my grandfather had to move on and change careers, so he taught himself to be an electrician, and eventually became so good that he soon had other electricians working for him. The financial rewards for his diligent work allowed him to raise three daughters as a widower as well as help other members of his extended family. He worked hard to be a good electrician, customers knew it, and he reaped the benefits.

Contrast my grandfather's work ethic to what I observed while employed as an intern with the federal government in the early 1970s, where the people I worked with were fine individuals, but they just didn't work very hard. Three, sometimes four-hour lunches were common, and so was leaving for the day a half or a full hour early. No one ever seemed especially busy.

Were my colleagues lazy? When I chatted with them about their lives away from work, they certainly didn't seem to be, with child rearing, home chores, and community service being important to most of them. Instead, it was the system that discouraged hard work at the office. Firing someone from a government job was (and still is) virtually impossible, so my office colleagues knew they'd always get paid. On top of that, raises were across-the-board, meaning if someone did work very hard, they'd get the same pay raise as someone who didn't.

In a capitalist system, workers who perform well and thereby help the company earn more profits tend to be rewarded more so than in a socialist system where profits aren't measured and where public bureaucrats give out pay raises. Mind you, the capitalist system isn't perfect in this regard, but it's better than the socialist alternative. The empirical literature supports the notion that the pay and performance incentives imbedded in capitalism result in a faster growing economy than with an alternative socialist system.[32]

Number two, the pursuit of profits in capitalism motivates businesses to constantly look for ways to give buyers what they want and at the lowest possible cost. Notice there are two benefits here: capitalist companies respond to the desires of buyers (the economic landscape is littered with examples of failed products, my personal favorite being yogurt shampoo),[33] and capitalist companies want to keep their costs low, which makes them frugal, less wasteful, and innovative. These companies are constantly trying to find better ways to do the same thing.

Capitalist companies are also customer-driven. In the days before streaming, cable companies had a virtual monopoly on TV service. Good luck getting a cable TV technician to come to your home for service. Now with competition from satellite and streaming, cable workers give a specific time for their arrival, and they rarely miss an appointment. The cable companies want to keep their customers happy.

Which leads to my third reason for choosing capitalism: the competition in capitalism keeps prices low, but not so low that shortages are created. In socialism, a central authority sets prices, but with the government's reputation and political viability on the line, there's a motivation to err on the low-side for prices. Yet if prices are so low that production isn't viable, then output levels fall and shelves become bare. If you doubt me, arrange a trip to Cuba and check out the shelves in a typical retail store. There are often more cobwebs than there are products.[34]

In capitalism, prices must be high enough to cover costs, and when they are, production keeps shelves stocked. But what if a company becomes greedy and pushes prices above the level needed to cover costs and provide a normal profit? Then other companies won't follow, and they'll take away the sales from the greedy company. So as long as there is competition, there's an automatic regulator on price levels, and that regulator is not a person, but is the capitalist system.

Number four is that capitalism is fast at moving economic resources to where they do the most good. Movement in prices tell resource owners where users ultimately want more or less. This resource allocation happens automatically, with no need for a public body to endlessly deliberate over a decision. In contrast, in socialism, public bodies make the decisions about resource use, and this decision-making can be slow and fraught with political considerations.

Despite its advantages, pure capitalism isn't enough—it needs to be augmented. It needs to become *capitalism-plus*. What's in the "plus" part? The previous chapters give the answer, but I'll summarize here.

First and foremost, we need to re-double our efforts to offer a quality Pre-K-12 education to our children so each of them has the opportunity to be adequately prepared for the economic world (Chapter 1). Furthermore, we need to institute reforms in how higher education is delivered so that individuals wishing to pursue college degrees can do so on a frugal budget (Chapter 2).

Households, and particularly children, need to be assured of an acceptable standard of living that is generous enough to meet basic needs but not so generous as to discourage self-sufficiency. The "social safety net" needs to be turned into a "social success net" (Chapters 6 and 7). Importantly, these basic needs include health-care (Chapter 4) and an adequate supply of affordable housing (Chapter 5). Particular attention should be given to providing parents of newborn children the opportunity to spend time caring for them in the formative years of the child's life, which means there should be a real financial possibility for this to happen (Chapter 8).

Job churning has always occurred in our economy, but international trade and technology are expanding it and making it quicker. We need to recognize that the number of workers changing occupations will likely accelerate in the future, and so we must have programs and finances ready for when the churning occurs (Chapters 9 and 10). We also need to reform our immigration system in ways beneficial to immigrants, domestic workers, and the broader economy (Chapter 16).

Infrastructure—roads in particular—are essential to personal mobility and economic vitality. Yet our capacity to finance infrastructure is shrinking under current financing methods, most specifically the gas tax. A new way of financing infrastructure should be adopted that relies on a miles-travelled fee-based system (Chapter 3).

One fault of the capitalist system is its inability to consider costs external to individual decisions, such as pollution. Capitalism-plus rectifies this omission by "internalizing" pollution costs through appropriate fees (Chapter 11).

Social Security has provided financial support to millions of people in their retirement since its inception over 70 years ago. To ensure continuation of this support, the system must be tweaked to put it on full funding for the next 50 years (Chapter 12).

I could stop here because I've covered the major economic issues facing families and people. In economics lingo, I've covered the "micro" issues, but there are several big-picture "macro" issues affecting all of us and impacting the ability of the federal government to function and meet its obligations. So, here are more "pluses" in capitalism-plus.

We need an improved federal tax system that is simple, transparent, and collects relatively more from wealthier households, but that is also broad-based and has all households contributing regardless of economic status (Chapter 15). We also need a reformed federal spending budget that separates current spending from capital spending, creates a Rainy Day Fund to be used during recessions, pays off a large part of the national debt in the next thirty years, and which rebalances federal spending to prioritize education, defense, and health-care over spending for special groups and industries (Chapters 13 and 14).

The creation of capitalism-plus should go far to convince doubters who believe only socialism can address the socio-economic issues facing us today.[35] Capitalism-plus can deliver the benefits of that system of organizing the economy to all parts of, and participants in, the economy.

I have one other very important point to make in this chapter: we need to be vigilant in preventing capitalism-plus from turning into

capitalism-plus-cronyism (crony capitalism), where vested interests "capture" the political system and rig the rules and regulations
to feather their own nests. Crony capitalism eats away at all the
benefits of capitalism and expands income equality while slowing
economic growth.[36] It will take private efforts at exposing crony
capitalism as well as public efforts to build roadblocks against it.
How this can be done is part of the next, and final, chapter.

▲ SUMMING UP

Fundament to any economy is its "economic operating system"—
the philosophy behind who owns resources, how prices are set, and
who makes decisions about what is made and what workers are
paid. Although there are many alternatives, the two major competing systems today are capitalism and socialism. Capitalism stresses
private ownership of resources and private decision making,
whereas socialism has resources owned by the public, with public
bodies making production, pricing, and payment decisions. I argue
that capitalism gives the best economic outcomes for standards of
living, efficiency, and productivity. But to address potential faults
of capitalism, we need a system I term "capitalism-plus," where the
"plus" adds sufficient social safety nets, educational opportunities,
and better federal taxing and budgeting systems to prevent the
potential pitfalls of pure capitalism.

Chapter 17 Endnotes

1. Amadeo, "History of Recessions in the United States"; National Bureau of Economic Research, *op. cit.*; and U.S. Bureau of Economic Analysis, "National Income and Product Accounts," *op. cit.* The Great Depression of the 1930s was composed of two separate recessions spanning 1929-1933 and 1937-1938. The recession with the longest duration occurred from 1879 to 1885.

2. Lott, "Americans Warming to Socialism Over Capitalism, Poll Shows."

3. Taber, "The Night I Invented Crony Capitalism."

4. Durden, "FANG Stocks Slump as Warren Calls for Breaking up 'Big Tech.'"

5. Sachs, "The Economics of Happiness"; and Chang, *23 Things They Don't Tell You about Capitalism.*

6. Picketty, *Capital.*

7. Rovira, "The Fortunes of Romantic Anti-Capitalism in William Blake's Thel and Oothoon."

8. Wilby, "Why Capitalism Crates a Throwaway Society."

9. Perry, "The General Public Thinks the Average Company Makes a 36% Profit Margin, Which is about 5X too High."

10. Snowdon, *Selfishness, Greed, and Capitalism.*

11. O'Toole, *Enlightened Capitalists: Cautionary Tales of Business Pioneers Who Tried to Do Well While Doing Good.*

12. Smith, *The Wealth of Nations*, Book 1.

13. Newman, *Socialism.*

14. Harrington, *Socialism: Past and Future.*

15. *Ibid.*

16. Nance, "Capitalism, Socialism, and the Environment."

17. Laurent, "Macron Preaches Change but Pulls his Punches."

18. Shleifer and Vishny, "Pervasive Shortages under Socialism."

19. *Ibid*; Rosati, "Venezuela's Bribing Menu Brings Transparency to Corruption."

20. Qian, *How Reform Worked in China.*

21. Ruparelia, Reddy, Harriss, and Corbridge, *Understanding India's New Political Economy: A Great Transformation.*

22. Thurow, *Head to Head.*

23. Abe, "Japan's Shrinking Economy."

24. Ross, "Is the United States a Market Economy or a Mixed Economy?"

25. Richman, "Fascism."

26. Goldberg, *Liberal Fascism.*

27. Sowell, Marxism.

28. Cook, "Vietnam Gears Up to Divest State-Owned Enterprises in 2018."

29. Semple, "New Cuba Constitution, Recognizing Private Property, Approved by Lawmakers."

30. Cha and Collins, "The Markets: Private Economy and Capitalism in North Korea?"

31. Gat, "The Return of Authoritarian Capitalism."

32. Wilson, "Capitalism and Economic Growth across the World"; McCloskey, *Bourgeois Equality*; Rosenberg, *How the West Grew Rich*; Gwartney, Holcombe, and Lawson, "Institutions and the Impact of Investment on Growth"; Conquest, *Dragons of Expectations: Reality and Delusion in the Course of History.*

33. Frohlich, "The 10 Worst Product Fails of All Time."

34. Lawson and Powell, *Socialism Sucks.*

35. *Ibid.*

36. Lindsey and Teles, *The Captured Economy.*

CHAPTER EIGHTEEN

PUTTING THE SOLUTIONS IN PLAY

CHANGING LANES

One of the popular phrases I hear from my students is "stay in your lane." The Urban Dictionary says this phrase is a modern version of "mind your own business," or "stop talking about things you don't understand."[1] I violate that advice in this final chapter by deviating from economics into political science and a little psychology. I guess I can partially justify my action because I do have an undergraduate minor in political science, and my wife was a few credits shy of having a double-major in education and psychology.

What is my goal? It stems from the dissatisfaction that I often feel when I conclude a book on public policy. It isn't because the recommendations don't make sense, but rather, the authors of these books do not venture far enough; that is, they do not explain how to sell their suggestions to both the public and government decision-makers. Hence, this chapter presents some ways of implementing the recommendations of capitalism-plus in our public decision-making process.

There are two parts to meeting this objective. For the major recommendations I've made, I highlight those parts to be emphasized so people will respond by saying, "I get it. That makes sense and we should do it." The focus is on how the recommendations should be packaged and presented to the public, all the while still being true to the core of the proposals. In completing this part, I'll use my experience in sitting on several state and local commissions in North Carolina that have dealt with thorny public policy questions.

For the second part, I really move outside of my lane by interrogating the current public policy-making system. For example, do some fundamental changes need to be made to our election process and to the ways elected officials interact with private vested interests? Can change be made using the current political system, or do we have to get under the hood and rework the internal operations of the public policy apparatus?

△ PACKAGING AND PROMOTING GOOD IDEAS

I believe I've made reasonable recommendations that would move us toward addressing the major socio-economic issues we face as a country. Yet proposals are useless if they remain in a book sitting on a shelf; rather, they must be packaged and promoted to convince enough people to push them toward adoption. In this section, I go through my key recommendations and discuss how to present and sell them to people who are not policy wonks.

Selling a Spending Surge for Pre-K–12 Education: Solving problems is easier if they're addressed earlier rather than later. Many of our important public issues, such as poverty, crime, income inequality, and failure in college, have their roots in individuals not obtaining the proper start in life through education. While a $400 billion annual program to fund more and better teachers, child and neighborhood counselors, pre-school and after-school programs, and out-reach to student families seems enormous, it will more than pay for itself with the enhanced economic opportunities and reduced social challenges successful students will have.

Importantly, the program recognizes education doesn't stop at the school. Having students succeed in school also requires a commitment from students' parents and neighborhoods, which is why the school spending surge recognizes the necessity to work with parents and neighborhoods in supporting school achievement. Without these fundamental changes, we'll continue to face the same issues in Pre-K-12 for generation after generation.

Selling the Transformation of College Education: College education needs to be shaken up; it is too expensive, too dependent on public money, and too entrenched with binding rules and regulations. Colleges, too, are rigid in incorporating alternative learning methods, and they have strayed too far from their core mission of providing students with the training for a marketable occupation.

Two simple changes will make colleges more affordable, more flexible, and more successful in student learning. One is to remove the control accrediting organizations have over the spending of colleges, and two is for students to pass a comprehensive national standardized test in their field before graduating so employees know they possess a minimal level of competence. Indeed, anyone who can pass the national test would be granted a degree in the field, regardless of the kind of college they attended, or whether they attended a college at all. This will put all learning methods and all colleges at the same level and focused on one clear objective for students: learning a given field of study. Individuals can still attend expensive colleges with lots of frills, but they at least will now have much more affordable options.

Selling a New Way to Pay for Transportation: Transportation is undergoing its biggest changes in 100 years! Vehicles are getting much better gas mileage. New fuels are being used, including all-electric, battery plus gas (hybrids), and on the horizon, natural gas and maybe hydrogen. Possibly the biggest change—self-driving vehicles—is being tested now, and some projections suggest going driverless could be the choice of over half of travelers within just a few decades.

All these changes mean the traditional way of paying for roads and other transportation infrastructure primarily with the gas tax won't get the job done. Fortunately, there's a simple alternative, a mileage fee. I call it the Pumfee, or public mobility fee, and it will work with any fuel and any mode of transportation. A Pumfee could be easily added to the increasingly sophisticated technology of new vehicles, and its information could be encrypted to prevent unauthorized spying and tracking of drivers. A rate of between 2 and 3 cents per mile traveled will replace the revenues collected by the gas tax. A Pumfee is easy, workable, and fair.

Selling a Plan to Simultaneously Expand Access to Health-Care and to Lower Health-care Prices: Our current health-care system is in a

vicious cycle that creates ever higher prices, secretive and manipulative price setting, and control by those reaping big profits. We
need to dismantle the system and empower health-care consumers,
just as occurs in most markets. More supply of health-care services,
more competition between health-care providers, and consumer
control over health-care spending are the keys to a health-care system that works for patients.

Three changes will make this happen. The power and control of our
health care by big corporations needs to end. This can be accomplished by using laws to prevent further consolidation of health-care
firms and by removing laws that limit new competitors. Permitting
more foreign medical doctors and nurses to migrate to the U.S.,
expanding the capacities of domestic medical schools, and relaxing
restrictions on the duties of physician assistants and nurses will
increase the supply of health-care professionals and services. Lastly,
Medicare, Medicaid, and other federal funding for patients should
be converted to health-care vouchers targeted at households with
less than the median income. More supply of health-care services,
more competition between health-care providers, and consumer
control over health-care spending are the keys to a system that
works for patients.

Selling Ways to Make Housing More Affordable: In economics, when
the price of something is too high, there's a simple way to bring the
price down: make more of it. If the price of housing is too high in some
communities, building more housing will make it less expensive.

There are three parts to this straightforward solution: build more housing units, use innovative and less expensive materials and procedures

to construct them, and allow different kinds of units that cater to limited income households, such as units with kitchens, dining areas, and lounge areas that are shared by multiple households, to be built in the community. What prevents these solutions from being implemented now? It's local building and zoning restrictions that keep new housing supply low and existing property values high. If these restrictions are adjusted, more housing units will be built and will become more affordable. It's that simple!

Selling an Approach to Containing Rising Income Inequality: It's important first to note what income inequality is not. Income inequality does not mean higher-income households are taking income away from middle and lower-income households. Instead, rising income inequality has mainly resulted from a shifting economy which values education and technical and cognitive abilities more than physical skills. It is this change that has resulted in highly-skilled workers receiving the largest pay boosts.

Providing more successful educational opportunities to a greater range of individuals, especially young people, will halt the widening income gap. So "ditto" the recommendations for Pre-K–12 education and college education. We must also correct the mistaken attitude that vocational education is not as worthwhile as a four-year college education. There are plenty community college programs that lead to occupations paying well above the average salary. Young students in high school should be made aware of these excellent opportunities in vocational training, especially in the construction trades.

Selling a Reform of Poverty Programs: Official poverty numbers are overstated because they don't count the resources provided to poor households through programs like SNAP (food stamps) and Medicaid. However, because these programs remove assistance at a rapid rate when the household's earnings rise, our current system of poverty programs actually encourages persistent dependence and poverty.

The challenge in helping poor individuals is providing enough assistance to meet minimal standard needs, but not so much assistance as to create long-term dependency. A "success net," not a "safety net," is needed. A system of cash grants targeted to particular kinds of spending, and which are reduced at a modest rate when the recipient's earnings increase, would provide protection from poverty and also encourage behaviors like schooling and working which lead to self-sufficiency. Ultimately, self-sufficiency is the solution to poverty.

Selling Solutions for Gender and Racial Pay Differences: As women have acquired more formal education and skills, and have increased their representation in higher-paying occupations, the average pay differences between women and men have substantially narrowed. Businesses increasingly see women and men with similar training, experience, and occupational talents as comparable for hiring. This is good.

Still, parents, and especially female parents, face a difficult choice in time use upon the birth of a child. The choice is between foregoing work and the earnings from work to spend time with a child in its formative years, or to work and earn but spend money on paid childcare. A partial solution to this choice is to provide public funds based on the income of the parents that can be used to either replace some of lost earnings if a parent remains at home, or to defray some of the cost of childcare if the parent works. The funds, termed CHILD (Child Help in Loving Dollars), would be targeted to low and middle-income households and would be reduced slowly as the household's earnings rose.

As the educational success and achievement of Black students have improved, racial pay gaps have narrowed. The recommendations for a spending surge in Pre-K–12 schools and for lowering the costs of higher education should result in further improvements and ultimate elimination of the racial pay gap. Also, allowing high school students to request release of their disciplinary records will deter employers from making negative assumptions about students simply based on an inherent characteristic like race.

Selling a Way to Make Global Trade Work for All: Although global trade is a net plus for the U.S. economy, it is important to realize the "net" includes both winners and losers. Consumers buying cheap imports and U.S. businesses making money selling to foreign buyers are winners, but U.S. workers who are displaced from their jobs due to foreign trade are losers. In the recent 25 years of more open world trade, we have largely forgotten the losers.

A direct way to correct this error is to place a small fee (one-tenth of 1%) on the retail sales of imported products to the U.S. and use the proceeds to support retraining of workers who have lost their jobs due to foreign trade. This change would move international trade to a "win-win" situation.

Selling a Plan to Retain Workers Displaced by Technology: Unemployment caused by technology will occur in the coming decades;

the question is just how much? Addressing this challenge requires a two-pronged approach. First, we need continuous monitoring of occupational and skill changes in the labor market. Educational institutions should use this information in altering and developing training and degree programs. Second, federal unemployment compensation programs should use existing and additional funding and be converted to programs to assist displaced workers in receiving skill upgrades.

Selling a Way to Save the Environment: While some want to ignore the truth, global warming is a measurable problem, and we know who the culprit is—us. We've been getting away with dumping our waste (carbon dioxide (CO_2)) into the atmosphere, and the results have caught up with us. A layer of CO_2 is wrapped around the earth and trapping heat below it, and we're undergoing a slow cooking!

Yet the solution is relatively simple: Attach a fee to any activity that involves releasing CO_2 into the atmosphere. This fee will help curtail CO_2-making activities, and if it doesn't, the fee is increased until it does. But to make sure the fee doesn't send us to the poorhouse, the revenue collected is remitted back to individuals on an equal per-person basis. This isn't counterproductive, because research shows we won't just use the rebates to pay the fees; instead, since CO_2 producing activities are now more expensive, we'll actually spend most of the rebate on other things while reducing our pollution.

Selling the Saving of Social Security: Social Security needs a fix to keep paying promised pensions, but there are plenty of fixes that can be used. Two that will do the job are using a less generous and more correct measure of inflation in calculating the beginning Social

Security pension amount, and reducing the increase in pensions that accompany higher average earnings. The last time Social Security was adjusted in the early 1980s, the fixes did a decent job but missed forecasting the faster drop in the birthrate and the increased longevity of senior citizens. However, forecasting these factors is tough.

In addition to some needed patches on Social Security, we need to return the program to its place outside of the federal budget and keep it separate from the issues related to federal spending and taxes.

Selling Ideas for Controlling the National Debt: Almost every business and government in the country except the federal government keeps two budgets—a current budget and a capital budget. The current budget for day-to-day operational expenditures must be balanced. The capital budget for long-lasting projects that provide benefits over many years can be financed with borrowing.

The first step in dealing with the national debt is for the federal government to institute the two budgets, current and capital, and restrict borrowing to the capital budget. The second step is to again follow the lead of many states and start a federal "Rainy Day Fund." During good economic times, this fund will be built up, and when the inevitable recessions hit and federal tax revenues drop, the Rainy Day Fund will be used to maintain or even increase federal spending to avoid the massive borrowing that has typically occurred during economic downturns.

These three ideas—current budget, capital budget, and Rainy Day Fund—will contain and control the national debt.

Selling Re-Prioritizing Federal Spending: Over time, federal spending should focus on four priorities: Pre-K–12 education, national security, assistance to limited-income households, and national infrastructure. Spending for special interests, including student loans and subsidized home mortgages, as well as tax concessions for special interest groups, should be eliminated. A new federal budget with the new spending priorities, an annual contribution to a Rainy Day Fund, and a 30-year pay-off of the majority of the national debt, will require no additional funds than the current budget when current tax loopholes are counted as spending. These changes will restore reason to the federal budget.

Selling an Improved Federal Tax System: The current federal tax system is complicated, unfair, and wasteful in terms of time and money spent complying with its vast rules and regulations. What is needed is a simple, broad-based, fair, and unobtrusive tax system.

A tax system based on all transactions and all wealth meets these goals. Dubbed the "3.8% Tax Solution," it would impose a 3.8% federal tax on any monetary transaction in which goods or services change hands. Additionally, it would place a 3.8% tax on household wealth above the median wealth level. Such a tax system will be universal, meaning everyone pays so everyone has "skin in the game." It will also be highly progressive, with the wealthy paying much more than the non-wealthy, and it will be easy to understand. After the 30-year pay-off of the majority of the national debt, the federal tax on monetary transactions and on wealth will be reduced to 3.1%.

Selling an Immigration Program Everyone Can Support: Immigration has historically been beneficial for the U.S. Particularly with the prospect of low domestic birth rates, immigration will become a key factor in keeping a sufficient labor force in the country.

But our current immigration system is disjointed and a source of deep division in the nation. Making it work and ensuring public support will involve four changes. First, undocumented immigrants currently in the country should be granted "permanent residence" status, but not citizenship, in exchange for becoming documented and paying a fine. Second, the border—the southern border in particular—must be controlled so we know who is entering. Third, quotas for immigrants should be shifted away from extended family members to only immediate family members plus those immigrants with educational and training skills needed by the country. Asylum applications should also be tightened. Fourth, the annual numerical limit for legal immigration should be set at close to 1 million. These are immigration principles most in the country should be able to back.

Creating Capitalism-Plus: Both in concept and in practice, capitalism beats socialism and the other "isms" in terms of organizing the economy. Harnessing private incentives to improve personal lives and the collective well-being is the major accomplishment of capitalism.

Still, there are rough edges to pure capitalism, which is why "capitalism-plus" is needed. Capitalism-plus retains the fundamental principles of capitalism—private ownership, private decision-making, and business competition—but adds public programs to help maximize individual success, support those who have not yet reached their potential, assist individuals who are coping with major disruptions in their lives and in the economy, and address widespread negative consequences of our collective behavior, like pollution.

△ A POLITICAL SYSTEM TO SUPPORT REAL SOLUTIONS

It's somewhat ironic that in the last section of this book I veer outside my lane of expertise and address politics and the political system. Because most of my solutions will require actions by our elected officials, it is necessary to think about our political decision-making process and how it can be improved.

There are two big concerns. First, our political system has been captured by big money interests. This issue appears in the health-care chapter (Chapter 4) as an example of crony capitalism. Many analysts see health-care interest groups like pharmaceutical companies and doctors using the clout they derive from funding political campaigns to prevent reform in the health-care industry and protect a system that feeds them a constant stream of money. Indeed, there's a general concern that companies in many industries try to mold public policies to their benefit and to the disadvantage of consumers.[2]

Second, increasing contentions between the two major political parties has barred political agreement; some say this is a recent phenomenon being driven by the fragmentation of the media into warring camps catered only to particular beliefs. With each side locked into their own point-of-view, there is less motivation for tolerance, compromise, and consensus.[3]

Several proposals have been put forth to limit the crony capitalism related to the first concern. Among them are term limits for U.S. Senate and House members,[4] prohibitions on elected officials voting on legislation affecting their donor's interests,[5] significantly raising the salaries of officeholders in order to attract better candidates,[6] and—perhaps most importantly—making political campaigns completely publicly financed. The last proposal would eliminate influence by big donors, thereby allowing politicians to shift time away from raising money to time used studying issues.[7]

Yet huge obstacles stand in the way of implementing any of the above ideas. Term limits would require a constitutional amendment, and achieving it is a multi-year process needing support from three-fourths of the states. Also, there is inconclusive evidence from state legislatures with such limits that they curtail outside influence.[8] Limitations on the legislation office holders could vote on would be highly subjective and could be bypassed with contributions made to PACS (political action committees). Higher pay for senators and congresspersons could be approved by those bodies, but would likely be unpopular among the public. And in localities where it has been adopted, even public financing hasn't resulted in less political fighting and polarization.[9]

A less drastic step would be to require significantly more disclosure for campaign donors prior to elections. This could be combined with the development and encouragement of non-partisan "issue analysis" organizations which provide straightforward and unbiased analysis of candidates' platforms and claims. Both ideas would help "raise the veil" currently covering political activities to the public.

Ultimately, the way to curtail crony capitalism is to reduce the incentives for businesses and others to influence, and ultimately control, political decision-making. Why do companies and interest groups spend so much on lobbying Congress and the president and contributing to political campaigns? It's because the federal government has considerable power over them through regulations, public spending, and programs. Health-care is an excellent example. Public funding of Medicare and Medicaid impacts the spending by patients on medical care. Regulatory oversight by the FDA controls the approval of pharmaceutical drugs. The health-care community wouldn't spend so much on trying to influence elected officials if those elected officials didn't have such a big impact on economic outcomes for health-care providers.

I'm not saying the government should not have a role in health-care as well as in many other areas. Government should have a role, as I've demonstrated. Still, we should keep in mind that the bigger and the more specific the public role, the more that private players will try to shape that role to their advantage. This is why I've tried to recommend approaches in which the government provides help, but the beneficiary of the help has maximum discretion over how specifically to use the assistance. The health insurance vouchers outlined in Chapter 4 and cash assistance targeted to broad spending described in Chapter 7 are good examples.

Unfortunately, the capture of government programs by economic interests is part of a large feed-back loop. The ability of businesses to benefit from government programs gives businesses the incentive to influence public decision-making through political donations. The more the businesses are successful at these efforts, the richer and more capable of continuing those efforts they become, and the more they have to lose if their influence is ended. Snapping the loop at either side by reducing the incentives for businesses to interfere, or reducing their abilities to interfere, becomes a high mountain to climb.

Reducing the incentive of officeholders to engage in political activity is one way to reduce the issue of political polarization. Lengthening the terms of federal officeholders would help accomplish this. Members of the House of Representatives serve terms of only two years. This means once elected, the representative must immediately think about gearing up to run again. In fact, newly elected members of the House are usually told to devote a minimum of four hours daily to fund-raising phone calls.[10] Four hours daily! That's half a typical workday. No wonder many House members have no time to study the issues, instead opting to use "talking points" provided by their party leadership or lobbyists representing large donors.

I recommend doubling the term of House members to four years. Senators serve six-year terms, which seems reasonable. The presidential term is four years, with a maximum of two terms. Yet in today's political world, a president can effectively govern and make substantive proposals in only the first two years of the term. Once past the half-way point in years three and four, it's all about posturing and campaigning for a second term, or, in the case of a second term, it's about legacy development and focusing on a successor.

I think expanding the presidential term to six years and keeping the two-term limit would give presidents more time to govern and less time to worry about campaigning. Many will disapprove of an apparent expansion of presidential authority, but we already have enough "checks" on the power of presidency. For example, both chambers must approve legislation, each chamber has investigatory power, and spending budgets must be initiated in and approved by Congress.

Once again, however, these are big proposals requiring heavy lifting over many years to accomplish. Even if there was a strong movement started today to push these ideas, it would likely be well past my lifetime before they succeeded.

What realistically can be done to adopt the ideas I've presented in this book? The answer neatly brings me back to one of my lanes: education. There are numerous political obstacles, however, it is possible to implement the solutions presented in this book because they are reasonable, logical, and workable. Scholars have shown how the interaction between our democratic system and capitalism has created needed adjustments to our economic system at several key points in our nation's history.[11] The process begins with discussing the problems and presenting the solutions. Books advocate answers to our most pressing problems, but so do op-ed articles, presentations to civic groups, and the recruitment of influential people. For those of you who agree with me—speak up, get organized or elected, and create change!

▲ SUMMING UP

Real solutions are worthless unless they are implemented. Two barriers must be addressed in the political system before change can be implemented. One is the control by private business interests over legislation, programs, and regulations impacting many of the issues addressed in the book. The other is the level of political polarization making major changes to existing government programs very difficult.

There are good ideas for addressing both of these impediments, but all have the challenge that they must be approved by the existing political system, which is often an obstacle to change. Therefore, the short-run solution is education and publicity about the issues and their solutions through writing, speaking, and organizing. History shows this is the way ground-breaking change has always occurred.

Chapter 18 Endnotes

1.   "Stay in Your Lane," *Urban Dictionary.*

2.   Holcombe, *Political Capitalism.*

3.   Duca and Saving, "Income Inequality, Media Fragmentation, and Increased Political Fragmentation."

4.   Greenberg, "Term Limits: The Only Way to Clean Up Congress."

5.   Hilton, *Positive Populism.*

6.   Hall, *Who Wants to Run?*

7.   Sheffield, "Could Public Financing of Elections Revolutionize Politics?"

8.   Miller, Nicholson-Crotty, and Nicholson-Crotty, "Reexamining the Institutional Effects of Term Limits in US State Legislatures."

9.   Hall, "How the Public Financing of Elections Increases Candidate Polarization."

10. *Ibid.*

11. Iversen and Soskice, *Democracy and Prosperity: Reinventing Capitalism through a Turbulent Century.*

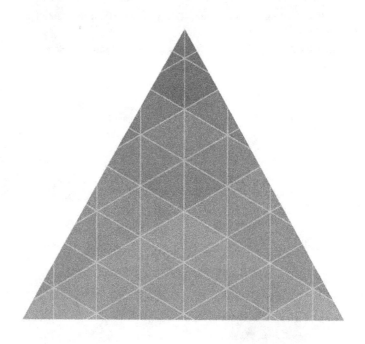

COSTS AND BENEFITS OF K-12 EDUCATION RECOMMENDATIONS

COSTS

Costs included are an increase in teacher pay, a reduction in class sizes, an expansion of school social workers, an expansion of after-school programs, and the institution of boarding schools. Because the required size of after-school programs is linked to the availability of boarding schools, two sets or estimates are provided for these two costs: one without boarding schools, and one with boarding schools.

Without Boarding Schools:

A. Increase Teacher Pay by 30%: The average teacher salary in 2016 (latest data available) was $55,120.[1] A 30% increase in salary is $16,536. There were 3,556,000 K-12 public school teachers in 2016. Multiplying $16,536 by 3,556,000 results in an annual expenditure of $59 billion.

B. Reduce Class Sizes by One-Third: Reducing class sizes by one-third will require a 50% increase in the number of teachers. Using the higher teacher salary calculated above, adding 50% more teachers requires an additional annual expenditure of $128 billion. Additional classrooms, or conversion of existing classroom (for example, dividing an existing classroom into two classrooms) would also be required. I propose dedicating $500 billion for new construction or conversion construction for this element. This is almost half the amount that would be needed to construct new facilities (excluding the land) for the current 50 million students in public school, so it should be sufficient.[2] Typically, construction of long-lasting projects is done through borrowing, following the idea that benefits from construction extend over a long period. Borrowing $500 billion at a 3% annual interest rate over 30 years requires an annual payment of $25 billion. Therefore, the total annual cost of reducing class sizes by one-third is $128 billion + $25 billion, or $153 billion.

C. Expand the Use of Social Workers in School: In 2015 (latest data available), 23% of high school students were in a fight at least one time during the school year.[3] Using this measure as a proxy for the proportion of K-12 students who are in challenging social and neighborhood environments, 11 million K-12 students are in this risk category. Assigning 15 students per social worker, this creates a need for 730,000 school social workers. Paying these workers the same augmented salary ($71,650) as teachers results in an annual expenditure of $52 billion.

D. Expand After-School Programs: Assuming they last 2 hours, after-school programs represent a 25% increase in the workday of a teacher. Currently, approximately 25% of students use after-school programs.[4] Assuming a goal of 50% of students using after-school programs, there would be a need for 50% of the teachers to add 25% of time to their workday. Using an annual salary expenditure for the now-increased 5.4 million teachers (50% more than the current 3.6 million) of $387 billion, the annual cost is 0.50 x 0.25 x $387 billion, or $48 billion.

E. Add Pre-K Classes for 3 and 4-Year-Olds: There are 7.9 million 3 and 4-year-old children. Keeping a class size of only 10 children requires the hiring of 790,000 new teachers. Paying these teachers the augmented salary of $71,650 yields an annual expense of $57 billion. Assuming new classrooms could be constructed adjacent to existing schools on land already owned by the school systems, and using a need of 90 square feet per child[5] at a cost of $250 per square foot,[6] there is a requirement of $178 billion in new school construction. Financing the construction over 30 years using a 3% interest rate gives an annual financing cost of $9 billion. So, the annual cost for the Pre-K classes is $66 billion.

F. Total: The total additional annual expenditure is $59 billion for increased salaries of existing teachers, $153 billion for the additional salaries and construction for smaller class sizes, $52 billion for social workers, + $48 billion for after-school programs, and $66 billion for salaries and construction of Pre-K programs, giving a grand total of $378 billion. This represents an increase of 70% over actual K-12 expenditures in 2015 (last year of available data).[7]

With Boarding Schools:

The additional expenses for increasing teacher pay, reducing class sizes, and adding social workers remain the same. Changes occur for the expenses for boarding schools and for after-school programs. With the focus on assisting at-risk students, boarding schools would presumably draw from students who participate in the expanded after-school programs, and thus, as boarding schools are added, expenses for after-school programs would decrease.

Based on the experience of existing boarding schools, their costs-per-student are twice as much as for students in traditional school.[8] Teacher costs are not needed in these calculations because teachers at traditional schools could be shifted to boarding schools. Doubling the current non-instructional costs-per-pupil results in a cost of $11,944 per student in a boarding school.[9] Using half of the 23% (11.5%) of students who are assumed to be from challenging social and neighborhood environments (see paragraph C in the above costs calculations), then the annual costs of boarding schools are $11,944 x 5,500,000 students, or $66 billion.

However, there would be an offsetting savings from a reduced need for teacher hours in after-school programs. Instead of 50% of students participating in the after-school programs, 38.5% (50%-11.5%) would participate. The savings in teacher time-costs for after-school programs would therefore be 0.115 x 0.25 x $387 billion, or $11 billion. Hence, the costs for after-school programs when boarding schools are available are $48 billion–$11 billion, or $37 billion.

Adding the $37 billion for boarding schools to the $378 billion additional annual cost without boarding schools gives a $415 billion additional annual expenditure with boarding schools. This is an 87% expenditure over current spending.

△ BENEFITS

While it is easy to logically assert that factors like lower class sizes and better-quality teachers will improve student learning, evidence confirming the expectations is challenging to find. This is because a careful statistical analysis is required comparing students in classrooms with and without the factor (such as with smaller class sizes versus with larger class sizes), and then making sure all other factors that affect student performance are controlled. Fortunately, there have been well-structured studies providing these estimates.

A. Increase Teacher Pay by 30%: Several studies have confirmed a link between teacher pay, teacher effectiveness, and student learning.[10] Chetty, Friedman, and Rockoff valued the kind of improvement in teacher quality and student learning resulting from a 30% increase in teacher salary at a $9,605 (in 2016 purchasing power dollars) increase in each student's lifetime income.[11] However, the study's results were based on improving teacher quality in one grade. The plan outlined here seeks to improve teacher quality in all grades. Hence, assuming the increase in teacher quality is comparable for all grades, Chetty, Friedman, and Rockoff's results are multiplied by 12 to give a value of $115,260 in additional lifetime income per student. Note that these lifetime additional incomes are not simply the sum of the additional yearly incomes over the working life of the student. Instead, each annual income boost is converted to a "present value" amount, which accounts for the fact that money is worth more now rather than later since prices will be higher in the future. By using 3.6 million annual graduates, 3.6 million x $115,260 gives a total annual value of $415 billion.

B. Reduce Class Sizes by One-Third: The best study of the impact on student performance from lowering class sizes is from Tennessee's STAR (student/teacher achievement ratio) project.[12] Here, class sizes were reduced by one-third in grades K-3 but kept the same in higher grades. By looking at the earnings later in life of the students experiencing the smaller K-3 class sizes, Chetty, Friedman, Hilger, Saez, Schanzenbach, and Yagan estimated the reduced class sizes increased lifetime incomes of the students by $10,179 (in 2016 purchasing power dollars).[13] However, this value only represents the impact of lower class sizes for grades K-3. My proposal is to lower class sizes for all grades. Assuming there is a comparable impact on lifetime earnings for all grades, the estimated value is $33,082 (13 total grades from K-12 divided by 4 grades from K-3 and then multiplied by $10,179). Further multiplying $33,082 by 3.6 million annual graduates gives a total annual benefit of $119 billion.

C. Expand the Use of Social Workers in Schools: While there is significant empirical support for more qualified teachers and smaller class sizes leading to improved student academic performance, unfortunately there are not similar studies for school social workers. Still, school social workers would be expected to especially work with students who are at-risk of dropping out of school and never graduating. Therefore, one tangible measure of the value of school social workers would be a reduction in the high school dropout rate.

The latest data show the high school dropout rate is 16%,[14] which measures the percentage of high school freshmen who never graduate, after adjusting for students who leave for other schools before graduating and for students who enter school after the freshman year. The average annual lifetime earnings difference between workers with a high school degree and workers who dropped out of high school is estimated at $207,000 (in 2016 purchasing power dollars).[15] It is not unreasonable to expect the intense counseling and parental-neighborhood interaction provided by the significant expansion in school social workers will reduce the annual number of high school dropouts (currently 571,000) by one-third, thus resulting in a continuing annual monetary benefit of $39 billion (571,000 x 0.33 x $207,000).

D. Expand After-School Programs: Numerous studies have found a positive impact on learning from after-school programs. The studies have indicated that the programs achieve student gains by reducing their crime and drug use and improving health.[16] Unfortunately, there are no studies to my knowledge directly estimating a monetary value from the programs. As an estimate, I treat after-school programs as an extension of the benefits of smaller class sizes. Using the same $33,082 per graduate value of smaller classes, the calculation that a 2-hour after school program would extend the school day by 30%,[17] and that the expanded after school program would accommodate 25% of students, then the calculation is $33,082 x 0.30 x 0.25 x 3.6 million, or $8.9 billion annually.

E. Add Pre-K Classes for 3 and 4-Year-Olds: Heckman, *et. al.* found lifetime earnings gains for students in pre-K programs 2.9 times higher than program costs, a benefit/cost ratio comparable to similar studies.[18] Costs include those for both classrooms and teachers. Multiplying 2.9 times the $66 billion annual cost yields benefits of $191 billion.

REAL SOLUTIONS: Common Sense Ideas for Solving our most Pressing Problems

F. Provide the Option of Boarding Schools: Since boarding schools are a relatively new concept with little current use, evidence on their performance is scant. One study does suggest their improvements in student academic performance are similar to those from improved teacher quality and smaller class sizes.[19] Hence, no additional benefits will be cited here. Still, it should be remembered that the concept of boarding schools is for those very high at-risk students whose home and neighborhood situations make learning difficult in traditional settings, even with the benefit of better teachers, smaller classes, after-school activities, and the help and guidance of social workers.

G. Other Benefits: It makes sense that improvements in our K-12 education system should lead to improvements in other areas of society, specifically in reduced crime, reduced public assistance, and reduced health-care costs. Indeed, research backs up this intuition.[20] Combining the results of this research show that every individual who graduates from high school (rather than drops out) saves society $57,826 over their lifetime in reduced crime costs, reduced public assistance, and reduced health-care costs. Assuming the annual number of drop-outs falls by one-third, total lifetime savings associated with each graduating class is $11 billion (571,000 x 0.33 x $57,826).

The sum of benefits is $415 billion + $119 billion + $39 billion + $8.9 billion + $191 billion + $11 billion or $784 billion (rounded). Using a different methodology, Hanushek, Peterson, and Woessmann have estimated even larger gains.[21]

Appendix Endnotes

1. National Center for Education Statistics, *op. cit.*, Table 330.10; U.S. Bureau of Labor Statistics, "All Employees, Thousands, Total Nonfarm, Seasonally Adjusted," and Hall and Rabushka, *op. cit.*

2. California Department of Education, "Completed Schools." Using 50 million students, 90 square feet per student. School Planning and Management, "School Costs – Did You Know...", and a cost per square foot of $250, the total cost of construction is $1.1 trillion.

3. *Ibid.* Table 231.10.

4. Afterschool Alliance, *America after 3 PM: Afterschool Programs in Demand.*

5. California Department of Education, "Complete Schools."

6. School Planning and Management, "School Costs – Did You Know..."

7. *Ibid.* Table 236.10.

8. Curto and Fryer, *op. cit.*

9. National Center for Education Statistics, *Digest of Education Statistics, 2016*, Tables 201.10, 236.10.

10. Dolton, Peter and Oscar Gutierrez, *Teachers' Pay and Pupil Performance*; Kane and *Staiger*, "Estimating Teacher Impacts on Student Achievement: An Experimental Evaluation"; Rivkin, Hanushek, and Kain, "Teachers, Schools, and Academic Achievement"; and Rockoff and Staiger, "Searching for Effective Teachers with Imperfect Information."

11. Chetty, Raj, John Friedman, and Jonah Rockoff. *The Long-Term Impacts of Teachers: Teacher Value-Added and Student Outcomes in Adulthood.*

12. Word, Johnston, Bain, Fulton, Achilles, Lintz, Folger, and Breda, "The State of Tennessee's Student/Teacher Achievement Ratio (STAR) Project: Technical Report 1985-1990."

13. Chetty, Raj, John Friedman, Nathaniel Hilger, Emmanuel Saez, Diane Schanzenbach, and Danny Yagan, "How Does Your Kindergarten Classroom Affect Your Earnings? Evidence from Project STAR."

14. National Center for Education Statistics, Public High School Graduation Rates.

15. U.S. Bureau of Labor Statistics, "Median Weekly Earnings by Educational Attainment." Based on a 40-year work career and a 3% discount rate.

16. American Institutes for Research, *Afterschool Programs Make a Difference: Findings from the Harvard Family Research Project*; McCoombs, Whitaker, and Yoo, *The Value of Out-of-School Time Programs.*

17. National Center for Education Statistics, *Schools and Staffing Survey.*

18. Heckman, Moon, Pinto, Savelyev, and Yavitz, *op. cit.*

19. Curto and Fryer, *op.cit.*

20. Alliance, for Excellent Education, *Healthier and Wealthier: Decreasing Health Care Costs by Increasing Educational Attainment*; Levin, Belfield, Muenning, and Rouse, *The Costs and Benefits of an Excellent Education for All of America's Children*; Lochner and Moretti. "The Effect of Education on Crime: Evidence from Prison Inmates, Arrests, and Self Reports."

21. Hanushek, Peterson, and Woessmann, *op. cit.*

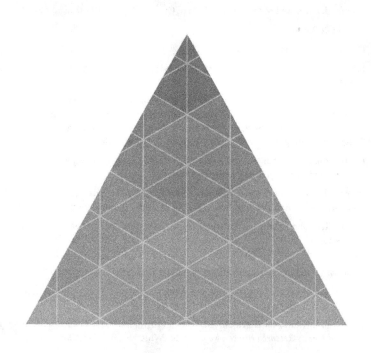

BIBLIOGRAPHY

"5 Forces Driving Hospital Consolidation." *Stratasan,* July 10, 2013. Available on-line at https://blog.stratasan.com/5-forces-driving-hospital-consolidation.

Aastveit, Knut, Bruno Albuquerque, and Andre Anundsen. "Time-Varying Housing Supply Elasticities and US Housing Cycles." Norges Bank and Ghent University, January 31, 2018. Available on-line at https://editorialexpress.com/cgi-bin/conference/download.cgi?db_name=IAAE2018&paper_id=397.

Abe, Naoki. "Japan's Shrinking Economy." *Brookings,* February 12, 2010. Available on-line at https://www.brookings.edu/opinions/japans-shrinking-economy/.

Abutaleb, Yasmeen. "U.S. Healthcare Spending to Climb 5.3% in 2018: Agency." *Reuters,* February 14, 2018. Available on-line at https://www.reuters.com/article/us-usa-healthcare-spending/us-healthcare-spending-to-climb-53-percent-in-2018-agency-idUSKCN1FY2ZD.

"Accreditation of Colleges and Universities: Who's Accrediting the Accreditors?" The Best Schools. Available on-line at https://thebestschools.org/degrees/accreditation-colleges-universities/.

"Accredited On-Line Colleges." *The Best Colleges.com.* Available on-line at https://www.bestcolleges.com/features/top-online-schools/.

Acemoglu, Daron, David Autor, David Dorn, Gordon Hanson and Brendan Price. "Import Competition and the Great U.S. Employment Sag of the 2000s." *Journal of Labor Economics,* Vol. 34, #S1, Part 2, pp. S141-S198, January 2016. Available on-line at https://www.journals.uchicago.edu/doi/10.1086/682384.

Acemoglu, Daron and Pascual Restrepo. "Automation and New Tasks: Now Technology Displaces and Reinstates Labor." Working Paper 25684, Cambridge, MA: National Bureau of Economic Research, March 2019. Available on-line at https://www.nber.org/papers/w25684.pdf.

Acemoglu, Daron and Pascual Restrepo. "Implications of Technology for Growth, Factor Shares, and Employment." Working Paper 22252, Cambridge, MA: National Bureau of Economic Research, June 2017. Available on-line at http://www.nber.org/papers/w22252.pdf.

Acemoglu, Daron and Pascual Restrepo. "Robots and Jobs: Evidence for U.S. Labor Markets." Working Paper 23285, Cambridge, MA: National Bureau of Economic Research, March 2017. Available on-line at http://www.nber.org/papers/w23285.pdf.

ACT, Inc. *The ACT Profile Report – National, Graduating Class 2018,* 2018. Available on-line at http://www.act.org/content/dam/act/unsecured/documents/cccr2018/P_99_999999_N_S_N00_ACT-GCPR_National.pdf.

Adinolfi, Joseph. "How Much of America Do Foreigners Really Own?" *MarketWatch,* September 27, 2016. Available on-line at marketwatch.com/story/how-much-of-america-do-foreigners-really-own-2016-09-27.

Agrawal, Asha. *Gas Taxes and Mileage Fees: What Does the Public Think?* San Jose, CA: Mineta National Transportation Finance Center, December 20, 2016. Available on-line at http://onlinepubs.trb.org/onlinepubs/futureinterstate/AgrawalAsha.pdf.

Afterschool Alliance. *America after 3 PM: Afterschool Programs in Demand.* Washington, D.C., 2014. Available on-line at http://afterschoolalliance.org/documents/AA3PM-2014/AA3PM_National_Report.pdf.

Akcigit, Ufuk, John Grigsby, Tom Nicholas, and Stefanie Stantcheva. "Taxation and Innovation in the 20th Century." Working Paper 24982, Cambridge, MA: National Bureau of Economic Research, September 2018. Available on-line at http://www.nber.org/papers/w24982.

Allcott, Hunt, Rebecca Diamond, and Jean-Pierre Dube. "The Geography of Food Deserts and Food Choices Across the U.S." Cambridge, MA: National Bureau of Economic Research Working Paper 24094, January 2018. Available on-line at https://papers.ssrn.com/sol3/papers.cfm?abstract_id=3095779.

Allegretto, Sylvia, Sean Corcoran, and Lawrence Mishel. *How Does Teacher Pay Compare? Methodological Challenges and Answers.* Washington, D.C.: Economic Policy Institute, 2004.

Allen, Treb, Caue de Castro Dobbin, and Melanie Morton. "Border Walls." Working Paper No. 25267, Cambridge, MA: National Bureau of Economic Research, November 2018. Available on-line at https://www.nber.org/papers/w25267.

Alliance for Excellent Education. *Healthier and Wealthier: Decreasing Health Care Costs by Increasing Educational Attainment.* Issue Brief, November 2006. Available on-line at http://www.all4ed.org/wp-content/uploads/HandW.pdf.

Almond, Douglas, Janet Currie, and Valentina Duque. "Childhood Circumstances and Adult Outcomes: Act II." *Journal of Economic Literature,* Vol. 56, No. 4, December 2018, pp. 1360-1446. Available on-line at https://pubs.aeaweb.org/doi/pdfplus/10.1257/jel.20171164.

Alpert, Terri. "5 Reasons Craftsmanship is Making a Return." *YoungUpStarts,* July 5, 2017. Available on-line at http://www.youngupstarts.com/2017/07/05/5-reasons-craftsmanship-is-making-a-return/.

Alston, Richard, J. Kearl, and Michael Vaughan. "Is there Consensus among Economists in the 1990s?" *American Economic Review,* Vol. 82, No. 3, 2001, pp. 203-209. Available on-line at https://www.weber.edu/wsuimages/AcademicAffairs/ProvostItems/global.pdf.

Altman, Nancy. *The Battle for Social Security.* New York: John Wiley and Sons, 2005.

Amadeo, Kimberly. "What is Wrong with Obamacare?" *The Balance,* March 21, 2019. Available on-line at https://www.thebalance.com/what-is-wrong-with-obamacare-3306076.

Amadeo, Kimberly. "The U.S. Trade Deficit and How It Hurts the Economy." *The Balance,* July 19, 2018. Available on-line at https://www.thebalance.com/u-s-trade-deficit-causes-effects-trade-partners-3306276.

Amadeo, Kimberly. "History of Recessions in the United States." *The Balance,* March 20, 2019. Available on-line at https://www.thebalance.com/the-history-of-recessions-in-the-united-states-3306011.

Amadeo, Kimberly. "Who Owns the US National Debt?" *The Balance,* May 25, 2019. Available on-line at https://www.thebalance.com/who-owns-the-u-s-national-debt-3306124.

American Immigration Council. "Foreign-Trained Doctors are Critical to Serving Many U.S. Communities." January 17, 2018. Available on-line at https://www.americanimmigrationcouncil.org/sites/default/files/research/foreign-trained_doctors_are_critical_to_serving_many_us_communities.pdf.

American Institutes for Research. *Afterschool Programs Make a Difference: Findings from the Harvard Family Research Project.* Cambridge, MA, 2008. Available on-line at http://www.sedl.org/pubs/sedl-letter/v20n02/afterschool_findings.html.

American Society of Civil Engineers. *2017 Infrastructure Report Card.* Washington, D.C., 2018. Available on-line at https://www.infrastructurereportcard.org/making-the-grade/report-card-history/.

American Society of Civil Engineers. *2017 Infrastructure Report Card – Roads.* Washington, D.C., 2018. Available on-line at https://www.infrastructurereportcard.org/wp-content/uploads/2017/01/Roads-Final.pdf.

Americans for Fair Taxation. *The Fair Tax.* Available on-line at https://fairtax.org.

Amuedo-Dorantes, Catalina and Jean Kimmel. "The Motherhood Wage Gap for Women in the United States: The Importance of College and Fertility Delay." *Review of Economics of the Household,* Vol. 3, No. 1, March 2005, pp. 17-48. Available on-line at https://link.springer.com/content/pdf/10.1007%2Fs11150-004-0978-9.pdf.

Anand, Priyanka. "Health Insurance Costs and Employee Compensation: Evidence from the National Compensation Survey." *Health Economics*, Vol. 26, No. 12, December 2017, pp. 1601-1616. Available on-line at https://onlinelibrary.wiley.com/doi/epdf/10.1002/hec.3452.

Anderson, Deborah, Melissa Binder, and Kate Krause. "The Motherhood Wage Penalty Revisited: Experience, Heterogeneity, Work Effort, and Work-Schedule Flexibility." *Industrial and Labor Relations Review*, Vol. 56, No. 2, January 2003, pp. 273-294. Available on-line at http://econ2.econ.iastate.edu/classes/econ321/rosburg/Anderson%20et%20al%20-%20The%20motherhood%20wage%20penalty%20revisted.pdf.

Anderson-Cook, Anna, Jared Maeda, and Lyle Nelson. "Prices for and Spending on Specialty Drugs in Medicare Part D and Medicaid." Washington, D.C.: Congressional Budget Office, March 19, 2019. Available on-line at https://www.cbo.gov/system/files/2019-03/55041-presentation.pdf.

Annie Casey Foundation. "Hunger a Harsh Reality for 14 Million Children Nationwide." April 2, 2018. Available on-line at http://www.aecf.org/blog/hunger-a-harsh-reality-for-14-million-children-nation wide/?msclkid=ae7ec0f483f11e733a2e9bc624aa5eeb&utm_source=bing&utm_medium=cpc&utm_campaign=AECF%20Site&utm_term=world%20hunger%20statistics&utm_content=Child%20Hunger.

Armour, Philip, Richard Burkhauser, and Jeff Larrimore. "Deconstructing Income and Income Inequality Measures: A Cross-Walk from Market Income to Comprehensive Income." *American Economic Review*, Vol. 103, No. 3, May 2013. Available on-line at https://pubs.aeaweb.org/doi/pdfplus/10.1257/aer.103.3.173.

Arntz, Melanie, Terry Gregory, and Ulrich Zierahn. *The Risk of Automation for Jobs in OECD Countries.* OECD Social, Employment, and Migration Working Paper 189, Paris, OECD, 2016. Available on-line at oecd-ilibrary.org/social-issues-migration-health/the-risk-of-automation-for-jobs-in-oecd-countries_5jlz9h56dvq7-en.

Arum, Richard and Josipa Roksa. *Academically Adrift.* Chicago: The University of Chicago Press, 2011.

Aryal, Gaurab, Manudeep Bhuller, and Fabian Lange. "Signaling and Employer Learning with Instruments." Working Paper 25885, Cambridge, MA: National Bureau of Economic Research, May 2019. Available on-line at https://www.nber.org/papers/w25885.pdf.

Ashenfelter, Orley and David Card. *Handbook of Labor Economics.* Vol. 4B, Amsterdam: Elsevier, North-Holland, 2011, pp. 1543-1590.

Ashford, Ellie. "South Carolina Puts Its Support Behind Apprenticeships." *Community College Daily,* December 19, 2019. Available on-line at: http://www.ccdaily.com/2018/08/south-carolina-supports-apprenticeships/.

Astariz, S., A. Vasquez, and C. Iglesias. "Evaluation and Comparison of the Levelized Cost of Tidal, Wave, and Offshore Wind Energy." *Journal of Renewable and Sustainable Energy*, Vol. 7, No. 5, September 2015. Available on-line at https://aip.scitation.org/doi/pdf/10.1063/1.4932154?class=pdf.

Atlas, Scott. *Restoring Quality Health Care.* Stanford, CA: Hoover Institution Press, 2016.

Atlas, Scott. "Single Payer's Misleading Statistics." *Wall Street Journal*, December 18, 2018.

"A Troubling Trend in Federal Investment Spending." *Concord Coalition.* Washington D.C., July 2, 2018. Available on-line at https://www.concordcoalition.org/issue-brief/troubling-trend-federal-investment-spending.

Aurand, Emmanuel, Yentel, and Errico. *The Gap: A Shortage of Affordable Housing.* Washington, D.C., The National Low Income Housing Coalition, 2017. Available on-line at http://nlihc.org/sites/default/files/Gap-Report_2017.pdf.

Austin, D. Andrew. "Has the U.S. Government Ever 'Defaulted'?" Congressional Research Service, December 8, 2016. Available on-line at https://fas.org/sgp/crs/misc/R44704.pdf.

Auten, Gerald and David Splinter. "Income Inequality in the United State: Using Tax Data to Measure Long-Term Trends." New York University School of Law, February 6, 2018. Available on-line at http://www.law.nyu.edu/sites/default/files/upload_documents/Income%20Inequality%20in%20the%20United%20States%20-%20Auten_1.pdf.

Autor, David. "The Unsustainable Rise of the Disability Rolls in the United States: Causes, Consequences, and Policy Options." Working Paper 17697, Washington, D.C.; National Bureau of Economic Research, December 2011. Available on-line at https://www.nber.org/papers/w17697.

Autor, David. "Work of the Past, Work of the Future." *AEA Papers and Proceedings*, Vol 109, 2019. Available on-line at https://pubs.aeaweb.org/doi/pdfplus/10.1257/pandp.20191110.

Autor, David and Mark Duggan. *A Proposal for Modernizing the U.S. Disability Insurance System*. Washington, D.C.: Center for American Progress and the Hamilton Project, December 2010. Available on-line at https://economics.mit.edu/files/6281.

Autor, David and Mark Duggan. "The Growth in the Social Security Disability Rolls: A Fiscal Crisis Unfolding." *Journal of Economic Perspectives*, Vol. 20, No. 3, Summer 2006. Available on-line at https://economics.mit.edu/files/597.

Autor, David and Mark Duggan. "The Rise in the Disability Rolls and the Decline in Unemployment." *Quarterly Journal of Economics*, Vol 118, No. 1, February 2003. Available on-line at https://economics.mit.edu/files/579.

Autor, David and Anna Salomons. "New Frontiers: The Evolving Content and Geography of New Work in the 20th Century." Available on-line at http://web.mit.edu/dautor/www/Autor-Salomons-NewFrontiers.pdf.

Auxier, Richard. "Reforming State Gas Taxes." Washington, D.C.: The Urban Institute, November 2014. Available on-line at https://www.urban.org/sites/default/files/publication/49811/413286-Reforming-State-Gas-Taxes.PDF.

"Average Life Expectancy in North America for those Born in 2018, by Gender and Region." *Statista*. Available on-line at https://www.statista.com/statistics/274513/life-expectancy-in-north-america/.

Badger, Doug and Edmund Haislmaier. "How Congress Can Reduce Obamacare Premiums." Washington, D.C.: The Heritage Foundation, July 5, 2018. Available on-line at https://www.heritage.org/health-care-reform/commentary/how-congress-can-reduce-obamacare-premiums.

Badger, Emily. "The Unbelievable Rise in Single Motherhood in America over the Last 50 Years." *The Washington Post*, December 18, 2014. Available on-line at *https://www.washingtonpost.com/news/wonk/wp/2014/12/18/the-unbelievable-rise-of*-single-motherhood-in-america-over-the-last-50-years/?noredirect=on&utm_term=.9081ad508509.

Badger, Emily. "Is It Time to Bring Back the Boarding House?" *Citylab*, July 18, 2013. Available on-line at https://www.citylab.com/equity/2013/07/it-time-bring-back-boarding-house/6236/.

Bai, Ge and Gerald Anderson. "Extreme Markup: The Fifty US Hospitals with the Highest Charge-to-Cost Ratios." *Health Affairs*, Vol. 34, No. 6, June, 2015. Available on-line at https://www.healthaffairs.org/doi/pdf/10.1377/hlthaff.2014.1414.

Bailey, Martha, Brad Hershbein, and Amalia Miller. "The Opt-In Revolution? Contraception and the Gender Gap in Wages." *American Economic Journal: Applied Economics*, Vol. 4, No. 3, July 2012. Available on-line at https://pubs.aeaweb.org/doi/pdfplus/10.1257/app.4.3.225.

Bailey, Martha, Shuqiao Sun, and Brenden Timpe. "Prep School for Poor Kids: The Long-Run Impacts of Head Start on Human Capital and Economic Self-Sufficiency." Department of Economics, University of Michigan, November 2018. Available on-line at http://www-personal.umich.edu/~baileymj/Bailey_Sun_Timpe.pdf.

Baily, Martin and Adam Looney. "The True Trade Deficit." *Brookings*, February 6, 2018. Available on-line at https://www.brookings.edu/blog/up-front/2018/02/06/the-true-trade-deficit/.

Bain, Marc. "Americans have Stopped Trying to Stuff More Clothes into their Closets." *Quartz*, February 26, 2018. Available on-line at https://qz.com/1212305/americans-have-stopped-trying-to-stuff-more-clothes-into-their-closets/.

Baker, Bruce, David Sciarra, and Danielle Farrie. *Is School Funding Fair: A National Report Card*. Education Law Center, Newark, NJ, 2015.

Baker, Michael, Jonathan Gruber, and Kevin Milligan. "The Long-Run Impacts of a Universal Child Care Program." *American Economic Review*, Vol. 11, No. 3, August 2019. Available on-line at https://pubs.aeaweb.org/doi/pdfplus/10.1257/pol.20170603.

Bakhshi, Hasan, Jonathan Downing, Michael Osborne, and Phillippe Schneider. *The Future of Skills: Employment in 2030*. London, Pearson and Nesta, 2017. Available on-line at https://futureskills.pearson.com/research/assets/pdfs/technical-report.pdf.

Baldwin, Richard. *The Globotics Upheaval*. Cambridge, UK: Oxford University Press 2019.

Banerjee, Pallavi. "A Systematic Review of Factors Linked to Poor Academic Performance of Disadvantaged Students in Science and Math in Schools." *Cogent Education*, Vol. 3, No. 1, May 2016. Available on-line at https://www.tandfonline.com/doi/pdf/10.1080/2331186X.2016.1178441?needAccess=true.

Barbier, Edward, Mikolaj Czajkowski, and Nick Hanley. "Is the Income Elasticity of the Willingness to Pay for Pollution Control Constant?" Working Paper No. 7, Faculty of Economic Sciences, University of Warsaw, 2015. Available on-line at https://www.wne.uw.edu.pl/files/5214/2559/0151/WNE_WP155.pdf.

Barbosa, Filipe, Jonathan Woetzel, Jan Mischke, Maria Ribeirinho, Mukund Sridhar, Matthew Parsons, Nick Bertram, and Stephanie Brown. *Reinventing Construction: A Route to Higher Productivity.* McKinsey Global Institute, February 2017. Available on-line at https://www.mckinsey.com/~/media/McKinsey/Industries/Capital%20Projects%20and%20Infrastructure/Our%20Insights/Reinventing%20construction%20through%20a%20productivity%20revolution/MGI-Reinventing-Construction-Executive-summary.ashx.

Barnard, Anne. "Demise of Gasoline Cars? What We Know about N.Y.'s Ambitious Climate Goals." *The New York Times,* June 20, 2019. Available on-line at https://www.nytimes.com/2019/06/20/nyregion/greenhouse-gases-ny.html.

Barnes, Peter. *With Liberty and Dividends for All.* San Francisco: Berrett-Koehler Publishers, 2014.

Barro, Josh. "Constitutional Concerns Are a Major Risk for Federal Wealth Tax." *Intelligencer,* February 2019. Available on-line at http://nymag.com/intelligencer/2019/02/constitutional-concerns-are-a-major-risk-for-a-wealth-tax.html.

Bauer, Elizabeth. "So Hey, Why Not Just Remove the Social Security Earnings Cap?" *Forbes,* April 28, 2018. Available on-line at https://www.forbes.com/sites/ebauer/2018/04/28/so-hey-why-not-just-remove-the-social-security-earnings-cap/#302815162b23.

Becker, Amanda. "Kamala Harris Proposes Equal Pay Measure to Close Gender Gap." *Reuters,* May 20, 2019. Available on-line at https://www.reuters.com/article/us-usa-election-harris/kamala-harris-proposes-equal-pay-measure-to-close-gender-gap-idUSKCN1SQ0YH.

Becker, Gary and Guity Becker. *The Economics of Life.* New York: McGraw-Hill, 1997.

Bennett. William. "Our Greedy Colleges." *The New York Times,* February 2, 1987. Available on-line at https://www.nytimes.com/1987/02/18/opinion/our-greedy-colleges.html.

Benson, Alan, Raimundo Esteva, and Frank Levy. "Dropouts, Taxes, and Risk: The Economic Return to College under Realistic Assumptions." *Researchgate.net,* 2015. Available on-line at https://www.researchgate.net/publication/314545280_Is_College_Worth_It_The_Economic_Return_to_College_Under_Realistic_Assumptions.

Bento, Antonio, Lawrence Goulder, Mark Jacobsen, and Roger von Haefen. "Distributional and Efficiency Impacts of Increased US Gasoline Taxes." *American Economic Review,* Vol. 99, No. 3, June 2009. Available on-line at https://pubs.aeaweb.org/doi/pdfplus/10.1257/aer.99.3.667.

Berdik, Chris. "To Ban or Not to Ban: Teachers Grapple with Forcing Students to Disconnect from Technology." *The Washington Post,* January 22, 2018. Available on-line at https://www.washingtonpost.com/news/grade-point/wp/2018/01/22/to-ban-or-not-to-ban-teachers-cope-with-students-driven-to-distraction-by-technology/?utm_term=.90be31e85d4c.

Berg, Andrew, Edward Buffie, and Luis-Felipe Zanna. "Should We Fear the Robot Revolution? The Correct Answer is Yes." *Journal of Monetary Economics,* Vol. 97, August 2018. Available on-line at https://bit.ly/2XkPkj7

Berger, Thor and Carl Frey. "Did the Computer Revolution Shift the Fortunes of U.S. Cities? Technology Shocks and the Geography of New Jobs." *Regional Science and Urban Economics,* Vol. 57, March 2016. Available on-line at https://bit.ly/3cRyBKV

Bertrand, Marianne. "The Glass Ceiling." Working Paper 2018-38, Becker-Friedman Institute, University of Chicago, June 2018. Available on-line at https://papers.ssrn.com/sol3/papers.cfm?abstract_id=3191467&download=yes.

Bertrand, Marianne. "New Perspectives on Gender." *Handbook of Labor Economics.* Vol. 4B, Amsterdam: Elsevier, North-Holland, 2011, pp. 1543-1590.

Bertrand, Marianne, Claudia Goldin, and Lawrence Katz. "Dynamics of the Gender Gap for Professionals in the Financial and Corporate Sectors." *American Economic Journal: Applied Economics,* Vol. 2, No. 3, July 2010. Available on-line at https://pubs.aeaweb.org/doi/pdfplus/10.1257/app.2.3.228.

Bertrand, Natasha. "Here's the Average SAT Scores for Every College Major." *Business Insider,* October 24, 2014. Available on-line at http://www.businessinsider.com/heres-the-average-sat-score-for-every-college-major-2014-10.

Besharov, Douglas and Neil Gilbert. *Marriage Penalties in the Modern Social-Welfare State.* Washington, D.C.:

R Street, Policy Study No. 40, September 2015. Available on-line at http://www.welfareacademy.org/pubs/family/Marriage_Penalties_in_the_Modern_Social-Welfare_State.pdf.

Bettinger, Eric, Torbjorn Haegeland, and Mari Rege. "Home with Mom: The Effects of Stay-at-Home Parents on Children's Long-Run Educational Outcomes." Discussion Paper 739, *Statistics Norway*, May 2013. Available on-line at https://www.ssb.no/forskning/discussion-papers/_attachment/113165?_ts=13ea1e1e480.

Bhat, Christine. "Cyber Bullying: Overview and Strategies for School Counselors, Guidance Officers, and All School Personnel." *Australian Journal of Guidance and Counseling*, 18(1). Available on-line at http://citeseerx.ist.psu.edu/viewdoc/download?doi=10.1.1.458.3987&rep=rep1&type=pdf

Bhattarai, Keshab, Jonathan Haughton, and David Tuerck. "The Economic Effects of the Fair Tax: Analysis of a Dynamic CGE Model of the U.S. Economy." *International Economics and Economic Policy*, July, Vol. 13, Issue 3. Available on-line at https://link.springer.com/content/pdf/10.1007%2Fs10368-016-0352-4.pdf.

Bialik, Kristen. "Most Americans Favor Stricter Environmental Laws and Regulations." *Pew Research Center*, December 14, 2016. Available on-line at http://www.pewresearch.org/fact-tank/2016/12/14/most-americans-favor-stricter-environmental-laws-and-regulations/.

Bier, David. "Why the Wall Won't Work." *The Cato Institute*, May 2017. Available on-line at https://www.cato.org/publications/commentary/why-the-wall-wont-work.

Biery, Mary Ellen and Sageworks Stats. "These are the 10 Most Profitable Industries in 2017." *Forbes*, August 6, 2017. Available on-line at https://www.forbes.com/sites/sageworks/2017/08/06/these-are-the-10-most-profitable-industries/#5556391515f0.

Bifulco, Robert and Helen Ladd. "Institutional Change and Coproduction of Public Services: The Effect of Charter Schools on Parental Involvement." *Journal of Public Administration Research and Theory*, Vol. 16, No. 4, October 2006. Available on-line at https://pdfs.semanticscholar.org/69ae/524a278fe06e1a14ef30e3b594b88665daeb.pdf.

Bilal, Qureshi. "From Wrong to Right: A U.S. Apology for Japanese Internment." *Code Switch*, August 9, 2013. Available on-line at https://www.npr.org/sections/codeswitch/2013/08/09/210138278/japanese-internment-redress.

Blau, Francine and Lawrence Kahn. "The Gender Wage Gap: Extent, Trends, and Explanations." *Journal of Economic Literature*, Vol. 55, No. 3, September 2017. Available on-line at https://pubs.aeaweb.org/doi/pdfplus/10.1257/jel.20160995.

Blinder, Alan. *After the Music Stopped: The Financial Crisis, the Response, and the Work Ahead*. New York: Penguin Press, 2013.

Block, Walter. "Rent Control." *The Concise Encyclopedia of Economics*. Library of Economics and Liberty, 2008. Available on-line at http://www.econlib.org/library/Enc/RentControl.html.

Board of Governors of the Federal Reserve System. "Changes in U.S. Family Finances from 2013 to 2016: Evidence from the Survey of Consumer Finances." *Federal Reserve Bulletin*, Vol. 103, No. 3, September 2017.

Board of Governors of the Federal Reserve System. *Financial Accounts of the United States, 3rd Quarter, 2018*. Washington, D.C., December 6, 2018. Available on-line at https://www.federalreserve.gov/releases/z1/20181206/z1.pdf.

Board of Governors of the Federal Reserve System. *Report on the Economic Well-Being of U.S. Households in 2017*. Washington, D.C., May 2018. Available on-line at https://www.federalreserve.gov/publications/files/2017-report-economic-well-being-us-households-201805.pdf.

Board of Trustees, Federal Old-Age and Survivors Insurance and Federal Disability Insurance Trust Funds. *The 1985 Annual Report*. Available on-line at: https://www.ssa.gov/oact/TR/historical/1985TR.pdf.

Board of Trustees, Federal Old-Age and Survivors Insurance and Federal Disability Insurance Trust Funds. *The 2018 Annual Report*. Available on-line at: https://www.ssa.gov/oact/TR/2018/tr2018.pdf.

"Board Policy 3225—Technology Responsible Use." *Wake County Public Schools*, 2019. Available on-line at https://www.wcpss.net/Page/13046.

Bolotnyy, Valentin and Natalie Emanuel. "Why Do Women Earn Less than Men? Evidence from Bus and Train Operators." Harvard University, April 29, 2019. Available on-line at https://scholar.harvard.edu/files/bolotnyy/files/be_gender_gap.pdf.

Book, Robert. "Medicare Administrative Costs are Higher, Not Lower, for Private Insurance." *The Heritage Foundation*, June 25, 2009. Available on-line at https://www.heritage.org/health-care-reform/report/medicare-administrative-costs-are-higher-not-lower-private-insurance.

Bosworth, Barry and Gary Burtless. "Privatizing Social Security: The Troubling Trade-Offs." *The Brookings Institute*, March 1, 1997. Available on-line at https://www.brookings.edu/research/privatizing-social-security-the-troubling-trade-offs/.

Bouffard, Suzanne. *The Most Important Year*, New York: Avery Publishing, 2017.

Bouie, Jamelle. "Where Do Americans Stand on Affirmative Action?" *The American Prospect*, June 13, 2013. Available on-line at http://prospect.org/article/where-do-americans-stand-affirmative-action.

Bound, John, Michael Lovenheim, and Sarah Turner. "Why Have College Completion Rates Declined? An Analysis of Changing Student Preparation and Collegiate Resources." *American Economic Journal: Applied Economics*, Vol. 2, No. 3, July 2010. Available on-line at https://pubs.aeaweb.org/doi/pdfplus/10.1257/app.2.3.129.

Bowles, Nellie. "Silicon Valley Came to Kansas Schools – that Started a Rebellion." *The New York Times*, April 21, 2019. Available on-line at https://www.nytimes.com/2019/04/21/technology/silicon-valley-kansas-schools.html?module=inline.

"BP Statistical Review of World Energy 2018." *British Petroleum*, London, June 2018. Available on-line at bp.com/content/dam/bp/business-sites/en/global/corporate/pdfs/energy-economics/statistical-review/bp-stats-review-2018-full-report.pdf.

Brainerd, Jackson. "State Equal Pay Laws." *National Conference of State Legislatures*, August 23, 2016. Available on-line at: http://www.ncsl.org/research/labor-and-employment/equal-pay-laws.aspx.

Bram, Jason and Nicole Gorton. "How Is Online Shopping Affecting Retail Employment?" *Liberty Street Economics*. Federal Reserve Bank of New York, October 5, 2017. Available on-line at http://libertystreeteconomics.newyorkfed.org/2017/10/how-is-online-shopping-affecting-retail-employment.html.

Bregman, Rutger. "Nixon's Basic Income Plan." *Jacobin*, May 5, 2016. Available on-line at https://www.jacobinmag.com/2016/05/richard-nixon-ubi-basic-income-welfare/.

Bricker, Darrell and John Ibbitson. *Empty Planet*. New York: Crown, 2019.

Brill, Steven. *America's Bitter Pill*. New York: Random House, 2015.

Brinlow, Adam. "SF Built One New Home for Every 10.4 New Jobs Last Year." *San Francisco Curb*, December 15, 2017. Available on-line at https://sf.curbed.com/2017/12/15/16782272/san-francisco-planning-commission-commerce-industry-inventory.

Britschgi, Christian. "America's Roads Are Getting Bumpier and More Dangerous," *Reason*, August 22, 2019. Available on-line at reason.com/2019/08122/Americas-roads-are-getting-bumpier-and-more-dangerous/.

Brook, Robert H., Emmett B. Keeler, Kathleen N. Lohr, Joseph P. Newhouse, John E. Ware, William H. Rogers, Allyson Ross Davies, Cathy D. Sherbourne, George A. Goldberg, Patricia Camp, Caren Kamberg, Arleen Leibowitz, Joan Keesey, and David Reboussin. "The Health Insurance Experiment: A Classic RAND Study Speaks to the Current Health Care Reform Debate." Santa Monica, CA: RAND Corporation, 2006. Available on-line at https://www.rand.org/pubs/research_briefs/RB9174.html.

Brown, Jeffrey. "Why do We Fund Social Security Differently from Other Government Programs?" *Forbes*, June 25, 2014. Available on-line at https://www.forbes.com/sites/jeffreybrown/2014/06/25/why-do-we-fund-social-security-differently-from-other-government-programs/#23e0ac5b52ca.

Bruenig, Matt. "Social Wealth Fund for America." *People's Policy Project*, 2018. Available on-line at https://www.peoplespolicyproject.org/projects/social-wealth-fund/.

Brummet, Quentin and Davin Reed. "The Effects of Gentrification on the Well-Being and Opportunity of Original Resident Adults and Children." Working Paper 19-30, Philadelphia: Federal Reserve Bank of Philadelphia, July 2019. Available on-line at https://cdn.theatlantic.com/assets/media/files/gentrification_final.pdf.

Buhayar, Noah. "To Fix Its Housing Crunch, One US City Takes Aim at the Single-Family Home." *Bloomberg Businessweek*, July 31, 2019. Available on-line at https://www.bloomberg.com/news/features/2019-07-31/to-fix-its-housing-crunch-one-u-s-city-takes-aim-at-the-single-family-home.

Bughin, Jacques, Eric Hazan, Susan Lund, Peter Dahlstrom, Anna Wiesinger, and Amresh Subramaniam.

Skill Shift: Automation and the Future of the Workforce. Washington, D.C., McKinsey and Company, 2018. Available on-line at https://www.mckinsey.com/~/media/McKinsey/Global%20Themes/Future%20of%20Organizations/Skill%20shift%20Automation%20and%20the%20future%20of%20the%20workforce/MGI-Skill-Shift-Automation-and-future-of-the-workforce-May-2018.ashx.

Bughin, Jacques, Eric Hanzan, Tera Allas, Klemens Hjartar, James Manyika, Pal Sjatil, and Irina Shigina. *Tech for Good*. Washington, D.C., McKinsey Global Institute, May 2019. Available on-line at https://www.mckinsey.com/~/media/McKinsey/Featured%20Insights/Future%20of%20Organizations/Tech%20for%20Good%20Using%20technology%20to%20smooth%20disruption%20and%20improve%20well%20being/Tech-for-good-MGI-discussion-paper.ashx.

Burke, Lindsey, Mary Clare Amselem, and Jamie Hall. *Big Debt, Little Study: What Taxpayers Should Know about College Students' Time Use*. Washington, D.C.: The Heritage Foundation, July 19, 2016. Available on-line at https://www.heritage.org/education/report/big-debt-little-study-what-taxpayers-should-know-about-college-students-time-use.

Burke, Lindsey and Stuart Butler. *Accreditation: Removing the Barrier to Higher Education Reform*. Washington, D.C.: The Heritage Foundation, September 21, 2012. Available on-line at https://www.heritage.org/education/report/accreditation-removing-the-barrier-higher-education-reform.

Burkhauser, Richard and Mary Daly. *The Declining Work and Welfare of People with Disabilities*. Washington, D.C.: The AEI Press, 2011.

Burman, Leonard. "The Trouble with the FairTax." Washington, D.C.: *Tax Policy Center*, May 27, 2015. Available on-line at https://www.taxpolicycenter.org/taxvox/trouble-fairtax.

Burris, Roddie. "Haier America to Expand Kershaw County Appliance Plant, Add 400 Jobs." *The State*, August 17, 2017. Available on-line at https://www.thestate.com/news/business/article31335002.html.

Burrows, Leah. "Large-Scale Wind Power Would Require More Land and Cause More Environmental Impact than Previously Thought." *Harvard News*, John A. Paulson School of Engineering and Applied Sciences, October 4, 2018. Available on-line at https://www.seas.harvard.edu/content/large-scale-wind-power-would-require-more-land-and-cause-more-environmental-impact-than-previously.

Burtless, Gary. "Income Growth and Income Inequality: The Facts May Surprise You." Washington, D.C.: The Brookings Institute, January 6, 2014. Available on-line at https://www.brookings.edu/opinions/income-growth-and-income-inequality-the-facts-may-surprise-you/.

Bush, Jeb and Clint Bolick. *Immigration Wars*. New York: Threshold Editions, 2013.

Calabresi, Guido and Philip Bobbitt. *Tragic Choices: The Conflicts Society Confronts in the Allocation of Tragically Scarce Resources*. New York: W.W. Norton, 1978.

California Department of Education. "Complete Schools." May 23, 2007. Available on-line at https://www.cde.ca.gov/ls/fa/sf/completesch.asp.

Canadian Institute of Health Insurance. "How Canada Compares: Results from the Commonwealth Fund's 2017 International Health Policy Survey of Seniors." Ottawa, 2018.

Caplan, Bryan. *Open Borders*. New York: First Second, 2019.

Caplan, Bryan. *The Case against Education*. Princeton: Princeton University Press, 2018.

Cappelli, Peter. *Will College Pay Off?* New York: Public Affairs, 2015.

Capps, Cory and David Dranove. "Hospital Consolidation and Negotiated PPO Prices." *Health Affairs*, Vol. 23, No. 2, March/April 2004. Available on-line at https://www.healthaffairs.org/doi/10.1377/hlthaff.23.2.175.

Carapezza, Kirk and Mallory Noe-Payne. "Stopping German Students in their Tracks." *Marketplace*, April 8, 2015. Available on-line at https://www.marketplace.org/2015/04/08/education/learning-curve/stopping-german-students-their-tracks.

Card, David, Ciprian Domnisoru, and Lowell Taylor. "The International Transmission of Human Capital: Evidence from the Golden Age of Upward Mobility." Working Paper 25000, Cambridge, MA: National Bureau of Economic Research, September 2018. Available on-line at https://www.nber.org/papers/w25000.pdf.

Carnevale, Anthony, Jeff Strohl, Ban Cheah, and Neil Ridley. *Good Jobs that Pay without a BA*. Center on Education and the Workforce, Georgetown University, 2017. Available on-line at https://goodjobsdata.org/wp-content/uploads/Good-Jobs-wo-BA-final.pdf.

Carr, Robert. "Average Office Rents Might Keep Rising Until 2018." *National Real Estate Investor*, November

10, 2016. Available on-line at http://www.nreionline.com/office/average-office-rents-might-keep-rising-until-2018.

Carr, Sarah. "Is Education a Waste of Time?" *The Washington Post*, February 16, 2018. Available on line at https://www.washingtonpost.com/outlook/is-education-a-waste-of-time-and-money/2018/02/16/7e3fdcfe-0a86-11e8-8890-372e2047c935_story.html?utm_term=.b9b4b86f9638.

Carter, Joe. "The Government Isn't Being Honest About Hunger in America." *Action Institute*, September 21, 2015. Available on-line at https://blog.acton.org/archives/82059-the-government-isnt-being-honest-about-hunger-in-america.html.

Carty, Sharon and *USA Today*. "Cash-for-Clunkers Bill Passes, Offers Up to $4500." *ABC News*. Available on-line at https://abcnews.go.com/Business/story?id=7880140&page=1.

Carson, Rachel. *Silent Spring.* New York: Houghton Mifflin, 1962.

Castle, Steve. "This Brick Laying Robot Can Build an Entire House in Two Days Flat." *Digital Trends,* June 29, 2015. Available on-line at https://www.digitaltrends.com/home/bricklaying-robot/.

Center on Budget and Policy Priorities. "Federal Tax Expenditures." April 9, 2018. Available on-line at https://www.cbpp.org/sites/default/files/atoms/files/policybasics-taxexpenditures.pdf.

Center on Budget and Policy Priorities. "Policy Basics: Understanding the Social Security Trust Funds." July 23, 2018. Available on-line at https://www.cbpp.org/research/social-security/policy-basics-understanding-the-social-security-trust-funds.

Center for Climate and Energy Solutions. "Cap and Trade Basics." 2017. Available on-line at https://www.c2es.org/content/cap-and-trade-basics/.

Center for Insurance Policy and Research. "The Relevance of the McCarran-Ferguson Act." 2017. Available on-line at https://www.naic.org/cipr_newsletter_archive/vol22_mccarran-ferguson.pdf?50.

Centers for Disease Control and Prevention. "Health, U.S., 2016 – Individual Charts and Tables." Available on-line at https://www.cdc.gov/nchs/hus/contents2016.htm#082.

Centers for Medicare and Medicaid Services. "Data on 2019 Individual Health Insurance Market Conditions." October 11, 2018. Available on-line at https://www.cms.gov/newsroom/fact-sheets/data-2019-individual-health-insurance-market-conditions.

Centers for Medicare and Medicaid Services. "NHE (National Health Expenditures) Fact Sheet." Baltimore, February 20, 2019. Available on-line at https://www.cms.gov/research-statistics-data-and-systems/statistics-trends-and-reports/nationalhealthexpenddata/nhe-fact-sheet.html.

Cha, Victor and Lisa Collins. "The Markets: Private Economy and Capitalism in North Korea?" *Beyond Parallel*, August 26, 2018. Available on-line at https://beyondparallel.csis.org/markets-private-economy-capitalism-north-korea/.

Chang, Ha-Joon. *23 Things They Don't Tell You about Capitalism*. New York: Bloomsbury Press, 2010.

Chanowitx, Max. "Do San Francisco's Zoning Laws that Prevent Neighborhoods from Building Tall Buildings for More People to Live in Hurt Residents and Drive up Rent?" *Quora*, April 16, 2014. Available on-line at https://www.quora.com/Do-San-Francisco-zoning-laws-that-prevent-neighborhoods-from-building-tall-buildings-for-more-people-to-live-in-hurt-its-residents-and-drive-up-rent.

Chantrill, Christopher. "U.S. Government Spending." 2018. Available on-line at https://www.usgovernmentspending.com/federal_budget_estimate_vs_actual_2018.

Chen, Xianglei and Sean Simone. *Remedial Course-Taking at U.S. Public 2 and 4-year Institutions: Scope, Experience, and Outcome.*, National Center for Education Statistics, U.S. Department of Education, NCES 2016-405, September 2016. Available on-line at https://nces.ed.gov/pubs2016/2016405.pdf.

Chetty, Raj, David Grusky, Maximilian Hell, Nathaniel Hendren Robert Manduca, and Jimmy Narang. "The Fading American Dream: Trends in Absolute Income Mobility since 1940." *Science*, April 2017. Available on-line at http://science.sciencemag.org/content/sci/early/2017/04/21/science.aal4617.full.pdf.

Chetty, Raj, John Friedman, and Jonah Rockoff. *Teacher Value-Added and Student Outcomes in Adulthood.* Working Paper No. 17699, Cambridge MA: National Bureau of Economic Research, January 2012. Available on-line at http://www.nber.org/papers/w17699.pdf.

Chetty, Raj, John Friedman, Nathaniel Hendren. Maggie Jones, and Sonya Porter. "The Opportunity Atlas: Mapping the Childhood Roots of Social Mobility." Working Paper No. 25147, Cambridge, MA: National Bureau of Economic Research, October 2018. Available on-line at https://www.nber.org/papers/w25147.pdf.

Chetty, Raj, Nathaniel Hendren, Maggie Jones, and Sonya Porter. "Race and Economic Opportunity in the United States: An Intergenerational Perspective." Harvard University, March 2018. Available on-line at www.equality-opportunity.org/assets/documents/race_paper.pdf.

Chetty, Raj, Nathaniel Hendren, Patrick Kline, Emmanuel Saez, and Nicholas Turner. "Is the United States Still a Land of Opportunity? Recent Trends in Intergenerational Mobility." *American Economic Review: Papers and Proceedings*, 104 (5), 2014. Available on-line at http://www.rajchetty.com/chettyfiles/mobility_trends_published.pdf.

Chetty, Raj, John Friedman, Nathaniel Hilger. Emmanuel Saez, Diane Schanzenbach, and Danny Yagan. "How Does Your Kindergarten Classroom Affect Your Earnings? Evidence from Project STAR." *The Quarterly Journal of Economics*, 126 (4), 2011. Available on-line at https://www.jstor.org/stable/pdf/41337175.pdf.

Child Trends Databank. *Children in Poverty*. December 2016. Available on-line at https://www.childtrends.org/indicators/children-in-poverty.

Child Trends Databank. *Neighborhood Safety*. May 2013. Available on-line at https://www.childtrends.org/wp-content/uploads/2013/05/indicator0.72789500 1369730886.html.

Chui, Michael, James Manyika, and Mehdi Miremadi. "Where Machines Could Replace Humans – and Where They Can't (Yet)." *McKinsey Quarterly*, July 2016. Available on-line at https://www.mckinsey.com/business-functions/digital-mckinsey/our-insights/where-machines-could-replace-humans-and-where-they-cant-yet.

Citizens Against Government Waste. *Prime Cuts*. 2017. Available on-line at https://www.cagw.org/sites/default/files/pdf/PrimeCuts2017Web.pdf.

City of Raleigh. *Affordable Housing in Raleigh*. Housing and Neighborhoods Department, 2018. Available on-line at https://affordablehousing.raleighnc.gov/.

"Classroom Design Overview." *Space Planning Working Group*. New York University, October 8, 2013. Available on-line at https://www.nyu.edu/content/dam/nyu/spacePriorities/documents/13-1008%20 USPWG%20Classrooms%20FINAL.pdf.

Clemens, Jeffrey. "Making Sense of the Minimum Wage." *The Cato Institute*, May 14, 2019.

Clemens, Michael. "Economics and Emigration: Trillion-Dollar Bills on the Sidewalk?" *Journal of Economic Perspectives*, Vol. 25, No. 3, Summer 2011. Available on-line at https://pubs.aeaweb.org/doi/pdf/10.1257/jep.25.3.83.

Clemens, Michael and Lant Pritchett. "The New Economic Case for Migration Restrictions: An Assessment." Bonn, Germany: The Institute for the Study of Labor, IZA DP No. 9730, February 2016. Available on-line at http://ftp.iza.org/dp9730.pdf.

Climate Leadership Council. "The Conservative Case for Carbon Dividends." February 2017. Available on-line at https://www.clcouncil.org/media/TheConservativeCaseforCarbonDividends.pdf.

Cocco, Federica. "Most U.S. Manufacturing Jobs Lost to Technology, Not Trade." *Financial Times*, December 2, 2016. Available on-line at https://www.ft.com/content/dec677c0-b7e6-11e6-ba85-95d1533d9a62.

Cochrane, John. "The Tax and Spend Healthcare Solution." *Wall Street Journal*, July 30, 2018.

Cohen, Kelly. "Majority of Americans Support Welfare Spending Restrictions." *Washington Examiner*, April 16, 2015. Available on-line at https://www.washingtonexaminer.com/majority-of-americans-support-welfare-spending-restrictions.

Cohn, Jonathan. "The Big New Idea for Reducing Health Care Costs is Actually Really Old." *Huffpost*, April 20, 2018. Available on-line at https://www.huffingtonpost.com/entry/california-health-care-price-control_us_5ad66dcde4b0e4d0715b21d8.

Coile, Courtney and Mark Duggan. "When Labor's Lost: Health, Family Life, Incarceration, and Education in a Time of Declining Economic Opportunity for Low-Skilled Men." *Journal of Economic Perspectives*, Vol. 33, No. 2, Spring 2019. Available on-line at https://pubs.aeaweb.org/doi/pdfplus/10.1257/jep.33.2.191.

College Board. *2016 College-Bound Seniors Total Group Profile Report*. 2016. Available on-line at https://reports.collegeboard.org/pdf/total-group-2016.pdf.

College Board. *Trends in Student Aid*. 2017. Available on-line at https://trends.collegeboard.org/sites/default/files/2017-trends-student-aid_0.pdf.

College Board. "Tuition and Fees over Time." *Trends in College Education*. Available on-line at https://trends.collegeboard.org/college-pricing/figures-tables/tuition-fees-room-board-over-time.

BIBLIOGRAPHY

Committee for a Responsible Federal Budget. "Q and A: Gross Debt vs. Debt Held by the Public." Washington, D.C., September 11, 2017. Available on-line at http://www.crfb.org/papers/qa-gross-debt-versus-debt-held-public.

Committee for a Responsible Federal Budget. "Senator Rand Paul Releases Flat Tax Plan." Washington, D.C., November 16, 2015. Available on-line at http://www.crfb.org/blogs/senator-rand-paul-releases-flat-tax-plan-0.

Committee for a Responsible Federal Budget. "The Tax Break-Down: Child Tax Credit." Washington, D.C., August 29, 2013. Available on-line at http://www.crfb.org/blogs/tax-break-down-child-tax-credit.

Confino, Jo. "We Buy a Staggering Amount of Clothing, and Most of It Ends Up in Landfills." *HuffPost*, September 14, 2016. Available on-line at https://www.huffingtonpost.com/entry/transforming-the-fashion-industry_us_57ceee96e4b0a48094a58d39.

Congressional Budget Office. *Analysis of the Long-Term Costs of the Administration's Goals for the Military.* Washington, D.C., December 2017. Available on-line at https://www.cbo.gov/system/files?file=115th-congress-2017-2018/reports/53350-costsofadministrationsgoalsformilitary.pdf.

Congressional Budget Office. *Effective Marginal Tax Rates for Low- and Moderate-Income Workers in 2016.* Washington, D.C., November 2015. Available on-line at https://www.cbo.gov/sites/default/files/114th-congress-2015-2016/reports/50923-marginaltaxrates.pdf.

Congressional Budget Office. *Federal Investment, 1962 to 2018.* Washington, D.C., June 2018. Available on-line at https://www.cbo.gov/system/files/2019-06/55375-Federal_Investment.pdf.

Congressional Budget Office. *Options for Reducing the Deficit: 2019 to 2028.* Washington, D.C.: Government Printing Office, December 2018. Available on-line at https://www.cbo.gov/system/files/2019-06/54667-budgetoptions-2.pdf.

Congressional Budget Office. *Social Security Policy Options.* Washington, D.C., December 2015. Available on-line at https://www.cbo.gov/sites/default/files/114th-congress-2015-2016/reports/51011-SSOptions.pdf.

Congressional Budget Office. *The 2018 Long Term Budget Outlook.* Washington, D.C., June 2018. Available on-line at https://www.cbo.gov/system/files?file=2018-06/53919-2018ltbo.pdf.

Congressional Budget Office. *The Distribution of Household Income, 2014.* Washington, D.C., March 2018. Available on-line at https://www.cbo.gov/system/files/115th-congress-2017-2018/reports/53597-distribution-household-income-2014.pdf.

Congressional Budget Office. *The Effects on Employment and Family Income of Increasing the Federal Minimum Wage.* Washington, D.C.: Government Printing Office, July 2019. Available on-line at https://www.cbo.gov/system/files/2019-07/CBO-55410-MinimumWage2019.pdf.

Conley, Paul. "Treasuries are the Safest Investment." *The Balance*, May 21, 2018. Available on-line at https://www.thebalance.com/what-is-the-safest-investment-417037.

Conquest, Robert. *Dragons of Expectations: Reality and Delusion in the Course of History.* New York: W.W. Norton, 2005.

Cok, Erin. "Vietnam Gears Up to Divest State-Owned Enterprises in 2018." *The Diplomat*, December 21, 2017. Available on-line at https://thediplomat.com/2017/12/vietnam-gears-up-to-divest-state-owned-enterprises-in-2018/.

Conover, Chris. "Why Bernie Sanders' Health Plan Will Cost at Least 40% More than Advertised." *Forbes*, January 20, 2016. Available on-line at https://www.forbes.com/sites/theapothecary/2016/01/20/why-bernie-sanders-health-plan-will-cost-at-least-40-more-than-advertised/#7fc0e0384426

Cooper, Preston. "New York Fed Highlights Underemployment among College Graduates." *Forbes*, July 13, 2017. Available on-line at https://www.forbes.com/sites/prestoncooper2/2017/07/13/new-york-fed-highlights-underemployment-among-college-graduates/#2059b0f640d8.

Copeland, Larry. "Biking to Work Increases 60% in Past Decade." *USA Today*, May 9, 2014. Available on-line at https://www.usatoday.com/story/news/nation/2014/05/08/bike-commuting-popularity-grows/8846311/.

Corak, Miles. "Income Inequality, Equality of Opportunity, and Intergenerational Mobility." *Journal of Economic Perspectives*, Vol. 27, No. 3, Summer 2013. Available on-line at https://pubs.aeaweb.org/doi/pdfplus/10.1257/jep.27.3.79.

Coren, Michael. "New Mexico is the Third State to Legally Require 100% Carbon-free Electricity." *Quartz*, March 13, 2019. Available on-line at https://qz.com/1571918/new-mexicos-electricity-will-be-100-renewable-by-2045/

Corker, Michael. "Hard Lessons Breathe New Life into Retail Stores." *The New York Times*, September 6, 2018. Available on-line at https://www.nytimes.com/2018/09/03/business/retail-walmart-amazon-economy.html.

Cornelissen, Thomas and Christian Dustmann. "Early School Exposure, Test Scores, and Noncognitive Outcomes." *American Economic Journal: Economic Policy*, Vol. 11, No. 2, May 2019. Available on-line at https://pubs.aeaweb.org/doi/pdfplus/10.1257/pol.20170641.

Coronado, Julia, Don Fullerton, and Thomas Glass. "The Progressivity of Social Security." Working Paper 7520, Boston: National Bureau of Economic Research, February 2000. Available on-line at https://www.nber.org/papers/w7520.pdf.

"Costs to Bring a Drug to Market Remains in Dispute." *Managed Care*, September 14, 2017. Available on-line at https://www.managedcaremag.com/news/20170914/costs-bring-drug-market-remain-dispute.

Council of Economic Advisers. *Addressing the Reskilling Challenge*. Washington, D.C.: The White House, July 2018. Available on-line at https://www.whitehouse.gov/wp-content/uploads/2018/07/Addressing-Americas-Reskilling-Challenge.pdf.

Council of Economic Advisers. *Economic Report of the President*. Washington, D.C.: The White House, March 2019. Available on-line at https://www.whitehouse.gov/wp-content/uploads/2019/03/ERP-2019.pdf.

"Country List Government Debt to GDP." *Trading Economics*. Available on-line at https://tradingeconomics.com/country-list/government-debt-to-gdp.

Cowen, Tyler and Alex Tabarrok. *Modern Principles of Economics*, New York: Worth Publishers, 2014.

CPA Practice Advisor. "Student Loan Debt Delays Homeownership by Millennials by 7 Years." Sept. 18, 2017. Available on-line at http://www.cpapracticeadvisor.com/news/12368514/student-loan-debt-delays-homeownership-for-millennials-by-7-years.

Craig, Glen. "What Do Your Property Taxes Pay For?" *Free from Broke*, April 28, 2014. Available on-line at https://freefrombroke.com/what-do-your-property-taxes-pay-for/.

Craig, Ryan. *A New U*. Dallas: BenBella Books, 2018.

Craig, Winston. "Health Effect of Vegan Diets." *The American Journal of Clinical Nutrition*, Vol. 89, No. 5, May 2009. Available on-line at https://academic.oup.com/ajcn/article/89/5/1627S/4596952.

Crisp, James. "Finland Ends Universal Basic Income." *The Telegraph*, April 24, 2018. Available on-line at https://www.telegraph.co.uk/news/2018/04/23/finland-ends-universal-basic-income-experiment/.

Cristobal, Ramon and Tim O'Shea. "Why Hiring More Judges Would Reduce Immigration Court Backlogs." *Bipartisan Policy Center*, July 25, 2018. Available on-line at https://bipartisanpolicy.org/blog/why-hiring-more-judges-would-reduce-immigration-court-backlogs/.

Cubanski, Juliette and Tricia Newman. "The Facts on Medicare Spending and Financing." *Henry J. Kaiser Family Foundation*. San Francisco, CA, June 22, 2018. Available on-line at https://www.kff.org/medicare/issue-brief/the-facts-on-medicare-spending-and-financing/.

Cullis, John, Philip Jones, and Carol Propper. "Waiting Lists and Medical Treatment: Analysis and Policies." In Anthony Culyer and Joseph Newhouse, *Handbook in Health Economics*, Vol. 1, Part B, 2000. Amsterdam: Elsevier.

Curto, Vilas and Roland Fryer, Jr. "The Potential of Urban Boarding Schools for the Poor: Evidence from SEED." *Journal of Labor Economics*, 32 (1). Available on-line at https://www.journals.uchicago.edu/doi/pdfplus/10.1086/671798.

Cutter, Chip. "Amazon to Retrain a Third of Its Workforce." *The Wall Street Journal*, July 11, 2019. Available on-line at https://www.wsj.com/articles/amazon-to-retrain-a-third-of-its-u-s-workforce-11562841120.

"Cuyahoga River Fire." *Ohio History Central*. Available on-line at http://www.ohiohistorycentral.org/w/Cuyahoga_River_Fire.

Dafny, Leemore. "Are Health Insurance Markets Competitive?" *American Economic Review*, Vol. 100, No. 4, September 2010. Available on-line at https://pubs.aeaweb.org/doi/pdfplus/10.1257/aer.100.4.1399.

Dalesio, Emery. "Chinese Tiremaker Picks NC Site for Major Plant." *USnews*, December 20, 2017. Available on-line at https://www.usnews.com/news/business/articles/2017-12-19/chinese-tire-maker-picks-north-carolina-site-for-major-plant.

D'Ambrosio, Conchita, Giorgia Menta, and Edward Wolff. "Income and Wealth: Evidence from Italy and the U.S. in the Past Two Decades," Working Paper 26527, Cambridge, MA: National Bureau of Economic Research, December 2019. Available on-line at www.nber.org/papers/w26527.pdf.

BIBLIOGRAPHY

D'Antonio, Patricia and Jean Whelan. "Counting Nurses: The Power of Historical Census Data." *Journal of Clinical Nursing*, Vol 18, No. 19, October 2009. Available on-line at https://www.ncbi.nlm,nih.gov/pmc/articles/pmc2756047/.

Darity, William and Kirsten Mullen. "How Reparations for American Descendants of Slavery Could Narrow the Racial Wealth Divide." *Think*, June 20, 2019. Available on-line at https://www.nbcnews.com/think/opinion/how-reparations-american-descendants-slavery-could-narrow-racial-wealth-divide-ncna1019691.

D'Aveni, Richard. *The Pan-Industrial Revolution.* Boston: Houghton, Mifflin, Harcourt, 2018.

Davies, Antony and James Harrigan. "The Economic Case for Immigration." *U.S. News*, February 6, 2018. Available on-line at https://www.usnews.com/opinion/economic-intelligence/articles/2018-02-06/from-an-economic-and-civic-standpoint-immigrants-are-good-for-society.

Davis, Karen, Cathy Schoen, and Farham Bandeali. "Medicare: 50 Years of Ensuring Coverage and Care." Publication 1812, Washington, D.C.: *The Commonwealth Fund*, April 2015. Available on-line at https://www.commonwealthfund.org/sites/default/files/documents/___media_files_publications_fund_report_2015_apr_1812_davis_medicare_50_years_coverage_care.pdf.

Davis, Lucas and Lutz Kilian. "Estimating the Effect of a Gasoline Tax on Carbon Emissions." Cambridge, MA: National Bureau of Economic Research, January 2009. Available on-line at https://www.nber.org/papers/w14685.pdf.

Davis, Lucas and James Sallee. "Should Electric Vehicle Drivers Pay a Mileage Tax?" Working Paper 26702, Cambridge, MA: National Bureau of Economic Research, July 2019. Available on-line at https://www.nber.org/papers/w26072.pdf.

Day, John and Charles Hall. *America's Most Sustainable Cities and Regions.* New York: Springer, 2016.

Day, John and Charles Hall. "The Myth of the Sustainable City." *Scientific American*, August 21, 2016. Available on-line at https://www.scientificamerican.com/article/the-myth-of-the-sustainable-city/.

Deaton, Angus. *The Great Escape: Health, Wealth, and the Origins of Inequality.* Princeton: Princeton University Press, 2013.

Dedrick, Jason, Greg Linden, and Kenneth Kraemer. "We Estimate China Only Makes $8.46 from an iPhone – and That's Why Trump's Trade War Is Futile." *The Conversation*, July 8. 2018. Available on-line at https://theconversation.com/we-estimate-china-only-makes-8-46-from-an-iphone-and-thats-why-trumps-trade-war-is-futile-99258.

Delaney, Kevin. "The Robot that Takes Your Job Should Pay Taxes, Says Bill Gates." *Quartz*, February 17, 2017. Available on-line at https://qz.com/911968/bill-gates-the-robot-that-takes-your-job-should-pay-taxes/.

De Leon, Benito. "Airport Financing and Development." Washington, D.C.: U.S. Department of Transportation, June 18, 2014. Available on-line at https://www.transportation.gov/content/airport-financing-and-development.

Delsol, Jean-Philippe, Nicolas Lecaussin, and Emmanuel Martin. *Anti-Piketty.* Washington, D.C.: The Cato Institute, 2017.

Del Real, Jose. "The Number of Undocumented Immigrants in the U.S. Has Dropped, a Study Says. Here are 5 Takeaways." *The New York Times*, November 27, 2018. Available on-line at https://www.nytimes.com/2018/11/27/us/illegal-immigrants-population-study.html.

Deming, David and Kadeem Noray. "STEM Careers and Technological Change." Working Paper 25065, Boston: National Bureau of Economic Research, September 2018. Available on-line at http://www.nber.org/papers/w25065.pdf.

"Demographic Characteristics of the Population 65 and Over." *Proximity*, March 6, 2019. Available on-line at proximityone.com/demographics65up.htm.

De Rugy, Veronique. "A Comprehensive Look at U.S. Debt." *Mercatus Center*, George Mason University. Available on-line at https://www.mercatus.org/system/files/debt-in-perspective-analysis.pdf.

De Rugy, Veronique. "Food Stamp Spending and Enrollment Double in Five Years." *Mercatus Center*, George Mason University, June 25, 2012. Available on-line at https://www.mercatus.org/publication/food-stamp-spending-and-enrollment-double-five-years.

Desmet, Klaus, David Nagy, and Esteban Rossi-Hansberg. "The Geography of Development." *Journal of Political Economy*, Vol. 126, No. 3, May 2018. Available on-line at https://www.journals.uchicago.edu/doi/pdfplus/10.1086/697084.

Dewey, Caitlin. "GOP Proposes Stricter Work Requirement for Food Stamp Recipients, a Step Toward a Major Overhaul of the Social Safety Net." *The Washington Post*, April 12, 2018. Available on-line at https://www.washingtonpost.com/news/wonk/wp/2018/04/12/gop-proposes-stricter-work-requirements-for-food-stamp-recipients-a-step-toward-a-major-overhaul-of-the-social-safety-net/?noredirect=on&utm_term=.08e76929b688.

Diamond, Peter and Emmanuel Saez. "The Case for a Progressive Tax: From Basic Research to Policy Recommendations," *Journal of Economic Perspectives*, Vol. 25, No. 1, Fall 2011. Available on-line at https://pubs.aeaweb.org/doi/pdfplus/10.1257/jep.25.4.165.

Diamond, Rebecca, Timothy McQuade, and Franklin Qian. "The Effects of Rent Control Expansion on Tenants, Landlords, and Inequality: Evidence from San Francisco." Working Paper No. 24181, Cambridge, MA: National Bureau of Economic Research, January 2018. Available on-line at http://www.nber.org/papers/w24181.

Diaz, Roderick. *Impacts of Rail Transit on Property Values*. Washington, D.C.: American Public Transit Association, 1999. Available on-line at http://reconnectingamerica.org/assets/Uploads/bestpractice083.pdf.

DiChristopher, Tom. "Sizing up the Trade Adjustment Assistance Act." *CNBC*, June 29, 2015. Available on-line at https://www.cnbc.com/2015/06/26/is-aid-to-trade-displaced-workers-worth-the-cost.html.

Dickow, Alice. "A Dysfunctional Market: What the Foundation is Doing to Control Healthcare Costs." *Inside Philanthropy*, September 12, 2018. Available on-line at https://www.insidephilanthropy.com/home/2018/9/12/a-dysfunctional-market-what-this-foundation-is-doing-to-control-healthcare-costs.

Diez, Frederico, Daniel Leigh, and Suchanan Tambunlertchai. "Global Market Power and its Macroeconomic Implications." Working Paper 18/137, Washington: International Monetary Fund, June 2018. Available on-line at file:///C:/Users/walden.WOLFTECH/Downloads/wp18137%20(1).pdf.

Dillard, Megan. "Customers Upset with Area Post Office for Unpredictable Midday Closures." *Fox4KC.com*, February 11, 2015. Available on-line at https://fox4kc.com/2015/02/11/customers-upset-with-area-post-office-for-unpredictable-midday-closures/.

Dlouhy, Jennifer and Christopher Flavelle. "Exxon Puts $1 Million into Quest for Carbon Tax and Rebate." *Bloomberg*, October 9, 2018. Available on-line at https://www.bloomberg.com/news/articles/2018-10-09/exxon-puts-1-million-into-quest-for-carbon-tax-and-rebate-plan.

"Do Economists All Favor a Carbon Tax?" *The Economist*, September 19, 2011. Available on-line at https://www.economist.com/free-exchange/2011/09/19/do-economists-all-favour-a-carbon-tax.

Dolfin, Sarah and Peter Schochet. *The Benefits and Costs of the Trade Adjustment Assistance (TAA) Program under the 2002 Amendments*. Mathematica Policy Research, December 2012. Available on-line at https://wdr.doleta.gov/research/FullText_Documents/ETAOP_2013_09.pdf.

Dolton, Peter and Oscar Gutierrez. "Teachers' Pay and Pupil Performance." *Centre for Economic Performance*, October 2011. Available on-line at http://cep.lse.ac.uk/pubs/download/cp352.pdf.

Dougherty, Conor. "A Factory-Made Answer to a Crisis." *The New York Times*, June 10, 2018. Available on-line at https://www.nytimes.com/2018/06/07/business/economy/modular-housing.html.

Drum, Kevin. "Raw Data: How Green are Our Cities?" *Mother Jones*, April 22, 2018. Available on-line at https://www.motherjones.com/kevin-drum/2018/04/raw-data-how-green-are-our-cities/.

Duca, John and Jason Saving. "Income Inequality, Media Fragmentation, and Increased Political Fragmentation." *Contemporary Economic Policy*, Vol. 35, No. 2, April 2019. Available on-line at https://onlinelibrary.wiley.com/doi/epdf/10.1111/coep.12191.

Duggan, Mark, Atul Gupta, and Emilie Jackson. "The Impact of the Affordable Care Act: Evidence from California's Hospital Sector." Working Paper 25488, Cambridge, MA: National Bureau of Economic Research, January 2019. Available on-line at https://www.nber.org/papers/w25488.

Dunn, Megan and James Walker. "Union Membership in the U.S." *Spotlight on Statistics*. U.S. Bureau of Labor Statistics, September 2016. Available on-line at https://www.bls.gov/spotlight/2016/union-membership-in-the-united-states/pdf/union-membership-in-the-united-states.pdf.

Durbin, Dee-Ann. "As Rents Soar, Co-Living a More Appealing Option." *The New York Times*, May 13, 2018.

Durden, Tyler. "FANG Stocks Slump as Warren Calls for Breaking up 'Big Tech.'" *ZeroHedge*, March 8, 2019. Available on-line at https://www.zerohedge.com/news/2019-03-08/fang-shares-slump-warren-calls-breaking-big-tech.

BIBLIOGRAPHY

Eby, Charles and Donald Cohodes. "What Do We Know about Rate Setting?" *Journal of Health Politics, Policy, and Law*, Vol. 10, No. 2, Summer 1985, pp. 299-327. Available on-line at https://read.dukeupress.edu/jhppl/article-abstract/10/2/299/12964/What-Do-We-Know-About-Rate-Setting?redirectedFrom=fulltext.

Eckard, Cindy. "Guidelines Needed for Screen Safety at School." *The Baltimore Sun*, February 1, 2016. Available on-line at https://www.baltimoresun.com/opinion/op-ed/bs-ed-children-technology-20160201-story.html.

Edmunds. "Used Car Report 2018." Santa Monica, CA. Available on-line at https://static.ed.edmunds-media.com/unversioned/img/car-news/data-center/2018/nov/used-car-report-q3.pdf.

Edwards, Chris. "Agricultural Subsidies." *Downsizing the Federal Government*, April 16, 2018. Available on-line at https://www.downsizinggovernment.org/agriculture/subsidies.

"Effects of Divorce on Children's Education." *Marripedia*. Available on-line at http://marripedia.org/effects_of_divorce_on_children_s_education.

Employment and Training Administration. *Trade Adjustment Assistance for Workers Program, Fiscal Year 2016*. U.S. Department of Labor, 2017. Available on-line at https://www.doleta.gov/tradeact/docs/AnnualReport16.pdf.

Eneriz, Ashley. "Benefits of Attending Community College for Two Years to Save Money." *Money Crashers*. Available on-line at https://www.moneycrashers.com/benefits-of-community-college/.

Ewert, Stephanie and Tara Wildhagen. "Educational Characteristics of Prisoners: Data from the ACS." *SEHSD*, Working Paper # 2011-8, Washington, D.C. March 31-April 2, 2011. Available on-line at https://www.census.gov/library/working-papers/2011/demo/SEHSD-WP2011-08.html.

Fajgelbaum, Pablo and Amit Khandelwal. "Measuring the Unequal Gains from Trade." Working Paper 20331, Cambridge, MA: National Bureau of Economic Research, July 2014. Available on-line at http://www.nber.org/papers/w20331.pdf.

Farber, Henry, Daniel Herbst, Ilyana Kuziemko, and Suresh Naidu. "Unions and Inequality Over the Twentieth Century: New Evidence from Survey Data." Working Paper 24587, Boston: National Bureau of Economic Research, May 2018. Available on-line at http://www.nber.org/papers/w24587.pdf.

Farley, Robert. "Is Illegal Immigration Linked to More or Less Crime?" *FactCheck.org*, June 27, 2018. Available on-line at https://www.factcheck.org/2018/06/is-illegal-immigration-linked-to-more-or-less-crime/.

Fazel-Zarandi, Mohammad, Jonathan Feinstein and Edward Kaplan. "The Number of Undocumented Immigrants in the U.S. Based on Demographic Modelling with Data from 1990-2016." *PlosOne*, September 21, 2018. Available on-line at https://journals.plos.org/plosone/article?id=10.1371/journal.pone.0201193.

Federal Highway Administration. *Highway Statistics 2016*. Washington, D.C., U.S. Department of Transportation, 2017. Available on-line at https://www.fhwa.dot.gov/policyinformation/statistics/2016/.

Federal Reserve Bank of New York. *Quarterly Report on Household Debt and Credit*. February 2018. Available on-line at https://www.newyorkfed.org/medialibrary/interactives/householdcredit/data/pdf/HHDC_2017Q4.pdf.

Federal Reserve Bank of St. Louis. "Delinquency Rate on Single Family Residential Mortgages." FRED Economic Data. Available on-line at https://fred.stlouisfed.org/series/DRSFRMACBS.

Federal Reserve Bank of St. Louis. "Effective Federal Funds Rate." FRED Economic Data. Available on-line at https://fred.stlouisfed.org/series/FEDFUNDS.

Federal Reserve Bank of St. Louis. "Federal Debt: Total Public Debt." FRED Economic Data. Available on-line at https://fred.stlouisfed.org/series/GFDEBTN.

Federal Reserve Bank of St. Louis. "Federal Outlays: Interest as a Percent of GDP." FRED Economic Data. Available on-line at https://fred.stlouisfed.org/series/FYOIGDA188S.

Federal Reserve Bank of St. Louis. "Moving 12-Month Vehicle Miles Traveled." FRED Economic Data. Available on-line at https://fred.stlouisfed.org/series/M12MTVUSM227NFWA.

Federal Reserve Bank of St. Louis. "Real Median Family Income in the United States." FRED Economic Data. Available on-line at https://fred.stlouisfed.org/series/MEFAINUSA672N.

Federal Reserve Bank of St. Louis. "S&P/Case-Shiller National Home Price Index." FRED Economic Data. Available on-line at https://fred.stlouisfed.org/series/CSUSHPINSA.

Ferguson, Niall. "Can the Great Recession Happen Again?" *The Boston Globe*, September 17, 2018. Available on-line at https://www.bostonglobe.com/opinion/2018/09/17/can-great-recession-happen-again/MMunlNWuThFmiSedkI6g3L/story.html.

Finkelstein, Amy, Nathaniel Hendren, and Erzo Luttmer. "The Value of Medicaid: Interpreting Results from the Oregon Insurance Experiment." Working Paper 21308, Boston: National Bureau of Economic Research, June 2015.

Fiorillo, Steve. "Average Net Worth by Age: Mean, Median, and How to Calculate." *TheStreet*, October 3, 2018. Available on-line at https://www.thestreet.com/personal-finance/average-net-worth-by-age-14730772.

Florida, Richard. "The Comeback and Competition of the Inner City." *Citylab*, May 2, 2016. Available on-line at https://www.citylab.com/life/2016/05/the-comeback-and-competition-of-the-inner-city/480720/.

Florida, Richard. "The Incredible Rise of Urban Real Estate." *Citylab*, February 25, 2016. Available on-line at https://www.citylab.com/equity/2016/02/rise-of-urban-real-estate/470748/.

Fogelson, Robert. *Downtown: Its Rise and Fall, 1880-1950*. New Haven: Yale University Press, 2001.

Fontenot, Kayla, Jessica Semega, and Melissa Kollar. *Income and Poverty in the United States, 2017*. Washington, D.C., U.S. Census Bureau, September 2018. Available on-line at https://www.census.gov/content/dam/Census/library/publications/2018/demo/p60-263.pdf.

Ford, Martin. *Rise of the Robots*. New York: Basic Books, 2015.

Fox, Linda. *The Supplemental Poverty Measure, 2017*. Washington, D.C.: US Bureau of the Census, September 2018. Available on-line at https://www.census.gov/content/dam/Census/library/publications/2018/demo/p60-265.pdf.

Frakes, Michael and Jonathan Gruber. "Defensive Medicine: Evidence from Military Immunity." Working Paper 24846, National Bureau of Economic Research, Boston, July 2018. Available on-line at https://www.nber.org/papers/w24846.pdf.

Frank, Charles. "Pricing Carbon: A Carbon Tax or Cap-and-Trade?" *The Brookings Institute*, August 22, 2014. Available on-line at https://www.brookings.edu/blog/planetpolicy/2014/08/12/pricing-carbon-a-carbon-tax-or-cap-and-trade/.

Frank, Robert. *Falling Behind: How Rising Inequality Harms the Middle Class*. Berkeley: University of California Press, 2007.

Frank, Robert. *Luxury Fever*, New York: The Free Press, 1999.

Frank, Robert. "Why Does the Government Pay Farmers Not to Grow Crops?" *PBS Newshour*, August 4, 2009. Available on-line at https://www.pbs.org/newshour/economy/why-does-the-govt-pay-farmers.

Frank, Robert and Philip Cook. *The Winner-Take-All Society*. New York: The Free Press, 1995.

Frankel, Matthew. "The 2018 Child Tax Credit Changes: What You Need to Know." *The Motley Fool*, January 9, 2018. Available on-line at https://www.fool.com/taxes/2018/01/09/the-2018-child-tax-credit-changes-what-you-need-to.aspx.

Frankel, Todd. "Build the Wall? It Could Take at Least 10 Years, Even with 10,000 Workers." *The Washington Post*, January 9, 2019. Available on-line at https://www.washingtonpost.com/business/economy/build-the-wall-it-could-take-at-least-10-years-even-with-10000-workers/2019/01/09/62d5eaae-1376-11e9-803c-4ef28312c8b9_story.html?utm_term=.fe43619ce169.

Freeman, Lance, and Frank Braconi. "Gentrification and Displacement: New York City in the 1990s." *Journal of the American Planning Association*, Vol. 70, No. 1, pp. 37-41, March 2004. Available on-line at https://www.researchgate.net/publication/249052109_Gentrification_and_Displacement_New_York_City_in_the_1990s.

Fremstad, Anders, and Mark Paul. "A Short-Run Distributional Analysis of a Carbon Tax in the United States." Working Paper 434, Political Economy Research Institute, University of Massachusetts Amherst, August 2017. Available on-line at file:///C:/Users/walden.WOLFTECH/Downloads/WP434.pdf.

Frey, Carl. *The Technology Trap*. Princeton: Princeton University Press, 2019.

Frey, Carl and Michael Osborne. "How Susceptible are Jobs to Computerisation?" *Technological Forecasting and Social Change*, vol. 114, June 2017, pp. 254-280. Available on-line at https://www.sciencedirect.com/science/article/pii/S0040162516302244.

Friedman, Benjamin. "A Plan to Cut Military Spending." *The Cato Institute*, Washington, D.C., August 1, 2017. Available on-line at https://www.downsizinggovernment.org/defense/plan-cut-military-spending.

BIBLIOGRAPHY

Friedman, Milton and Anna Schwartz. *Monetary Trends in the United States and United Kingdom.* Chicago: The University of Chicago Press, 1982.

Frohlich, Thomas. "The 10 Worst Product Fails of All Time." *Time,* March 6, 2014. Available on-line at Fry, Richard and Paul Taylor. "The Rise of Residential Segregation by Income," *Pew Research Center,* August 1, 2012. Available on-line at http://www.pewsocialtrends.org/2012/08/01/the-rise-of-residential-segregation-by-income/.

"From Horseless to Driverless." *The Economist,* July 1, 2015. Available on-line at http://worldif.economist.com/article/12123/horseless-driverless.

Fry, Richard and Paul Taylor. "The Rise of Residential Segregation by Income." *Pew Research Center,* August 1, 2012. Available on-line at http://www.pewsocialtrends.org/2012/08/01/the-rise-of-residential-segregation-by-income/.

Furman, Jason. "Barriers to Growth: The Case of Land Use Regulation and Economic Rent." Washington D.C.: The Urban Institute, November 20, 2015. Available on-line at https://obamawhitehouse.archives.gov/sites/default/files/page/files/20151120_barriers_shared_growth_land_use_regulation_and_economic_rents.pdf.

Gabaix, Xavier and Augustin Landier. "Why has CEO Pay Increased So Much?" *The Quarterly Journal of Economics,* Vol 123, No. 1, February 2008, pp. 49-100. Available on-line at https://academic.oup.com/qje/article/123/1/49/1889842.

Gardiner, Beth. "China's Surprising Solutions to Clear Killer Air." *National Geographic,* May 5, 2017. Available on-line at https://news.nationalgeographic.com/2017/05/china-air-pollution-solutions-environment-tangshan/.

Gardner, Howard. *Frames of Mind: The Theory of Multiple Intelligences.* New York: Basic Books, 1983.

Gavura, Scott. "What Does a New Drug Cost?" *Science-Based Medicine,* April 11, 2011. Available on-line at https://sciencebasedmedicine.org/what-does-a-new-drug-cost/.

Gat, Azar. "The Return of Authoritarian Capitalism." *The New York Times,* June 14, 2007. Available on-line at https://www.nytimes.com/2007/06/14/opinion/14iht-edgat.1.6137311.html.

Gaynor, Martin. "Examining the Impact of Health Care Consolidation." Washington, D.C., February 14, 2018. Available on-line at https://docs.house.gov/meetings/IF/IF02/20180214/106855/HHRG-115-IF02-Wstate-GaynorM-20180214.pdf.

Gaynor, Martin and William Vogt. "Competition Among Hospitals." Boston, MA: National Bureau of Economic Research, paper 9471, January 2003. Available on-line at https://www.nber.org/papers/w9471.pdf.

Gayou, Gerald. "A Trade Deficit Isn't a Mortgage." *The Wall Street Journal,* November 15, 2018. Available on-line at https://www.wsj.com/articles/a-trade-deficit-isnt-a-mortgage-1542327085.

Geloso, Vincent and Youcef Msaid. "Adjusting Inequalities for Regional Price Parities: Importance and Implications." *Journal of Regional Analysis and Policy,* Vol. 4, No. 4, August 2018, pp. 1-8. Available on-line at https://jrap.scholasticahq.com/article/4229-adjusting-inequalities-for-regional-price-parities-importance-and-implications.

Gershgorn, Dave. "After Decades of Decline, No-Car Households are Becoming More Common in the U.S." *Quartz,* December 28, 2016. Available on-line at https://qz.com/873704/no-car-households-are-becoming-more-common-in-the-us-after-decades-of-decline/.

Gibson, Dale. "Duke Outpaces Other Hospitals in Market Share." *Triangle Business Journal,* February 27, 2006. Available on-line at https://www.bizjournals.com/triangle/stories/2006/02/27/tidbits1.html.

Glaeser, Edward and Joseph Gyourko. "The Impact of Zoning on Housing Affordability." Working Paper 8335, Boston, MA: National Bureau of Economic Research, March 2002. Available on-line at http://www.nber.org/papers/w8335.pdf.

Glaeser, Edward. *Triumph of the City.* New York: The Penguin Press, 2011.

Global Climate Change. *Responding to Climate Change.* Available on-line at https://climate.nasa.gov/solutions/adaptation-mitigation/.

Gneezy, Uri, Ernan Haruvy, and Hadas Yafe. "The Inefficiency of Splitting the Bill." *The Economic Journal,* Vol. 114, Issue 495, April 2004, pp. 265-280. Available on-line at https://rady.ucsd.edu/faculty/directory/gneezy/pub/docs/splitting-bill.pdf.

Goldberg, David. *Discontented America: The United States in the 1920s,* Baltimore: Johns Hopkins University Press, 1999.

Goldberg, Jonah. *Liberal Fascism*. New York: Doubleday, 2008.

Goldberg, Wendy, JoAnn Prause, Rachel Lucas-Thompson, and Amy Himsel. "Maternal Employment and Children's Achievement in Context: A Meta-Analysis of Four Decades of Research." *Psychological Bulletin*, Vol. 134, No. 1, 2008, pp. 77-108. Available on-line at https://psycnet.apa.org/record/2007-19419-004?doi=1.

Goldman, Anna, Steffie Woolhandler, David Himmelstein, David Bor, and Danny McCormick. "Out-of-Pocket Spending and Premium Contributions after Implementation of the Affordable Care Act." *JAMA Internal Medicine*, Vol. 178, No. 3, January 2018, pp. 347-355. Available on-line at https://jamanetwork.com/journals/jamainternalmedicine/fullarticle/2669908.

Goldstein, Steve. "Sanders Rolls Out 'Bezos Act' that Would Tax Companies for Welfare their Employees Receive." *MarketWatch*, September 5, 2018. Available on-line at https://www.marketwatch.com/story/sanders-rolls-out-bezos-act-that-would-tax-companies-for-welfare-their-employees-receive-2018-09-05.

Goldstein, Joshua and Staffan Qvist. *A Bright Future*. New York: PublicAffairs, 2019.

Goodman, John. "Six Problems with the ACA that Aren't Going Away." *Health Affairs Blog*, January 25, 2015. Available on-line at https://www.healthaffairs.org/do/10.1377/hblog20150625.048781/full/.

Goodwin, Barry and Vincent Smith. *The Economics of Crop Insurance and Disaster Aid*. Washington, D.C.: American Enterprise Institute, 1995.

Gordon, Grey and Aaron Hedlund. *Accounting for the Rise in College Tuition*. Working Paper 21967, Boston: National Bureau of Economic Research, February 2016. Available on-line at https://www.newyorkfed.org/medialibrary/media/research/staff_reports/sr733.pdf.

Gordon, Linda and Felice Batlan. "AFDC: The Legal History." *VCU Libraries Social History Program*. Available on-line at https://socialwelfare.library.vcu.edu/public-welfare/aid-to-dependent-children-the-legal-history/.

Gordon, Robert and Ian Dew-Becker. "Controversies About the Rise of American Inequality: A Survey." Working Paper 13982, Cambridge, MA: National Bureau of Economic Research, May 2008. Available on-line at https://www.nber.org/papers/w13982.pdf.

Gould, Elise and Tanyell Cooke. "High Quality Child Care is out of Reach for Working Families." *Economic Policy Institute*, October 6, 2015. Available on-line at https://www.epi.org/publication/child-care-affordability/.

Goulder, Lawrence and Andrew Schein. "Carbon Taxes vs. Cap and Trade: A Critical Review." Working Paper 19338, Cambridge, MA: National Bureau of Economic Research, August 2013. Available on-line at http://www.nber.org/papers/w19338.

Gowrisankaran, Gautam, Aviv Nero, and Robert Town. "Mergers when Prices are Negotiated: Evidence from the Hospital Industry." *American Economic Review*, Vol. 105, No. 1, January 2015, pp. 172-203. Available on-line at http://faculty.wcas.northwestern.edu/~ane686/research/GNT_AER2015.pdf.

Graham, Carol. *Happiness for All?* Princeton, NJ: Princeton University Press, 2017.

Gramlich, John. *The Gap between the Number of Blacks and Whites in Prison is Shrinking*. Pew Research Center, January 12, 2018. Available on-line at http://www.pewresearch.org/fact-tank/2018/01/12/shrinking-gap-between-number-of-blacks-and-whites-in-prison/.

Grawe, Nathan. *Demographics and the Demand for Higher Education*. Baltimore: Johns Hopkins University Press, 2018.

Greenberg, Ashley and Sara Moore. *Faculty Workload Policies at Public Universities*. Washington, D.C.: Education Advisory Board, February 2013. Available on-line at http://www.uky.edu/ie/sites/www.uky.edu.ie/files/uploads/BP_Faculty%20Workload%20Policies%20at%20Public%20Universities.pdf.

Greenberg, Dan. "Term Limits: The Only Way to Clean Up Congress." *Backgrounder*, No. 994, August 10, 1994, Washington, D.C.: The Heritage Foundation. Available on-line at http://thf_media.s3.amazonaws.com/1994/pdf/bg994.pdf.

Greenwood, Jeremy, Ananth Seshadri, and Mehmet Yorukoglu. "Engines of Liberation." *Review of Economic Studies*, Vol. 72. No. 1, January 2005, pp. 109-133. Available on-line at https://www.jstor.org/stable/pdf/3700686.pdf.

Grennes, Thomas, Qingliang Fan, and Mehmet Caner. "New Evidence on Debt as an Obstacle to US Economic Growth." *Mercatus Center*, George Mason University, Arlington, VA, March 2019. Available on-line at https://www.mercatus.org/system/files/grennes-debt-obstacle-growth-mercatus-working-paper-v2.pdf.

Guilfore, Gwynn. "The Obama Administration Accidentally Accelerated the Corolla Conquest of American Roads." *Quartz*, August 2, 2017. Available on-line at https://qz.com/1042742/why-did-cash-for-clunkers-fail-a-new-paper-explains-how-obamas-stimulus-program-backfired/.

Gulker, Max. "The Job Guarantee: A Critical Analysis." *American Institute for Economic Research*, October 2018. Available on-line at https://www.aier.org/sites/default/files/Files/WYSIWYG/blog/9338/JobGuarantee.pdf.

Gwartney, James, Randall Holcombe, and Robert Lawson. "Institutions and the Impact of Investment on Growth." *Kyklos*, Vol. 59, No. 2, May 2006, pp. 255-273. Available on-line at https://papers.ssrn.com/sol3/papers.cfm?abstract_id=898234.

Haas-Wilson, Deborah and Christopher Garmon. "Hospital Mergers and Competitive Effects: Two Retrospective Analyses." *International Journal of the Economics of Business*, Vol. 18, No. 1, February 2011, pp. 17-32. Available on-line at https://www.tandfonline.com/doi/abs/10.1080/13571516.2011.542952.

Habitat for Humanity. *Habitat for Humanity's Milestones in History*, 2018. Available on-line at https://www.habitat.org/about/history/timeline.

Hafstead, Marc. "The Year of the Carbon Pricing Proposal." *Resources*, August 2, 2019. Available on-line at https://www.resourcesmag.org/common-resources/the-year-of-the-carbon-pricing-proposal/.

Hagquist, Ron. "Higher Gas Efficiency Equals Lower Fuel Revenues." *Public Roads*, Federal Highway Administration Research and Technology, November/December 2008. Available on-line at https://www.fhwa.dot.gov/publications/publicroads/08nov/03.cfm.

Hahn, Heather, Eleanor Pratt, Eva Allen, Genevieve Kenney, Diane Levy, and Elaine Waxman. "Work Requirements in Social Safety Net Programs." Washington, D.C.: The Urban Institute, December 2017. Available on-line at https://www.urban.org/sites/default/files/publication/95566/work-requirements-in-social-safety-net-programs.pdf.

"Half of Millennials Don't Believe Social Security Will Exist when They Retire: Poll." *HuffPost,* May 2, 2013. Available on-line at https://www.huffingtonpost.com/2011/10/20/millenials-social-security_n_1021602.html.

Hall, Andrew. *Who Wants to Run?* Chicago: The University of Chicago Press, 2019.

Hall, Andrew. "How the Public Funding of Elections Increases Candidate Polarization." Working Paper, Dept. of Government, Harvard University, August 13, 2014. Available on-line at http://www.andrewbenjaminhall.com/Hall_publicfunding.pdf.

Hall, Robert and Alvin Rabushka. *The Flat Tax, 2ⁿᵈ edition*. Stanford, California: Hoover Institution Press, 1995.

Hamilton, Gayle, Stephen Freedman, Lisa Gennetian, Charles Michalopoulos, Johanna Walter, Diana Adams-Ciardullo, and Anna Gassman-Pines. "National Evaluation of Welfare-to-Work Strategies." Washington, D.C.: U.S. Department of Health and Human Services and U.S. Department of Education, December 2001. Available on-line at https://www.mdrc.org/sites/default/files/full_391.pdf.

Hamilton, Laura. "More Is More or More Is Less? Parental Financial Investments During College." *American Sociological Review*, 78(1):70-95, February 2013. Available on-line at http://journals.sagepub.com/doi/pdf/10.1177/0003122412472680.

Hanushek, Eric and Paul Peterson. "The Achievement Gap Fails to Close." *Education Next*, Vol 19, No. 3, Summer 2019, pp. 1-9. Available on-line at https://www.educationnext.org/achievement-gap-fails-close-half-century-testing-shows-persistent-divide/.

Hanushek, Eric, Paul Peterson, and Ludger Woessmann. *Endangering Prosperity*. Washington, D.C.: Brookings Institution Press, 2013.

Harari, Yuval Noah. *21 Lessons for the 21ˢᵗ Century*. New York: Spiegel and Grau, 2018.

Harasztosi, Peter and Attila Lindner. "Who Pays the Minimum Wage?" *American Economic Review*, Vol. 109, No. 8, August 2019, pp. 2693-2727. Available on-line at https://pubs.aeaweb.org/doi/pdfplus/10.1257/aer.20171445.

Harrington, Michael. *Socialism: Past and Future*. New York: Little Brown & Co., 1989.

"Harry S Truman on Economy and Economics." *Quotationsbook.com*. Available on-line at http://quotationsbook.com/quote/11809/.

Hartford, Tim. *Fifty Inventions that Shaped the Modern Economy.* New York: Riverhead Books, 2017.

Hathaway, Ian and Mark Muro. "Ridesharing Hits Hyper-Growth." Washington, D.C.: The Brookings Institute, June 1, 2017. Available on-line at https://www.brookings.edu/blog/the-avenue/2017/06/01/ridesharing-hits-hyper-growth/.

Heal, Geoffrey and Wolfram Schlenker. "Coase, Hotelling, and Piguo: The Incidence of a Carbon Tax and CO_2 Emissions." Working Paper 26086, Cambridge, MA: National Bureau of Economic Research. Available on-line at https://www.nber.org/papers/w26086.pdf.

Heathcote, Jonathan and Fabrizio Perri. "Wealth and Volatility." *The Review of Economic Studies*, Vol. 85, No. 4, October 2018, pp. 2173-2213. Available on-line at https://academic.oup.com/restud/article/85/4/2173/4793245.

Heckman, James. *Giving Kids a Fair Chance.* Cambridge, MA: The MIT Press, 2013.

Heckman, James and Alan Krueger. *Income Inequality in America: What Role for Human Capital Policies?* Cambridge, MA: The MIT Press, 2003.

Heckman, James, Seong Hyeok Moon, Rodrigo Pinto, Peter Savelyev, and Adam Yavitz. "The Rate of Return to the HighScope Perry Preschool Program." *Journal of Public Economics*, Vol. 94, No. 1, 2010, pp. 114-128. Available on-line at https://www.sciencedirect.com/science/article/pii/S0047272709001418.

Hegewisch, Ariane and Emma Williams-Brown. *The Gender Wage Gap: 2017.* Institute for Women's Policy Research, March 2018. Available on-line at https://iwpr.org/wp-content/uploads/2018/03/C464_Gender-Wage-Gap-2.pdf.

Helland, Eric and Alex Tabarrok. "Why Are the Prices So Damn High?" *Mercatus Center*, George Mason University, 2019. Available on-line at https://www.mercatus.org/system/files/helland-tabarrok_why-are-the-prices-so-damn-high_v1.pdf.

Hendren, Nathaniel and Ben Sprung-Keyser. "A Unified Welfare Analysis of Government Policies." Cambridge, MA: Harvard University, July 2019. Available on-line at https://scholar.harvard.edu/files/hendren/files/welfare_vnber.pdf.

Hersch, Joni and Leslie Stratton. "Housework and Wages." *Journal of Human Resources*, Vol. 37, No. 1, Winter, 2002, pp. 217-229. Available on-line at https://www.jstor.org/stable/pdf/3069609.pdf.

Hilton, Steve. *Positive Populism.* New York: Crown Forum, 2018.

Hilzik, Michael. "Disproving the Notion of the Social Security 'Lockbox.'" *The Los Angeles Times,* March 8, 2011. Available on-line at http://articles.latimes.com/2011/mar/08/business/la-fi-hiltzik-20110305.

Ho, Jessica and Samuel Preston. "US Mortality in an International Context: Age Variations." *Population and Development Review*, Vol. 36, No. 4, December 2010, pp. 749-773. Available on line at https://onlinelibrary.wiley.com/doi/abs/10.1111/j.1728-4457.2010.00356.x.

Hoffman, David and Erik Lundh. "'Huge' Trade Deficits are Smaller than You Think." *Bloomberg*, March 18, 2018. Available on-line at https://www.bloomberg.com/view/articles/2018-03-18/big-u-s-china-trade-deficit-is-smaller-than-it-appears.

Holan, John, Diane Rowland, Judith Feder, and David Heslam. "Explaining the Recent Growth in Medicaid Spending." *Health Affairs*, Vol. 12, No. 3. Available on-line at https://www.healthaffairs.org/doi/10.1377/hlthaff.12.3.177.

Holcombe, Randall. *Political Capitalism.* Cambridge, UK: Cambridge University Press, 2018.

Hollingsworth, Joseph, Breena Copeland, and Jeremiah Johnson. "Are E-Scooters Polluters? The Environmental Impacts of Shared Dockless Electric Scooters." *Environmental Research Letters*, Vol. 14, No. 8, August 2019. Available on-line at https://iopscience.iop.org/article/10.1088/1748-9326/ab2da8/pdf.

Holpuch, Amanda. "I Don't Want to Go Back: What's next for the Central American Migrant Caravan?" *The Guardian*, December 8, 2018. Available on-line at https://www.theguardian.com/world/2018/dec/08/central-american-migrant-caravan-tijuana.

Holtz-Eakin, Douglas and Gordon Gray. "Wealth Taxes and Workers." *American Action Forum*, January 10, 2020. Available on-line at americanactionforum.org/research/wealth-taxes-and-workers/.

Holzer, Harry, Diane Schanzenbach, Greg Duncan, and Jens Ludwig. "The Economic Costs of Childhood Poverty in the United States." *Journal of Children and Poverty*, Vol. 14, No. 1, March 2008, pp. 41-61. Available on-line at https://www.tandfonline.com/doi/full/10.1080/10796120701871280.

Hooper, Charles. "Pharmaceuticals: Economics and Regulation." *The Library of Economics and Policy.* Available on-line at https://www.econlib.org/library/Enc/PharmaceuticalsEconomicsandRegulation.html.

Horowitz, John, Julie-Anne Cronin, Hannah Hawkins, Laura Konda, and Alex Yuskavage. "Methodology for Analyzing a Carbon Tax." Working Paper 115, Office of Tax Analysis, The Department of the Treasury, January 2017. Available on-line at https://www.clcouncil.org/wp-content/uploads/2017/02/Treasury_Analysis.pdf.

"H.R. 2095: Fair Pay Act of 2017." *Govtrack.* Available on-line at https://www.govtrack.us/congress/bills/115/hr2095.

Hsieh, Chang-Tai and Enrico Moretti. "Housing Constraints and Spatial Misallocation." *American Economic Journal: Macroeconomics*, Vol. 11, No. 2, April 2019, pp. 1-39. Available on-line at https://pubs.aeaweb.org/doi/pdfplus/10.1257/mac.20170388.

Hsu, Shi-Ling. *The Case for a Carbon Tax.* Washington: Island Press, 2011.

Hui, T. Keung. "How Did Wake County Schools Perform Last Year?" *The News and Observer*, September 7, 2017. Available on-line at https://www.newsobserver.com/news/local/education/article171733222.html.

Illanes, Pablo, Susan Lund, Mona Mourshed, Scott Rutherford, and Magnus Tyreman. "Retraining and Reskilling Workers in the Age of Automation." McKinsey and Company, January 2018. Available on-line at https://www.mckinsey.com/featured-insights/future-of-work/retraining-and-reskilling-workers-in-the-age-of-automation.

Impact of Poverty on Student Outcomes. Hanover Research, January 2015. Available on-line at http://gssaweb.org/wp-content/uploads/2015/04/Impact-of-Poverty-on-Student- Outcomes-1.pdf.

Institute for Energy Research. *Gas Tax Revenues Will Plummet with Large Increases in Electric Vehicles.* Washington, D.C., August 23, 2017. Available on-line at https://instituteforenergyresearch.org/analysis/gas-tax-revenues-will-plummet-large-increase-electric-vehicles/

Ip, Greg. "The Problem with a Federal Jobs Guarantee (Hint: It's Not the Price Tag), *The Wall Street Journal*, May 2, 2018. Available on-line at https://www.wsj.com/articles/the-problem-with-a-federal-jobs-guarantee-hint-its-not-the-price-tag-1525267192.

Irwin, Douglas. "Does Trade Reform Promote Economic Growth? A Review of Recent Evidence." Working Paper 25927, Cambridge, MA: National Bureau of Economic Research, June 2019. Available on-line at https://www.nber.org/papers/w25927.pdf.

"Is Human Activity Primarily Responsible for Global Climate Change?" *ProCon.org,* October 11, 2018. Available on-line at https://climatechange.procon.org/.

Iskyan, Kim. "China's Middle Class is Exploding." *Business Insider*, August 27, 2016. Available on-line at https://www.businessinsider.com/chinas-middle-class-is-exploding-2016-8.

Issacs, Julia. "The Costs of Benefit Delivery in the Food Stamp Program: Lessons from Cross-Program Analysis." Contract and Cooperator Report No. 39, U.S. Department of Agriculture, March 2008. Available on-line at https://www.brookings.edu/wp-content/uploads/2016/06/03_food_stamp_isaacs.pdf.

Iversen, Torben and David Soskice. *Democracy and Prosperity: Reinventing Capitalism through a Turbulent Century*, Princeton: Princeton University Press, 2019.

Jackson, Abby. "3 Big Ways No Child Left Behind Failed." *Business Insider*, March 25, 2015. Available on-line at https://www.businessinsider.com/heres-what-no-child-left-behind-got-wrong-2015-3.

Jackson, Eric. "The Rise and Fall of the African-American Community in OTR Cincinnati." *The Voice of Black Cincinnati*, August 7, 2018. Available on-line at https://thevoiceofblackcincinnati.com/otr-cincinnati-african-americans/.

Jackson, James. *Foreign Direct Investment in the United States: An Economic Analysis.* Washington, D.C.: Congressional Research Service, June 29, 2017. Available on-line at https://fas.org/sgp/crs/misc/RS21857.pdf.

Jackson, Kirabo. "Does School Spending Matter: The New Literature on an Old Question?" Working Paper 25368, Cambridge, MA: National Bureau of Economic Research, December 2018. Available on-line at https://www.nber.org/papers/w25368.pdf.

Jackson, Rebecca. "The Case Against Group Projects: What Parents and Teachers Can Learn from Them." *HuffPost*, March 6, 2015. Available on-line at https://www.huffpost.com/entry/why-group-projects-fail-w_b_6804104.

Jaffe, Susan. "No More Secrets: Congress Bans Pharmacist 'Gag Orders' on Drug Prices." *Kaiser* Health *News*, October 10, 2018. Available on-line at https://khn.org/news/no-more-secrets-congress-bans-pharmacist-gag-orders-on-drug-prices/.

Japsen, Bruce. "States Ease More Restrictions to Physician Assistants as Team Care Takes Hold." *Forbes*, May 13, 2018. Available on-line at https://www.forbes.com/sites/brucejapsen/2018/05/13/states-ease-more-restrictions-to-physician-assistants-as-team-care-takes-hold/#6321c3e37d99.

Jargowsky, Paul and Mohamed El Komi. "Before or After the Bell? School Context and Neighborhood Effects on Student Achievement." *The Urban Institute*, Working Paper 28, Washington, D.C.; National Center for Analysis of Longitudinal Data in Education Research. Available on-line at https://eric.ed.gov/?id=ED509690.

Jaschik, Scott. "Closing Arguments in the Harvard Case." *Inside Higher Ed*, February 18, 2019. Available on-line at https://www.insidehighered.com/admissions/article/2019/02/18/critics-and-defenders-affirmative-action-submit-their-closing-briefs.

Jascik. Scott. "Grade Inflation, Higher and Higher." *Inside Higher Ed*, March 29, 2016. Available on-line at https://www.insidehighered.com/news/2016/03/29/survey-finds-grade-inflation-continues-rise-four-year-colleges-not-community-college.

Jenkins, Jesse. "How Much Land Does Solar, Wind, and Nuclear Energy Require?" *The Energy Collective Group*, June 25, 2015. Available on-line at https://www.energycentral.com/c/ec/how-much-land-does-solar-wind-and-nuclear-energy-require.

Johnsen, Dawn and Walter Dellinger. "The Constitutionality of a National Wealth Tax." *Indiana Law Journal*, Vol. 93, Issue 1, Winter 2018, pp. 111-137. Available on-line at https://www.repository.law.indiana.edu/cgi/viewcontent.cgi?article=11279&context=ilj.

Johnson, Janna and Morrie Kleiner. "Is Occupational Licensing a Barrier to Interstate Migration?" Working Paper 24107, Cambridge: National Bureau of Economic Research, December 2017. Available on-line at https://www.nber.org/papers/w24107.pdf.

Johnston, Katie. "Efforts to Regulate CEO Pay Gain Traction." *The Boston Globe*, October 26, 2014. Available on-line at https://www.bostonglobe.com/business/2014/10/25/growing-effort-limit-ceo-pay/1VKKZCuZMkXJvaQRmUb4RN/story.html.

Joint Committee on Taxation, U.S. Congress. "Estimates of Federal Tax Expenditures for Fiscal Years 2017-2021." Washington, D.C., May 25, 2018. Available on-line at https://www.jct.gov/publications.html?func=startdown&id=5095.

Jones, Charles I. "Taxing Top Incomes in a World of Ideas." Columbia Business School, September 6, 2018. Available on-line at https://www8.gsb.columbia.edu/faculty-research/sites/faculty-research/files/finance/Macro%20Workshop/toptax.pdf.

Jones, Jeffrey. "In U.S., Positive Attitudes toward Foreign Trade Stay High." *Gallup*, March 1, 2018. Available on-line at https://news.gallup.com/poll/228317/positive-attitudes-toward-foreign-trade-stay-high.aspx.

Jones, John. "How Does Electronic Reading Affect Comprehension?" *dmlcentral*, November 5, 2013. Available on-line at https://dmlcentral.net/how-does-electronic-reading-affect-comprehension/.

Josephson, Amelia. "All About Child Tax Credits." *Smartasset*, August 7, 2018. Available on-line at https://smartasset.com/taxes/all-about-child-tax-credits.

Kabali, Hilda, Matilde Irigoyen, Rosemary Nunez-Davis, Jennifer Budacki, Sweta Mohanty, Kristen Leister, and Robert Bonner. "Exposure and Use of Mobile Media Devices by Young Children." *Pediatrics*, 136 (6): 1-7, 2015. Available on-line at www.pediatrics.aappublications.org/content/pediatrics/early/2015/10/28/peds.201502151.full.pdf.

Kagan, Julia. "Cascade Tax." *Investopedia*, May 8, 2018. Available on-line at https://www.investopedia.com/terms/c/cascade-tax.asp.

Kahn, Joan, Javier Garcia-Manglano, and Suzanne Bianchi. "The Motherhood Penalty in Midlife: Long-Term Effects of Children on Women's Careers." *Journal of Marriage and the Family*, Vol. 76, No. 1, February 2014, pp. 56-72. Available on-line at https://www.academia.edu/17310234/The_Motherhood_Penalty_at_Midlife_Long-Term_Effects_of_Children_on_Womens_Careers?auto=download.

Kaiser Family Foundation. "10 Essential Facts about Medicare and Prescription Drug Spending." January 29, 2019. Available on-line at https://www.kff.org/infographic/10-essential-facts-about-medicare-and-prescription-drug-spending/.

Kaiser Family Foundation. *Employer Health Benefits, 2018.* Available on line at http://files.kff.org/attachment/ Summary-of-Findings-Employer-Health-Benefits-2018.

Kaiser Family Foundation. *Employer Health Benefits 2018 Annual Survey.* San Francisco: Kaiser Family Foundation. Available on-line at http://files.kff.org/attachment/Report-Employer-Health-Benefits-Annual-Survey-2018.

Kaiser Family Foundation. "Peterson-Kaiser Health Tracker System." Available on-line at https://www. healthsystemtracker.org/indicator/spending/per-capita-spending/.

Kaiser Family Foundation. *State Health Facts, Health Coverage of the Total Population, 2017.* Available on-line at https://www.kff.org/other/state-indicator/total-population/?dataView=1&currentTimeframe=0&sortMo del=%7B%22colId%22:%22Location%22,%22sort%22:%22asc%22%7D.

Kaiser Family Foundation. "Summary of the Affordable Care Act." *Focus on Health Reform*, April 23, 2013. Available on-line at http://files.kff.org/attachment/fact-sheet-summary-of-the-affordable-care-act.

Kandel, William. "U.S. Family-Based Immigration Policy." Washington, D.C.: Congressional Research Service, CRS Report R43145, February 9, 2018. Available on-line at https://fas.org/sgp/crs/homesec/R43145.pdf.

Kane, Thomas and Douglas Staiger. "Estimating Teacher Impacts on Student Achievement: An Experimental Evaluation." Working Paper 14607, Cambridge, MA: National Bureau of Economic Research, December 2008. Available on-line at http://www.nber.org/papers/w14607.

Kantarjian, Hagop and S. Vincent Rajkumar. "Why are Cancer Drugs so Expensive in the United States, and What are the Solutions?" *Mayo Clinic Proceedings*, Vol. 90, No 4, April 2015, pp. 500-504. Available on-line at https://mfprac.com/web2018/07literature/literature/Health_Costs/CostCA-Rx_Kantarjian.pdf.

Kaplan, Steven and Joshua Rauh. "It's the Market: The Broad-Based Rise in the Return to Top Talent." *Journal of Economic Perspectives*, Vol. 77, No. 3, Summer 2013, pp. 35-56. Available on-line at https://pubs.aeaweb. org/doi/pdfplus/10.1257/jep.27.3.35.

Kaufman, Eric. *White Shift: Populism, Immigration, and the Future of White Majorities.* New York: Abrams Press, 2019.

Kearney, John. "Social Security and the 'D' in OASDI: The History of a Federal Program Insuring Earners against Disability." *Social Security Bulletin*, Vol. 66, No. 3, August 2006. Available on-line at https://www. ssa.gov/policy/docs/ssb/v66n3/v66n3p1.html.

Keckley, Paul. "Medical Necessity and Unnecessary Care." *The Healthcare Blog*, January 29, 2015. Available on-line at https://thehealthcareblog.com/blog/2015/01/29/medical-necessity-and-unnecessary-care/.

Keith, Katie. "Federal Judge Strikes Down Entire ACA; Law Remains in Effect." *Health Affairs*, December 15, 2018. Available on-line at https://www.healthaffairs.org/do/10.1377/hblog20181215.617096/full/.

Kellough, J. Edward. "Affirmative Action in Government Employment." *Annuals of the American Academy of Political and Social Science*, Vol. 523, September 1992, pp. 117-130. Available on-line at https://www.jstor. org/stable/1047585?seq=1#metadata_info_tab_contents.

Kelton, Stephanie. "How We Think About the Deficit is Mostly Wrong." *The New York Times*, October 5, 2017. Available on-line at https://www.nytimes.com/2017/10/05/opinion/deficit-tax-cuts-trump.html.

Kerr, William. *The Gift of Global Talent.* Stanford, CA: Stanford University Press, 2019.

Kessler, Glenn. "The Trump Administration's Claim that the U.S. Government Certified 700,000 Jobs Lost by NAFTA." *The Washington Post*, August 18, 2017. Available on-line at https://www.washingtonpost.com/ news/fact-checker/wp/2017/08/18/the-trump-administrations-claim-that-the-u-s-government-certified-700000-jobs-lost-by-nafta/?noredirect=on&utm_term=.d925f52ec765.

Kessler, Sarah. "What I Learned in 12 Weeks of Therapy for Social Media Addiction." *FastCompany*, January 8, 2016. Available on-line at https://www.fastcompany.com/3055149/what-i-learned-in-12-weeks-of-therapy-for-social-media-addiction.

Keynes, John M. "Economic Possibilities for our Grandchildren." *Essays in Persuasion.* London: Palgrave MacMillan, 1930, pp. 321-334. Available on-line at http://www.econ.yale.edu/smith/econ116a/keynes1.pdf.

Khachaturian, Tamar and David Riker. *Economic Impact of Trade Agreements Implemented Under Trade Authorities Procedures, 2016 Report.* Publication # 4614, Washington, D.C.: U.S. International Trade Commission, June 2016. Available on-line at https://www.usitc.gov/publications/332/pub4614.pdf.

Kiplinger, Knight. "How Can the Approval Process for New Drugs Be Speeded Up?" *Kiplinger Personal Finance.* Available on-line at https://www.kiplinger.com/article/investing/T027-C013-S002-how-can-approvals-for-new-drugs-be-faster.html.

Kirp, David. *The College Dropout Scandal.* Cambridge, UK: Oxford University Press, 2019.

Kliff, Sarah, and Dylan Scott. "We Read Democrats' 9 Plans for Expanding Health Care. Here's How They Work." *Vox*, March 20, 2019. Available on-line at https://www.vox.com/2018/12/13/18103087/medicare-for-all-explained-single-payer-health-care-sanders-jayapal.

Knight, Will. "This is the Most Dexterous Robot Ever Created." *MIT Technology Review*, March 26, 2018. Available on-line at https://www.technologyreview.com/s/610587/robots-get-closer-to-human-like-dexterity/.

Kohn, Alfie. *No Contest: The Case against Competition.* Boston: Houghton-Mufflin, 1992.

Kolko, Jed. "Millennials Delay Marriage and Kids, but Are Still Eager to Become Homeowners." *Emarketer*, January 22, 2016. Available on-line at https://www.emarketer.com/Article/Millennials-Delay-Marriage-Kids-Still-Eager-Become-Homeowners/1013492.

Kolko, Jed. "Where the Fast-Growing Jobs Are." *Jedkolko.com*, December 9, 2009. Available on-line at http://jedkolko.com/2015/12/09/where-the-fast-growing-jobs-are/.

Komisar, Erica. *Being There: Why Prioritizing Motherhood in the First Three Years Matter.* New York: Tarcher-Perigee, 2017.

Konish, Lorie. "If You Can't Wait Until 70, this is the Next Best Age to Claim Social Security Benefits." *CNBC*, July 12, 2018. Available on-line at https://www.cnbc.com/2018/07/11/if-you-cant-wait-until-70-this-is-the-next-best-age-to-claim-social-.html.

Konish, Lorie. "Trump's Budget Calls for Six Weeks' Paid Family Leave." *CNBC*, February 12, 2018. Available on-line at https://www.cnbc.com/2018/02/12/trumps-budget-calls-for-six-weeks-paid-family-leave.html

Koru, Omer. "Automation and Top Income Inequality." Working Paper 19-004, Penn Institute for Economic Research, University of Pennsylvania, March 2019. Available on-line at https://papers.ssrn.com/sol3/papers.cfm?abstract_id=3360473.

Kotlikoff, Laurence. "The Economic Impact of Replacing Federal Income Taxes with a Sales Tax." Cato Policy Analysis, No. 1939, Washington, D.C., April 1993. Available on-line at https://www.cato.org/sites/cato.org/files/pubs/pdf/pa193.pdf.

Krogstad, Jens, Jeffrey Passe, and D'Vera Cohn. "5 Facts about Illegal Immigration in the U.S." Washington, D.C.: Pew Research Center, November 28, 2018. Available on-line at http://www.pewresearch.org/fact-tank/2018/11/28/5-facts-about-illegal-immigration-in-the-u-s/.

Kruzel, John. "Majority of Undocumented Immigrants Show Up for Court, Data Show." *Punditfact*, June 26, 2018. Available on-line at https://www.politifact.com/punditfact/statements/2018/jun/26/wolf-blitzer/majority-undocumented-immigrants-show-court-data-s/.

Kuhn, Moritz, Moritz Schularick, and Ulrike Steins. *Income and Wealth Inequality in America, 1949-2016.* Working Paper 9, Opportunity and Inclusive Growth Institute, Federal Reserve Bank of Minneapolis, June 2018. Available on-line at https://www.minneapolisfed.org/institute/working-papers-institute/iwp9.pdf.

Kulish, Nicholas. "What It Costs to Be Smuggled Across the U.S. Border." *The New York Times*, June 30, 2018. Available on-line at https://www.nytimes.com/interactive/2018/06/30/world/smuggling-illegal-immigration-costs.html.

Lacey, T. Alan, Mitra Toossi, Kevin Dubina, and Andrea Gensler. "Projections Overview and Highlights, 2016-2026." *Monthly Labor Review*, October 2017. Available on-line at https://www.bls.gov/opub/mlr/2017/article/projections-overview-and-highlights-2016-26.htm.

Lanfear, Denny. "How Big Pharma Suppresses 'Biosimilars'." *The Wall Street Journal*, June 23, 2019. Available on-line at https://www.wsj.com/articles/how-big-pharma-suppresses-biosimilars-11561317460.

Lang, Kevin and Jee-Yeon Lehmann. "Racial Discrimination in the Labor Market: Theory and Empirics." *Journal of Economic Literature*, Vol. 50, No. 4, December 2012: pp. 959-1006. Available on-line at https://pubs.aeaweb.org/doi/pdfplus/10.1257/jel.50.4.959.

Langer, Ashley, Vikram Maheshri, and Clifford Winston. "From Gallons to Miles: A Disaggregate Analysis of Automobile Travel and Externality Taxes." *Journal of Public Economics*, Vol. 152, August 2017, pp. 34-46. Available on-line at https://www.brookings.edu/wp-content/uploads/2017/06/jpube-vmt-paper.pdf.

Lankford, James. "Senator Lankford Released Federal Fumbles, Vol. 3," Washington, D.C., November 27, 2017. Available on-line at https://www.lankford.senate.gov/news/press-releases/senator-lankford-releases-federal-fumbles-vol-3.

BIBLIOGRAPHY

Lattier, David. "Did Public Schools Really Improve American Literacy?" *Foundation for Economic Freedom*, September 13, 2016. Available on-line at https://fee.org/articles/did-public-schools-really-improve-american-literacy/.

Laugesen, Miriam. *Fixing Medical Prices*. Cambridge: Harvard University Press, 2016.

Laurent, Lionel. "Macron Preaches Change but Pulls his Punches." *Bloomberg*, September 18, 2018. Available on-line at https://www.bloomberg.com/opinion/articles/2018-09-18/macron-s-medicine-for-france-s-economy-is-too-weak.

LawLogix. "Immigration Case Management Blog: What is the DREAM Act and Who are the DREAMers?" July 19, 2013. Available on-line at https://www.lawlogix.com/what-is-the-dream-act-and-who-are-dreamers/.

Lawson, Robert and Benjamin Powell. *Socialism Sucks*. Washington, D.C.: Regnery Publishing, 2019.

Layzer, Jean and Nancy Burstein. *National Study of Child Care for Low-Income Families: Patterns of Care Use among Low-Income Families*. Washington, D.C., U.S. Department of Health and Human Services, September 2007. Available on-line at https://www.acf.hhs.gov/sites/default/files/opre/patterns_cc_execsum.pdf.

Leatherby, Lauren. "Medical Spending among the U.S. Elderly." *Journalist's Resource*, February 22, 2016. Available on-line at https://journalistsresource.org/studies/government/health-care/elderly-medical-spending-medicare/.

Lee, Changju and John Miller. "Lessons Learned from the Rise, Fall and Rise of Toll Roads in the United States and Virginia." University of Virginia and Virginia Center for Transportation Innovation and Research, 2015. Available on-line at http://www.p3virginia.org/wp-content/uploads/2015/06/Rise-Fall-and-Rise-of-Toll-Roads-John-Miller-2015.pdf.

Levin, Henry, Clive Belfield, Peter Muenning, and Ceclia Rouse. *The Costs and Benefits of an Excellent Education for All of America's Children*. Columbia University, January 2007. Available on-line at file:///C:/Users/walden/AppData/Local/Temp/Education_final_report.pdf.

Levinson, Marc. *The Box: How the Shipping Container Made the World Smaller and the Economy Bigger*. Princeton, NJ: Princeton University Press, 2006.

Levkovich, Or, Jan Rouwendal, and Ramona van Marwijk. "The Effects of Highway Development on Housing Prices." *Transportation*, V0l. 43, No. 2, March 2016, pp. 379-405. Available on-line at https://link.springer.com/article/10.1007/s11116-015-9580-7.

"Life Expectancy in the USA, 1900-1998." Available on-line at http://www.demog.berkeley.edu/~andrew/1918/figure2.html.

Lindeke, Bill. "Chart of the Day: Vehicle Weight vs. Road Damage Levels." *Streets.mn*, July 7, 2017. Available on-line at https://streets.mn/2016/07/07/chart-of-the-day-vehicle-weight-vs-road-damage-levels/.

Lindsey, Rebecca. "Climate Change: Global Sea Level." *National Oceanic and Atmospheric Administration*, August 1, 2018. Available on-line at https://www.climate.gov/news-features/understanding-climate/climate-change-global-sea-level.

Lindsey, Brink and Steven Teles. *The Captured Economy*. Oxford: Oxford University Press, 2017.

Lino, Mark, Kevin Kuczynski, Nestor Rodriguez, and TusaRebecca Schap. *Expenditures on Children, 2015*, Washington, D.C.: Center for Nutrition Policy and Promotion, US Department of Agriculture, Report No. 152802015, March 2017. Available on-line at https://fns-prod.azureedge.net/sites/default/files/crc2015_March2017_0.pdf.

Livingston, Gretchen. "Fewer than Half of U.S. Kids Today Live in a 'Traditional' Family." *Pew Research Center*, December 22, 2014. Available on-line at http://www.pewresearch.org/fact-tank/2014/12/22/less-than-half-of-u-s-kids-today-live-in-a-traditional-family/.

Lochner, Lance and Enrico Moretti. "The Effect of Education on Crime: Evidence from Prison Inmates, Arrests, and Self Reports." *American Economic Review*, 94 (1): 155-189, March 2004. Available on-line at https://www.aeaweb.org/articles?id=10.1257/000282804322970751.

Loria, Joe. "You Can't Eat Meat and Be an Environmentalist. Period." *Mercy for Animals*, April 20, 2017. Available on-line at https://mercyforanimals.org/you-cant-eat-meat-and-be-an-environmentalist.

Lott, Maxim. "Americans Warming to Socialism Over Capitalism, Poll Shows." *Fox News*, January 4, 2019. Available on-line at https://www.foxnews.com/politics/americans-warming-to-socialism-over-capitalism-polls-show.

Loudenback, Tanza. "Alexandria Ocasio-Cortez Has a Plan to Tax the Wealthiest Americans 60% to 70%, and it Highlights a Detail about Taxes Most People Get Wrong." *Business Insider*, January 13, 2019. Available on-line at https://www.businessinsider.com/us-progressive-taxes-alexandria-ocasio-cortez-tax-plan-2019-1.

Lowrey, Annie. *Give People Money*. New York: Crown Publishing, 2018.

Lu, Denise and Derek Watkins. "Court Backlog May Prove Bigger Barrier for Migrants than Any Wall." *The New York Times*, January 24, 2019. Available on-line at https://www.nytimes.com/interactive/2019/01/24/us/migrants-border-immigration-court.html.

Lubin, Joann. "When Pregnancies and Bigger Jobs Go Hand in Hand." *The Wall Street Journal*, July 10, 2019. Available on-line at https://www.wsj.com/articles/when-pregnancies-and-bigger-jobs-go-hand-in-hand-11562768534.

Lucas, Suzanne. "Benefits and Drawbacks of a Four-Day Workweek." *Careers*, April 15, 2019. Available on-line at https://www.thebalancecareers.com/benefits-and-drawbacks-four-day-workweek-4158304.

Lucca, David, Taylor Nadauld, and Karen Shen. *Credit Supply and the Rise in College Tuition: Evidence from the Expansion in Federal Student Aid Programs*. Staff Report No. 733, Federal Reserve Bank of New York, February 2017. Available on-line at https://www.newyorkfed.org/medialibrary/media/research/staff_reports/sr733.pdf.

Luscombe, Belinda. "Workplace Salaries: At Last, Women on Top." *Time*, September 1, 2020. Available on-line at http://content.time.com/time/business/article/0,8599,2015274,00.html.

Maag, Elaine, C. Eugene Steuerle, Ritadhi Chakravarti, and Caleb Quakenbush. "How Marginal Tax Rates Affect Families at Various Levels of Poverty." *National Tax Journal*, December 2012, Vol. 65, No. 4, pp. 759-782. Available on-line at https://www.urban.org/sites/default/files/alfresco/publication-pdfs/412722-How-Marginal-Tax-Rates-Affect-Families-at-Various-Levels-of-Poverty.PDF.

Mahtani, Shibani. "From Ailing to Artisanal: The Transformation of a Cincinnati Neighborhood." *The Wall Street Journal*, August 22, 2017. Available on-line at https://www.wsj.com/articles/from-ailing-to-artisanal-the-transformation-of-a-cincinnati-neighborhood-1503403202.

Mandelker, Daniel. "Zoning Barriers to Manufactured Housing." Washington University in St. Louis School of Law Research Paper 16-08-01, August 23, 2016. Available on-line at https://papers.ssrn.com/sol3/papers.cfm?abstract_id=2828268.

MacKenzie, Christopher. "The True Operating Costs between Bus and Light Rail." *Thought Co.*, July 10, 2017. Available on-line at https://www.thoughtco.com/bus-and-light-rail-costs-2798852.

MacLeod, W. Bentley, Evan Riehl, Juan Saavedra, and Miquel Urquiola. *The Big Sort: College Reputation and Labor Market Outccomes*. Working Paper 21230, Boston: National Bureau of Economic Research, 2015. Available on-line at www.nber.org/papers/w21230.

Mangan, Dan. "This Map Shows How Much of the United States Could See Zero or Few Obamacare Insurers Selling Health Coverage Next Year." *CNBC*, June 13, 2017. Available on-line at https://www.cnbc.com/2017/06/13/map-shows-where-people-could-see-zero-few-obamacare-insurers-in-2018.html.

Mark, Michelle, Skye Gould, and Andy Kiersz. "As the Government Shutdown over Trump's Border Wall Rages, a Journey Along the Entire 1933 Mile US-Mexico Border Shows the Monumental Task of Securing It." *Business Insider*, January 12, 2019. Available on-line at https://www.businessinsider.com/us-mexico-border-wall-photos-maps-2018-5.

Markstein, Don. "Keeping Up with the Joneses." 2010. Available on-line at http://www.toonopedia.com/joneses.htm.

Marron, Donald and Eric Toder. "Tax Policy in Designing a Carbon Tax." *The American Economic Review: Papers and Proceedings*, Vol. 104, No. 5, May 2014, pp. 563-568. Available on-line at https://www.jstor.org/stable/pdf/42920999.pdf?refreqid=excelsior%3Ad05d0613fa7da12b229a6b59f5dfe917.

Martin, Patricia and David Weaver. "Social Security: A Program and Policy History." *Social Security History*, vol. 66, no. 1, 2005. Available on-line at https://www.ssa.gov/policy/docs/ssb/v66n1/v66n1p1.html.

Mason, Deirdre. "EPA Releases Report on Progress Made to Reduce Water Pollution from Non-points Sources." *Association of Drinking Water Administrators*, November 10, 2016. Available on-line at https://sourcewaternews.asdwa.org/2016/11/10/epa-releases-report-on-progress-made-to-reduce-water-pollution-from-nonpoint-sources/.

Matthews, Anna and Melanie Evans. "Hospitals Keep Doctors to Keep Referrals In-House." *Wall Street Journal*, December 28, 2018, pp. A1 & A9.

Maxwell, Locke, and Ritter. "Do the Rich Give the Most to Charity?" October 23, 2016. Available on-line at https://www.mlrpc.com/articles/do-the-rich-give-most-to-charity/.

Maynard, Micheline. *The Selling of the American Economy.* New York: Crown Business Publishing, 2009.

McBride, James. "The U.S. Trade Deficit: How Much Does It Matter?" *Backgrounder.* Council on Foreign Relations, October 17, 2017. Available on-line at https://www.cfr.org/backgrounder/us-trade-deficit-how-much-does-it-matter.

McClelland, Robert and Shannon Mok. *A Review of Recent Research on Labor Supply Elasticities.* Working Paper 2012-12, Washington, D.C., Congressional Budget Office, October 2012. Available on-line at http://www.cbo.gov/sites/default/files/cbofiles/attachments/10-25-2012-Recent_Research_on_Labor_Supply_Elasticities.pdf.

McCloskey, Deirdre. *Bourgeois Equality.* Chicago: University of Chicago Press, 2016.

McCombs. Jennifer, Anamarie Whitaker, and Paul Yoo. *The Value of Out-of-School Time Programs.* Santa Monica: The RAND Corporation, 2017. Available on-line at https://www.rand.org/content/dam/rand/pubs/perspectives/PE200/PE267/RAND_PE267.pdf.

McCully, Clinton, Brian Moyer, and Kenneth Stewart. "Comparing the Consumer Price Index and the Personal Consumption Expenditures Index." *Survey of Current Business,* Vol. 87, No. 11, November 2007, pp. 26-33. Available on-line at https://www.bea.gov/scb/pdf/2007/11%20November/1107_cpipce.pdf.

McDonald, Bruce and D. Ryan Miller. "Welfare Programs and the State Economy." *Journal of Policy Modeling,* Vol. 32, No. 6, November-December 2010, pp. 719-732. Available on-line at https://bit.ly/3cXY4Ci

McDonald, Kerry. *Unschooled.* Chicago: Chicago Review Press, 2019.

McDonough, John. "Tracking the Demise of State Hospital Rate Setting." *Health Affairs,* Vol. 16, No. 1, January/February, 1997, pp. 142-149. Available on-line at https://www.healthaffairs.org/doi/pdf/10.1377/hlthaff.16.1.142.

McFarland, Joel, Bill Hussar, Cristobal de Brey, and Tom Snyder. *The Condition of Education 2017.* Washington, D.C.: National Center of Education Statistics, May 2017. Available on-line at https://nces.ed.gov/pubs2017/2017144.pdf.

McLanahan, Sara and Isabel Sawhill. "Marriage and Child Wellbeing: Introducing the Issue." *The Future of Children,* Vol. 25, No 2, Fall 2015, pp. 3-9. Available on-line at https://files.eric.ed.gov/fulltext/EJ1079423.pdf.

Mendenhall, James. "WTO Panel Report on Consistency of China Intellectual Property Standards." *American Society of International Law,* April 3, 2009. Available on-line at https://www.asil.org/insights/volume/13/issue/4/wto-panel-report-consistency-chinese-intellectual-property-standards.

Mehta, Suketu. *This Land is Our Land.* New York: Farrar, Straus and Giroux, 2019.

Mertens, Karel and Morton Ravn. "Dynamic Effect of Personal and Corporate Income Tax Changes in the U.S." *American Economic Review,* Vol. 103, No. 4, June 2013: pp. 1212-1247. Available on-line at https://pubs.aeaweb.org/doi/pdfplus/10.1257/aer.103.4.1212.

Metcalf, Gabriel. "Sand Castles Before the Tide: Affordable Housing in Expensive Cities." *Journal of Economic Perspectives,* Vol. 32, No. 1, Winer 2019, pp. 59-80. Available on-line at https://pubs.aeaweb.org/doi/pdfplus/10.1257/jep.32.1.59.

Meyer, Bruce and James Sullivan. "Annual Report on U.S. Consumption Poverty: 2017." University of Chicago and University of Notre Dame, October 31, 2018. Available on-line at https://www.aei.org/wp-content/uploads/2018/11/2017-Consumption-Poverty-Report-Meyer-Sullivan-final.pdf.

Meyer, Bruce and James Sullivan. "Winning the War: Poverty from the Great Society to the Great Recession," *Journal of Economic Perspectives,* Vol. 26, No. 3, Fall, 2012, pp. 111-136. Available on-line at https://www.brookings.edu/wp-content/uploads/2012/09/2012b_meyer.pdf.

Michigan Land Institute. *10 Principles of New Urbanism.* April 27, 2006. Available on-line at http://www.mlui.org/mlui/news-views/articles-from-1995-to-2012.html?archive_id=678#.XVRU05NKilF.

Migration Policy Institute. "Legal Immigration in the U.S.: 1820-Present." Washington, D.C. Available on-line at https://www.migrationpolicy.org/programs/data-hub/charts/Annual-Number-of-US-Legal-Permanent-Residents.

Migration Policy Institute. "Major US Immigration Laws, 1790-Present," Washington, D.C., 2013. Available on-line at file:///C:/Users/walden.WOLFTECH/Downloads/CIR-1790Timeline.pdf.

Miller, Claire. "The Gender Pay Gap Is Largely Because of Motherhood." *The New York Times*, May 13, 2017. Available on-line at https://www.nytimes.com/2017/05/13/upshot/the-gender-pay-gap-is-largely-because-of-motherhood.html.

Miller, Susan, Jill Nicholson-Crotty, and Sean Nicholson-Crotty. "Reexamining the Institutional Effects of Term Limits in US State Legislatures." *Legislative Studies Quarterly*, Vol. 36, No. 1, February 2011, pp. 71-97. Available on-line at https://onlinelibrary.wiley.com/doi/epdf/10.1111/j.1939-9162.2010.00004.x.

Minarik, Joseph and Caroline Ferguson. "Immigration is Best Solution for Shortage of Workers in America." *The Hill*, July 6, 2018. Available on-line at https://thehill.com/opinion/finance/395790-immigration-is-best-solution-for-shortage-of-workers-in-america.

Minter, Steve. "Why Business is Worried about EPA." *IndustryWeek*, December 1, 2014. Available on-line at https://www.industryweek.com/regulations/why-business-worried-about-epa.

Mishel, Lawrence and Jessica Schieder. "CEO Pay Remains High Relative to the Pay of Typical Workers and High-Wage Earners." *Economic Policy Institute*. Washington, D.C., July 20, 2017. Available on-line at https://www.epi.org/files/pdf/130354.pdf.

Mislinski, Jill. "The Fed's Financial Assets: What Is Uncle Sam's Largest Asset?" *Advisor Perspective*, March 15, 2018. Available on-line at https://www.advisorperspectives.com/dshort/commentaries/2018/03/15/the-fed-s-financial-accounts-what-is-uncle-sam-s-largest-asset.

Mislinski, Jill. "U.S. Household Incomes: A 51 Year Perspective." *Advisor Perspective*, October 16, 2018. Available on-line at https://www.advisorperspectives.com/dshort/updates/2018/10/16/u-s-household-incomes-a-51-year-perspective.

Mitchell, David. "If You Want to Control Fiscal Policy, Forget the Balanced Budget Amendment and Pursue Spending Caps." *Forbes*, March 2, 2015. Available on-line at https://www.forbes.com/sites/danielmitchell/2015/03/02/if-you-want-good-fiscal-policy-forget-the-balanced-budget-amendment-and-pursue-spending-caps/#54c88b1f5eac.

Mitchell, Matthew. "Certificate of Need Laws: Are They Achieving their Goals?" Mercatus Center, George Mason University, April 2017. Available on-line at https://www.mercatus.org/system/files/mercatus-mitchell-con-qa-mop-v1.pdf.

Mitra, Dana. *Pennsylvania's Best Investment: The Social and Economic Benefits of Public Education*. College Park, PA: Penn State University, June 27, 2011. Available on-line at https://www.elc-pa.org/wp-content/uploads/2011/06/BestInvestment_Full_Report_6.27.11.pdf.

"Monitoring the Future: A Continuing Survey of American Youth." *University of Michigan*. Available on-line at www.monitoringthefuture.org.

Morath, Eric. "Seven Years Later, Recovery Remains Weakest of the Post World War II Era." *The Wall Street Journal*, July 29, 2016. Available on-line at https://blogs.wsj.com/economics/2016/07/29/seven-years-later-recovery-remains-the-weakest-of-the-post-world-war-ii-era/.

Moretti, Eric. "Real Wage Inequality." *American Economic Journal: Applied Economics*, Vol. 5, No. 1, January 2013, pp. 65-103. Available on-line at https://pubs.aeaweb.org/doi/pdfplus/10.1257/app.5.1.65.

Moseller, Frederick. "The Tennessee Study of Class Size in the Early School Grades." *The Future of Children*, 5 (2): 113-127. Available on-line at https://www.princeton.edu/futureofchildren/publications/docs/05_02_08.pdf.

Moynihan, Daniel Patrick. *The Negro Family: The Case for National Action*. Washington, D.C., Office of Policy Planning and Research, U.S. Department of Labor, 1965.

Muhlhausen, David. "Building a Better Border: What the Experts Say." *Backgrounder*. The Heritage Foundation, No. 1952, July 17, 2006. Available on-line at https://www.heritage.org/immigration/report/building-better-border-what-the-experts-say.

Mui, Ylan and Suzy Khimm. "College Dropout have Debt but no Degree." *The Washington Post*, May 28, 2012. Available on-line at https://www.washingtonpost.com/business/economy/college-dropouts-have-debt-but-no-degree/2012/05/28/gJQAnUPqwU_story.html?utm_term=.ed5f8c5381fa.

Mullin, Emily. "A Simple Artificial Heart Could Permanently Replace a Failing Human One." *MIT Technology Review*, March 16, 2018. Available on-line at https://www.technologyreview.com/s/610462/a-simple-artificial-heart-could-permanently-replace-a-failing-human-one/.

Munnell, Alicia, editor. *Lessons from the Income Maintenance Experiments*. Boston: Federal Reserve Bank of Boston and The Brookings Institution, 1986.

BIBLIOGRAPHY

Munnell, Alicia and Michael Tanner. "Should the Social Security Fund be Invested in the Stock Market? It's Complicated." *MarketWatch*, April 18, 2017. Available on-line at https://www.marketwatch.com/story/should-the-social-security-fund-be-invested-in-the-stock-market-its-complicated-2017-04-18.

Murphy, Ryan. "Virginia Ahead of Curve in Transportation Funding, But Revenue Lags Projections." *Daily Press*, February 22, 2015. Available on-line at https://www.dailypress.com/news/transportation/dp-nws-transportation-ap-highway-funding-20150222-story.html.

Murray, Charles. *In Our Hands: A Plan to Replace the Welfare State*. Washington, D.C.: The American Enterprise Institute, 2016.

Murray, Charles. *Real Education*. New York: Crown Forum, 2008.

Musumeci, MaryBeth and Julia Zur. "Medicaid Enrollees and Work Requirements: Lessons from the TANF Experiment." Issue Brief, The Kaiser Family Foundation, August 2017. Available on-line at http://files.kff.org/attachment/Issue-Brief-Medicaid-and-Work-Requirements-New-Guidance-State-Waiver-Details-and-Key-Issues.

Nadeau, Cary. "Living Wage Calculator." *Department of Urban Studies and Planning*. MIT University, December 30, 2018. Available 0n-line at http://livingwage.mit.edu/resources/Living-Wage-User-Guide-and-Technical-Notes-2018.pdf.

Nagayach, Rakshita. "Do Polluted Rivers Play Any Role in Cleaning Themselves?" *Quora*, November 28, 2015. Available on-line at https://www.quora.com/Do-polluted-rivers-play-any-role-in-cleaning-themselves.

Nance, Kevin. "Capitalism, Socialism, and the Environment." *In Defense of Marxism*, September 3, 2009. Available on-line at https://www.marxist.com/capitalism-socialism-environment.htm.

Nasrawi, Salah. "Iraq: Oil Overproduction is Tantamount to Military Aggression." *Associated Press*, July 18, 1990. Available on-line at https://www.apnews.com/357fa34e6325da60ddcd61f3aaad7523.

National Academies of Sciences, Engineering, and Medicine. *The Economic and Fiscal Consequences of Immigration*. Washington, D.C.: The National Academies Press, 2017.

National Academies of Sciences, Engineering, and Medicine. *The Integration of Immigrants into American Society*. Washington, D.C.: The National Academies Press, 2015.

National Academy of Sciences. *Hidden Costs of Energy: Unpriced Consequences of Energy Production and Use*. Washington, D.C.: National Academies Press, 2010. Available on-line at http://www.ourenergypolicy.org/wp-content/uploads/2012/06/hidden.pdf.

National Assessment of Educational Progress. *The Nation's Report Card*, 2019. Available on-line at https://nces.ed.gov/nationsreportcard/.

National Association of Realtors. *Existing Home Sales Statistics, 2018*. Washington, D.C. Available on-line at https://www.nar.realtor/sites/default/files/documents/ehs-11-2018-summary-2018-12-19.pdf.

National Association of State Budget Officers. *State Expenditure Report, fiscal years 1999-2000 and 2015-2016*. Available on-line at https://www.nasbo.org/mainsite/reports-data/state-expenditure-report.

National Bureau of Economic Research. "U.S. Business Cycle Expansions and Contractions." Available on-line at http://www.nber.org/cycles.html.

National Center for Education Statistics. *Digest of Education Statistics, 2016*. Available on-line at https://nces.ed.gov/programs/digest/2016menu_tables.asp.

National Center for Education Statistics. *Public High School Graduation Rates*. Table 219.71. Available on-line at https://nces.ed.gov/programs/coe/indicator_coi.asp.

National Center for Education Statistics. *Schools and Staffing Survey*. Available on-line at https://nces.ed.gov/surveys/sass/tables/sass0708_035_s1s.asp.

National Conference of State Legislatures. "Affirmative Action: Court Decisions." June 2016. Available on-line at http://www.ncsl.org/research/education/affirmative-action-court-decisions.aspx.

National Conference of State Legislatures. "Background on Federal Balanced Budget Amendment Proposals." July 20, 2011. Available on-line at http://www.ncsl.org/research/fiscal-policy/balanced-budget-amendment.aspx.

National Conference of State Legislatures. "Con-Certificate of Need State Laws." Washington, D.C., February 28, 2019. Available on-line at http://www.ncsl.org/research/health/con-certificate-of-need-state-laws.aspx.

National Student Clearinghouse Research Center. *Completing College: Eight-Year Completion Outcomes, Fall 2010 Cohort*. February 2019. Available on-line at: https://nscresearchcenter.org/wp-content/uploads/NSC_Signature-Report_12_Update.pdf

National Student Clearinghouse Research Center. *Snapshot Report: Yearly Success and Progress Rates*. March 19, 2018. Available on-line at https://nscresearchcenter.org/snapshot-report-yearly-success-and-progress-rates/.

Nededog, Jethro. "The Number of U.S. Homes without a TV Doubled in Just Six Years." *Business Insider,* March 1, 2017. Available on-line at https://www.businessinsider.com/how-many-tvs-in-american-homes-number-us-department-energy-2017-3.

Nelson, Edward and Jasen Buol. "Budget Deficits and Interest Rates: What Is the Link?" *Central Banker*. Federal Reserve Bank of St. Louis, Summer 2004. Available on-line at https://www.stlouisfed.org/publications/central-banker/summer-2004/budget-deficits-and-interest-rates-what-is-the-link.

Neumark, David and William Wascher. *Minimum Wages*. Cambridge, MA: The MIT Press, 2008.

New, Michael. "The Effect of State Regulations on Health Insurance Premiums: A Preliminary Analysis." Washington, D.C.: Center for Data Analysis, The Heritage Foundation, CDA05-07, October 27, 2005. Available on-line at https://www.heritage.org/health-care-reform/report/the-effect-state-regulations-health-insurance-premiums-preliminary.

Newburger, Harriet, Eugenie Birch, and Susan Wachter. *Neighborhood and Life Changes: How Place Matters in Modern America*. Philadelphia: University of Pennsylvania Press, 2011, pp. 50-72.

Newman, Michael. *Socialism*. Oxford, UK: Oxford University Press, 2005.

NHS. "Guide to Waiting Times in England." Available on-line at https://www.nhs.uk/using-the-nhs/nhs-services/hospitals/guide-to-nhs-waiting-times-in-england/.

Nikolewski, Rob. "Can California Hit a 100% Renewable Energy Target?" *San Diego Union Tribune*, June 9, 2017. Available on-line at http://www.sandiegouniontribune.com/business/energy-green/sd-fi-california-100percent-20170601-story.html.

Noel, Amber, Patrick Stark, Jeremy Redford, and Andrew Zukerberg. "Parental and Family Involvement in Education, from the National Household Education Surveys Program, 2012." *National Center for Education Statistics*, June 2016. Available on-line at https://nces.ed.gov/pubs2013/2013028rev.pdf.

Noonan, Mary, Mary Corcoran, and Paul Courant. "Pay Differences among the Highly Trained: Cohort Differences in the Sex Gap in Lawyer's Earnings." *Social Forces*, Vol. 84, No. 2, December 2005, pp. 853-872. Available on-line at https://www.jstor.org/stable/pdf/3598482.pdf.

Nordhaus, William. *A Question of Balance*. New Haven: Yale University Press, 2008.

Nordhaus, William. "Projections and Uncertainties about Climate Change in an Era of Minimal Climate Policies." *American Economic Journal: Economic Policy*, Vol. 10, No. 3, August 2018, pp. 333-360. Available on-line at https://pubs.aeaweb.org/doi/pdfplus/10.1257/pol.20170046.

Nuclear Energy Agency. *Comparing Nuclear Accident Risks with Those from Other Energy Sources*. Organization for Economic Co-Operation and Development, NEA No. 6861, 2010. Available on-line at https://www.oecd-nea.org/ndd/reports/2010/nea6861-comparing-risks.pdf.

"Number of Heart Transplantations in the U.S. from 1975 to 2017." *Statista*. Available on-line at https://www.statista.com/statistics/671451/heart-transplants-number-us/.

"Number of Hospital Beds in the U.S. from 1975 to 2016." *Statista*. Available on-line at https://www.statista.com/com/statistics/185860/number-of-all-hospital-beds-in-the-us-ince-2001/.

Nunn, Ryan. "Occupational Licensing and American Workers." Washington, D.C.: The Brookings Institute, June 21, 2016. Available on-line at https://www.brookings.edu/wp-content/uploads/2016/07/occupational_licensing_and_the_american_worker.pdf.

O'Dowd, Niall. "Stop U.S. Tax-Paying Law-Abiding Undocumented Immigrants Right Now." *IrishCentral*, August 13, 2018. Available on-line at https://www.irishcentral.com/opinion/niallodowd/stop-us-tax-paying-law-abiding-undocumented-immigrants-right-now.

Office of Management and Budget. *Historical Tables*. Washington, D.C., U.S. Government Printing Office, 2019. Available on-line at https://www.whitehouse.gov/omb/historical-tables/.

Office of the Historian, U.S. Department of State. "The Immigration Act of 1924." Available on-line at https://history.state.gov/milestones/1921-1936/immigration-act.

BIBLIOGRAPHY

Office of the United States Trade Representative. "Economy and Trade." Available on-line at https://ustr.gov/issue-areas/economy-trade.

Ohlemacher, Stephen. "House Investigators: Social Security Disability Judges Too Lax." *The Seattle Times*, June 26, 2013. Available on-line at https://www.seattletimes.com/seattle-news/politics/house-investigators-social-security-disability-judges-too-lax/.

Oliveira, Erneson, Jose Andrade, Jr., and Hernan Makse. "Large Cities are Less Green." *Scientific Reports*, Vol. 4, Article 4235, February 28, 2014. Available on-line at https://www.nature.com/articles/srep04235.

Orben, Amy, Tobias Dienlin, and Andrew Przybylski. "Social Media's Enduring Effect on Adolescent Life Satisfaction." *Proceedings of the National Academy of Sciences of the United States of America*, May 6, 2019. Available on-line at https://www.pnas.org/content/early/2019/04/30/1902058116.

Oregon State University. "Minimum Wage History." June 19, 2015. Available on-line at https://oregonstate.edu/instruct/anth484/minwage.html.

Organization for Economic Cooperation and Development. *Innovating Education and Education for Innovation*, Paris: OECD Publishing, 2016.

Organization for Economic Cooperation and Development. *Looking to 2060: Long-Term Global Growth Prospects*. Paris: OECD Publishing, 2012. Available on-line at https://www.oecd.org/eco/outlook/2060%20policy%20paper%20FINAL.pdf.

Organization for Economic Cooperation and Development. "Tax Revenue, 2017." Paris. Available on-line at https://data.oecd.org/tax/tax-revenue.htm.

Organization for Economic Development. *Under Pressure: The Squeezed Middle Class*. Paris: OECD Publishing, April 2019.

Ortman, Jennifer and Christine Guarneri. "U.S. Population Projections: 2000 to 2050." *U.S. Bureau of the Census*, 2009. Available on-line at https://www.census.gov/content/dam/Census/library/working-papers/2009/demo/us-pop-proj-2000-2050/analytical-document09.pdf.

O'Toole, James. *Enlightened Capitalists: Cautionary Tales of Business Pioneers Who Tried to Do Well While Doing Good*. New York: HarperBusiness, 2019.

Ozimek, Adam, Kenan Fikri, and John Lettieri. "From Managing Decline to Building the Future: Could a Heartland Visa Help Struggling Regions?" *Economic Innovation Group*. Washington, D.C., April 2019. Available on-line at https://eig.org/wp-content/uploads/2019/04/Heartland-Visas-Report.pdf.

Pachavri, Rajendra and Leo Meyer (eds.). *Climate Change 2014 Synthesis Report*, Intergovernmental Panel on Climate Change, Geneva, Switzerland, 2015. Available on-line at http://ar5-syr.ipcc.ch/ipcc/ipcc/resources/pdf/IPCC_SynthesisReport.pdf.

Paletta, Damian and Max Ehrenfreund. "Trump Considers Value Added, Carbon Taxes as Part of Tax Code Overhaul." *Chicago Tribune*, April 4, 2017. Available on-line at http://www.chicagotribune.com/news/nationworld/politics/ct-trump-tax-code-overhaul-20170404-story.html.

Panhans, Matthew. "Adverse Selection in ACA Exchange Markets: Evidence from Colorado." *American Economic Journal: Applied Economics*, Vol. 11, No. 2, April 2019: pp. 1-36. Available on-line at https://pubs.aeaweb.org/doi/pdfplus/10.1257/app.20170117.

Pant, Paula. "REPAYE: Everything You Need to Know about the Revised Pay as You Earn Program." *Studentloanhero.com*, June 2, 2017. Available on-line at https://studentloanhero.com/featured/repaye-revised-pay-as-you-earn-program-guide/.

Parker, Will and Jimmy Vielkind. "New York Passes Overhaul of Rent Laws, Buoying Wider Movement to Tackle Housing Crunch." *New York Times*, June 14, 2019. Available on-line at https://www.wsj.com/articles/new-york-passes-overhaul-of-rent-laws-revving-up-nationwide-movement-to-tackle-housing-crunch-11560544718.

Parry, Ian, Margaret Walls, and Winston Harrington. "Automobile Externalities and Policies." *Journal of Economic Literature*, Vol. 45, No. 2, June 2007, pp. 373-399. Available on-line at pubs.aeaweb.org/doi/pdfplus/10.1257/jel.45.2.373.

Partridge, Mark and Amanda Weinstein. "Rising Inequality in an Era of Austerity: The Case of the U.S." *European Planning Studies*, Vol. 21, Issue 3, pp. 388-410. Available on-line at https://www.tandfonline.com/doi/pdf/10.1080/09654313.2012.716247.

Pathe, Simone. "Too Many College Grads? Or Too Few?" *PBS News Hour,* February 21, 2014. Available on-line at https://www.pbs.org/newshour/nation/many-college-grads.

Paul, Rand. "Chairman Paul's Penny Plan Budget: A Budget for Fiscal Year 2019." Washington, D.C., U.S. Senate Committee on Homeland Security and Governmental Affairs, Subcommittee on Federal Spending Oversight, April 2018. Available on-line at https://www.paul.senate.gov/sites/default/files/page-attachments/ReportonBalancedBudgetProposal.pdf.

Paul, Rand. "Senator Paul Highlights $1.8 Billion in Wasteful Spending through Weekly Waste Report." 2018. Available on-line at https://www.paul.senate.gov/news/sen-rand-paul-highlights-18-billion-wasteful-spending-through-weekly-waste-reports.

Perry, Mark. "The General Public Thinks the Average Company Makes a 36% Profit Margin, which is about 5X too High." *Carpe Diem, American Enterprise Insitute,* January 15, 2018. Available on-line at http://www.aei.org/publication/the-public-thinks-the-average-company-makes-a-36-profit-margin-which-is-about-5x-too-high-part-ii/.

Peterson, Hayley. "McDonald's Shoots Down Fears it is Planning to Replace Cashiers with Kiosks." *Business Insider,* June 23, 2017. Available on-line at http://www.businessinsider.com/what-self-serve-kiosks-at-mcdonalds-mean-for-cashiers-2017-6.

Pethokoukis, James. "Not Only did Obama Ignore Simpson-Bowles, but Now He's Doing the Opposite of What They Recommended." *AEIdeas,* July 9, 2012. Available on-line at http://www.aei.org/publication/not-only-did-obama-ignore-simpson-bowles-but-now-hes-doing-the-opposite-of-what-they-recommended/.

Pew Research Center. "More than Half of Black Children Now Live with a Single Parent." *Social and Demographic Trends,* June 21, 2016. Available on-line at https://pewsocialtrends.org/2016/06/27/1-demographic-trends-and-economic-well- being/st_2016-06-27_race-inequality-ch2-09/.

Pew Research Center. "The American Middle Class is Losing Ground." *Social and Demographic Trends,* December 9, 2015. Available on-line at http://www.pewsocialtrends.org/2015/12/09/the-american-middle-class-is-losing-ground/.

Pew Research Center. "The Rising Cost of Not Going to College." *Social and Demographic Trends,* February 11, 2014. Available on-line at http://www.pewsocialtrends.org/2014/02/11/the-rising-cost-of-not-going-to-college/.

Phelps, Edmund. *Rewarding Work.* Cambridge, MA: Harvard University Press, 1997.

Picketty, Thomas. *Capital in the 21st Century.* Cambridge, MA: The Belknap Press of Harvard University, 2014.

Pinker, Steven. *Enlightment Now.* New York: Viking Press, 2018.

Plumer, Brad. "Only 27% of College Grads have a Job Related to their Major." *Washington Post,* May 20, 2013. Available on-line at https://www.washingtonpost.com/news/wonk/wp/2013/05/20/only-27-percent-of-college-grads-have-a-job-related-to-their-major/?utm_term=.051011bc1694.

Podolsky, Anne, Tara Kini, Joseph Bishop, and Linda Darling-Hammond. "Solving the Teacher Shortage: How to Attract and Retain Excellent Educators." Learning Policy Institute, Sept. 15, 2016. Available on-line at https://learningpolicyinstitute.org/product/solving-teacher-shortage-brief.

Pollin, Robert, James Heintz, Peter Arno, Jeannette Wicks-Lim, and Michael Ash. "Economic Analysis of Medicare for All." *Political Economy Research Institute.* University of Massachusetts Amherst, November 2018. Available on-line at https://www.peri.umass.edu/publication/item/1127-economic-analysis-of-medicare-for-all.

Pollock, Alex. "Colleges Need to Have Skin in the Game to Tackle Student Loan Debt." *The Hill,* May, 7, 2019. Available on-line at https://thehill.com/opinion/education/442497-colleges-need-to-have-skin-in-the-game-to-tackle-student-loan-debt.

Pomerleau, Kyle and Huaqun Li. "How Much Revenue would a 70% Tax Rate Raise? An Initial Analysis." *Tax Foundation,* January 14, 2019. Available on-line at https://taxfoundation.org/70-percent-tax-initial-analysis.

Popovich, Nadja, Livia Albeck-Ripka, and Kendra Pierre-Lovis. "76 Environmental Rules on the Way out under Trump." *New York Times,* October 5, 2017. Available on-line at https://nytimes.com/interactive/2017/10/05/climate/trump-environment-rules-reversed.html

Porter, Eduardo. "The Politics of Income Inequality." *The New York Times,* May 13, 2014. Available on-line at https://www.nytimes.com/2014/05/14/business/economy/the-politics-of-income-inequality.html.

Pradhan, Tejesh and James Capretta. *Disability Insurance Needs Reform*. Washington, D.C.: The American Enterprise Institute, January 5, 2018. Available on-line at http://www.aei.org/publication/disability-insurance-needs-reform/.

President's Council of Economic Advisers. *The Economics of Early Childhood Investments*, Washington, D.C.: The White House, January 2015. Available on-line at https://obamawhitehouse.archives.gov/sites/default/files/docs/early_childhood_report_update_final_non-embargo.pdf.

President's Council of Economic Advisers. *Economic Report of the President, 1975*. Washington, D.C.: Superintendent of Documents, February 1975. Available on-line at http://www.presidency.ucsb.edu/economic_reports/1975.pdf.

Pretis, Felix. "Does a Carbon Tax Reduce CO_2 Emissions? Evidence from British Columbia." University of Victoria and University of Oxford, February 8, 2019. Available on-line at https://papers.ssrn.com/sol3/papers.cfm?abstract_id=3329512.

Pritchett, Lant. *Let Their People Come*. Washington: Center for Global Development, 2006.

Prosperity Now. "Asset Limits in Public Benefit Programs." 2016. Available on-line at https://scorecard.prosperitynow.org/2016/measure/asset-limits-in-public-benefit-programs.

Pryde, Joan. "A National Sales Tax to Pay for Health Care?" *Kiplinger*, July 1, 2009. Available on-line at https://www.kiplinger.com/article/taxes/T056-C012-S001-a-national-sales-tax-to-pay-for-health-care.html.

Puentes, Robert. "The Problem with the Gas Tax in Three Charts." Washington D.C.: The Brookings Institute, June 18, 2015. Available on-line at https://www.brookings.edu/blog/the-avenue/2015/06/18/the-problem-with-the-gas-tax-in-three-charts/.

Pula, Kevin. "Variable Rate Gas Taxes." *National Conference of State Legislatures*, July 19, 2017. Available on-line at http://www.ncsl.org/research/transportation/variable-rate-gas-taxes.aspx.

Qian, Yingyi. *How Reform Worked in China*. Cambridge, MA: MIT Press, 2017.

Quincy, Lynn and Amanda Hunt. "Revealing the Truth about Healthcare Price Transparency." Washington, D.C.: Altarum Healthcare Value Hub, Research Brief 27, June 2018. Available on-line at https://www.healthcarevaluehub.org/files/4315/3003/4068/RB_27_-_Revealing_the_Truth_About_Healthcare_Price_Transparency.pdf.

Quinlan, Paul. "Cap-and-Trade for Water Pollution – Trendy, Hip, Glitzy, and Controversial." *Greenwire*, May 8, 2012. Available on-line at https://www.eenews.net/stories/1059964052.

Quintana, Chris. "Free College Plans Such as Elizabeth Warren's Are Pretty Pricey. Some Say her Plan Would Benefit the Rich Most." *USA Today*, April 28, 2019. Available on-line at https://www.usatoday.com/story/news/education/2019/04/26/fafsa-elizabeth-warren-student-loans-forgiveness-free-college-debt-relief/3572444002/.

Raab, Barbara. "Has Disability Become a 'de facto welfare program'?" *NBC News*, March 28, 2013. Available on-line at https://www.nbcnews.com/feature/in-plain-sight/has-disability-become-de-facto-welfare-program-v17459470.

Rabushka, Alvin. "The Colonial Roots of American Taxation: 1607-1700." *Policy Review*. Stanford, CA: Hoover Institution, April 1, 2002. Available on-line at https://www.hoover.org/research/colonial-roots-american-taxation-1607-1700.

Rachidi, Angela. *The Earned Income Tax Credit and Marriage Penalties: Does a Childless Worker Expansion make Them Worse?* Washington, D.C.: American Enterprise Institute, November 2015. Available on-line at http://www.aei.org/wp-content/uploads/2015/10/The-earned-income-tax-credit-and-marriage-penalties.pdf.

Radford, Jynnah. "Facts on U.S. Immigrants, 2016." *Pew Research Center*, September 14, 2018. Available on-line at http://www.pewhispanic.org/2018/09/14/facts-on-u-s-immigrants/.

"Raleigh Leaders Approve Front-Yard Parking Ban." *WRAL-TV*, June 19, 2012. Available on-line at https://www.wral.com/news/local/story/11224367/.

Ramseur, Jonathan. *U.D. Carbon Dioxide Emissions Trends and Projections: Role of the Clean Power Plan and Other Factors*. Congressional Research Service Report 7-5700, May 31, 2017. Available on-line at https://fas.org/sgp/crs/misc/R44451.pdf.

Ramsey, Austin. "Beijing's Olympic War on Smog." *Time*, April 15, 2008. Available on-line athttp://content.time.com/time/world/article/0,8599,1730918,00.html.

RAND Education. "Effect of Teacher Pay on Student Performance." *The RAND Corporation*, Paper No. WR-378-EDU, April 2006. Available on-line at https://www.rand.org/content/dam/rand/pubs/working_papers/2006/RAND_WR378.pdf.

Rauch, Kate. "Prefab Housing Complex for UC Berkeley Students Goes Up in Four Days." *Berkeleyside*, August 2, 2018. Available on-line at https://www.berkeleyside.com/2018/08/02/prefab-housing-complex-for-uc-berkeley-students-built-in-four-days.

Rector, Robert. *How Welfare Undermines Marriage and What to Do About It*. Issue Brief, no. 4302, Washington, D.C.: The Heritage Foundation, November 17, 2014. Available on-line at https://www.heritage.org/welfare/report/how-welfare-undermines-marriage-and-what-do-about-it.

Regan. Ed. *The Motor Fuel Tax: A Critical System at Risk*, Boston, MA: CDM Smith, 2017.

Reuters. "Finland's Basic Income Trial Boosts Happiness, Not Employment." *The New York Times*, February 9, 2019. Available on-line at https://www.nytimes.com/2019/02/09/world/europe/finland-basic-income.html.

Reynolds, Kara and John Palatucci. "Does Trade Adjustment Assistance Make a Difference?" *Contemporary Economic Policy*, Vol. 30. No. 1, January 2012: 43-59. Available on-line at https://onlinelibrary.wiley.com/doi/epdf/10.1111/j.1465-7287.2010.00247.x.

Richards, Julian and Elizabeth Schaefer. "Jobs Attributable to Foreign Direct Investment in the U.S." *Office of Trade and Economic Analysis, International Trade Administration, Industry and Analysis Economics Brief*, February 2016. Available on-line at https://www.trade.gov/mas/ian/build/groups/public/@tg_ian/documents/webcontent/tg_ian_005496.pdf.

Richman, Sheldon. "Mandated Paid Family Leave Harms Its Intended Beneficiaries." *American Institute for Economic Research*, June 27, 2017. Available on-line at https://www.aier.org/research/mandated-paid-family-leave-harms-its-intended-beneficiaries.

Richman, Sheldon. "Fascism." *The Library of Economics and Liberty*. Available on-line at https://www.investopedia.com/ask/answers/031815/united-states-considered-market-economy-or-mixed-economy.asp.

Riggs, Liz. "The Myth of a Teacher's Summer Vacation." *The Atlantic*, July 2, 2015. Available on-line at https://www.theatlantic.com/education/archive/2015/07/myth-of-teacher-summer-vacation/397535.

Riley, Naomi. *Be the Parent, Please*. West Conshohocken, PA: Templeton Press, 2018

Rivkin, Steven, Eric Hanushek, and John Kain. "Teachers, Schools, and Academic Achievement." *Econometrica*, 73 (2): 417-458, 2005. Available on-line at https://www.econometricsociety.org/publications/econometrica/2005/03/01/teachers-schools-and-academic-achievement.

Robson, Nate. "For Many Students, Community College is the End of the Academic Road." *Oklahoma Watch*, February 11, 2016. Available on-line at http://oklahomawatch.org/2016/02/11/bachelors-degree-eludes-8-of-10-in-community-colleges/.

Rodden, Jonathan. *Why Cities Lose*. New York: Basic Books, 2019.

Rodgers, Luke. "Give Credit Where? The Incidence of Child Care Tax Credits." *Journal of Urban Economics*, October 2018. Available on-line at https://bit.ly/2ZtaFtx.

Rogers, Paul and Katy Murphy. "California Mandates 100% Clean Energy by 2045." *The Mercury News*. September 10, 2018. Available on-line at https://www.mercurynews.com/2018/09/10/california-mandates-100-percent-clean-energy-by-2045/.

Rohaly, Jeffrey. "Reforming the Child and Dependent Tax Credit." *Tax Policy Center*. Washington, D.C., May 30, 2007. Available on-line at https://www.urban.org/sites/default/files/publication/46496/411474-reforming-the-child-and-dependent-care-tax-credit.pdf.

Rosati, Andrew. "Venezuela's Bribing Menu Brings Transparency to Corruption." *Bloomberg*, November 11, 2018. Available on-line at https://www.bloomberg.com/news/articles/2018-11-27/venezuela-s-bribing-menu-brings-transparency-to-corruption.

Rosenberg, Nathan. *How the West Grew Rich*. London: I.B. Tarvis & Co., 1986.

Rosenthal, Elisabeth. *An American Sickness*. New York: Penguin Press, 2017.

Ross, Sean. "Is the United States a Market Economy or a Mixed Economy?" *Investopedia*, June 15, 2018. Available on-line at https://www.investopedia.com/ask/answers/031815/united-states-considered-market-economy-or-mixed-economy.asp.

Rovira, James. "The Fortunes of Romantic Anti-Capitalism in William Blake's Thel and Oothoon." *Text, Identity, and Subjectivity*. April 18, 2013. Available on-line at http://scalar.usc.edu/works/text-identity-subjectivity/the-fortunes-of-romantic-anti-capitalism-in-william-blakes-thel-and-oothoon.

Rubb, Stephen and Scott Sumner. *Economic Principles*. New York: Worth Publishers, 2019.

Rubin, Stacey and H. Ray Wooten. "Highly Educated Stay-at-Home Mothers: A Study of Commitment and Conflict." *The Family Journal: Counseling and Therapy for Couples and Families*, Vol. 15, No. 4, October 2007, pp. 336-335. Available on-line at https://journals.sagepub.com/doi/pdf/10.1177/1066480707304945.

Ruparelia, Sanjay, Sanjay Reddy, John Harriss, and Stuart Corbridge (eds.). *Understanding India's New Political Economy: A Great Transformation*. Abington-on-Thames: Routledge, 2011.

Russell, Jason. "Look How Many Pages are in the Federal Tax Code." *Washington Examiner*, April 15, 2016. Available on-line at https://www.washingtonexaminer.com/look-at-how-many-pages-are-in-the-federal-tax-code.

Ryan, Kevin. "Richard Branson is the Latest Entrepreneur to Show Support for Universal Basic Income." *Inc.*, August 15, 2017. Available on-line at https://www.inc.com/kevin-j-ryan/richard-branson-supports-universal-basic-income.html.

Sachs, Jeffrey. "The Economics of Happiness." *Project-Syndicate.org*, August 29, 2011. Available on-line at https://www.earth.columbia.edu/sitefiles/file/Sachs%20Writing/2011/ProjectSyndicate_2011_TheEconomicsofHappiness_08_29_11.pdf.

Saez, Emmanuel, Joel Slemrod, and Seth Giertz. "The Elasticity of Taxable Income with Respect to Marginal Rates." *Boston: National Bureau of Economic Research*, NBER Working Paper 15012, May 2009. Available on-line at https://www.nber.org/papers/w15012.pdf.

"Safety Net Programs." *Federal Safety Net*. Available on-line at http://federalsafetynet.com/safety-net-programs.html.

Sahadi, Jeanne. "Bush's Plan for Social Security." *CNN Money*, March 4, 2005. Available on-line at https://money.cnn.com/2005/02/02/retirement/stofunion_socsec/.

Salam, Reihan. *Melting Pot or Civil War?* New York: Sentinel, 2018.

Sanders, Bernie. "The Medicare for All Act of 2019." Washington, D.C., April 10, 2019. Available on-line at https://www.sanders.senate.gov/download/medicare-for-all-2019-summary-by-title?id=2CC6F6CB-2978-4149-B9C0-A455E8DD2A3D&download=1&inline=file.

Saringo-Rodriguez, John. "Studies Show Depression Affects Academic Progress, Causes Stress and Chemical Imbalance." *The Sundial*, November 21, 2013. Available on-line at https://sundial.csun.edu/2013/11/studies-show-depression-affects-academic-progress-causes-stress-and-chemical-imbalance/.

Sawhill, Isabel. *The Forgotten Americans*. New Haven: Yale University Press, 2018.

Scarboro, Morgan and Joseph Bishop-Henchman. *How Are Your State's Roads Funded?* Washington, D.C.: The Tax Foundation, July 13, 2017. Available on-line at https://taxfoundation.org/state-road-funding-2017/.

Schochet, Peter, John Burghardt, and Sheena McConnell. "Does Job Corps Work? Impact Findings from the National Job Corps Study." *American Economic Review*, vol. 98, no. 5, pp. 1864-1886, December 2008. Available on-line at https://www.jstor.org/stable/pdf/29730155.pdf?refreqid=excelsior%3Ab7c6aa808692cbe80f8a022a6fac3471.

Scholz, John, Hyunpyo Moon, and Sang-Hyop Lee. *Social Policies in the Age of Austerity: A Comparative Analysis of the U.S. and Korea*. Northampton, MA: Edward Elgar Publishing, 2015, pp. 107-136.

Schumpeter, Joseph. *Capitalism, Socialism, and Democracy*. New York: Harper and Brothers, 1942.

Schencker, Lisa. "More Doctors Embrace Membership Fees, Shunning Health Insurance." *Chicago Tribune*, June 22, 2018. Available on-line at https://www.chicagotribune.com/business/ct-biz-membership-medicine-20180529-story.html.

Scherer, F.M. "The F.T.C., Oligopoly, and Shared Monopoly." *Faculty Research Working Paper Series*, RWP13-031, Harvard Kennedy School of Government, September 2013. Available on-line at https://research.hks.harvard.edu/publications/getFile.aspx?Id=978.

Schleith, Kevin. *Implications of Electric Vehicles on Gasoline Tax Revenues*. Washington, D..C: Electric Vehicle Transportation Center, December 2015. Available on-line at http://www.fsec.ucf.edu/en/publications/pdf/FSEC-CR-2011-15.pdf.

"School Costs: Did You Know…" *Spaces4Learning,* July 1, 2015. Available on-line at https://webspm.com/Articles/2015/07/01/School-Costs.aspx.

Schwartz, John. "A Conservative Climate Solution: Republican Group Calls for Carbon Tax." *The New York Times,* February 2, 2017. Available on-line at https://www.nytimes.com/2017/02/07/science/a-conservative-climate-solution-republican-group-calls-for-carbon-tax.html.

Scott, Robert and Zane Mokhiber. "The China Toll Deepens." Washington, D.C.: Economic Policy Institute, October 23, 2018. Available on-line at https://www.epi.org/publication/the-china-toll-deepens-growth-in-the-bilateral-trade-deficit-between-2001-and-2017-cost-3-4-million-u-s-jobs-with-losses-in-every-state-and-congressional-district/.

Seabrook, Elizabeth, Margaret Kern, and Nikki Rickard. "Social Networking Sites, Depression, and Anxiety: A Systematic Review." *JMIR Mental Health,* 3 (4), 2016. Available on-line at https://www.ncbi.nlm.nih.gov/pmc/articles/PMC5143470/.

"Secret Ways to Get Student Loan Forgiveness." *The College Investor,* March 19, 2018. Available on-line at https://thecollegeinvestor.com/11856/secret-student-loan-forgiveness/.

Seibold, Michael. "Impact of Commercial Over-Reimbursement on Hospitals: The Curious Case of Central Indiana." *International Journal of Health Economics Management,* September 6, 2018. Available on-line at https://www.researchgate.net/publication/327476421_Impact_of_commercial_over-reimbursement_on_hospitals_the_curious_case_of_central_Indiana.

Semple, Kirk. "New Cuba Constitution, Recognizing Private Property, Approved by Lawmakers." *The New York Times,* July 22, 2018. Available on-line at https://www.nytimes.com/2018/07/22/world/americas/cuba-constitution.html.

Semuels, Alana. "The Case for Trailer Parks." *The Atlantic,* October 21, 2014. Available on-line at https://www.theatlantic.com/business/archive/2014/10/the-case-for-trailer-parks/381808/.

"Senior Living History: 1930-1939." *Seniorliving.org.* Available on-line at https://www.seniorliving.org/history/1930-1939/.

"Share of Old Age Population (65 Years and Older) in the Total US. Population from 1950 to 2050." *Statista.* Available on-line at https://www.statista.com/statistics/457822/share-of-old-age-population-in-the-total-us-population/.

Sheffield, Rachel and Robert Rector. *Understanding Poverty in the U.S.: Surprising Facts About America's Poor.* Washington, D.C.: The Heritage Foundation, September 13, 2011. Available on-line at https://www.heritage.org/poverty-and-inequality/report/understanding-poverty-the-united-states-surprising-facts-about.

Sheffield, Matthew. "Could Public Funding of Elections Revolutionize Politics?" *Salon,* February 20, 2018. Available on-line at https://www.salon.com/2018/02/20/could-public-funding-of-elections-revolutionize-politics/.

Shell, Ellen. *The Job.* New York: Currency Publishing, 2018.

Shi, Leiyu. "The Impact of Primary Care: A Focused Review." *Scientifica,* December 2012. Available on-line at https://www.ncbi.nlm.nih.gov/pmc/articles/PMC3820521/.

Shiller, Robert. "Modern Monetary Theory Makes Sense, Up to a Point." *The New York Times,* March 29, 2019. Available on-line at https://www.nytimes.com/2019/03/29/business/modern-monetary-theory-shiller.html.

Shingler, Benjamin. "Quebec's New Basic Income Plan Has Proponents Dreaming Big, Others Skeptical." *CBC News,* December 12, 2017. Available on-line at https://www.cbc.ca/news/canada/montreal/quebec-basic-income-plan-francois-blais-1.4442902.

Shleifer, Andrei and Robert Vishny. "Pervasive Shortages under Socialism." *The RAND Journal of Economics,* Vol. 23, No. 2, Summer 1992, pp. 237-246. Available on-line at https://www.jstor.org/stable/pdf/2555986.pdf?refreqid=excelsior%3A1a15f844d0e63865a8811bc2cc39aebe.

Shoener, Sara. "Two Parent Households Can Be Lethal." *The New York Times,* June 21, 2014. Available on-line at https://www.nytimes.com/2014/06/22/opinion/sunday/domestic-violence-and-two-parent-households.html.

Silver, Charles and David Hyman. *Overcharged: Why Americans Pay Too Much for Health Care.* Washington, D.C.: The Cato Institute, 2018.

Silverstein, Stuart. "This Is Why Your Prescriptions Cost so Damn Much." *Mother Jones,* October 21, 2016. Available on-line at https://www.motherjones.com/politics/2016/10/drug-industry-pharmaceutical-lobbyists-medicare-part-d-prices/.

BIBLIOGRAPHY

Simler, Kevin and Robin Hanson. *The Elephant in the Brain*. Oxford, UK: Oxford University Press, 2016.

Sink, Justin and Andrew Mayeda. "Trump Asks China for Plan to Cut $100 Billion Off U.S. Trade Gap." *Bloomberg*, March 8, 2018. Available on-line at https://www.bloomberg.com/news/articles/2018-03-08/trump-asks-china-for-plan-to-cut-100-billion-off-u-s-trade-gap.

Sintia, Radu. "How Soon Will You Be Working from Home?" *U.S. News*, February 16, 2018. Available on-line at https://www.usnews.com/news/best-countries/articles/2018-02-16/telecommuting-is-growing-but-still-not-unanimously-embraced.

Sisson, Patrick. "How Air Conditioning Shaped Modern Architecture – and Changed Our Climate." *Curbed*, May 9, 2017. Available on-line at https://www.curbed.com/2017/5/9/15583550/air-conditioning-architecture-skyscraper-wright-lever-house.

Sitaraman, Ganesh and Anne Alstott. *The Public Option*. Cambridge, MA: Harvard University Press, 2019.

Smith, Adam. *The Wealth of Nations*. London: W. Strahan and T. Cadell, 1776.

Smith, Jack. "$37 Screws, a $7622 Coffee Maker, $640 Toilet Seats: Suppliers to our Military Just Won't be Oversold." *Los Angeles Times*, July 30, 1986. Available on-line at https://www.latimes.com/archives/la-xpm-1986-07-30-vw-18804-story.html.

Smith, Noah. "Who Has the World's No. 1 Economy? Not the U.S." *Bloomberg Opinion*, October 18, 2017. Available on-line at https://www.bloomberg.com/view/articles/2017-10-18/who-has-the-world-s-no-1-economy-not-the-u-s.

Snowden, Christopher. *Selfishness, Greed, and Capitalism*. London: The Institute of Economic Affairs, 2015.

Social Security Administration. "Annual Statistical Report on the SSDI Program." *Office of Retirement and Disability Policy*. Washington, D.C., Social Security Administration, 2017. Available on-line at https://www.ssa.gov/policy/docs/statcomps/di_asr/2016/charts-text.html#chart3.

Social Security Administration. "Life Expectancy for Social Security." *Social Security History*. Available on-line at https://www.ssa.gov/history/lifeexpect.html.

Social Security Administration. "OASI Trust Fund, A Social Security Fund." *Office of the Chief Actuary*. Available on-line at https://www.ssa.gov/oact/STATS/table4a1.html.

Social Security Administration. "Report of the National Commission on Social Security Reform, January 1983." *Social Security Reports and Studies*. Available on-line at https://www.ssa.gov/history/1983amend.html.

Social Security Administration. "Summary of Social Security Amendments of 1983 – Signed on April 20, 1983." *Social Security History*. Available on-line at https://www.ssa.gov/history/1983amend.html.

Social Security Administration. *Understanding the Benefits*, January 2018. Available on-line at https://www.ssa.gov/pubs/EN-05-10024.pdf.

Song, Sha. "Here's How China Is Going Green." *World Economic Forum*, April 26, 2018. Available on-line at https://www.weforum.org/agenda/2018/04/china-is-going-green-here-s-how/.

Sorkin, Amy. "Economic Inequality: A Matter of Trust." *The New Yorker*, December 4, 2013. Available on-line at https://www.newyorker.com/news/amy-davidson/economic-inequality-a-matter-of-trust.

Sowell, Thomas. *Marxism,* New York: William Morrow, 1985.

Staiger, Douglas and Jonah Rockoff. "Searching for Effective Teachers with Imperfect Information," *Journal of Economic Perspectives*, 24 (3): 97-117. Available on-line at https://pubs.aeaweb.org/doi/pdfplus/10.1257/jep.24.3.97.

"Stay in Your Lane." *Urban Dictionary*, January 28, 2007. Available on-line at https://www.urbandictionary.com/define.php?term=stay%20in%20your%20lane.

Stossel, John. "Debunking Popular Nonsense About Income Mobility in America." *Reason*, June 4, 2014. Available on-line at http://reason.com/archives/2014/06/04/income-mobility-myths.

Su, Yichen. "The Rising Value of Time and the Origin of Urban Gentrification." Stanford University, November 16, 2017. Available on-line at https://pdfs.semanticscholar.org/a651/b2ef58e3ad750caad5d9d44c2f357295084b.pdf.

Sullivan, Thomas. "Defensive Medicine Adds $45 Billion to the Cost of Healthcare." *Policy and Medicine*, May 5, 2018. Available on-line at https://www.policymed.com/2010/09/defensive-medicine-adds-45-billion-to-the-cost-of-healthcare.html.

Sumner, Jenny, Lori Bird, and Hillary Smith. *Carbon Taxes: A Review of Experience and Policy Design.* Golden CO: National Renewable Energy Laboratory, 2009. Available on-line at http://www.nrel.gov/docs/fy10osti/47312.pdf.

Sundheim, Doug. "Do Women Take as Many Risks as Men?" *Harvard Business Review*, February 27, 2013. Available on-line at https://hbr.org/2013/02/do-women-take-as-many-risks-as.

Swanson, Ana. "American Presidents Have a Long History of Walking Back Tough Talk on China." *Washington Post*, December 6, 2016. Available on-line at https://www.washingtonpost.com/news/wonk/wp/2016/12/06/american-presidents-have-a-long-history-of-walking-back-tough-talk-on-china/?utm_term=.fbe0bcd211e0.

Taber, George. "The Night I Invented Crony Capitalism." *Knowledge@Wharton*, November 3, 2015. Available on-line at http://knowledge.wharton.upenn.edu/article/the-night-i-invented-crony-capitalism/.

Tax Policy Center. "Motor Fuel Tax Revenue." Washington, D.C., October 18, 2017. Available on-line at https://www.taxpolicycenter.org/statistics/motor-fuel-tax-revenue.

Taylor, Jerry. "The Conservative Case for a Carbon Tax." March 23, 2015. Available on-line at http://niskanencenter.org/wp-content/uploads/2015/03/The-Conservative-Case-for-a-Carbon-Tax1.pdf.

Tehrani, James. "The History of Retirement Pensions." *Workforce*. Available on-line at https://www.workforce.com/2016/06/21/the-history-of-retirement-benefits/.

The Billion Prices Project. Massachusetts Institute of Technology and Harvard University. Available on-line at http://www.thebillionpricesproject.com/.

"The Complexities of Physician Supply and Demand: Projections from 2015 to 2030." *IHS Markit*. Washington, D.C., February 28, 2017. Available on-line at https://aamc-black.global.ssl.fastly.net/production/media/filer_public/a5/c3/a5c3d565-14ec-48fb-974b-99fafaeecb00/aamc_projections_update_2017.pdf.

"The Moment of Truth." *National Commission on Fiscal Responsibility and Reform*, December 2010. Available on-line at https://www.aau.edu/sites/default/files/AAU%20Files/Key%20Issues/Innovation%20%26%20Competitiveness/The-Moment-of-Truth_Report-of-the-National-Commission-on-Fiscal-Responsibility-and-Reform_2010.pdf.

"The Salary You Must Earn to Afford a Home in the Largest 50 Metros." *HSH.com*, February 22, 2018. Available on-line at https://www.hsh.com/finance/mortgage/salary-home-buying-25-cities.html#national.

"The State of the Nation's Housing, 2017." *Joint Center for Housing Studies at Harvard University*. Cambridge, MA: Harvard University, 2017. Available on-line at http://www.jchs.harvard.edu/sites/jchs.harvard.edu/files/harvard_jchs_state_of_the_nations_housing_2017.pdf.

The White House. "President Signs Landmark No Child Left Behind." January 2002. Available on-line at https://georgewbush-whitehouse.archives.gov/news/releases/2002/01/20020108-1.html.

Thimou, Theo. "When Paying Cash for Prescriptions Beats Using Insurance." *Clark*, August 8, 2018. Available on-line at https://clark.com/health-health-care/prescriptions-paying-cash-vs-insurance/.

Thomas, Diana and Devon Gorry. *Regulation and the Cost of Child Care*. Mercatus Working Paper, George Mason University, August 2015. Available on-line at https://www.mercatus.org/system/files/Thomas-Regulation-Child-Care.pdf.

Thompson, Derek. "Is Our Debt Burden Really $100 Trillion?" *The Atlantic*, November 28, 2012. Available on-line at https://www.theatlantic.com/business/archive/2012/11/is-our-debt-burden-really-100-trillion/265644/.

Thurow, Lester. *Head to Head*. New York: William Morrow, 1993.

Timmons, Edward. "Healthcare License Turf Wars." Arlington, VA: Mercatus Center, George Mason University, January 2016. Available on-line at https://www.forbes.com/sites/brucejapsen/2018/05/13/states-ease-more-restrictions-to-physician-assistants-as-team-care-takes-hold/#6321c3e37d99.

Timpe, Brenden. "The Long-Run Effects of America's First Paid Maternity Leave Policy." University of Michigan, February 2, 2019. Available on-line at /file.

Topol, Eric. *Deep Medicine*. New York: Basic Books, 2019.

"Top Ten Jokes for Tax Season." *ATBS*. January 2014. Available on-line at https://www.atbs.com/knowledge-hub/top-10-jokes-for-tax-season.

Torjesen, Ingrid. "Drug Development: The Journey of a Medicine from Lab to Shelf." *Tomorrow's Pharmacist*, May 12, 2015. Available on-line at http://paa2019.populationassociation.org/uploads/193674.

"Total Number of Doctors of Medicine in the U.S., 1949-2015." *Statista*. Available on-line at https://www.statista.com/statistics/186260/total-doctors-of-medicine-in-the-us-since-1949/.

Town, Robert and Gregory Vistnes. "Hospital Competition in HMO Networks." *Journal of Health Economics*, Vol. 20, No, 5, September 2001, pp. 733-753. Available on-line at https://ac.els-cdn.com/S0167629601000960/1-s2.0-S0167629601000960-main.pdf?_tid=c7034026-6d96-415c-8d2a-cc8390c92e6c&acdnat=1552063746_cc4fc5813efff860785c1901983b71bc.

Trabandt, Mathias and Harald Uhlig. "The Laffer Curve Revisited." *Journal of Monetary Economics*, Vol. 58, 2011, pp. 305-327. Available on-line at https://ac.els-cdn.com/S030439321100064X/1-s2.0-S030439321100064X-main.pdf?_tid=1c148e56-d923-4fbb-b307-aa3aa7e0a9c2&acdnat=1547580163_bf077b1695d9495e4f44c0510a549ed6.

Trilling, David. "Robots are Taking Jobs but Also Creating Them." *Journalist's Resource*, February 12, 2017. Available on-line at https://journalistsresource.org/studies/economics/jobs/robots-jobs-automation-artificial-intelligence-research.

"Trump Signs 'Right to Try' Allowing Gravely Ill Patients to Bypass FDA for Experimental Medicines." *CNBC*. May 30, 2018. Available on-line at https://www.cnbc.com/2018/05/30/trump-signs-right-to-try-legislation-on-experimental-medicines.html.

Tuerck, David, Jonathan Haughton, Paul Bachman, Alfonso Sanchez-Penalver, and Phong Viet Ngo. "A Distributional Analysis of Adopting the FairTax: A Comparison of the Current Tax System and the FairTax Plan." *The Beacon Hill Institute*. Boston, MA, February 2007. Available on-line at http://www.beaconhill.org/FairTax2007/DistributionalAnalysis%20FairTaxBHI4-25-07.pdf.

Tuttle, Brad. "Alexandria Ocasio-Cortez Suggested a 70% Tax Rate on the Rich. Here's How It Would Work." *Money*, January 7, 2019. Available on-line at http://time.com/money/5495760/alexandria-ocasio-cortez-70-percent-tax-rate-rich/.

Twenge, Jean. "Why So Many Teens Today Have Become Depressed." *Psychology Today*, August 25, 2017. Available on-line at https://www.psychologytoday.com/us/blog/our-changing-culture/201708/why-so-many-teens-today-have-become-depressed.

Twenge, Jean. *IGen; Why Today's Super-Charged Kids Are Growing Up Less Rebellious, More Tolerant, Less Happy – and Completely Unprepared for Adulthood*. New York: Atria Books, 2017.

United Health Foundation. *America's Health Rankings, 2016 Annual Report*. Available on-line at https://www.americashealthrankings.org/learn/reports/2016-annual-report/comparison-with-other-nations.

"United States Gross Federal Debt to GDP." *Trading Economics*. Available on-line at https://tradingeconomics.com/united-states/government-debt-to-gdp.

"U.S. 10 Year Treasury." *CNBC*. Available on-line at https://www.cnbc.com/quotes/?symbol=US10Y.

"U.S. Average Hourly Wages." *Trading Economics*. Available on-line at https://tradingeconomics.com/united-states/wages.

U.S. Bureau of the Census. *Historical Statistics of the U.S.: Colonial Times to 1970*. Available on-line at https://www2.census.gov/library/publications/1975/compendia/hist_stats_colonial-1970/hist_stats_colonial-1970p1-chK.pdf.

U.S. Bureau of the Census. "Poverty Thresholds." 2017. Available on-line at https://www.census.gov/data/tables/time-series/demo/income-poverty/historical-poverty-thresholds.html.

U.S. Bureau of the Census. "U.S. and World Population Clock." Available on-line at https://www.census.gov/popclock/.

U.S. Bureau of the Census. "Mean Earnings of Workers 18 Years and Over, by Educational Attainment, Race, Hispanic Origin, and Sex, 1975-2015." Washington, D.C. Available on-line at https://www.census.gov/data/tables/2016/demo/education-attainment/cps-detailed-tables.html.

U.S. Bureau of the Census. *State and Local Government Finance*. Washington, D.C. Available on-line at https://www.census.gov/govs/local/.

U.S. Bureau of the Census. *United States Summary: 2010, Population and Housing Unit Counts*. CPH-2-1, September 2012. Available on-line at https://www.census.gov/prod/cen2010/cph-2-1.pdf.

U.S. Bureau of the Census. *U.S. Trade in Goods and Services – Balance of Payments Basis*. June 6, 2018.

Available on-line at https://www.census.gov/foreign-trade/statistics/historical/gands.pdf

U.S. Bureau of Economic Analysis. "Real Gross Domestic Product, Chained Dollars." Available on-line at https://apps.bea.gov/iTable/iTable.cfm?isuri=1&reqid=19&step=2&0=survey.

U.S. Bureau of Economic Analysis. "Real Gross Domestic Product by Major Type of Product, Quantity Indexes." Available on-line at https://www.bea.gov/iTable/iTable.cfm?reqid=19&step=2#reqid=19&step=3&isuri=1&1910=x&0=-99&1921=survey&1903=17&1904=1978&1905=2018&1906=a&1911=0.

U.S. Bureau of Economic Analysis. "Wages and Salaries by Industry." Available on-line at https://www.bea.gov/iTable/iTable.cfm?reqid=19&step=2#reqid=19&step=3&isuri=1&1921=survey&1903=189.

U.S. Bureau of Economic Analysis. "U.S. Economic Accounts." Available on-line at https://www.bea.gov/.

U.S. Bureau of Economic Analysis. "National Income and Product Accounts." Available on-line at https://apps.bea.gov/iTable/iTable.cfm?reqid=19&step=2#reqid=19&step=2&isuri=1&1921=survey.

U.S. Bureau of Economic Analysis. "International Data." Available on-line at https://apps.bea.gov/iTable/iTable.cfm?ReqID=62&step=1#reqid=62&step=9&isuri=1&6210=4.

U.S. Bureau of Economic Analysis. "Industry Data – Gross Output by Industry." Available on-line at https://apps.bea.gov/iTable/iTable.cfm?ReqID=51&step=1.

U.S. Bureau of Economic Analysis. "Gross Domestic Product by State." Available on-line at https://apps.bea.gov/itable/iTable.cfm?ReqID=70&step=1.

U.S. Bureau of Economic Analysis. "Real Personal Income for States and Metropolitan Areas." 2017. Available on-line at https://www.bea.gov/news/2019/real-personal-income-states-and-metropolitan-areas-2017.

U.S. Bureau of Labor Statistics. "All Employees, Thousands, Manufacturing, Seasonally Adjusted." Available on-line at https://data.bls.gov/pdq/SurveyOutputServlet.

U.S. Bureau of Labor Statistics. "All Employees, Thousands, Retail Trade, Seasonally Adjusted." Available on-line at https://data.bls.gov/pdq/SurveyOutputServlet.

U.S. Bureau of Labor Statistics. "All Employees, Thousands, Total Nonfarm, Seasonally Adjusted." Available on-line at https://data.bls.gov/cgi-bin/surveymost.

U.S. Bureau of Labor Statistics. "Average Paid Holidays and Days of Vacation and Sick Leave for Full-Time Employees." Available on-line at https://www.bls.gov/news.release/ebs.t05.htm.

U.S. Bureau of Labor Statistics. "Current Employment Statistics." Available on-line at https://data.bls.gov/cgi-bin/surveymost?ce.

U.S. Bureau of Labor Statistics. "Usual Weekly Earnings of Wage and Salary Workers." July 17, 2018. Available on-line at https://www.bls.gov/news.release/pdf/wkyeng.pdf.

U.S. Bureau of Labor Statistics. "Consumer Expenditure Surveys." 2016. Available on-line at https://www.bls.gov/cex/2016/combined/decile.pdf.

U.S. Bureau of Labor Statistics. "Consumer Expenditure Surveys." 2017, Table 1203, Income before Taxes. Available on-line at https://www.bls.gov/cex/2017/combined/income.pdf

U.S. Bureau of Labor Statistics. "Consumer Price Index." Available on-line at https://data.bls.gov/PDQWeb/cu.

U.S. Bureau of Labor Statistics. "Current Employment Statistics." Available on-line at https://www.bls.gov/ces/.

U.S. Bureau of Labor Statistics. "Employment, Hours, and Earnings from the Current Employment Statistics Survey." Available on-line at https://data.bls.gov/pdq/SurveyOutputServlet.

U.S. Bureau of Labor Statistics. "Employment Projections: Employment by Detailed Occupation." Available on-line at https://www.bls.gov/emp/tables/emp-by-detailed-occupation.htm.

U.S. Bureau of Labor Statistics. "Occupational Employment Statistics." Available on-line at https://www.bls.gov/oes/#data.

U.S. Bureau of Labor Statistics. "Databases, Tables and Calculators by Subject." Available on-line at https://data.bls.gov/pdq/SurveyOutputServlet.

U.S Bureau of Labor Statistics. "U.S. Median Earnings by Educational Attainment." Available on-line at https://www.bls.gov/opub/ted/2015/median-weekly-earnings-by-education-gender-race-and-ethnicity-in-2014.htm.

U.S. Bureau of Labor Statistics. "Unemployment Rates and Earnings by Educational Attainment." 2017.

Available on-line at https://www.bls.gov/emp/chart-unemployment-earnings-education.htm.

U.S. Bureau of Labor Statistics. *Women in the Labor Force: A Databook, 2004*, Report 985, Washington, D.C., May 2005, Table 11. Available on-line at https://www.bls.gov/cps/wlf-databook-2005.pdf.

U.S. Bureau of Labor Statistics. *Women in the Labor Force: A Databook, 2016*. Report 1071, Washington, D.C., November 2017, Table 11. Available on-line at https://www.bls.gov/opub/reports/womens-databook/2017/home.htm.

U.S. Bureau of Labor Statistics. "Worker Displacement: 2013-2015." USDL 16-1731, August 25, 2016. Available on-line at https://www.bls.gov/news.release/pdf/disp.pdf.

U.S. Bureau of Labor Statistics. "Average Expenditure, Share and Standard Error Tables." 2017. Available on-line at https://www.eia.gov/tools/faqs/faq.php?id=427&t=3.

U.S. Department of Agriculture. "Food Security Status of Households with Children in 2016." Available on-line at https://www.ers.usda.gov/topics/food-nutrition-assistance/food-security-in-the-us/key-statistics-graphics.aspx#children.

U.S. Departments of Health and Human Services, Treasury, and Labor. *Reforming America's Healthcare System through Choice and Competition*. 2018. Available on-line at https://www.hhs.gov/sites/default/files/Reforming-Americas-Healthcare-System-Through-Choice-and-Competition.pdf.

U.S. Department of Justice. *Equal Access to Education: Forty Years of Title IX*. Washington, D.C., June 23, 2012. Available on-line at https://www.justice.gov/sites/default/files/crt/legacy/2012/06/20/titleixreport.pdf.

U.S. Department of the Treasury. *Tax Expenditures*. 2018. Available on-line at https://www.treasury.gov/resource-center/tax-policy/Documents/Tax-Expenditures-FY2018.pdf.

U.S. Department of the Treasury. "The Debt to the Penny and Who Holds It." Available on-line at https://treasurydirect.gov/NP/debt/current.

U.S. Department of the Treasury. "Daily Treasury Yield Curve Rates." 2019. Available on-line at https://www.treasury.gov/resource-center/data-chart-center/interest-rates/pages/TextView.aspx?data=yieldYear&year=2019.

U.S. Department of the Treasury and Federal Reserve Board. "Major Foreign Holders of Treasury Securities." September 2018. Available on-line at http://ticdata.treasury.gov/Publish/mfh.txt.

U.S. Energy Information Agency. *Annual Energy Outlook 2018*, p. 111. Washington, D.C.: U.S. Department of Energy, February 6, 2018. Available on-line at https://www.eia.gov/outlooks/aeo/pdf/AEO2018.pdf.

U.S. Energy Information Administration. "Weekly U.S. Product Supplied of Finished Gasoline." Available on-line at https://www.eia.gov/dnav/pet/hist/LeafHandler.ashx?n=PET&s=wgfupus2&f=W.

U.S. Energy Information Administration. "Weekly U.S. Imports of Total Gasoline." Available on-line at https://www.eia.gov/dnav/pet/hist/LeafHandler.ashx?n=PET&s=WGTIMUS2&f=W.

U.S. Energy Information Administration. "What Is the U.S. Electricity Generation by Energy Source?" Available on-line at https://www.eia.gov/tools/faqs/faq.php?id=427&t=3.

U.S. Environmental Protection Agency. "Greenhouse Gas Emissions." Available on-line at https://www.epa.gov/ghgemissions/inventory-us-greenhouse-gas-emissions-and-sinks.

U.S. Environmental Protection Agency. *National Water Quality Inventory: Report to Congress*. EPA 841-R-16-011, August 2017. Available on-line at https://www.epa.gov/sites/production/files/2017-12/documents/305brtc_finalowow_08302017.pdf.

U.S. Environmental Protection Agency. "Nutrient Pollution – The Problem." Available on-line at https://www.epa.gov/nutrientpollution/problem.

U.S. Environmental Protection Agency. "Nutrient Pollution – The Effects: Human Health." Available on-line at https://www.epa.gov/nutrientpollution/effects-human-health.

U.S. Environmental Protection Agency. *Overview of Greenhouse Gases*. Available on-line at https://www.epa.gov/ghgemissions/overview-greenhouse-gases#methane.

U.S. Environmental Protection Agency. *Fact 962: Vehicles per Capita*. June 30, 2017. Available on-line at https://www.energy.gov/eere/vehicles/fact-962-january-30-2017-vehicles-capita-other-regionscountries-compared-united-states.

U.S. Food and Drug Administration. "Fast Track, Breakthrough Therapy, Accelerated Approval, Priority

Review." February 23, 2018. Available on-line at https://www.fda.gov/patients/learn-about-drug-and-device-approvals/fast-track-breakthrough-therapy-accelerated-approval-priority-review

U.S. Government Accounting Office. *Discipline Disparities for Black Students, Boys, and Students with Disabilities*. GAO-18-258, Washington, D.C., March 2018. Available on-line at https://www.gao.gov/assets/700/690828.pdf.

U.S. Government Accounting Office. "Savings from Generic Drug Use." GAO-12-371R, Washington, D.C., January 31, 2012. Available on-line at https://www.gao.gov/assets/590/588064.pdf.

U.S. Government Printing Office. "Recognizing the Duty of the Federal Government to Create a Green New Deal." 116th Congress, 1st Session, February 5, 2019. Available on-line at https://www.congress.gov/116/bills/hres109/BILLS-116hres109ih.pdf.

U.S. History. "Unemployment Statistics during the Great Depression." Available on-line at https://www.u-s-history.com/pages/h1528.html.

"U.S. Homes Add Even More TV Sets in 2010." *Newswire*, April 28, 2010. Available on-line at https://www.nielsen.com/us/en/insights/news/2010/u-s-homes-add-even-more-tv-sets-in-2010.html.

U.S. House Budget Committee. *The War on Poverty: 50 Years Later*. Washington, D.C., 2014. Available on-line at https://budget.house.gov/initiatives/war-on-poverty/.

"U.S. National Health Expenditures as a Percent of GDP for 1960—2019." *Statista*. Available on-line at https://www.statista.com/statistics/184968/us-health-expenditure-as-percent-of-gdp-since-1960/.

"U.S. Population." *Trading Economics*. Available on-line at https://tradingeconomics.com/united-states/population.

"U.S. Population throughout History." *ThoughtCo.*, December 4, 2018. Available on-line at https://www.thoughtco.com/us-population-through-history-1435268.

U.S. Postal Service. *U.S. Postal Service FY2018 Annual Report to Congress*. Washington, D.C., 2018. Available on-line at https://about.usps.com/who-we-are/financials/annual-reports/fy2018.pdf.

U.S. Senate, Committee on Homeland Security and Governmental Affairs. "Securing Israel: Lessons from a Nation under Constant Threat of Attack." Washington, D.C., February 1, 2017. Available on-line at https://www.hsgac.senate.gov/imo/media/doc/Feb.%202017_Securing%20Israel%20Lessons%20learned%20from%20a%20nation%20under%20constant%20threat%20of%20attack.pdf.

"U.S. Will Become a Net Oil Exporter within 10 Years, Says IEA." *The Guardian*, November 14, 2017. Available on-line at https://www.theguardian.com/business/2017/nov/14/us-net-oil-exporter-iea-international-energy-agency.

Upcounsel. "How Long Does a Drug Patent Last?" Available on-line at https://www.upcounsel.com/how-long-does-a-drug-patent-last.

Using, Yu. "Estimating the Laffer Curve and Policy Implications." *Journal of Socio-Economics*, Vol. 25, No. 3, pp.395-401. Available on-line at https://ac.els-cdn.com/S105353579690013X/1-s2.0-S105353579690013X-main.pdf?_tid=c57f4625-0987-4053-ada8-762ecd8b5f5c&acdnat=1547580491_33a6aedac5ef0bd3321070418d8175a8.

Vallas, Rebecca and Joe Valenti. "Asset Limits are a Barrier to Economic Security and Mobility." Washington, D.C.: Center for American Progress, September 10, 2014. Available on-line at https://www.americanprogress.org/issues/poverty/reports/2014/09/10/96754/asset-limits-are-a-barrier-to-economic-security-and-mobility/.

Valletta, Robert. *Recent Flattening in the Higher Education Wage Premium: Polarization, Skill Degrading, or Both?* Federal Reserve Bank of San Francisco, Working Paper 2016-17, August 2016. Available on-line at https://www.frbsf.org/economic-research/files/wp2016-17.pdf.

Valverde, Miriam. "Border Fence in Israel Cut Illegal Immigration 99%, GOP Senator Says." *Politifact*, February 13, 2017. Available on-line at https://www.politifact.com/truth-o-meter/statements/2017/feb/13/ron-johnson/border-fence-israel-cut-illegal-immigration-99-per/.

Van Parijs, Philippe and Yannick Vanderborght. *Basic Income*. Cambridge, MA: Harvard University Press, 2017.

Varathan, Preeti. "Modern Parents Spend More Time with their Kids than their Parents Spent with Them." *Quartz*, November 30, 2017. Available on-line at https://qz.com/1143092/study-modern-parents-spend-more-time-with-their-kids-than-their-parents-spent-with-them/.

Vedder, Richard. *Restoring the Promise*. Oakland, CA; Independent Institute, 2019.

Vedder, Richard. "Immigration Reform: A Modest Proposal." In Benjamin Powell, ed., *The Economics of Immigration*, Oxford: Oxford University Press, 2015, pp. 145-166.

Vernon, Steve. "Americans Fear Social Security Will Go Broke, Poll Shows." *MoneyWatch*, September 29, 2017. Available on-line at https://www.cbsnews.com/news/social-security-goes-broke-americans-fear/.

Vijaya, Ramya. "Broken Fever: How Trade Adjustment Assistance Fails American Workers." *Demos*, 2010. Available on-line at https://www.demos.org/sites/default/files/publications/Broken_Buffer_FINAL.pdf.

Vita, Michael and Seth Sacher. "The Competitive Effects of Not-for-Profit Hospital Mergers: A Case Study." *Journal of Industrial Economics*, Vol. 49, No. 1, March 2001, pp. 63-84. Available on-line at https://onlinelibrary.wiley.com/doi/epdf/10.1111/1467-6451.00138.

Wachter, Robert. *The Digital Doctor*. New York: McGraw-Hill, 2015.

Walden, Michael L. "Labor Market Hollowing-Out in North Carolina: Measurement and Causes." *The Journal of Regional Studies*, Vol. 49, No. 1, 2019. Available on-line at https://rrs.scholasticahq.com/article/7931-labor-market-hollowing-out-in-north-carolina-measurement-and-analysi.

Wallace-Wells, David. *The Uninhabitable Earth*. New York: Tim Duggan Books.

Walsh, Matt. "Businesses Don't Pay Taxes, Consumers Do." *Business Observer*, February 15, 2013. Available on-line at https://www.businessobserverfl.com/article/businesses-dont-pay-taxes-consumers-do.

Weinick, Robin, Rachel Burns, and Ateev Mehrotra. "How Many Emergency Department Visits Could be Managed at Urgent Care and Retail Clinics?" *Health Affairs*, Vol. 29, No. 9, September 2010, pp. 1630-1636. Available on-line at https://www.healthaffairs.org/doi/pdf/10.1377/hlthaff.2009.0748.

Weirsch, Ann Marie. *The Cost of College: Student Loan Debt on the Rise*. Federal Reserve Bank of Cleveland, January 31, 2014. Available on-line at https://www.clevelandfed.org/en/newsroom-and-events/publications/forefront/ff-v5n01/ff-v5n014501-the-cost-of-college-student-loan-debt.aspx.

Weissmann, Jordan. "Is Going to College Still Worth It if You Dropout?" *The Atlantic*, June ll, 2013. Available on-line at https://www.theatlantic.com/business/archive/2013/06/is-going-to-college-still-worth-it-if-you-drop-out/276757/.

Weissmann, Jordan. "Why Are College Textbooks So Absurdly Expensive?" *The Atlantic*, January 3, 2013. Available on-line at https://www.theatlantic.com/business/archive/2013/01/why-are-college-textbooks-so-absurdly-expensive/266801/.

"What is the Typical Teaching Load for University Faculty?" *Higher Ed Professor,* May 11, 2015. Available on-line at http://higheredprofessor.com/2015/05/11/what-is-the-typical-teaching-load-for-university-faculty/.

Whitten Sarah. "McDonald's to Add Self-Order Kiosks to 1000 Stores Each Quarter." *CNBC*, June 4, 2018. Available on-line at https://www.cnbc.com/2018/06/04/mcdonalds-to-add-self-order-kiosks-to-1,00-stores-each-quarter.html.

"Why the FDA has an Incentive to Delay the Introduction of New Drugs." *The Independent Institute*, 2019. Available on-line at http://www.fdareview.org/issues/why-the-fda-has-an-incentive-to-delay-the-introduction-of-new-drugs/.

Wiederspan, Jessica, Elizabeth Rhodes, and H. Luke Shaefer. "Expanding the Discourse on Antipoverty Policy: Reconsidering a Negative Income Tax." *Journal of Poverty*, Vol. 19, No. 2, February 2015, pp. 218-238. Available on-line at https://www.tandfonline.com/doi/abs/10.1080/10875549.2014.991889.

Wilby, Peter. "Why Capitalism Creates a Throwaway Society." *New Statesman America*, August 28, 2008. Available on-line at https://www.earth.columbia.edu/sitefiles/file/Sachs%20Writing/2011/ProjectSyndicate_2011_TheEconomicsofHappiness_08_29_11.pdf.

Wilcox, W. Bradford, Joseph Price, and Angela Rachidi. *Marriage, Penalized*. Washington, D.C. American Enterprise Institute, July 26, 2016. Available on-line at https://www.aei.org/wp-content/uploads/2016/07/IFS-HomeEconReport-2016-Final-072616.pdf.

Wilkie, Dana. "When Two Workers Doing the Same Job Earn Different Pay." *SHRM*, February 2, 2017. Available on-line at https://www.shrm.org/resourcesandtools/hr-topics/employee-relations/pages/pay-disparity-for-same-job.aspx.

Wilkinson, Richard and Kate Pickett. *The Inner Level: How More Equal Societies Reduce Stress, Restore Sanity and Improve Everyone's Well-Being*. New York: Penguin Press, 2019.

Wilson, Sy. "Capitalism and Economic Growth across the World." *SSRN*, September 18, 2016. Available on-line at https://dx.doi.org/10.2139/ssrn.2840425.

Winship, Scott. *Poverty after Welfare Reform*. Report 19, New York: The Manhattan Institute, August 2016. Available on-line at https://www.manhattan-institute.org/html/poverty-after-welfare-reform.html.

Wodtke, Geoffrey, David Harding, and Felix Elbert. "Neighborhood Effects in Temporal Perspective: The Impact of Long-Term Exposure to Concentrated Disadvantage on High School Graduation." *American Sociological Review*, 76(5): 713-736. Available on-line at http://journals.sagepub.com/doi/pdf/10.1177/0003122411420816.

Wogan, J. B. "No Cut in Premiums for Typical Family." *Politifact*, August 31, 2012. Available on-line at https://www.politifact.com/truth-o-meter/promises/obameter/promise/521/cut-cost-typical-familys-health-insurance-premium-/.

Wolff, Edward. *A Century of Wealth in America*. Cambridge, MA: Harvard University Press, 2017, Table 9.1.

Wolverton, Brad, Ben Hallman, Shane Shifflett, and Sandhya Kambhampti, "The $10 Billion Sports Tab." *The Chronicle of Higher Education*, November 15, 2015. Available on-line at https://www.chronicle.com/interactives/ncaa-subsidies-main#id=table_2014.

Woodruff, Judy. "Who's Behind the Chinese Takeover of World's Largest Pork Producer." *PBS News Hour*, September 12, 2014. Available on-line at https://www.pbs.org/newshour/show/whos-behind-chinese-takeover-worlds-biggest-pork-producer.

Woolhandler, Steffie and David Himmelstein. "Single Payer Reform: The Only Way to Fulfil the President's Pledge of More Coverage, Better Benefits, and Lower Costs." *Annuals of Internal Medicine*, April 18, 2017. Available on-line at https://annals.org/aim/fullarticle/2605414/single-payer-reform-only-way-fulfill-president-s-pledge-more.

Word, Elizabeth, John Johnston, Helen Bain, Dewayne Fulton, Charles Achilles, Martha Lintz, John Folger, and Carolyn Breda. "The State of Tennessee's Student/Teacher Achievement Ratio (STAR) Project: Technical Report 1985-1990." *Tennessee State Department of Education*, 1990. Available on-line at https://eric.ed.gov/?id=ED328356.

World Health Organization. "Ambient (Outdoor) Air Quality and Health." May 2, 2018, Geneva Switzerland. Available on-line at http://www.who.int/news-room/fact-sheets/detail/ambient-(outdoor)-air-quality-and-health.

World Nuclear Association. "Nuclear Power in France." September 2018. Available on-line at http://www.world-nuclear.org/information-library/country-profiles/countries-a-f/france.aspx.

Wright, Joshua. "America's Skilled Trades Dilemma: Shortages Loom as Most-In-Demand Group of Workers Retires." *Forbes*, March 7, 2013. Available on-line at https://www.forbes.com/sites/emsi/2013/03/07/americas-skilled-trades-dilemma-shortages-loom-as-most-in-demand-group-of-workers-ages/#3c10ec896397.

Yang, Andrew. "Silicon Valley is Right—Our Jobs are Already Disappearing." *Quartz*, February 2, 2017. Available on-line at https://qz.com/895681/silicon-valley-is-right-our-jobs-are-already-disappearing-due-to-automation/.

Yaw, Lim Hui. "The Effect of Single Parenting on Student Academic Performance in Secondary Schools in Brunei." *The Social Sciences*, vol. 11, pp. 698-703. Available on-line at https://www.medwelljournals.com/abstract/?doi=sscience.2016.698.703.

Yeginsu, Ceylan. "N.H.S. Overwhelmed in Britain, Leaving Patients to Wait." *New York Times*, January 3, 2018. Available on-line at https://www.nytimes.com/2018/01/03/world/europe/uk-national-health-service.html.

York, Erica. "Summary of the Latest Federal Income Tax Data, 2017 Update." *Tax Foundation*, Tax Foundation, January 17, 2018. Available on-line at https://taxfoundation.org/summary-federal-income-tax-data-2017/.

Zarroli, Jim. "Study: Upward Mobility No Tougher in US than Two Decades Ago." *National Public Radio*, January 23, 2014. Available on-line at https://www.npr.org/2014/01/23/265356290/study-upward-mobility-no-tougher-in-u-s-than-two-decades-ago.

Ziol-Guest, Kathleen, Greg Duncan, and Ariel Kalil. "One-Parent Students Leave School Earlier." *Education Next*, Spring 2015, pp. 37-41. Available on-line at www.educationnext.org/one-parent-students-leave-school-earlier/.

Zuk, Miriam, Ariel Bierbaum, Karen Chapple, Karolina Gorska, Anastasia Loukaitou-Sideris, Paul Ong, and Trevor Thomas. "Gentrification, Displacement and the Role of Public Investment: A Literature Review." Community Development Investment Center, Federal Reserve Bank of San Francisco, Working Paper 2015-05, August 2015. Available on-line at https://www.frbsf.org/community-development/files/wp2015-05.pdf.

Zweig, Phillip and Frederick Blum. "When Does the Law Against Kickbacks Not Apply? Your Hospital." *Wall Street Journal*, May 18, 2018, p. A17.

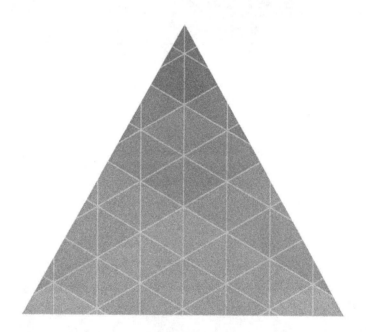

INDEX

ABOUT THE AUTHOR

Michael L. Walden, Ph.D., is a Reynolds Distinguished Professor at North Carolina State University, where he has taught since 1978. A prolific writer and speaker, Walden has authored fourteen books and over 300 articles and reports. He broadcasts a daily radio program, writes weekly and monthly columns, and makes scores of presentations to a variety of groups annually. Walden has received several national, state, and university awards. He resides in Raleigh with his wife.

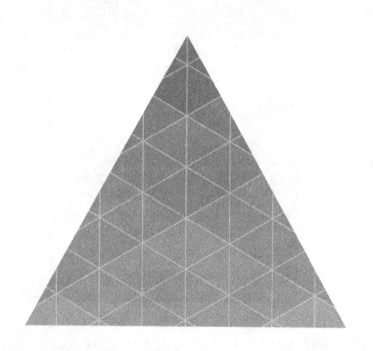

CPSIA information can be obtained
at www.ICGtesting.com
Printed in the USA
BVHW031933200721
612447BV00013B/69